ORGANIZATIONAL
LEADERSHIP

Selected, Edited, and with Introductions and Summaries by

Joyce Huth Munro
Chestnut Hill College

Contemporary
Learning Series

Photo Acknowledgement
Royalty-Free/CORBIS

Cover Acknowledgement
Maggie Lytle

Compositor: Hurix Systems

Copyright © 2008 by McGraw-Hill Contemporary Learning Series,
A Division of The McGraw-Hill Companies, Inc., Dubuque, Iowa 52001

Roundtable Viewpoints™ trademark application pending by the
McGraw-Hill Companies, Inc.

Manufactured in the United States of America

First Edition

1234567890DOCDOC987

MHID: 0-07-352782-3
ISBN: 978-0-07-352782-6
ISSN: 1934-4236

Printed on Recycled Paper

CONTENTS IN BRIEF

UNIT 1   CONTEXTUAL ISSUES IN ORGANIZATIONAL LEADERSHIP   1

Issue 1   What Are the Newest Approaches to Organizational Leadership?   4

Issue 2   Why Is It Important for Leaders to Understand the Role of Social Responsibility in Organizations?   31

Issue 3   What Does It Take for an Organization to Act Ethically?   65

Issue 4   Does Organizational Culture Link to Success or Profitability?   98

Issue 5   How Can Leaders Capitalize on Diversity in the Workplace?   132

Issue 6   How Is Globalization Affecting Organizations around the World?   171

UNIT 2   OPERATIONAL ISSUES IN ORGANIZATIONAL LEADERSHIP   210

Issue 7   How Can a Systems Approach Help Organizational Leaders?   212

Issue 8   What Performance Measures Should Organizational Leaders Consider Today?   246

Issue 9   Has Strategic Planning Been Left Behind?   269

Issue 10   How Will Organizations Function in the Future?   315

CONTENTS

Preface xii
Guided Tour xiv
Introduction xvi

UNIT 1 CONTEXTUAL ISSUES IN ORGANIZATIONAL LEADERSHIP 1

Issue 1 **What Are the Newest Approaches to Organizational Leadership? 4**

    1.1 Gary Yukl and Richard Lepsinger, from "Improving Performance Through Flexible Leadership," *Leadership in Action* (September/October 2005) 6

    1.2 Wilfred H. Drath, from "Leading Together: Complex Challenges Require a New Approach," *Leadership in Action* (March/April 2003) 9

    1.3 Lynn Barendsen and Howard Gardner, from "Is the Social Entrepreneur a New Type of Leader?" *Leader to Leader* (Fall 2004) 16

    1.4 Tim Field, from "Successful Leaders Possess Emotional Intelligence," *Media and Entertainment Insights* (October 2003) 24

Issue 2 **Why Is It Important for Leaders to Understand the Role of Social Responsibility in Organizations? 31**

    2.1 *GolinHarris*, from "Doing Well by Doing Good 2005: The Trajectory of Corporate Citizenship in American Business," *GolinHarris* (2005) 34

2.2   *Journal of Financial Planning*, from "10 Questions with . . . David Henderson on the Role of Business Today: Does It Include Corporate Social Responsibility?" *Journal of Financial Planning* (August 2005)   43

2.3   Deborah Doane, from "The Myth of CSR," *Stanford Social Innovation Review* (Fall 2005)   48

2.4   T.E. Bostock, from "The Dangers of Weasel Words: 'Corporate Social Responsibility' as a Banner for Left-Wing Politics," *National Observer* (Spring 2005)   57

Issue 3   What Does It Take for an Organization to Act Ethically?   65

3.1   Curtis C. Verschoor, from "Ethical Culture: Most Important Barrier to Ethical Misconduct," *Strategic Finance* (December 2005)   67

3.2   Amey Stone, from "Putting Teeth in Corporate Ethics Codes," *Business Week Online* (February 19, 2004)   70

3.3   Dean L. Bottorff, from "Advancing from Compliance to Performance," *Quality Progress* (April 2006)   73

3.4   David Gebler, from "Creating an Ethical Culture," *Strategic Finance* (May 2006)   87

Issue 4   Does Organizational Culture Link to Success or Profitability?   98

4.1   Anne D'Innocenzio, from "Wal-Mart Tries to Modify Corporate Culture," *ABCNews.com* (April 16, 2006)   101

4.2   Susan Davidson, from "The Irresolute American," *Executive Action* (May 2006)   103

4.3   Jennifer A. Chatman and Sandra Eunyoung
       Cha, from "Leading by Leveraging Culture,"
       California Management Review (2003)   109

4.4   Gary L. Neilson, Bruce A. Pasternack, and Karen E.
       Van Nuys, from "The Passive-Aggressive
       Organization," *Harvard Business Review*
       (October 2005)   119

**Issue 5   How Can Leaders Capitalize on Diversity in the
Workplace?   132**

5.1   Nancy R. Lockwood, from "Workplace Diversity:
       Leveraging the Power of Difference for Competi-
       tive Advantage," *HR Magazine* (vol. 50, no. 6, June
       2005)   134

5.2   Joseph Coates, from "An Increasingly Diverse Work-
       force Makes Traditional Diversity Programs Passé,"
       Employment Relations Today (March 2006)   148

5.3   Susan P. Eisner, from "Managing Generation Y,"
       SAM Advanced Management Journal (Autumn
       2005)   157

**Issue 6   How Is Globalization Affecting Organizations around the
World?   171**

6.1   Dick Martin, from "Rebuilding Brand America:
       Corporate America's Role," *Journal of Business
       Strategy* (2006)   174

6.2   Richard Seline, from "2005 National Innovation
       Survey," *New Economy Strategies* (2005)   185

6.3   Karen Crennan, Paul F. Nunes, and Marcia A. Halfin,
       from "Making the Trend Your Friend," *Outlook*
       (2006)   196

UNIT 2   OPERATIONAL ISSUES IN ORGANIZATIONAL LEADERSHIP   210

Issue 7   How Can a Systems Approach Help Organizational Leaders?   212

7.1   Russell L. Ackoff, from "On Learning and the Systems That Facilitate It," *The SOI Journal* (August 1999)   214

7.2   George E. Reed, from "Leadership and Systems Thinking," *Defense AT&L* (May/June 2006)   231

7.3   Nelda Cambron-McCabe and Luvern L. Cunningham, from "Suspending the Elephant Over the Table," *The School Administrator* (November 2004)   237

Issue 8   What Performance Measures Should Organizational Leaders Consider Today?   246

8.1   Jena McGregor, from "The Struggle to Measure Performance," *Business Week* (January 9, 2006)   249

8.2   Howard M. Guttman and Andrew Longman, from "Project Teams: How Good Are They?" *Quality Progress* (February 2006)   252

8.3   Ralph Jacobson, from "Assessment Alternatives: Appraising Organizational Performance," *Chief Learning Officer* (November 2005)   259

Issue 9   Has Strategic Planning Been Left Behind?   269

9.1   Michael C. Mankins and Richard Steele, from "Stop Making Plans: Start Making Decisions," *Harvard Business Review* (January 2006)   272

9.2   Robert W. Rowden, from "The Learning Organization and Strategic Change," *SAM Advanced Management Journal* (Summer 2001)   284

9.3   Mike Freedman, from "The Genius Is in the Implementation," *Journal of Business Strategy* (March/April 2003)   294

9.4   John Vogelsang, from "Futuring: A Complex Adaptive Systems Approach to Strategic Planning," *Support Center for Nonprofit Management* (2004)   303

Issue 10   How Will Organizations Function in the Future?   315

10.1   *SCM* Editorial Board, from "Fast Forward: Future Trends in Corporate Communication," *Strategic Communication Management* (December 2005/January 2006)   317

10.2   Eric D. Beinhocker, from "The Adaptable Corporation," *McKinsey Quarterly* (2006)   325

10.3   John Seely Brown and John Hagel III, from "Creation Nets: Getting the Most from Open Innovation," *McKinsey Quarterly* (2006)   332

10.4   Sabine Flambard-Ruaud, from "Relationship Marketing in Emerging Economies: Some Lessons for the Future," *The Journal for Decision Makers* (July-September 2005)   341

Contributors   357
Credits   363
Index   366

PREFACE

———————————————————————————————————●

This book is about some of the most pressing issues that organizational leaders face today. They are thorny, complex issues—the kind of issues that do not come with simple answers. So expect no magic formulas or absolutes in this book. Instead, expect to find multiple viewpoints on each issue that enlarge your perspective and assist you in examining ways leadership is carried out in organizations.

As the title suggests, this book is meant to be more than a collection of readings—it is a stimulus for deeper thought and wiser action. The idea of having a roundtable discussion of issues is an extension of traditional debate, where an issue is polarized into two positions. By taking one side of an issue, the debater's goal is to win the argument by appealing to emotions. Nothing is wrong with this approach, but a roundtable discussion sets in motion other goals than winning an argument. Think of sitting at a conference table in an office building somewhere with a group of people who are sharing their perceptions and ideas about an important issue facing the organization. Your task is to learn as much as possible about the issue. Everyone at the table enters the discussion—demonstrating that your group is committed to "thinking systemically." This book is like a virtual roundtable discussion. The multiple viewpoints in these pages enable you to learn more about the issues, make connections, and relate the author's statements to yourself in the role of organizational leader.

All of the readings have been selected because they are relevant and current. More importantly, they align with latest theoretical developments and best practices. Issues such as corporate social responsibility and globalization are incredibly volatile, eliciting strong responses. Other issues like strategic planning, while not as controversial, still need to be considered from a variety of angles.

The readings in this volume address 10 issues that are contextual (Unit 1) and operational (Unit 2). Among the contextual issues are emerging leadership approaches, social responsibility, ethical climate, diversity, culture, and globalization. The operational issues include performance measures, strategic planning, systems, and organizational functioning in the future.

An underlying theme of the book is the importance and benefit of considering organizational issues from a systems perspective. Systems has been a traditional way to analyze the mechanical components of an organization, like a production line, but recently the approach has been adapted to managing emotional, relational systems. Systems thinking is becoming the foundation on which leaders analyze issues and build enduring change. This approach to leadership is presented in the introductory essay and reinforced through the book.

The purpose of Roundtable Viewpoints is to enable potential organizational leaders to be sensitive to issues in order to be better guides in a chaotic world and into the future. With a systems approach in mind, read and analyze each issue and consider how you would lead if you were in a key leadership position right now.

STRUCTURE OF *ROUNDTABLE VIEWPOINTS: ORGANIZATIONAL LEADERSHIP*

This book is organized in two units: "Contextual Issues in Organizational Leadership," and "Operational Issues in Organizational Leadership." Unit 1 consists of six issues and Unit 2 consists of four. Each issue is addressed through multiple readings that provide a range of viewpoints. The issues and accompanying readings can be thought of as chapters; in each chapter is an introduction that frames the readings in a larger context and a summary that ties the viewpoints together. The marginal notes contain Challenge Questions to encourage students to form an educated opinion about the issue. The summary is accompanied by several features that extend learning. These features are Highlights, Critical Thinking, and Additional Reading Resources. These end-of-chapter resources are opportunities for application and skill development. The book concludes with Contributors—a listing of authors of the readings and their biographical sketches. The authors are an interesting variety of professionals, including organizational leaders, scholars, reporters, and consultants.

ACKNOWLEDGMENTS

My work on this book began with a conversation with Larry Loeppke on another topic altogether. But as he talked about his idea of a new series that would tackle professional issues from multiple perspectives, my writing began to take a different direction. So I am grateful to Larry for introducing me to the Roundtable Viewpoints series and to Susan Brusch for shepherding the drafts and permissions and other vagaries of writing for a new series. I am also grateful to James Munro, a seasoned organizational leader, who allowed himself to be a sounding board throughout the writing process. Jamie is not only knowledgeable about the field of leadership; he is a good systems thinker who knows how to help organizations get unstuck.

GUIDED TOUR

UNIT OPENER

Designed to outline related issues and capture student interest, each unit opener provides general information for the upcoming issues. The unit openers conclude with a list of issue questions covered in each unit.

ISSUE INTRODUCTIONS

Designed to introduce the issue to the reader, the issue introduction states an issue question, provides history, current events, a list of the upcoming article selections for the issue, and relevant information about the issue to help facilitate discussion.

ISSUE SUMMARIES

Issue summaries appear at the end of each issue text. The summary brings the readings together, offers concluding observations, and suggests new directions for the student to take to further explore the issue.

CHALLENGE QUESTIONS

EFFECTIVE LEADERSHIP

What constitutes an effective leader? An effective leader brings out the best in the organization's people in terms of their aspirations, potential, performance and contribution. They encourage collegial, collaborative and supportive work styles and use this to build strong teams.

Leaders seek and welcome feedback and are comfortable analyzing both their successes as well as their failures.

The core competency underlying these effective leadership skills is emotional intelligence. As defined by Daniel Goleman (1995, 1998), emotional intelligence has five components. Three are self-management skills and include self-awareness, self-regulation and motivation. The remaining two, empathy and social skill, involve the ability to manage relationships with others. For the purposes of this article, I will focus on self-awareness, self-regulation and social skill.

While intelligence and technical skills are certainly important for success, it has been shown that emotional intelligence is twice as important in achieving excellent performance for jobs at all levels of an organization. The importance of emotional intelligence becomes even stronger in senior leadership positions where it has been found that 90% of the difference between top and average senior management performance is due to emotional intelligence and not to cognitive abilities.

Is emotional intelligence a necessary characteristic of organizational leaders?

Each issue contains challenge questions, in the form of marginal notes, designed to stimulate critical thinking and discussion. The challenge questions are thought-provoking and relevant to the issue and its selections.

ISSUE HIGHLIGHTS

ISSUE HIGHLIGHTS

- A corporation with a reputation for ruthless competition can attempt to recast its culture by being more transparent and responsive to critics.
- A corporation attempting to change its culture must recognize that its core business model will be affected.
- Massive culture-changing will inevitably result in public skepticism and questioning the organizations' true intent of change.
- Around the world, American organizations have the reputation for cultural virtues such as speaking one's mind, open exchange of ideas, and initiative, yet in many organizations the culture is not that open and honest.
- One perspective on organizational culture involves intentional efforts to socialize and train employees, a preventive measure.

Highlights appear at the end of each issue and help to identify important information and details about the issue. The main points covered in the readings are recapped in the issue highlights.

CRITICAL THINKING

CRITICAL THINKING

Culture is a complex social system. It consists of processes, patterns, and events. The tendency is for leaders to focus on the events themselves; however, a systems approach requires taking a "balcony view." Looking at the processes and patterns rather than the events per se, is what Peter Senge refers to as personal mastery of the situation: "continually clarifying and deepening our personal vision, of focusing our energies, of developing patience, and of seeing reality objectively" (1990, p. 7). When leaders have clarified the big picture, they can then form a mental image of the culture: "Mental models are deeply ingrained assumptions, generalizations, or even pictures or images that influence how we understand the world and how we take action" (p. 8).

Any participant in an organization can reach this stage in systems thinking yet still not influence the culture, but leaders take the next step by sharing their mental model: "If any one idea about leadership has inspired organizations for thousands of years, it's the capacity to hold a shared picture of the future we seek to create" (p. 9).

For Senge, shared vision is necessary to culture change, but it is not sufficient. The way to change a culture is through a group approach: "Team learning is vital because teams, not individuals, are the fundamental learning unit in modern organizations" (p. 10). It is a simple strategy, but tremendously ignored—through dialogue shared understandings emerge and the culture is changed.

Found at the end of each issue, this essential feature provides key strategies for using critical thinking skills in discussing the issues and forming an educated and well-thought-out opinion.

ADDITIONAL READING RESOURCES

ADDITIONAL READING RESOURCES

Kim S. Cameron & Robert E. Quinn, *Diagnosing and Changing Organizational Culture: Based on the Competing Values Framework*. John Wiley & Sons, 2006.

James L. Gibson, John M. Ivancevich, James H. Donnelly, Jr., & Robert Konopaske, Organizational culture. *Organizations: Behavior, Structure, Processes*. McGraw-Hill, 2003.

John P. Kotter & James L. Heskett, *Corporate Culture and Performance*. Simon & Schuster, 1992.

Peter Senge, *The Fifth Discipline*. Doubleday, 1990.

For more on improvement of organizational culture, visit these sites:

http://eqmextra.cqm.org/cqmjournal/nd/reprints/rp09100
http://www.novalearning.com/html/institutional_formation.htm
http://www.strategic-organizational-change.com

This feature encourages further research relevant to each issue. Many perspectives frame each issue, and these resources provide additional material related to the topic being discussed.

INTRODUCTION

TOWARD A SYSTEMS APPROACH TO ISSUES IN ORGANIZATIONAL LEADERSHIP

This book of roundtable viewpoints on leadership is tied tightly to organizations. The readings are about leadership located in an organization, be it educational, professional, industrial, technological, military, or commercial. In effect, the organization is the lens for examining a set of issues that affects how leadership is practiced.

While other leadership books and articles focus solely on the person as leader, this book is about the interface of person-as-leader, place, and participants. Some scholars and researchers refer to this interface as situated leadership. The readings selected for this book address organizational leadership issues from multiple perspectives, because in truth there is no single correct answer to any of the issues. From the perspective of situated leadership, the best answer is "it depends." Firm and fast rules or tried and true principles are less reliable when the focus shifts from solitary leader to interaction of key leadership factors. For this reason, it is important to consider different viewpoints on the practice of leadership in organizations for a deeper understanding of personal leadership.

The authors of these readings speak with a variety of voices from different settings. It may be tempting to pick up separate pieces and cobble together a picture of how an organizational leader should deal with issues. To counter the temptation, this essay explores concepts of leadership over time and examines the direction leadership is taking today. The essay ends with an explanation of the systems approach, a useful way for leaders to think about organizational issues. While many experts and scholars decry shallow (but popular) depictions of leadership as a bag of tricks or a quick fix, the search continues for a wholly new way to conceive of the organizational leader in today's world. Unfortunately, the tendency is to return to time-honored notions of effective leadership. This is where systems thinking comes in. We begin with a look back at these time-honored concepts of leadership as they play out in the organizational setting.

Since the sixteenth century when Machiavelli proposed leadership qualities for a political system (from an extreme point of view), many experts and pundits have explored the nature of organizational leadership. At the beginning, researchers of organizational leadership were preoccupied with traits of leaders, a point of view that continues to be accepted. The problem with the traits perspective (a psychological construct) is it narrowly categorizes leadership as the personality of an individual. Moreover, there are as many lists of "most desirable traits" as there are leadership experts and consultants. This is not to denigrate traits of leaders; in fact, exploration of essential personality factors is reappearing in current organizational literature. But leadership in today's organizations is far more complex than a certain set of traits displayed by an individual.

Parallel to the traits perspective of leadership in management literature runs the concept of control. During the late nineteenth century and into the early twentieth, small family-owned companies were replaced by large-scale organizations—America had entered the age of bureaucratic operations. As the economy grew so did industry, business, and government.

For some time, the leadership model was the "big man," an appropriate match to big business, big industry, and big government. The suggestion behind the image was that only a few leaders knew the "big picture."

For some people, it is impossible to conceive of leadership without thinking of authority, order, and power. The notion that leadership is about control is ubiquitous.

> The word "management" with its connotations of control is no longer restricted to a technical or indeed political function *within* organizations. It is currently used to encompass areas as diverse and grandiose as the management of the environment, the management of the economy, the management of the African elephant, the management of emotion, or still more ambitiously the management of the planet. . . . For practicing managers, the issue has become one of technique and search for efficiency—how best to control people, information and other resources in the light of continuous change and uncertainty. (Gabriel, 1998, p. 257)

Classic leadership literature is replete with examples of leaders' attempts to predict, categorize, classify, and control for every variable imaginable within organizations. But what if organizations were unpredictable and impossible to control?

More and more, organizational scholars are looking to theoretical constructs that paint a picture of leadership as fluid, emergent, or connected. The result is concepts of chaos theory and complexity science are edging out control in organizational leadership literature. These new sciences cast leadership in a setting that is more like an ecosystem than a machine. Two decades ago, Tom Peters, a well-published expert on organizational leadership, set the tone for thinking about leadership in a chaotic environment. "The winners of tomorrow will deal *proactively* with chaos, will look at the chaos per se as the source of market advantage, not as a problem to be got around. Chaos and uncertainty are (will be) market opportunities; capitalizing on fleeting market anomalies will be the successful business's greatest accomplishment" (1987, p. 3).

Exactly what it means for leaders to deal proactively with chaos is currently under debate. Leadership experts and think tanks are delving into the nature of leadership in an unpredictable world. At one of these think tanks, the Center for Creative Leadership, research is giving direction for a new conception of leadership that is more suitable for settings where discontinuity and uncertainty are key features. "Leadership is changing and approaches focusing on flexibility, collaboration crossing boundaries and collective leadership are expected to become a high priority" (2005, p. 3). One of the questions addressed in the CCL study is whether there is a move away from *leader* development toward *leadership* development, which would indicate that attention is shifting from the person to the process. The answer is yes—it makes sense to consider organizational leadership as a process.

Embedded leadership—leadership that is influenced and shaped by the organization where it is practiced—is an appropriate phrase for this new view of leadership. In recognition that organization and leadership are interdependent, current research is framing leadership as a set of qualities, imperatives, or elements. Devoid of a location, leadership can be boiled down to "tips" or "points," but in practice, leader work is highly complex, with many crucial areas of organizational life that must be addressed for an organization to be successful. Pervasive and escalating change has shaken our ability to think about effective leadership without thinking about its settings and circumstances.

To correct the tendency to study leadership in the abstract, Zaccaro and Klimoski (2001) have formed a set of defining elements of leadership embedded in organizations. Taken together, these elements provide a robust definition of organizational leadership in a world that new sciences are showing us is turbulent and chaotic.

- Organizational leadership involves processes and proximal outcomes that contribute to the development and achievement of organizational purpose.
- Organizational leadership is identified by the application of nonroutine influence on organizational life.
- Leader influence is grounded in cognitive, social, and political processes.
- Organizational leadership is inherently bounded by system characteristics and dynamics, that is, leadership is contextually defined and caused. (pp. 2–3)

Out of these elements comes a more holistic view of the true nature of organizational leadership. Look again at the essence of these elements—achieving organizational purpose, problem solving, relationship building, sense-making, contextualizing. This is very sophisticated work. The good news is leadership work is being reconceptualized as work done together over time. The other news is that organizational leadership-as-process has a feel and momentum unique to a particular setting. How leadership is conducted in one place will not look the same as another place. This fact creates another dilemma; it is difficult to examine new leadership work without relying on past theories. While some leadership work is grounded in ancient practices, other work takes new forms as the system adapts to the people in it.

Regardless of the approach, the current and pressing challenge is to find standards of excellence for leadership that is embedded, holistic, contextualized. The encouraging news is the elements of embedded leadership can be captured through systems thinking so they can be learned and practiced.

SYSTEMS THINKING IN THE SERVICE OF ORGANIZATIONAL LEADERSHIP

Systems are all around us and we are part of various systems. Our bodies are composed of several systems, one of which is the respiratory system. The earth is part of a solar system (which has recently seen its number of planets reduced). We talk of the earth's systems—ecosystems, weather systems. Organizations are also systems, in this case theoretical or conceptual rather than natural. Essentially, systems are self-organizing and evolving. They are not merely the sum or even the product of parts.

Historically, organizational systems have been cast in linear terms—input, feedback, output. When such terms are used for work, it is easy to see why organizations have been viewed as machines. The settings were manufacturing or industry and assembly-line problems were fairly well defined. Linear systems were appropriate for the industrial age because the science of industry naturally led to the need for efficiency, error-free production and quality control. By the 1940s, this approach to systems, referred to as a hard approach, spilled over into nonindustrial endeavors, particularly information science.

The journey from industry to the information era has not been easy and organizational systems have not always kept pace with new work realities. People still tend to think of organizations as stable systems that operate by set rules and formulas. Many have been reluctant to change their ways of thinking about organizations, preferring to cling to age-old ideas like the dichotomy of leaders and followers, the preoccupation with personality enhancement, and the power and control model of leadership. It has taken some effort to recast systems as open (inclusive of external forces and factors) and densely interdependent. Thinking about systems as open means avoiding the tendency to dichotomize, which people do when they frame situations as either/or or cause and effect. Instead, systems thinking looks for connections, patterns, relationships, spirals, and dynamics. These concepts help leaders move away from nineteenth century mechanics ideas about organizations.

In recent decades, chaos theory has influenced systems thinking and led to terms like sensitivity to conditions, equilibrium, and homeostasis. Discoveries in natural and biological sciences and quantum physics have increased our awareness of patterns in the midst of confusion and of order despite irregularity.

New ways of thinking about leadership have also challenged traditional bureaucratic models of organizations characterized by standardized procedures, division of labor, and expert leaders. Chaos theory contradicts Max Weber's concepts of bureaucracy—impersonalizing of the system and vertical hierarchy of authority. The question remains: How useful is chaos theory if leaders are never sure what the outcome of an action will be? On the surface, it seems that chaos is simply randomness and that is risky business for any organization. But experts in the new sciences would caution against equating chaos with organizational anarchy.

> Chaos theory does not leave us in a position of powerlessness and confusion: it enables us to observe and analyze such systems, unravel patterns, establish boundaries (e.g., no snowstorms in the Sahara), note similarities, identify areas of tranquility and make short-term forecasts. (Gabriel, 1998, p. 261)

Chaos theory comes into play as a way for leaders to deal with ambiguity while unraveling patterns and establishing boundaries within organizations. What we are coming to understand is that it is not the rational, settled organization that will thrive but the less stable system. This is because the need for homeostasis (stability and identity) actually interferes with attempts to learn, stay ahead, and innovate. In combination, systems thinking and chaos theory can help an organization keep a sense of security while moving in new directions.

RELATIONSHIPS AS CAPITAL FOR ORGANIZATIONAL LEADERSHIP

One of the striking findings of the 2005 research done by The Center for Creative Leadership is the increasing importance of leader skill in building and mending relationships. Historically, this "soft skill" has ranked low in surveys. Relationship building is currently the second most important skill (behind another soft skill: leading employees). The high ranking of relationships indicates that the days of casting a private vision—acting unilaterally and making decisions in isolation—are on the wane. It also says that treating employees as problems is no longer valid; rather, employees are a wealth that has been undervalued.

Attention to relationships becomes even more important due to the changing nature of work. Today employees move across functional boundaries to solve problems or implement new programs or collaborate with external partners. This is quite different from a traditional work group led by a single person who is responsible for getting the job done. In a networked organization, the assignment is shared, leadership is shared, and problems and decisions are shared.

Shared work is a practice that fits well in a "complex, no-one-in-charge, shared-power world" (Crosby & Bryson, 2005, p. 4). This paradigm could lead to the idea that sharing power preempts leadership—a troubling notion—until it is placed in perspective.

> All this does not mean that the in-charge leadership image has disappeared or completely lost its usefulness. The connective or quiet leader sometimes has to make a decision and implement it using whatever powers and controls he or she has. Similarly, leaders who are formally in charge know they often must consult and compromise with other powerful people before acting. In a shared-power situation, however, leadership that encourages the participation of others must be emphasized because only it has the power to inspire and mobilize those others. In the effort to tackle public problems, leadership and power must be consciously shared with a view to eventually creating power-sharing institutions within a regime of mutual gain. (p. 32)

Work that is shared heightens the importance of relationships in organizations and makes relationship building a central skill for leaders. Interaction skills like consultation, negotiation, compromise, and conflict management are an integral part of daily life for leaders in organizations that tackle public problems and operate by sharing power. Shared work and shared power also mean more investment in team building, group learning, and culture formation.

LEADERSHIP AS AN EMOTIONAL PROCESS (FROM A SYSTEMS POINT OF VIEW)

In the industrial age, when organizations were thought of as machines, employees were expected to leave personal issues at home. Concerns and emotions were left behind when employees arrived at work. Eventually human resource departments began to address "people problems," partly in recognition of employees as whole persons. But the expectation did not change—concerns and emotions were separate from work.

Today, organizations acknowledge the emotional nature of work. (Keep in mind that emotional is more than feelings—it is the instinctual response of humans to change, tension, and threat.) Teamwork in particular is emotion-filled work. Individuals in teams are in vulnerable positions because their knowledge and expertise are on display in front of others. Every aspect of shared work is done publicly and constant interaction is difficult for some individuals. Stress and anxiety are bound to be present in teams and there are no quick fixes for relationships that are stressful and anxious.

The emotional side of organizational life is a hot topic these days in both popular and academic literature. One practitioner whose work has broken new ground on the connections between emotional process at home and at work is Edwin Friedman. His premise (carried forward by Beal and Treadwell) is that emotional processes in society negatively impact American leadership. These processes are so powerful that tinkering with the mechanics or trying harder does not help.

> Administrative, technical, and managerial solutions (such as centralizing, de-centralizing, re-centralizing, deconstructing, downsizing, right-sizing, or otherwise re-engineering) may often alleviate the symptoms of an organization. But they rarely modify the malignant chronic anxiety that could have been part of that institution's "corporate culture" for generations, and that will, if left unmodified, resurface periodically in different shapes and forms. (Beal & Treadwell, 1999, p. 80)

Psychological or sociological theories are not sufficient to support leaders in a "leadership-toxic climate." Climate change begins by recognizing that negative or regressive emotional processes at work are systemic and must be dealt with throughout the organization.

A long-term approach to relationship building involves understanding that work is emotion-filled and knowing how to address negative emotions, particularly anxiety. Relationship systems can be thought of in ways similar to the natural systems of biology and physics (open, fluid, interactive, and adaptive). Rather than viewing the culture of an organization as a collection of individuals acting out emotional, relational processes, culture is the medium for these processes played out. This focus on relationship processes rather than on the individuals lends itself to applying emotional systems thinking in the workplace.

The paradox of emotional systems theory is that instead of trying to fix relationships or motivate people, leaders deliberately shift attention to their own ways of relating and communicating. The chief goal of leaders is to focus on their own integrity and capacity for dealing with the emotional processes of the organization (Beal & Treadwell, 1999, p. 11). Leaders do this by taking well-defined stands, treating conflict as natural, and determining the limits of consensus for good decision making. By dealing with the organization as an emotional system, leaders are less likely to become enmeshed in anxious, risk-averse processes in the organization. Having gained some amount of autonomy (self-differentiation), leaders are better able to connect with work teams, without reverting to the tendency to blame or correct. In some ways, this leadership approach to relationship systems is the same as a strengths approach. By looking for and supporting strengths, leaders move the organization in a positive direction rather than enabling it to be reactive or regressive.

Fundamental in the systems approach is a nonlinear view of organizational relationships. Instead of dyadic or two-person interaction, relationships are conceived as emotional triangles, with the third element being an unseen person, an issue, or another relationship. Emotional triangles have both positive and negative effects in the workplace. By analyzing triangles, leaders can be more objective in understanding what is happening and can influence the climate and effectiveness of the entire organization. Perhaps the most important effect of leaders who employ a systems approach to organizational relationships is the increase in opportunities for growth and learning.

Poorly defined leaders unwittingly compromise growth and learning by avoiding the emotional processes within their organizations. The best way to lead is "by taking the kind of stands that set limits to the invasiveness of those who lack self-regulation" (Beal & Treadwell, 1999, p. 11). In other words, leadership must be decisive in dealing with negative processes in the workplace.

In shared work settings, leadership ". . . .increasingly depends upon the power of creative relationships and all that is required in establishing, sustaining, nurturing, and bearing the anxiety involved in working through the medium of creative relationships" (Krantz, 1998, p. 11). The job of leaders in dealing with issues that organizations face is to be courageous, take a stand and stick to it, and then stay connected to those who are charged with carrying out the mission. This is a matter of finding the right balance, not finding a quick fix. Friedman portrays the balance a leader needs to find in an emotional system as a continuum.

On the left side of the continuum are behaviors that Friedman calls weak leadership and on the right side are strong leadership behaviors. A leader may be weak in one and strong in another, but through training and practice the pattern of behavior can be strengthened. The goal is to stay balanced in order to effectively lead emotional work systems.

Lean on others	←——————→	Stay accountable
Get information	←——————→	Be decisive
Keep distance	←——————→	Stay connected
Sustain anxiety	←——————→	Defuse anxiety
Do nothing	←——————→	Make decisions
Seek consensus	←——————→	Commit to seeing it through
Seek stability	←——————→	Take risks
Blame others	←——————→	Be objective
Fuse with others	←——————→	Take a stand
Stay in triangles	←——————→	Avoid being triangulated

Continuum of Leadership Functioning in Emotional Systems.
Adapted from Beal & Treadwell, 1999, p. 303.

It is important to emphasize that taking a systems approach is not the same as a systematic search for more data or the right technique. The more leaders try to help people by fixing the situation, the less likely the organization is to grow and improve. If leaders these days are to be successful, they must find ways of living within the system while remaining steadfast in defense of the common good for the organization.

> The twin problems confronting leadership in our society today, the failure of nerve and the desire for a quick fix, are not the result of overly strong self but of weak or no self. There certainly is reason to guard against capricious, irrational, autocratic, vainglorious leadership in any form of organized life. But democratic institutions have far more to fear from lack of self in their leaders and the license this gives to factionalism (which is not the same as dissent) than from too much strength in the executive power. (Beal & Treadwell, 1999, p. 217)

Ronald Heifetz, a leadership expert at Harvard University, takes a compatible approach to leadership of emotional systems at work. Adaptive leadership for today's organizations requires leaders who have courage to "interrogate reality." As he describes it, the leader's role in an emotional/social system is twofold: to help people face reality and conflict and to mobilize them to make change. In doing so, a leader must be a diagnostician and, when resistance starts, avoid taking things personally:

> It's dangerous to challenge people in a way that will require changes in their priorities, their values, their habits. It's dangerous to try to persuade people to take more responsibility than they feel comfortable with. And that's why so many leaders get marginalized, diverted, attacked, seduced. You want to be able to stir the pot without letting it boil over. You want to regulate disequilibrium, to keep people in a productive discomfort zone.

Courage. . . . diagnosis. . . . adaptive work. . . . relationship. These are the main functions of leadership for our day and time. Leading today is not just about dealing with conflict, it is also about bringing value and change to an organization. With so much at stake for organizations in the age of the quick fix, leaders must first find a sense of self that is capable of guiding an organization through the long haul.

RESOURCES

Edward W. Beal & Margaret M. Treadwell, A failure of nerve: Leadership in the age of the quick fix. Edwin Friedman Estate/Trust, 1999.

Barbara C. Crosby & John M. Bryson, *Leadership for the Common Good: Tackling Public Problems in a Shared-Power World.* Jossey-Bass, 2005.

Yiannis Gabriel, The hubris of management. *Administrative Theory and Praxis*, 1998.

Ronald Heifetz, *Leadership without Easy Answers.* Harvard University Press, 1994.

Kristina Jaskyte, Transformational leadership, organizational culture, and innovativeness in nonprofit organizations." *Nonprofit Management & Leadership,* Winter 2004.

James Krantz, Anxiety & the new order. *Leadership in the 21st Century.* International Universities, 1998.

Andre Martin, The changing nature of leadership. The Center for Creative Leadership, 2005.

Tom Peters, *Thriving on Chaos: Handbook for a Management Revolution.* Knopf, 1987.

Warren Smith, Chaos theory and postmodern organization. *International Journal of Organizational Theory and Behavior*, 2001.

Daniel J. Svyantek & Richard P. DeShon, Organizational attractors: A chaos theory explanation of why cultural change efforts often fail. *Public Administration Quarterly*, 1993.

William C. Taylor, The leader of the future: Harvard's Ronald Heifetz offers a short course on the future of leadership. Fast Company, May 1999. www.fastcompany.com/online/25/heifetz.html

Stephen J. Zaccaro & Richard J. Klimoski, *The Nature of Organizational Leadership: Understanding the Performance Imperatives Confronting Today's Leaders.* Jossey-Bass, 2001.

For more information check these sites:

www.ccl.org
www.ksg.harvard.edu/leadership
www.situational.com
www.blanchardtraining.com

UNIT 1

Contextual Issues in Organizational Leadership

The lead issue focuses attention directly on leadership with the question, "What Are the Newest Approaches to Organizational Leadership?" The readings present divergent perspectives on this opening question. The first approach is "flexible" leadership, a term that acknowledges the practice of leadership cannot be rigid or controlling. The second approach is "leading together," which moves leadership in the direction of a process. The third approach calls for an entirely different type of leader—the social entrepreneur. And the final approach focuses on the emotional intelligence needed by successful leaders. In assessing the validity of each approach, consider the four elements presented in the Zaccaro and Klimoski reading by asking questions like, Is one approach more "embedded" than another? What is the cognitive, social, or political grounding for this approach? and How is each approach contextually defined and caused?

Chaos theory and systems theory are germane to several of the issues addressed in Unit 1 of this book, particularly "Does Organizational Culture Matter?" and "How Is Globalization Affecting Organizations around the World?" The culture of an organization has covert and open dimensions. The public may think it knows an organization by its behavior, but the very next day something shocking happens within the organization that proves its true culture was hidden all along. The reason, from a systems perspective, is that internal culture is really a web that consists of component systems, some of which may interfere with the "public persona" that the organization attempts to purvey. The four readings on organizational culture deal with the root problem: Should ethics be treated as a matter of compliance or performance?

In systems terms, leadership that understands an organization's adaptive skill, its openness, and its response to irregular processes will be better able to handle the intangible nature of globalization. The readings chosen for globalization look at the unexpected consequences of incremental changes across the globe on American organizations. Keep in mind that one of the characteristics of chaotic systems is very small changes in conditions elsewhere will lead to completely different outcomes for an organization. Applied to the effects of globalization, what is happening in Peking today can have far-reaching consequences for an American organization that does not even intend to go global.

Three of the issues in Unit 1 of this book focus on relationships within teams and across the organization. The readings selected for each of these issues compose an intriguing and important conversation about fundamentals of organizational life. The questions show just how important these issues are: "Why Is It Important for Leaders to Understand the Role of Social Responsibility in Organizations?" "What Does It Take for an Organization to Act Ethically?" and "How Can Leaders Capitalize on Diversity in the Workplace?"

The readings selected for social responsibility confirm that this issue is causing deep cleavage in organizations these days. Some experts warn that it is dangerous for organizations to place political goals ahead of business goals. They point to the chief purpose of business—creating wealth—and express concern that political goals will thwart this purpose. For other organizations, social responsibility *is* the chief purpose and business goals are secondary. Leaders of nonprofits and NGOs do well to pay attention to the debate about the place of social responsibility in any organization.

What to do about ethics is one of the biggest challenges facing organizations today. Scholars, consultants, critics, and pundits today agree that organizations are in great need of better ethics. But what are leaders doing about this Achilles' heel of organizations? The readings addressing ethics paint a picture of leadership that is in a quandary. Leaders are divided over whether ethical conduct in the workplace is a matter of compliance with a code of ethics or part of a larger issue of corporate culture. Four readings provide different perspectives for leaders to consider. As you consider each reading, reflect on whether the perspective deals exclusively with the structural aspects of workplace ethics without considering the new reality of work in a "shared-power" world. And there is an underlying question to consider—whether it is possible for leadership to address ethics in a "no-one-in-charge" world.

Is workforce diversity an opportunity or impediment to organizations? This is the fundamental question behind this contextual issue for today's organizations. The readings look at the diversity issue from several angles— competitive advantage, traditional diversity programming, and strategic challenges of diverse age groups.

Issue 1: What Are the Newest Approaches to Organizational Leadership?

Issue 2: Why Is It Important for Leaders to Understand the Role of Social Responsibility in Organizations?

Issue 3: What Does It Take for an Organization to Act Ethically?

Issue 4: Does Organizational Culture Link to Success or Profitability?

Issue 5: How Can Leaders Capitalize on Diversity in the Workplace?

Issue 6: How Is Globalization Affecting Organizations around the World?

ISSUE 1

What Are the Newest Approaches to Organizational Leadership?

INTRODUCTION

There is no question that effective leadership is key to an organization's success. What is in question is whether one approach is better than another. Should a leader be in charge, out front, an expert? Or should a leader be a catalyst, visionary, empowering? Is leadership a matter of temperament and talent or training and practice? Should a leader focus on data and products/services or on people and processes?

These long-standing questions are dealt with in the readings for this section. In two of the readings, the authors set the stage for a new approach by showing a contrast with a model that was considered effective in the past. In the remaining two articles, the authors integrate previous models into a contemporary version. Taken together, the readings provide a multi-perspective look at the question of what defines organizational leadership today.

In "Improving Performance Through Flexible Leadership," two management experts provide a model of leadership that deals with the question: Does a leader focus on data and products/services or on people and processes? For Yukl and Lepsinger, leadership quality comes down to how well a leader influences three factors of an organization's success—efficiency, adaptation, and human resources. These authors contend that the essential element is flexibility. They identify three guidelines for flexible leadership: understanding both the external and internal processes, using systems thinking, and bringing people together in support of a shared purpose.

Drath presents the argument for a bold new perspective on leadership that is inclusive and collective, making the tasks of leading more compatible with current economic, social, and political realities. In "Leading Together: Complex Challenges Require a New Approach," Drath identifies several dynamics that organizations have never faced before. Today's problems are far more complex and are spread across traditional functional boundaries. Work teams share responsibility and no one person may be in charge. What is called for is a new approach—connected leadership—where shared sense-making leads to shared understanding, where structures are flexible, and where the strategy, as well as the outcome, is emergent.

4

The perspective on leadership provided by authors Barendsen and Gardner is within the domain of public, nonprofit, and educational organizations. "Is the Social Entrepreneur a New Type of Leader?" defines a unique type of leader whose focus is social problems and whose approach is entrepreneurial. This is a caring professional who also has business acumen—a powerful leadership combination according to the authors. What makes this leader unique is not simply a set of skills, but the integration of the individual's personality and beliefs with the ability to handle social problems in a business-like manner.

The final reading, "Successful Leaders Possess Emotional Intelligence," deals with the temperament question. Tim Field posits that it is not sufficient for a leader to have business savvy—people savvy is also necessary. While this area of leadership has always been intriguing, it is only recently that theorists and researchers have begun a systematic investigation into the underlying factor—emotional intelligence. Field defines three aspects of emotional intelligence that are vital to effective leadership: self-awareness, self-regulation, and social skill. It is the ability to understand and manage one's own emotions, in tandem with understanding others' emotions that enable a leader to help the organization make good decisions.

Will the questions posed at the beginning of this introduction ever be answered once and for all? Consider what Pierce and Newstrom (2006) say is happening to leadership:

> Increasingly, organizations are modifying the role of yesterday's manager, changing the role to that of a leader charged with the responsibility to gain follower recognition and acceptance and become a facilitator and orchestrator of group activity, while also serving as coach and cheerleader. It is feasible that many of these roles (e.g., servant, teacher, coach, cheerleader) will become a common part of the conceptualization of leader and leadership as the twenty-first century continues to unfold. (p. 11)

It seems evident that the meaning of leadership changes as organizations change. Because organizations will continue to vary in purpose, size, and structure, undoubtedly leadership approaches will continue to evolve.

SOURCES

Gary Yukl & Richard Lepsinger, Improving performance through flexible leadership. *Leadership in Action,* September/October 2005.

Wilfred H. Drath, Leading together: Complex challenges require a new approach. *Leadership in Action,* March/April 2003.

Lynn Barendsen & Howard Gardner, Is the social entrepreneur a new type of leader? *Leader to Leader,* Fall 2004.

Tim Field, Successful leaders possess emotional intelligence. *Media & Entertainment Insights,* October 2003.

ARTICLE 1.1

Improving Performance Through Flexible Leadership

Gary Yukl and Richard Lepsinger

In most industries there are companies that consistently outperform competitors that have similar business strategies and operating models and must deal with the same economic conditions. Examples include Southwest Airlines versus America West, Dell versus Gateway, and Wal-Mart versus Kmart. The key factor in explaining the difference in long-term performance for these firms is the quality of leadership.

Leaders of successful companies are able to influence three key determinants of company performance—efficiency, adaptation, and human resources. A business organization is more likely to prosper and survive when it has efficient and reliable operations, when it is adaptable and innovative in providing the products and services that customers want at prices they are willing to pay, and when it has people with a high level of skill, commitment, and mutual trust. There are two basic approaches for influencing these performance determinants.

One is the use of specific leadership behaviors. Efficiency can be improved through task-oriented behaviors such as short-term planning, clarifying work roles and task objectives, and monitoring operations and employee performance. Adaptation to the external environment can be improved through change-oriented behaviors such as identifying external threats and opportunities, explaining the need for change, articulating a vision for the future, and encouraging innovative thinking. And human relations and resources can be improved through relations-oriented behaviors such as empowering employees and providing support, recognition, and coaching.

The second approach that leaders can take to influence the performance determinants is the use of management programs, systems, structural forms, and external initiatives. Efficiency can be improved through process-improvement and cost-reduction programs and standardization and functional specialization in the design of work processes and sub-units. Adaptation can be improved through programs to learn about customer preferences and competitor actions, programs to encourage and facilitate innovation, structural forms to facilitate innovation, and external initiatives to enhance growth and diversification. Human resources and relations can be improved through quality-of-work-life programs; employee benefit, development, and empowerment programs; and talent management programs. The authority to initiate or modify management programs and systems is usually reserved for top management, but a new

6

program or system is unlikely to be successful without the support and coopera-tion of managers at all levels of the organization.

WORKING TOGETHER

These two different approaches for influencing performance determinants are complementary rather than mutually exclusive, and they can be used together in a mutually supportive way. Some leadership behaviors can be used to facilitate the implementation of new programs or systems and help make them successful. Some management programs and systems can enhance the effects of the leader-ship behaviors or reduce the need for them.

Efforts by leaders to influence improvements in efficiency, adaptation, and human resources are complicated by the complex relationships and potential trade-offs among these performance determinants and by changing conditions that can alter their relative importance. There is no simple formula to guarantee success in dealing with these leadership challenges, but flexibility is an essen-tial ingredient. Here are several useful guidelines for flexible leadership:

Maintain situational awareness. Situational awareness involves knowledge about external and internal processes that affect a leader's organization or team. It is difficult to diagnose the causes of a problem and identify good solutions without a clear understanding of the prior events and decisions that determined how the organization got to where it is, the attitudes of people who will be affected by major change, and the political processes that determine how stra-tegic decisions are approved. To obtain up-to-date information about relevant events and trends, it is usually necessary for leaders to develop an extensive network of contacts inside and outside the organization. These contacts can provide information that is not available from formal communications or from the regular information systems. Even when the company has a good informa-tion system, leaders can improve their understanding of organizational pro-cesses and problems by visiting facilities, observing operations firsthand, and meeting with employees, customers, and suppliers.

How is "managing by walking around" different from maintaining situational awareness?

Embrace systems thinking. Systems thinking is needed to understand the complex interdependencies among performance determinants and the short- and long-term effects of attempts to influence them. In large organizations, actions invariably have multiple outcomes, including unintended side effects. Complex problems often have multiple causes, which may include actions taken earlier to solve other problems. Changes often have delayed effects. A change in one part of a system will eventually affect other parts of it, and any short-term benefits may be lost as effects of the change eventually ripple through the system. Unless a new program or initiative is compatible with the competitive strategy, the organizational culture, and other programs and systems, the potential benefits will not be attained. It is essential to identify trade-offs and consider potential consequences in preparing for a change or new initiative, and leaders should look for ways to achieve synergy among different programs, systems, and structures.

How does building commitment to a core ideology differ from the traditional notion that a leader casts the vision?

Build commitment to a core ideology. To achieve sustained high performance in a large organization, the actions of the various leaders must be compatible with one another and with the competitive strategy. It is difficult to achieve the necessary level of cooperation and coordination unless each leader's decisions and actions are guided by a core organizational ideology. This ideology usually includes shared values and beliefs about the mission and purpose of the organization, the quality of products and services, and the rights and obligations of individuals.

A primary responsibility of leadership at the top is to help members come together in support of a shared purpose or mission for the organization. A primary responsibility of the leadership at the middle and lower levels is to build support for the core ideology by ensuring that it is clear and by explicitly using it to guide decisions and actions. When decisions are made, the ideals and values should be emphasized more than the policies and procedures that supposedly reflect them. In other words, the "spirit of the law" should be emphasized more than the "letter of the law" when the two are inconsistent.

The core ideology also provides a mental compass to help leaders identify appropriate forms of adaptation. Successful adaptation requires a good understanding of customer needs, but it is not appropriate to do anything that customers want just to increase sales. For example, clients of auditing, consulting, and financial firms may prefer to get rosy reports that overlook or minimize serious problems. However, a biased report designed to ensure future business from a client is inconsistent with the ideal of providing accurate and objective appraisals and recommendations.

Lead by example. Setting an example through one's own behavior is an important form of influencing that can be used to emphasize any of the performance determinants. When top executives act in highly visible ways that emphasize the importance of efficiency, innovation, or human relations, the effects can cascade down through the organization. For example, selling the corporate jet and the limousines used by executives is a way to communicate the importance of reducing costs. Setting a bad example can be as powerful as setting a good example, and it is essential to keep decisions and actions consistent with espoused values and the core ideology. Unethical behavior and decisions based primarily on the leader's self-interest can undermine the trust and commitment of employees.

A HELPFUL MODEL

The importance of efficiency, adaptation, and human resources may seem obvious, but many business failures and derailed management careers are largely a result of a lack of understanding and appreciation of the complex relationships among the performance determinants and their joint effects on the long-term performance of an organization. Even though there is no simple formula for success, it is helpful to have this model as a reminder that the combined effects of all three determinants should be considered when planning improvements in organizational effectiveness.

Leading Together: Complex Challenges Require a New Approach

Wilfred H. Drath

Leadership has become more difficult because of challenges that are not just complicated but also unpredictable. Such challenges demand that people and organizations fundamentally change, and make it virtually impossible for an individual leader to accomplish the work of leadership. What is needed is a more inclusive and collective leadership, a prospect that although difficult to achieve holds much potential.

People in organizations want and need to work together effectively and productively. Individuals long to be part of a bigger picture that connects them to a larger purpose. This is what they expect leadership to accomplish. They expect leadership to create the direction, alignment, and commitment that will enable them, working together, to achieve organizational success.

The trouble is, it's getting harder and harder to make this happen. Creating direction, alignment, and commitment—the work of leadership—is becoming more difficult than ever.

There are a number of reasons for this. As organizations break down functional silos and develop greater global reach, people more often work with others who are not like them. It's harder to get people who don't share a common set of values and perspectives to get behind a common direction, to align, and to commit to one another.

Adding to this difficulty, people don't work side by side as much anymore. People working together might be scattered over several regions and time zones, even over different countries. Subtle and not-so-subtle barriers to communication and trust are created by the lack of simply being in the same room together. It's harder to shape a common purpose and get people aligned, and it's more difficult for people who don't see each other face to face to commit effectively to one another.

It's also getting harder to make leadership work because of changes in the attitude toward traditional ways of practicing leadership. Increasingly people without formal authority want to be involved in setting their own direction and in designing their own work and how they will coordinate with others. They are less willing to commit themselves to work in which they have had no say. Yet people may not be prepared to participate effectively in leadership this way. They may knock on the door demanding to be let in on leadership without actually knowing how to enter into it. It's harder to create direction, alignment, and commitment when there are different and sometimes competing ideas of how to best accomplish this leadership work and when people have differing levels of readiness for participating in leadership.

FACING THE UNKNOWN

In general, leadership is more difficult today because of what Ronald A. Heifetz, in his book *Leadership Without Easy Answers*, calls *adaptive challenges*, which can also be thought of as complex challenges. A complex challenge is more than just a very complicated problem. Complexity implies a lack of predictability. Complex challenges confront people with the unknown and often result in unintended consequences.

This unpredictability also means that a complex challenge is quite different from a technical problem. Technical problems are predictable and solvable. Using assumptions, methods, and tools that already exist, people can readily define the nature of a technical problem and prepare a solution with some confidence in the results. So, for example, if a key supplier changes the pricing on critical components, and such changes are expected to happen from time to time (the problem is already understood), and there are established ways of responding (tools for solving the problem already exist), then this is a technical problem. A technical problem arises and is solved *without any fundamental change* in assumptions, methods, or tools. Also, the people who solve a technical problem don't themselves have to change.

A complex challenge cannot be dealt with like this. Existing assumptions, methods, or tools are no good in the face of a complex challenge and may even get in the way. To be faced successfully, complex challenges require altered assumptions, different methods, and new tools not yet invented. Complex challenges require people and organizations to change, often in profound and fundamental ways. This is where things get unpredictable. Some examples of current complex challenges are the need for companies that have merged to bring about culture change, for the health care industry to address the nursing shortage, for many companies to make the transformation from product push to customer pull, and for social agencies to get diverse constituents with differing perspectives to work together on such deep-rooted issues as reducing the number of youthful offenders.

Complex challenges are made even more difficult by the fact that no one can say with any authority or accuracy just how things need to change. This is where leadership starts to get a lot harder. Because the complex challenge lies beyond the scope of existing assumptions, the frameworks that people use to try to understand the nature of the challenge itself are not adequate. So, for example, it's not just that people in an organization that needs to undergo a culture change don't know how to make the change happen. It's worse than that. They have no way of being sure what sort of new culture is needed. No one who is part of the existing organization has any kind of especially gifted insight into the needs of the new, changed, still-unknown organization of the future. Everyone has ideas, of course, and everyone has a point of view and may be quite attached to it. Only by virtue of position and authority are anyone's ideas given special status. Unfortunately, although having a lot of authority may make it possible for a person to make sure his or her views hold sway, that doesn't guarantee the effectiveness of those views.

If all of this makes it sound as though a complex challenge requires a lot of talk and reflection among a lot of people in an organization, it does. And all that talk and reflection takes a lot of time. Because the complex challenge is not only complex but also a challenge, however, it demands a response now, not someday. So facing a complex challenge puts people in a bind and ensures that they will experience some stress as they try to think and reflect together without letting analysis lead to paralysis.

What can a leader do to ease stress when an organization faces a complex challenge?

NO GOING IT ALONE

In the face of complex challenges, a leader, no matter how skilled and otherwise effective, cannot simply step into the breach, articulate a new vision, make some clarifying decisions, and proclaim success. Because a complex challenge requires a whole system and all the people in it to change, it lies beyond the scope of any individual person to confront. Complex challenges make it virtually impossible for an individual leader to accomplish the work of leadership, and individual leadership therefore reaches a distinct limit in the face of complex challenges.

Since about the 1920s (in the writings of Mary Parker Follett) there has been talk of the possibility of distributing or sharing leadership and making leadership more inclusive and collective. If leadership is still needed (and who can deny that it is), and if no individual alone can provide leadership in the face of a complex challenge, then perhaps what is needed is the collective action of many people. It's conceivable, even compelling, that everyone in an organization could contribute in some way to facing a complex challenge. The possibility that a more inclusive and collective way of leadership could help organizations meet complex challenges and be more effective is promising.

The problem has always been—and remains today—*how* to get more people involved in leadership, and *how* to make leadership more inclusive and collective.

Two critical problems continuously block the way. The first could be called the *too-many-chefs* problem: the effort to make more people into leaders seems doomed to collapse in a cacophony of differing visions and values as too many individuals exhibit leadership. The second could be called the *diffused accountability* problem: when people share leadership, it seems inevitable that accountability will also get shared until, as everyone becomes accountable, no one is really accountable at all.

Both of these problems are real. Attempts to make leadership more inclusive and collective have often—if not always—foundered on just these obstacles. Such failures have made many people realistically pessimistic about the utility of a more inclusive and collective approach to leadership. Yet the promise of such leadership grows brighter as complex challenges surpass the ability of the individual leader to respond.

The problem is how to develop more inclusive and collective ways of making leadership happen without running afoul of the twin problems of too many chefs and diffused accountability. Somehow we need to develop the whole process by which direction, alignment, and commitment are created—not just develop individual leaders. We at CCL call the development of individual leaders *leader development*; the development of the whole process for creating direction, alignment, and commitment we call *leadership development*. Both leader development and leadership development are needed. But even though leadership development is becoming more critically important every day, it lags far behind leader development in most organizations.

DEFINING THE TASKS

A good place to start developing a more inclusive and collective leadership is to think of leadership (both individual and collective) as a process that is used to accomplish a set of *leadership tasks.* This makes it possible to focus not on the way leadership is practiced but rather on what people hope to *accomplish* with leadership. A useful question is, What work is leadership expected to get done? As already suggested, leadership is expected to set direction, create alignment, and generate commitment—or some similar list of desired outcomes.

The too-many-chefs problem that often comes up in trying to share leadership is created when organizations try to get more people to act as leaders and exhibit leadership. This is subtly but importantly different from getting more people involved in the process of accomplishing the leadership tasks.

Getting more people to act like leaders does little more than multiply the individual leader approach. In the face of a complex challenge, simply having more people trying to say what should be done is unlikely to be effective.

In the same way, the diffused accountability problem is created when organizations make more people accountable by designating more people as leaders. This is also little more than a way to multiply individual leaders. Many ways of trying to share leadership in order to make it more inclusive and collective are actually still firmly rooted in the tradition of the individual leader—designating more leaders can just add to the difficulty of accomplishing the leadership tasks in the face of complex challenges.

So having more leaders is not the answer. Instead the answer is to create richer and more complex processes of accomplishing the leadership tasks. Focus on how to create direction, alignment, and commitment in the face of complex challenges, and forget about how many people are, or are not, leaders.

Putting the accomplishment of the leadership tasks at the heart of leadership frames different and more useful questions: What are the obstacles to clear direction, effective alignment, and solid commitment? What resources exist in the organization for creating direction, alignment, and commitment as a complex challenge is being confronted? What different approaches to accomplishing the leadership tasks are possible for the organization? How might people act in new and different ways to accomplish the leadership tasks?

Answering questions like these can help organizations avoid the traditional problems of shared leadership by getting them past the idea that more inclusive and collective approaches require making more people individual leaders.

THREE CAPABILITIES

Complex challenges require richer and more complex ways of creating direction, alignment, and commitment. The ways people talk, think, and act together—the culture of the organization along with its systems and structures—are what need to become richer and more complex.

At first this may seem to be a bad idea. When facing a complex challenge, surely the last thing needed is more complexity. Yet the very complexity of the challenge calls for an equally complex capacity to respond. A complex capacity to respond means something different from just a more complicated process. It means a more varied, less predictable, more layered process capable of greater subtlety. At CCL we believe that making the leadership process more collective, pushing the process beyond one that depends primarily on individuals, enriches the process of leadership to the level of sensitivity and responsiveness required by a complex challenge. Continuing to depend on individual leaders (no matter how many) to lead people through basic and profound changes is risky. This is because any individual leader, no matter how capable, may be unable to make such changes personally. Getting more people working together in more ways increases the likelihood that people who are able to make the needed changes themselves will become influential in the leadership process. We call this *connected leadership.*

Three collective capabilities can be useful for organizations needing to achieve connected leadership: shared sense-making, connection, and navigation.

Shared sense-making • Complex challenges do not come wrapped with an explanation. By their nature they cause confusion, ambiguity, conflict, and stress. They are immediate, so they press for a solution now. But they also force people to change toward the unknown, so they also require reflection. Moving too fast can make things worse. What seems to be required is the capability to engage in shared sense-making.

This is not problem solving; it's not even problem defining. It's a process that must come before a challenge can even be thought of as a problem with solutions. The outcome of this sense-making is shared understanding. It involves people in paying attention to both the parts and the whole of the challenge. It requires people to experience multiple perspectives and to hold conflicting views in productive tension. It answers the persistent question about difficult change: Why change? Without an understanding of why change is required, people are rightly suspicious of it.

Connection • The process of leadership is realized in the connections between people, groups, teams, functions, and whole organizations. Complex challenges threaten existing connections. Think of what happens in an organization seeking to become more customer focused. The existing structures and boundaries that differentiate and coordinate such entities as production, marketing, sales, and finance begin to be more like impediments than workable ways of organizing. Facing complex challenges requires people and organizations to develop and enrich their forms of connection.

The outcome is relationships made to work in new ways both within and between groups and communities. Getting relationships to work in new ways requires people to see patterns of connection (and disconnection) in order to explore the root causes of the complex challenge and clarify differing and sometimes conflicting values. Often, new language emerges.

Navigation • Because a complex challenge is not a familiar problem to be solved but a reality to be faced through change and development, the process is one of learning from shared experiments, small wins, innovations, and emergent strategies. No one can set a goal whose achievement will resolve the complex challenge. It is a journey whose destination is unpredictable and unknown. A key to success is the ability to be keenly sensitive to the forces of change as they happen, like mariners who sail a ship by making minute, mutual adjustments to one another and to the elements of wind and current.

These capabilities cannot be taken on by individuals. They can be developed only between individuals and between groups, functions, and whole organizations. Too often the move to more inclusive and collective approaches to leadership is attempted without making this move into the space in between. More inclusive approaches to leadership have often been expected to flow from a change in the competencies of individual leaders, such as when leaders are called on to be more empowering and inclusive and to share leadership. The persistence of the obstacles to more inclusive and collective leadership comes from the failure to let go of long-held and long-valued assumptions about the individual nature of leadership.

MAKING GAINS

In facing complex challenges, people, organizations, and communities can develop ways of accomplishing the leadership tasks that give more people a sense of being responsible for setting direction, creating alignment, and generating commitment. Successfully facing complex challenges will support a sense of shared power and collective competence.

It will also create the possibility for leadership strategy. Because strategy means making choices among alternatives, no strategy is possible without alternatives to consider. So if the development of connected leadership, of a more inclusive and collective leadership process, adds to the alternative ways that leadership can be carried out, it also creates the possibility that choices can be made about leadership. Leadership then would no longer be a matter of making a single kind of practice work for every context. Instead of seeing leadership as simply a natural force to which humans are subject and that comes in only one naturally determined version (such as the forceful leader taking charge), people would come to see leadership as a process that humans control and that can be shaped to human needs through intentional choices.

ARTICLE 1.3

Is the Social Entrepreneur a New Type of Leader?

Lynn Barendsen and Howard Gardner

*S*ocial entrepreneur is a new term, much in the news these days. Social entrepreneurs are individuals who approach a social problem with entrepreneurial spirit and business acumen. Whereas business entrepreneurs create businesses, social entrepreneurs create change. But is social entrepreneurship actually something new? What, if anything, distinguishes the social entrepreneur from other workers?

To find out, we carried out a careful study of individuals who conform to our conception of social entrepreneurs. They have formed a wide array of organizations: one lends money to small businesses in South America, a second is dedicated to urban education, a third started a for-profit Web development company that hires extensively in disadvantaged urban neighborhoods. We chose two other groups with whom to compare them: a group of business entrepreneurs (to control for entrepreneurial talent and dedication) and a group of young service professionals working in the Albert Schweitzer Fellowship Program (to control for a commitment to social missions). Individuals were selected on the basis of recommendations of experts in the three fields. We discovered that social entrepreneurs are more like the Schweitzer service professionals, but they *act* more like business entrepreneurs.

HISTORY OF SOCIAL ENTREPRENEURSHIP

Social entrepreneurship is not a new phenomenon. While the name and description may be relatively new, individuals who adopt entrepreneurial strategies to tackle social issues are not. William Lloyd Garrison founded the Anti-Slavery Society in 1833. Publisher of the first anti-slavery newspaper, the *Liberator*, Garrison campaigned tirelessly for abolition throughout his lifetime. Jane Addams, social worker and reformist, founded the social settlement Hull House in Chicago in 1889. Hull House provided a welfare center for the neighborhood poor and offered a new model that was later replicated throughout the nation. Social histories are filled with many examples, both in the United States and abroad.

Only in recent years have these changemakers become known as social entrepreneurs. The emergence of social entrepreneurship as a recognizable field is most likely due to a variety of factors, including current dissatisfaction with the pace and management of standard charities and foundations. We might point as well to the emergence of funding for social entrepreneurial ventures.

Certainly one of the reasons for this recognition and movement is William Drayton. Drayton, a MacArthur Fellow, is often credited with introducing the term social entrepreneur. In 1980, Drayton founded Ashoka in the belief that social entrepreneurs have the greatest potential for solving social problems. Ashoka is one of the very first ventures designed explicitly to fund *social entrepreneurs*. Its purpose was and remains to empower social entrepreneurs with financial resources and a professional network within which they are able to disseminate ideas and solutions.

BACKGROUND AND EARLY LIFE

Social entrepreneurs are unusual in a number of ways. Like many of us, social entrepreneurs have deeply rooted beliefs, and like many of us, these beliefs are formed early. Social entrepreneurs are exceptional, however, in *what* they believe and in *how* these beliefs originate.

Several social entrepreneurs experienced some kind of trauma early in life. One person's mother committed suicide after a lengthy depression. Others were the children of divorce. One individual's father uprooted his family and moved from a "pristine" campus environment to a housing project. The headmaster at a prestigious prep school, he decided to give up his career to become a volunteer and an activist for the disadvantaged.

These traumatic events fill in our picture of social entrepreneurs as individuals and help explain how their beliefs develop. Priorities suddenly become clear when life seems short or when one faces a stark choice. Under such circumstances, a calling may be discovered. One individual, the victim of violence at a very early age, describes his reaction as follows:

"And then as I mentioned, just some of my own experiences with violence growing up, and without going into details, just not feeling safe for significant parts of my life to the point where I wasn't sure if I wanted to be alive. So just this real sense of helplessness and anger at a fairly young age, and that is really interesting. I was ten, and had really decided that life just wasn't so great. So I was sitting there contemplating not living anymore, and I remember sitting there and thinking that life is like this big equation and that for everything bad that happens on this side, something good is going to happen on this other side and I wasn't going to check out until I got to the other side of the equation. And, this again, I was in fourth grade so I must have been nine or ten. This really strong feeling, not of entitlement because I didn't feel like someone else owed me something, but it really turned into the sense of righteous anger that this isn't okay, that this is not my fault, and that things have to be different because it is wrong."

All too often, the victims of violence eventually become perpetrators themselves. According to the social entrepreneur just quoted, a very committed and sensitive mentor kept him from following this more typical route. It is also clear from this passage that, in spite of his trauma, he maintained a belief that good existed in the world and he had an early determination to find it.

Of those social entrepreneurs who do not experience extreme trauma, several describe some kind of deeply transformative experience. These experiences include living abroad and gaining perspective, combating depression, alcohol, or drug use, or working with troubled youth. One social entrepreneur was changed during his time as a camp counselor. He asked a young camper about a half-moon-shaped scar on his shoulder. In matter-of-fact tones, the child explained that he was hurt when his mother was beating his brother with an extension cord. The counselor describes himself as permanently changed by this encounter.

About half of the social entrepreneurs and half of the Schweitzer fellows had a traumatic or deeply transformative experience at an early age. Schweitzer fellows either lost someone close to them early in life or grew up in a troubled family environment. This is not true of business entrepreneurs. Although business entrepreneurs talk about transformative experiences, these experiences are usually very different in nature from those the other two groups describe. Some talk about the experience of starting and building a company, and one mentions the intellectual "epiphany" of attending MIT.

Many of the social entrepreneurs were involved with social issues at an early age. Several had role models or parents who were politically active. One young social entrepreneur grew up in the labor movement, another describes himself as the son of "broke, biracial lesbians." Other social entrepreneurs were involved in groups such as Amnesty International, the Lutheran Volunteer Corps, Big Brother, or other local groups. One started an organization in his school to help students with disabilities.

Once again, the social entrepreneurs resemble the other caring professionals. Most of the Schweitzer fellows describe early participation in some kind of service work. These include volunteering at hospitals, visiting nursing homes regularly, or helping out at homeless shelters. By contrast, fewer than half of the business entrepreneurs mention early evidence of their entrepreneurial tendencies. A few started businesses in high school. One collected golf balls and then sold them at the local golf course. Two had parents who were themselves entrepreneurs. But again, the *nature* of this early involvement is different.

PERSONALITY

Social entrepreneurs are energetic, persistent, and usually confident, with an ability to inspire others to join them in their work. Typically they feel responsible to a cause or a mission. Social entrepreneurs are usually quite pragmatic, able to describe their business plans down to the small details. If they do not enjoy practical planning, they are able to recognize this in themselves and hire others to handle these tasks. Social entrepreneurs are also very independent. This does not mean that they are loners, or that they see themselves as operating independent of market forces. In fact, they work with a clear understanding how their particular goals fit into a larger framework.

But there is no one type of social entrepreneur. Some are truly charismatic speakers, full of energy, polished, well dressed, and at home in the boardroom. Others are more soft-spoken and quietly persistent, describing their work in pragmatic, matter-of-fact tones; it is the scope of their work, the deeds themselves, that speak most eloquently. Some entrepreneurs consider politics as a possible future career. If they are unable to achieve their goals through current work, they are willing to consider entering the political arena in order to effect greater change.

Several social entrepreneurs we interviewed specifically mention feeling isolated or never fitting in. One was born with a bone condition that caused his legs to be much shorter than they should be. He could not play sports as a child, which made him feel "different." Feeling isolated does not always mean, however, that social entrepreneurs felt excluded in school; in fact, most of them were popular growing up and often leaders in their schools. They describe a sense of isolation because they are working on unusual issues or working with marginalized groups.

Some social entrepreneurs still feel like outsiders. One describes the difficulties he has had since graduating from college and starting his organization. He realizes that, throughout his lifetime, he has felt isolated: "That is a pretty consistent theme of not feeling like I had a peer group. High school and college were similar in that I had a lot of people who respected me but didn't understand me." Some social entrepreneurs feel isolated because the work they do is so unusual. The organizations they form are typically breaking new ground.

For many social entrepreneurs, feeling like an outsider begins in childhood and helps to inspire or explain why they identify with a particular cause. As the organization is established and work begins, that feeling of isolation often increases. There are few if any peers to consult and not many understand the work being attempted.

Several Schweitzer fellows also saw themselves as outsiders during childhood. Some identify themselves as marginalized because they are immigrants, racial minorities, homosexual, or poor. Business entrepreneurs also see themselves as outside the norm: however, *outsider* takes on a different sensibility in this group. They distinguish themselves from "regular" businesspeople and from peers who have chosen professions with more directed paths (typical MBA recipients, lawyers, doctors). According to one business entrepreneur, business skills can be learned, whereas the entrepreneurial mindset cannot. Once again, social entrepreneurs are similar to the Schweitzer fellows in that they feel like outsiders. Their *actions* are similar to business entrepreneurs in that they have chosen nontraditional paths in their work.

BELIEFS

We have argued that unusual events help shape the social entrepreneur. Their beliefs are sometimes inspired by trauma, sometimes by early activism. The beliefs themselves are also unusual.

In a number of studies of young professionals in different domains, ranging from journalism to theater, we have found that religion is rarely invoked. Social entrepreneurs are very different. With one exception all the social entrepreneurs describe themselves as spiritual or religious. Indeed, one social entrepreneur plans to become a Unitarian Universalist minister. Some social entrepreneurs' beliefs stem directly from spiritual or religious upbringing. One refers to the Judaic ideal of *tikkun olam*, or the "repair of the world." According to this person, repairing the world is what we're here for. Another social entrepreneur, who describes himself as "spiritual" but not formally following any religion, describes his beliefs in these terms: "I believe that . . . we all come from a higher power and that, while even though society is very segmented, that there's a responsibility to reach out to those pockets of society that are less served."

Somewhat surprisingly this religious orientation also turned up in both the caring and business professions. A majority of both Schweitzer fellows and business entrepreneurs say that religious or spiritual beliefs are important to them. The caring professionals are often inspired and sustained by their beliefs. The business entrepreneurs are less easy to explain. Some say they actively follow their faith and believe that a greater power has a plan in mind.

Social entrepreneurs not only believe that they should create change, they believe as well that they are able to make this change happen. Maybe this faith is a prerequisite to survival in the caring professions, because the Schweitzer fellows say much the same thing. Both groups believe in human potential, or the possibility of change. As one social entrepreneur explains: "I still have hope in the basic human spirit of folks. Of folks who, when there is something wrong, or something that is unjust or—people want to do something to change it, and they do want to make it better. . . . I also believe that we all have, each and every one of us has, amazing talents, so sometimes the vehicles are not there for them to come forth."

CHALLENGES

Like most professionals, social entrepreneurs face many challenges. But social entrepreneurs typically see possibility rather than problems. (For a brief look at how social entrepreneurs confront challenges. . . .) With respect to ethical issues, in particular, there is quite a difference between Schweitzer fellows and social entrepreneurs. Schweitzer fellows wonder about the wisdom of passing condoms out to high school students. They worry about counseling people as budding medical professionals, questioning their own level of expertise. Although social entrepreneurs consider parallel issues, they do not typically mention them as challenges. Instead, much like their counterparts in business, their primary concerns involve challenges to running their organizations. The organizations are then able to grapple with and address larger ethical issues. So although social entrepreneurs see the same issues that Schweitzer fellows see, they tackle them in a manner reminiscent of business entrepreneurs.

For some social entrepreneurs, it becomes difficult to differentiate between professional and personal goals. Questions of balance between work and life become moot as the lines between the two blur. Discussions of this particular challenge again demonstrate that social entrepreneurship is a combination of entrepreneurship and the caring professions. Business entrepreneurs are very personally involved in their professions; their companies are their babies. Schweitzer fellows become personally attached to the individuals they serve. Social entrepreneurs feel both of these pulls.

Although social entrepreneurs face other obstacles, the financial pressures involved in keeping their organizations running are their greatest challenge. Most social entrepreneurs depend on the financial assistance of individuals and on private and government foundations to fulfill the needs of their organizations. While social entrepreneurs express excitement about their work and passion for the various causes they represent, many describe the fundraising process as restrictive and frustrating.

NEGOTIATING THE ETHICAL FAULT LINE

Although the social entrepreneurs we studied are exceptional in many ways, even they occasionally cut ethical corners. Because of financial pressures, one social entrepreneur reports "spinning" the truth in a way that funders might find attractive. Another refers to "mission creep," or what happens when an entrepreneur revises the goals of a venture to satisfy a funder's expectations. One social entrepreneur raised $20,000 on the promise of a challenge grant. The initial funder later withdrew her promise and the entrepreneur failed to return the $20,000.

There are also examples of social entrepreneurs who face these tensions, grapple with their principles, and make choices that are more in line with the beliefs and values they espouse. Unfortunately, however, sometimes values and standards are sacrificed in the name of organizational growth and "larger purpose." Those that do cross ethical lines—and in our sample these are not a majority—may believe they are doing so as a form of civil disobedience, breaking a law to support a higher ideal.

To be sure, as we have confirmed in other studies, other young professionals face similar challenges. Young journalists find the change from high school or college journalism to professional journalism particularly difficult. With little or no mentorship, they have little choice in assignment and are often expected to follow either the most mundane (local court hearings) or the least desirable stories (following up on tragic events). Many describe circumstances under which they are willing to sacrifice honesty early on in order to further their careers. Unlike journalists and social entrepreneurs, scientists have a clear, prescribed apprenticeship process. As they negotiate their way through the various hoops necessary to fulfill the requirement of Ph.D., postdoctoral, and professional research, they also face ethical choices. Should they choose research that will serve a greater good or be financially rewarding?

Professionals all develop tools to tackle these various challenges, and social entrepreneurs are no exception. They organize and delegate and assess their work much as other professionals do. In particular, their process resembles that of business entrepreneurs. In two methods, however, they are unusual. First, they have the comfort of their convictions. Sometimes, less comfortably, they feel they have no choice but to continue in their work:

"As a founder, you feel so invested that it is not a job that you can just quit. I really couldn't just quit and walk away and say, 'Well I did my best, and whatever happens, happens.' I don't have that luxury, and there are probably many days where if I did, I would have. But it's a situation where you've got an extraordinary burden on your shoulders that you just can't turn away from under any circumstances."

Second, they have the ability to see that something positive, such as a commitment to a cause or working with an underserved population, can emerge from a painful situation. They often learn this lesson in childhood and apply it as adults.

A NEW LEADER?

What types of organizations match well with the social entrepreneur approach?

Social entrepreneurs are not new, but they are unusual: in terms of their compelling personal histories, their distinctive profile of beliefs, and their impressive accomplishments in the face of odds. What to make of the recent prominence of the social entrepreneur? On one hand, social entrepreneurs are finally receiving the accolades they deserve. On the other, they are taking on issues and populations that governments either can't or won't tackle. Their example is impressive, indeed inspiring. But to the extent that they are truly inspiring, they should inspire others to join in their pursuits, if not as leaders, then at least as strong supporters. The rest of society shouldn't rely on a new species of independent contractor to address concerns brushed aside by others.

Three Strategies Social Entrepreneurs Use

Three strategic approaches help social entrepreneurs in their work: reframing challenges, adhering to a sense of obligation, and discerning measures of success.

Reframing Challenges

Some social entrepreneurs have the ability to see that something positive, such as a commitment to a cause or to working with an underserved population, can emerge from a painful or tragic situation. Those who have experienced trauma—social entrepreneurs and Schweitzer fellows—demonstrate an ability to reframe these challenges into opportunities for growth.

Sense of Obligation

Individuals we interviewed in all three groups express a strong sense of obligation to their work and to the people it affects. Schweitzer fellows feel responsible to the communities or causes they serve; business entrepreneurs speak about responsibilities to investors and employees. Social entrepreneurs feel all these obligations, and in some cases this leads to the feeling that they have no alternative but to continue their work. It is important to recognize, however, that although individuals may say they have "no choice" but to continue in their work, they of course choose to do so. Because of their deep convictions, these individuals are willing to respond to and act on their obligations.

Measuring Success

Social entrepreneurs regularly evaluate their work. Many describe standards by which they measure success. In assessing the value of their work, social entrepreneurs feel the challenges of the other caring professions and face these challenges with businesslike organization and methods. Measuring the impact on a particular population or on behalf of a particular cause is not always easy, and the social entrepreneurs share this challenge with the Schweitzer fellows. For-profit social entrepreneurs face this challenge in a very businesslike manner, by looking at their financial profits. Other, nonprofit social entrepreneurs create clear programmatic methods of assessment that are very much like business plans.

ARTICLE 1.4

Successful Leaders Possess Emotional Intelligence

Tim Field

No one questions that effective leadership determines the success of an organization. Management that places a strong focus on high impact leadership can instill trust and passionate commitment to the organization's goals, mission and vision, even during turbulent times. It is that commitment that drives profitability.

How does an organization define "high impact leadership" today, and how is that different from management models of the past? The biggest change and trend in leadership has been a shift from a "command and control" model where decisions and orders are dictated from the highest levels to a model that works to inspire and motivate people through empowerment and active participation in decision-making processes.

As an organizational consultant, one of the most common requests I receive today is for assistance in creating a strategic leadership plan that will implement this new model, focusing on identifying and developing key internal talent and linked to succession planning. This is even more critical as organizations become leaner and there is greater reliance on teams.

How critical is this new leadership model? In the March 2001 Harvard Business Review, Larry Bossidy (Chairman and CEO of AlliedSignal from 1991–1999) states: "I'm convinced that AlliedSignal's success was due in large part to the amount of time and emotional commitment I devoted to leadership development."

In preparing this article, I spoke with several colleagues to obtain different perspectives on this subject, with particular reference to unique leadership challenges in entertainment and media. My colleagues, Tom Cairns, SVP Human Resources NBC West Coast, and Bill Simon, of Korn/Ferry, independently identified similar key issues.

In our discussions of leadership characteristics, there was good agreement about what is critical. First, there was an underlying assumption that the individual has to have a good understanding of the business and to have "business savvy." Beyond this, however, Tom and Bill both felt that some of the most important leadership characteristics were strong "people skills," i.e., ability to build relationships internally and externally, and agility in managing constant change. Both also agreed on the importance of someone who could create and articulate a vision, but strongly linked this skill to the ability to motivate people toward that vision.

Their emphasis on "people skills" as a critical leadership competency is not surprising. Research into the art and science of effective leadership has consistently identified "people skills" as the critical variable underlying not only successful leaders but organizations that are successful long term.

EFFECTIVE LEADERSHIP

What constitutes an effective leader? An effective leader brings out the best in the organization's people in terms of their aspirations, potential, performance and contribution. They encourage collegial, collaborative and supportive work styles and use this to build strong teams.

Leaders seek and welcome feedback and are comfortable analyzing both their successes as well as their failures.

The core competency underlying these effective leadership skills is emotional intelligence. As defined by Daniel Goleman (1995, 1998), emotional intelligence has five components. Three are self-management skills and include self-awareness, self-regulation and motivation. The remaining two, empathy and social skill, involve the ability to manage relationships with others. For the purposes of this article, I will focus on self-awareness, self-regulation and social skill.

Is emotional intelligence a necessary characteristic of organizational leaders?

While intelligence and technical skills are certainly important for success, it has been shown that emotional intelligence is twice as important in achieving excellent performance for jobs at all levels of an organization. The importance of emotional intelligence becomes even stronger in senior leadership positions where it has been found that 90% of the difference between top and average senior management performance is due to emotional intelligence and not to cognitive abilities.

How important is emotional intelligence to bottom-line profitability? Harvard Psychologist David McClelland (1996), in studying a large global food and beverage company, found that division leaders with high levels of emotional intelligence out-performed yearly earnings goals by 20%, those without under-performed by almost the same amount.

It is worth looking at a few of the emotional intelligence skills more closely as they paint a very accurate perspective of what a successful leader needs to be in today's constantly changing environment. The first component, self-awareness, is the ability to recognize and understand your moods, emotions and drives and in particular the impact these have on those around you and the work environment. Executives who have good self-awareness present as self-confidant without being arrogant, can voice unpopular views and are decisive in the face of uncertainty.

The second skill is self-regulation. This refers to the ability to manage one's potentially disruptive emotions and impulses effectively, to remain composed during challenging moments and to be able to think clearly and remain focused when under pressure.

As an Executive Coach, the skill of self-regulation is one that I find of critical importance. One of the more common reasons I am asked to provide individual coaching to an executive is because of overly aggressive behavior, the "bull-in-a-china-shop syndrome." Typically the individual is technically brilliant, but they leave a human path-of-destruction everywhere they go.

While this type of behavior can occur in any organization, it seems more prominent in the entertainment industry. Much of this relates to organizational culture, and what is defined as acceptable behavior. In more traditional industries there tend to be more clearly defined guidelines of what is acceptable and what will not be tolerated. When problems occur, this allows them to be addressed more quickly.

In cultures where aggressive behavior is tolerated, problems can manifest for years. Two executives that I coached in entertainment had been exhibiting these behaviors for over ten years each. In both cases, their behavior was actually rewarded and fostered. Eventually, however, the aggressiveness became so destructive that their technical expertise no longer compensated for what they were able to accomplish using those behaviors.

It is difficult to motivate others in environments where this occurs, and the costs can be enormous. There is not only the liability issue, but also decreased morale, decreased productivity, increased turnover and most importantly the risk of losing key talent. As Bill Simon of Korn/Ferry told me, "the days of the jumpers, screamers and throwers is gone."

The final emotional intelligence component I would like to review is social skill, which is proficiency in managing relationships and building networks. This includes a number of skills such as the ability to influence and persuade others without coercion, to listen openly, to manage conflict effectively, to inspire and guide individuals as well as groups and being able to serve as a change catalyst.

For Tom Cairns of NBC, the social skill component is critical for a successful executive because of its necessity in managing key internal and external relationships. This includes being able to balance business issues with the creative side of the business when there are no longer unlimited resources available. As resources dwindle, maintaining motivation and focus becomes imperative.

AGILITY

The second area identified by both Bill and Tom regarding leadership skills was agility, i.e., the ability to be flexible and adaptable in a constantly and rapidly changing environment. Many organizations are beginning to look at agility as a critical organizational skill, and differentiate this from older "change management" approaches.

In the older organizational models, change was talked about as going from Point A to Point B in a certain amount of time. Once you got to Point B the process was over and that's where you stayed. That model often doesn't work today as changes occur so fast that before you get to Point B, something is guiding you in a different direction Point C, and before you get to Point C it starts changing again.

Agile executives are ones that are able to quickly change their mindset and direction and not stay locked into ideas that forces are indicating are no longer relevant or important. Additionally, agile executives are ones that are flexible in their leadership style and know how to apply different leadership approaches to meet the unique demands of the individuals they manage or the situations they encounter.

This agility is also linked to emotional intelligence as the agile executive has to have the ability to lead others through constant change while keeping them motivated and focused. The most effective executives use a collection of distinct leadership styles—each in the right measure, at just the right time. Such skill is unique and very high-level; and while such agility is tough to put into action, it pays off in overall organizational performance. And the good news is, this high-level executive skill can be learned.

Agility may be a more critical skill in entertainment and media than in some other industries. Strong competition for viewers/users, rapidly changing viewer interests and ever-increasing entertainment choices make agility a critical leadership skill.

One of the leadership challenges facing the entertainment and media industry will be sorting through what historically has made them successful, from what they perceive to be drivers of organizational performance in the future. Some E&M [entertainment and media] companies, e.g., were built by highly entrepreneurial types that utilized aggressive tactics to become successful. The question now becomes whether this approach will continue to be effective, and whether it will grow, develop, retain and attract the top talent needed to run the organization in the future.

The bottom line on effective leadership is that while there are certainly unique business skills needed in entertainment and media as in any industry, the core of leadership regarding people skills and motivating and inspiring others to a shared vision are the same in most industries. How that occurs or is supported is unique to each organization and its culture. Regardless of the industry, however, leadership always starts at the top.

ISSUE SUMMARY

●

Taken together, these readings on the newest approaches to organizational leadership may best be understood by the larger question: What is organizational leadership today? Foremost, the readings indicate that leadership is a group process, not a set of traits or skills embodied in a single person. If this premise is true, organizational leadership involves more than personality, influence, power, or role. Its context is broader, involving actions of all participants, accountability of all participants, and success or failure of all participants.

Having considered the readings, now reflect on this contemporary definition of organizational leadership:

> Leadership is a dynamic and working relationship, built over time, involving an exchange between leader and follower in which leadership is a resource embedded in the situation, providing direction for goal attainment. (Pierce & Newstrom, 2006, p. 6)

If you give credence to this definition, these concepts or models may be less important:

- The traits model of leadership
- Leadership tasks
- Position power
- Transactional leadership
- Followership

All of the authors make the case for situating leadership in a specific context of time and place. But beyond the situation, organizational leadership is a relational phenomenon. We are left with the notion that leadership happens because of the relationship that exists between leader and participants. Leadership has psychological, sociological, and demographic characteristics that are not just interesting—they are vital to understanding the nature of the process. The future of organizational leadership lies in how we will advance leadership as a resource.

ISSUE HIGHLIGHTS

- The key factor in organizational success is leadership quality and flexibility.
- The success of an organization does not depend on a single leader.
- Leadership today is more difficult because of unpredictable challenges.
- One emerging approach to leadership involves adapting to changing situations, maintaining efficiency, and using a systems approach.

- Complex challenges require leadership that is more inclusive, yet decisive.
- An approach, labeled "connected leadership," occurs through shared sense-making, relationships, and emergent strategizing.
- The "social entrepreneur," another type of leader, adopts entrepreneurial strategies to tackle social problems.
- "Emotional intelligence" captures a different perspective on the core competencies of leadership and includes self-management, empathy, and social skill.

CRITICAL THINKING

Compelling evidence shows organizational leadership is undergoing fundamental changes in perspective and approach. But the proliferation of books, Web sites, and resources on leadership, intended to be helpful, can actually make it more difficult to sort out the nature and direction of the changes. The sheer quantity of resources shows that effective leadership looks different to different people.

One way to sort out the essentials for yourself is to adopt a definition of leadership that takes into account multiple perspectives of the readings. Rather than choosing one specific approach over another (connected leadership vs. social entrepreneur), a definition can include elements of several approaches. Obviously, not all definitions will suffice. Start by comparing the following definitions of leadership:

> Leadership is an influence relationship among leaders and followers who intend real changes that reflect their mutual purposes. (Rost, 1993, p. 102)
> Leadership is: knowing what to do next, knowing why it is important, and knowing how to bring appropriate resources to bear on the need at hand. (Biehl, n.d.)
> Leadership is a dynamic and working relationship, built over time, involving an exchange between leader and follower in which leadership is a resource embedded in the situation, providing direction for goal attainment. (Pierce & Newstrom, 2006, p. 6)

On the surface, these contemporary descriptions of leadership emphasize similar elements. First, leadership is understood as a process that places the emphasis on the interaction, not on the individual. Second, the process of leading is one of influence. Third, the context is a group or community. But take a closer look at the way "resources" is used in the second and third definitions. Resources are understood in very different ways. In one definition, resources are external to the interaction and must be supplied by the leader and in the other definition, leadership itself is a resource. Also take a look at the use of the terms "purposes" and "goal attainment" in definitions one and three. These terms differ in their level of complexity and in extent. Any of these definitions may be useful, but questions like these help determine whether they are equally valid for capturing the direction of new approaches in organizational leadership.

Finally, using the three definitions as reference overlay the clusters of concepts described in the readings. In reading one the concepts are situational awareness, systems thinking, commitment to core ideology. In reading two the concepts are complex challenges, inclusive and collective leadership, shared sense-making, relationships, navigation. In reading three the concepts are entrepreneurial spirit, business acumen, spiritual orientation, sense of obligation, reframing challenges into opportunities. In reading four the concepts are motivation through empowerment, self-management skills, empathy, relationships. At this point, the fundamental question is whether one of these definitions is sufficient to capture the concepts you value most or will you need to look elsewhere for a better definition?

This process of aligning a definition with clusters of concepts provides a framework for organizing your understanding of new approaches to organizational leadership. Essentially, you are looking for the direction of the preponderance of evidence.

ADDITIONAL READING RESOURCES

Bernard M. Bass & Ronald E. Riggio, *Transformation Leadership*. Lawrence Erlbaum, 2005.

Bobb Biehl, *Minute Motivators*, accessed at http://www.ahcnet.org/pdf/searchlight_winter_02.pdf

Barbara C. Crosby & John M. Bryson, *Leadership for the Common Good: Tackling Public Problems in a Shared-Power World*. Jossey-Bass, 2005.

Ronald Heifetz, *Leadership Without Easy Answers*. Harvard University Press, 1994.

Jeffrey S. Luke, *Catalytic Leadership: Strategies for an Interconnected World*. Jossey-Bass, 1998.

Peter G. Northouse, *Leadership: Theory and Practice*. Sage, 2004.

Jon L. Pierce & John W. Newstrom, Introduction to leadership. *Leaders & the Leadership Process*. McGraw-Hill/Irwin, 2006.

Joseph C. Rost, *Leadership for the Twenty-First Century*. Praeger, 1993.

Gary Yukl, *Leadership in Organizations*. Prentice Hall, 2006.

For more information check these sites:

www.ccl.org
www.conference-board.org
www.leadershipcentre.gov.bc.ca
www.leadertoleader.org
www.situational.com

Why Is It Important for Leaders to Understand the Role of Social Responsibility in Organizations?

INTRODUCTION

Corporate social responsibility is not a new concept for organizations with social purpose, but it *is* new for many other organizations. In fact, due to public pressure from a variety of interest groups, corporate social responsibility (also known as corporate citizenship) is becoming a mandate for some companies. However, it is a mandate that can be difficult to figure out, largely because of varying definitions of the concept. Consider this definition:

> **Corporate social responsibility (CSR)** is an expression used to describe what some see as a company's obligation to be sensitive to the needs of **all** of the stakeholders in its business operations.
> A company's stakeholders are all those who are influenced by, or can influence, a company's decisions and actions. These can include (but are not limited to): employees, customers, suppliers, community organizations, subsidiaries and affiliates, joint venture partners, local neighborhoods, investors, and shareholders (or a sole owner).
> CSR is closely linked with the principles of "Sustainable Development" in proposing that enterprises should be obliged to make decisions based not only on the financial/economic factors but also on the social and environmental consequences of their activities. (http://en.wikipedia.org/wiki/Corporate_social_responsibility)

The Wikipedia definition is a good starting point, but the exact meaning of social responsibility depends on many other factors, including the scope of the organization's mission and which interest group is adding the pressure. For many people, social responsibility simply means acting ethically, behaving responsibly and no one can argue with that. For others, the fundamental question is whether ethical or socially responsible investments are good business practice. Some see CSR as the counterbalance to decades of detrimental actions of big business, for example, actions that have exploited laborers or plundered the environment. The readings selected for this issue provide an overview of the many different purposes and types of corporate social responsibility that companies are undertaking today.

The first reading is a report on the state of corporate citizenship across the nation. "Doing Well by Doing Good 2005" is the third annual study commissioned by GolinHarris, a business support firm. This public opinion survey of Americans' expectations of companies and organizations is an eye-opener. What is clear is that citizens do not believe companies are very good citizens. The report verifies that the attributes most important to Americans are personal ones: honesty and ethical behavior. What is also clear is that Americans are placing ever-increasing expectations on its companies to deal with national social issues. (See Figure 1 in the first reading.)

"David Henderson on the Role of Business Today: Does It Include Corporate Social Responsibility?" is an insightful interview with a leading economist and business consultant. Just how many social objectives are the duty of companies? Is CSR becoming the new doctrine that will transform companies? Henderson claims that confusion over the definition of CSR is part of the problem in sorting out an appropriate role of organizations. Henderson, who views CSR as a matter of economics, is concerned that established fiscal and trade principles are being overlooked as companies move to adopt broader social responsibilities.

In "The Myth of CSR," Deborah Doane discusses four fundamental limits of social responsibility. Doane makes the case for a significant difference between what is good for an organization and what is good for society. If the driving force behind a company is capitalism, it only makes sense that the modus operandi is less about benevolence and more about capital. And while "ethical consumerism" is becoming a popular stance for people to take, consumers are not consistent when they are making purchases or dealing with companies. Due to these practical realities, CSR may not make a significant difference over time. Doane argues that if CSR is to be more than a public relations campaign, the legal structure of organizations will need to be altered.

T. E. Bostock pulls no punches in "The Dangers of Weasel Words: 'Corporate Social Responsibility' as a Banner for Left-Wing Politics." Bostock has experience as a partner in international law firms that represent corporations and organizations. Out of this context, Bostock argues that social responsibility (when practiced aggressively) is incongruent with fundamentals of corporate law, which deal with an organization's obligation to shareholders and outside parties. Keep in mind that for Bostock, shareholders are a legally defined entity. For others, the entity is stakeholders, a much broader, more diffuse group. His critique hinges on an essential question: Is corporate social responsibility a sure foundation for developing policy, practice, and procedure?

With so much attention given to corporate social responsibility today, it is time to ask: Is CSR a myth, a mandate, or a movement?

SOURCES

GolinHarris, Doing well by doing good 2005: The trajectory of corporate citizenship in American business. *GolinHarris*, 2005.

Journal of Financial Planning, 10 questions with David Henderson on the role of business today: Does it include corporate social responsibility? *Journal of Financial Planning*, August 2005.

Deborah Doane, The myth of CSR. *Stanford Social Innovation Review*, Fall 2005.

T. E. Bostock, The dangers of weasel words: "Corporate social responsibility" as a banner for left-wing politics. *National Observer*, Spring 2005.

Doing Well by Doing Good 2005: The Trajectory of Corporate Citizenship in American Business

GolinHarris

A GLIMMER OF HOPE? HOW CONSUMERS ARE RESPONDING TO CORPORATE CITIZENSHIP

Everywhere you look companies seem to be committing themselves to good corporate citizenship. From reducing greenhouse gases to awareness-building through rubber bracelets and walk-a-thons to more stringent corporate governance to a proliferation of Corporate Social Responsibility reports, companies are certainly getting the message that doing good deeds can be good for business.

And they are increasingly getting much more sophisticated about how they approach this work—making sure that the programs they invest in fit with their business, achieving real business-oriented goals, as well as societal ones, and engaging employees and customers.

Our third annual study on corporate citizenship shows that the downward spiral may be over when it comes to how people perceive corporate citizenship and companies' commitment in this area. It is one of the first signs that Americans may be ready to put the controversy of corporate scandals behind them and get back to business. Only now, there will be a new set of rules for what it means to be a "good" corporate citizen, both in a very real legal reporting sense and in terms of consumers' expectations for how companies behave in the marketplace and in the community.

But the alarm continues to sound as there is still a large number of Americans who are not ready to give companies any credit at this stage, even with what appears to be a renewed commitment on the part of business. In fact, 44% of the respondents to our survey say that American business is headed in the wrong direction when it comes to corporate citizenship. Now is not the time for any company to rest on its laurels as consumers and other stakeholders will continue to hold American business to a new and increasingly rigorous set of standards. Companies who have made corporate citizenship a company value and reaped the benefits of an improved reputation will not be able to slow down as a new group of companies figures out how to make this strategy work for them. What we will see in the coming years is a growing sophistication of this discipline and strategy as it continues to evolve from "nice-to-do" to "must-do."

We are pleased to present the results of *Doing Well by Doing Good 2005*, our third annual national opinion study based on interviews with 3,500 Americans on their attitudes and expectations of corporate citizenship and its role in business; the qualities that make a good corporate citizen; and people's perceptions of corporate citizenship performance by 108 brands.

AMERICANS' EXPECTATIONS REGARDING CORPORATE CITIZENSHIP ARE STILL UNMET

For all of the efforts companies are making in the area of corporate citizenship, Americans are still not giving business high marks in this area. More consumers report companies are doing a bad job when it comes to corporate citizenship. And what's worse, they don't see any sign that companies are getting any better. Nearly half (44%) of Americans think business performance in corporate citizenship is headed in the wrong direction.

Some of this sentiment is residual from the wave of corporate scandals and continuing coverage of corporate misdeeds.

However, it is clear that some companies that are making investments in this area simply have not figured out how to maximize the return on their investment.

GOOD CORPORATE CITIZENSHIP BUILDS TRUST

Companies have a real opportunity to build powerful bonds with key stakeholder groups by maximizing their corporate citizenship investments. They can encourage consumers to try their products for the first time, and they can improve the morale of their employees and improve recruitment and retention efforts of the best and brightest employees. Good corporate citizenship also inspires people to spread the word about a company: Both customers and employees report that they would "recommend" a company for its products and services, or as a place to work because of good corporate citizenship. This ability to inspire word-of-mouth is very powerful in a time when people rely on friends and family more than advertising and other communications vehicles for their information. *See tables below.*

Corporate Citizenship Rating

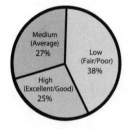

Corporate Citizenship Direction

Corporate Citizenship Influence on Consumer Opinions/Behavior (Top 5)

1. Be willing to try the company's products for the first time
2. Welcome the company into my community
3. Recommend the company's products and services to friends and family
4. Improve my overall trust for the company, its people and products
5. Improve my overall opinion of the company's reputation

Corporate Citizenship Influence on Employee Opinions/Behavior (Top 5)

1. Increase morale, spirit and pride by me and my fellow employees
2. Increase the trust I have in my employer
3. Enhance my employer's overall reputation in the community, in my opinion
4. Enable my employer to attract and retain the best, most talented people
5. Recommend my employer to others as a place to work, if asked my opinion

Information Sources (Top 5)

1. Through people and organizations helped by the company's corporate citizenship
2. News coverage on television and radio
3. News coverage on newspapers and magazines
4. Through partnering with non-profit organizations, educational institutions government, etc.
5. Community events, fundraisers, sponsorships, symbols (e.g. ribbons, bracelets)

TOP CONCERNS FOR BUSINESS TO ADDRESS

Most everyone has a story to tell about a work experience they had that was really positive and one that was not so great. These memories, both good and bad, stay etched in our psyche for a long time and they play a key role in how we judge companies and their record in corporate citizenship. Little wonder that when it comes to issues consumers believe business ought to address, the primary concern among all demographic groups is worker treatment—providing safe working conditions, job training and healthcare benefits. So to the degree a company is seen as having innovative programs in this area and is recognized as a leader, that company will enjoy the benefit of an improved reputation in the area of corporate citizenship. Issues related to the environment and education rank high with the American public. African Americans tend to favor issues that address local, community problems. Hispanics tend to focus on helping those less fortunate. Older Americans are interested in holding companies accountable for standing by product safety. *See Figure 1.*

COMMUNICATING ABOUT CORPORATE CITIZENSHIP

Americans are increasingly savvy when it comes to processing information coming from companies. What was once perhaps a healthy dose of skepticism a few years ago has turned into downright denial on the part of the public to take any information they receive at face value. What's more, consumers have the ability to check facts themselves on the internet going directly to sources of information rather than waiting for the information to come to them. What this means is that, more than ever before, companies must rely on objective, third-party, credible sources to communicate their commitment to corporate citizenship for them. And in order to maximize their communications efforts they need to find ways to engage consumers and other stakeholders through programs that are experiential and demonstrate a company's commitment by encouraging participation.

ATTRIBUTES OF GOOD CORPORATE CITIZENSHIP

The 2005 study identifies 12 key drivers that are important in building a company's reputation as a good corporate citizen. How a company treats its employees and how it is perceived as an ethical and honest company are still the two most critical factors when consumers judge a company's performance as a good corporate citizen. In this year's survey two additional attributes were considered that consumers ended up ranking as the third and fourth most important factors in corporate citizenship: "Goes beyond what is required to provide safe and reliable products and services" (50%), and "Responsibly markets and advertises its products and services" (40%). *See Figure 2 for complete listing.*

CHANGE CORPORATE CITIZENSHIP INDEX (CCI)

The *Change* Corporate Citizenship Index (CCI) is a proprietary metric that weights, integrates and consolidates the full range of corporate citizenship drivers into a single number score that enables "apples-to-apples" brand comparison. Using the CCI, a company can measure its own corporate citizenship against direct competitors, peer groups of brands sharing similar qualities, gold-standard brands whose corporate citizenship provides an aspirational model

Figure 1   Top 5 Corporate Citizenship Concerns

All	Men	Women	African American	Hispanic/Latino	Age: 55+
Worker welfare: rights, working conditions	Worker welfare: rights, working conditions	Worker welfare: rights, working conditions	Worker welfare: rights, working conditions	Worker welfare: rights, working conditions	Worker welfare: rights, working conditions
Promoting product safety	Guarding privacy concerns	Promoting product safety	Promoting human rights	Promoting human rights	Promoting product safety
Guarding privacy concerns	Preserving, renewing environmental resources	Guarding privacy concerns	Helping fight poverty, hunger	Helping fight poverty, hunger	Guarding privacy concerns
Preserving, renewing environmental resources	Promoting product safety	Improving quality of education	Helping redevelop neighborhoods, inner cities	Helping people with physical/mental disabilities	Preserving, renewing environmental resources
Improving quality of education	Promoting human rights	Preserving, renewing environmental resources	Improving quality of education	Helping cure illnesses	Promoting human rights

Figure 2   Top 12 Corporate Citizenship Drivers

Rank	Importance When Evaluating a Company's Corporate Citizenship	"Ranked Very High in Importance"
1.	Values and treats its employees well and fairly	69%
2.	Executives and business practices are ethical, honest, responsible and accountable	67%
3.	Goes beyond what is required to provide safe and reliable products and services	50%
4.	Responsibly markets and advertises its products and services	40%
5.	Committed to social responsibility, economic opportunity, environmental protection, etc.	38%
6.	Committed to diversity (gender, race, etc) in the workplace and its business practices	38%
7.	Listens to community or customer input before making business decisions	34%
8.	Is active and involved in the communities where it does business	33%
9.	Company's products and services enhance peoples' lives	31%
10.	Corporate values and business practices are consistent with my own beliefs	29%
11.	Donates or invests its fair share of profits, goods or services to benefit others	27%
12.	Supports a cause or issue that has led to improvement and positive change	26%

Figure 3   2005 Ranking Guide

Rank	CCI Score	Number of Brands
Excellent	65–100	4
Good	55–64	41
Average	50–54	39
Fair	45–49	18

and the company's own performance over time with customers, employees or investors.

In 2005, *Change* evaluated 108 brands for the CCI. This year CCI scores ranged from a high of 67 to a low of 39, with 52 as the average CCI score across all brands tested. Once the brands receive their CCI scores, they are classified using one of five performance grades from excellent to poor. *See Figure 3.*

While Americans perceive business in general as heading in the wrong direction and not living up to its corporate citizenship commitment, the 2005 CCI demonstrates that Americans can and do make strong distinctions between brands that are pace-setters, leaders, followers and laggards.

All brands included in the 2005 survey have their own unique corporate citizenship strengths and weaknesses, and approximately 40 percent of the 108 brands ranked "Good" or "Excellent" with the CCI scores of 55 or greater.

These 10 brands are examples of companies that not only have embraced corporate citizenship, but have also succeeded in making corporate citizenship an essential and vital part of their business strategy, value proposition and stakeholder relationships. *See Figure 4.*

What are some of the issues related to corporate social responsibility that would be unique to non-profits?

Figure 4   Top Corporate Citizenship Brands

Brand	CCI Score
Johnson & Johnson	67
Ben & Jerry's	66
Disney	65
Whole Foods	65
SC Johnson	64
Kraft	62
3M	61
McDonald's	61
Procter & Gamble	61
Southwest Airlines	61

IMPLICATIONS FOR COMMUNICATING ABOUT CORPORATE CITIZENSHIP

Don't be Shy

Any fear of being perceived as self-serving should be outweighed by the risk in not communicating what you are doing. Communication around a company's corporate citizenship record should be loud and clear to all important stakeholder groups. Companies should avoid "spin" and focus on sincerity and authenticity.

Use the Most Credible Communications Vehicles

Choose a signature cause that your most important stakeholders will care about and that is a natural fit with your business. Partner with your customers and get their help in your efforts to give back to the community. Communicate through third-party non-profit organizations and through local media relations programs.

Engage Employees as CSR Ambassadors

This works for your business on multiple levels—you will be seen as a company that treats its employees well if you have a well thought out volunteerism program while you will also be seen as a company that gives back in the community. Treating your employees well and giving back are huge drivers of a reputation as a good corporate citizen. This strategy will create a great ripple effect.

Take Advantage of Multiple Touch Points

If you are a retailer, use "cause branding" to connect your company with your efforts. Consider cause-related information on your packaging. Talk about your efforts at industry conferences. Promote your issues through suppliers and enlist their support of your cause.

ABOUT THE GOLINHARRIS DOING WELL BY DOING GOOD 2005 CORPORATE CITIZENSHIP SURVEY

Doing Well by Doing Good 2005 was designed by GolinHarris *Change* and fielded through InsightExpress, a leading online market research firm.

The 3,500 online interviews were conducted with Americans in April 2005, with participant demographics weighted and balanced to provide a representative sample and conform to the 2002 US census for gender, age, education, household income, marital status, presence of children age 18 or younger in the household, state of residence and racial/ethnic origin. The margin of error is $\pm$ 3%.

ABOUT GOLINHARRIS

GolinHarris is a full-service firm with world-class credentials in marketing and brand strategy, corporate and employee communications, healthcare, public affairs and technology. The firm's mission is to build long-term partnerships based on mutual trust. This philosophy is based on Founder Al Golin's belief that people want to do business with companies they know and trust. For nearly 50 years, the firm has specialized in long-term partnerships with some of the best-known and most-trusted brand names and companies in the world.

ABOUT CHANGE—GOLINHARRIS' APPROACH TO CORPORATE CITIZENSHIP

Change is a full-service practice, housed within GolinHarris, that specializes in delivering strategic philanthropy, corporate social responsibility, social marketing, cause-related marketing and public education services to corporations, brands, non-profits and government agencies.

Change helps companies and brands establish stronger connections with key stakeholders by setting clear, strategic priorities for their corporate citizenship efforts. Armed with a proprietary research approach and insights born from nearly a half century of experience with leading brands, *Change* helps clients transform corporate citizenship into a powerful tool for building brand value, competitive advantage and stakeholder loyalty.

Change helps clients to view corporate citizenship as an essential business asset that is baked into the very essence of a brand at every level—helping to define and drive brand character, express and shape the company's mission, vision and values, and build deep and lasting trust, leadership and preference.

This business-critical perspective on corporate citizenship, pioneered and implemented by *Change*, is at the heart of *Doing Well by Doing Good 2005: The Trajectory of Corporate Citizenship and American Business.*

10 Questions with...
David Henderson on the Role of Business Today: Does It Include Corporate Social Responsibility?

I t's not often that words fail your Voice editor. But this month, in order to properly and concisely describe and "set up" the topic of our "10 Questions" interview, Voice turned to *uber*-capitalist Steve Forbes, founder and editor of *Forbes* magazine. Well, not directly.

Forbes wrote the foreword for a new book, *The Role of Business in the Modern World*, by economist David Henderson, which examines what Henderson—and Forbes—call the misguided movement for corporate social responsibility (CSR) and its impact on business and individual prosperity around the globe. What's wrong with CSR? Is it anti-capitalism? How much morality in the boardroom should we expect? What kind of public policy does it result in? Why should we care about it? Forbes describes how he—and Henderson—view the new zeal for corporate social responsibility:

> CSR seeks to force firms to accept responsibility for a number of social objectives beyond their duty to shareholders. CSR may be viewed as the collectivists' backhanded compliment to the success of the modern corporation. . . . Utopians no longer reject the market; rather, they now seek to geld and harness it "to serve mankind." The modern corporation, CSR advocates argue, has power greater than many states—that power should be harnessed to ensure social justice, sustainable development, and global stability. . . . If adopted widely, the CSR approach would radically transform the corporation. . . . Profit [to many CSR advocates] is a dirty word—but profits are the seed corn for future advances in our standard of living, as well as rewards for past and current risk-taking. Under the label of CSR, firms are to take on a non-wealth-producing agenda of goals. . . . The fact that the corporation already plays its most effective role in these areas by profit maximization is little understood by CSR advocates. . . . Shifting the firm's attention to non-economic goals will stall economic progress, harming workers, consumers, and shareholders—in short, all of society.

A prominent and vocal critic of CSR, Henderson has served at numerous international economic institutions, including the Organization for Economic Cooperation and Development, and has taught at Oxford University and the

University College of London. Voice recently talked with Henderson about corporate social responsibility, global salvationism, the nature of capitalism and competitive markets, profits and virtue, and "woolly thinking" about what the role of business really is.

1 You've been Described as the Strongest Critic of the CSR "Movement." Are You Totally Against the Concept of Corporate Social Responsibility?

Not at all. But let's be clear about the differences between what I refer to as lowercase corporate social responsibility and uppercase Corporate Social Responsibility. The former expects that businesses should act responsibly, which I have always supported. And the dialogue about how companies ought to behave is nothing new; it's been around for centuries. The latter is a dangerous new doctrine, which I oppose. Ardent advocates of CSR believe that what is involved is nothing less than a complete "corporate transformation" and an entirely new concept of business's mission. If you look at economic history of the last 50 or 60 years, the role of business in a market economy is strongly positive and I see no reason to question or redefine it. Extraordinary advances have been made in countries that were previously seriously economically disadvantaged. My conclusion is that the material progress of people everywhere depends on the dynamism of the economies in which they live and work, and that rapid progress is now to be expected wherever the political and economic conditions exist for a market economy to operate efficiently. The adoption of CSR carries with it a high probability of cost increases and diminished performance.

2 So, Just What is CSR and How are Companies Supposed to Behave Differently if They Embrace it?

There is no one good definition of CSR, and that's the problem. But I'll answer that by using some of the stock phrases that have come into use. CSR-oriented firms are supposed to embrace corporate citizenship and adopt as their goal "sustainable development." They must pursue sustainable development in conjunction with an array of different stakeholders—in fact, they should buy into multi-stakeholder engagement. This notion of sustainable development also doesn't have one good, accepted definition. CSR advocates call it working to meet the triple bottom line: financial, environmental, and social.

3 What's Wrong with Those Goals?

The dangerous part of this push for CSR is that many CSR advocates, some of whom are virulently anti-business, although not all, ignore the fundamental role of the corporation: to make profits for shareholders. In my view, CSR advocates view profits with suspicion, as a manifestation of "greed," and as merely the happy outcome of virtuous conduct. In other words, if a business does the right thing, it will be profitable. That's absurd. Too many CSR advocates don't pay enough attention to the social function of profits.

Let me put it this way—how do you test what "good" a business is doing for society? My test is very simple: it's if the company is innovative, responsive, and competitive. Competitive businesses respond to what people show themselves willing to pay for. In a competitive market economy, the prima facie test of how well a company is doing is whether it's making money. In other words, enterprise profits are performance related. They're not doing good because they wish to do good and meet society's expectations; they're doing good because they're providing what people want. Corporations that have fallen in with the views of CSR think that by pursuing sustainable development, they're pleasing government and doing the right thing by society. Many governments have bought the CSR argument because of vocal and often extreme public opinion that globalization has "changed everything," which I think is wrong.

Are organizations that divert earnings to CSR initiatives robbing investors of their returns?

4 To What do You Ascribe Hostility Toward Globalization?

It's widely believed that when you bring down barriers to trade and foreign investment, which is a large element of globalization, this creates new opportunities for "excessive profits" for businesses—that it gives corporations new power and new gains that they don't deserve. That is very misleading—globalization actually brings companies more competition. This line of thinking about businesses getting more than their "fair share" is very one-sided.

5 Do CSR Advocates Believe Business Would not "Do The Right Thing" if not Pressured to do so, and that Business has not Upheld its Moral Obligations to Society?

There are different schools of thought on that. Some reasonably pro-business advocates of CSR say corporations are generally enlightened, do the right thing, and are mostly sincere about it. But they'd like more. Then there's a very anti-business segment that believes corporations are insincere, morally shallow, and are putting on an act when they talk about being good corporate citizens. These groups constantly pressure business to do more and to shoulder responsibilities that are not necessarily in their best interest, in my view, and I think it's harmful. Profit-oriented businesses always have moral as well as legal obligations. And let's not forget that managers have moral responsibilities to owners—shareholders.

6 How and Why did CSR Catch on with Corporations?

In a word, weakness. Historically, the business world has not been very strong in contributing ideas to public debate. With CSR, it's worse. They're acquiescing and falling in with things they ought to be opposing. Let me point this out: scarcely a single person involved with any of these CSR issues at any company has any training in economics or knowledge of economic history. They're all genuine professionals, in areas such as environmental issues, human resources, occupational safety and health, investor relations, and so on, but they're liable to make serious mistakes when it comes to issues of economics. It's a blank in their minds, or filled with very strange beliefs, such as that we've let corporations conspire to run the world. Nonsense, all of it. It's depressing that business is not standing up to these special-interest groups with their radical agenda.

Governments all over the world have fallen in with it, too. In the U.K. we even have a minister charged with the duty of promoting CSR. And the European Union is deeply committed to these notions. Somehow they think that adding this burden of a new cost and a new corporate agenda will make the EU more competitive. There's even an effort underway by the International Organisation for Standardization to create an ISO standard on CSR.

7 You Say That the Rise of Non-Governmental Organizations (NGOs) has Fueled the CSR Movement and that they are the Ones Who Really have Unprecedented Power. How so?

NGOs, which may be involved in environmental issues, organized labor, movements for social justice, the protection of indigenous peoples, and so on, are extremely well-off. They have enormous coffers. They've acquired power because people trust them and believe their goals are worthy, unlike those of "evil businessmen." But make no mistake: they want power and influence, too. And it's very debatable that what they want would make us better off. They're often obsessed with opposing freedom of cross-border trade and capital flow, and with what they see as the damaging effects of globalization. Many simply exhibit a general hostility to capitalism and the market economy.

8 What is Global Salvationism and Why do you Think it's Dangerous?

One of its big elements is deeply pessimistic and alarmist views about the situation and prospects of our world, primarily the environment and poverty. The environmental alarmist view is that problems, threats, and disasters around every corner are a result of profit-oriented economic activity. The alarmist view of poor countries is that they are evidence of remediable injustice and that their progress *depends* on assistance from outside. This thinking totally overlooks the measurable progress made on many fronts, from the environment to lifting people out of poverty to significant improvements in life expectancy, health, and educational standards in many places around the world.

Those who preach global salvationism believe, of course, that "solutions" are at hand—and they're typically radical collectivist prescriptions for the entire world, where one size solution fits all. I'm not entirely surprised at the rise of global salvationism thinking. I think there's something very deep in human nature for us to believe that things are bad, we're making them worse, and if we would only mend our ways and go through a process of redemption, we could make them right.

To suggest that "business" must have gone through a complete psychological and motivational revolution to "help" the economies of countries such as Malaysia, Thailand, Chile, Hong Kong, South Korea, or even to tackle the more difficult cases such as Sudan, Liberia, Haiti, is ridiculous.

9 Why Should we Care About this, Whether we're Financial Advisor, Investor, Businessperson, or Just Plain Old Citizen?

If you work for or invest in a large multinational company, you should be paying attention to the costs of CSR. Nike, for example, has a CSR department with something like 90 people in it. There are new bureaucratic procedures for monitoring, reporting, and auditing. You have to bring in outside stakeholders who can inquire into what you're doing. It makes your products and services more expensive.

If that isn't enough, then there's also the expectation that your suppliers and vendors are meeting CSR expectations. We have to remember how markets work and what their purpose is. If you offer me a job and I'm glad to take it, I don't think it's anybody's business in an NGO whether I ought to be accepting the conditions or you ought to be offering them, whether I'm a Bangladeshi dockworker or an old gentleman sitting in London.

10 Final Thoughts on Business and Corporate Social Responsibility?

In a competitive market economy, businesses should be free to take the path of CSR but also free to reject it. I believe it's far too simplistic to view business conduct in terms of a choice between profit-oriented and altruistic behavior. There are too many other motives involved. Again the acid test: if business conduct is well-directed, it will be revealed in performance-related profitability.

ARTICLE 2.3

The Myth of CSR

Deborah Doane

The Corporate Social Responsibility (CSR) movement has grown in recent years from a fringe activity by a few earnest companies, like The Body Shop, and Ben & Jerry's, to a highly visible priority for traditional corporate leaders from Nike to McDonald's. Reports of good corporate behavior are now commonplace in the media, from GlaxoSmithKline's donation of antiretroviral medications to Africa, to Hewlett-Packard's corporate volunteering programs, to Starbucks' high-volume purchases of Fair Trade coffee. In fact, CSR has gained such prominence that the *Economist* devoted a special issue to denouncing it earlier this year.

Although some see CSR as simply philanthropy by a different name, it can be defined broadly as the efforts corporations make above and beyond regulation to balance the needs of stakeholders with the need to make a profit. Though traces of modern-day CSR can be found in the social auditing movement of the 1970s, it has only recently acquired enough momentum to merit an *Economist* riposte. While U.S. and European drivers for CSR have differed slightly, key events, such as the sinking of Shell's Brent Spar oil rig in the North Sea in 1996, and accusations of Nike and others' use of "sweatshop labor," triggered the first major response by big business to the uprisings against the corporate institution.

Naomi Klein's famous tome, "No Logo,"[1] gave voice to a generation that felt that big business had taken over the world, to the detriment of people and the environment, even as that generation was successfully mobilizing attacks on corporate power following the Seattle antiglobalization riots in 1999.

Rather than shrink away from the battle, corporations emerged brandishing CSR as the friendly face of capitalism, helped, in part, by the very movement that highlighted the problem of corporate power in the first place. NGOs, seeing little political will by governments to regulate corporate behavior, as free-market economics has become the dominant political mantra, realized that perhaps more momentum could be achieved by partnering with the enemy. By using market mechanisms via consumer power, they saw an opportunity to bring about more immediate change.

So, organizations that address social standards in supply chains, such as the Fair Label Association in the United States or the United Kingdom's Ethical Trading Initiative, have flourished. The United Nations partnered with business to launch its own Global Compact, which offered nine principles relating to human rights and the environment, and was hailed as the ethical road map for the future. And while socially responsible investment had been popular in some circles for years, eventually the mainstream investment community cottoned onto CSR: In 1999, Dow Jones created the Dow Jones Sustainability Indexes, closely followed by the FTSE4Good. All of these initiatives have been premised on the notion that companies can 'do well' and 'do good' at the same time—both saving the world and making a decent profit, too.

The unprecedented growth of CSR may lead some to feel a sense of optimism about the power of market mechanisms to deliver social and environmental change. But markets often fail, especially when it comes to delivering public goods; therefore, we have to be concerned that CSR activities are subject to the same limitations of markets that prompted the movement in the first place.

MAKING MARKETS WORK?

At face value, the market has indeed been a powerful force in bringing forward some measurable changes in corporate behavior. Most large companies now issue a voluntary social and environmental report alongside their regular annual financial report; meanwhile the amount of money being poured into socially responsible investing (SRI) funds has been growing at an exponential rate, year over year. Some socially linked brands, such as Fair Trade, are growing very quickly. Ethical consumerism in the United Kingdom was worth almost £25 billion in 2004, according to a report from the Co-operative Bank.[2]

The *Economist* article argued that the only socially responsible thing a company should do is to make money—and that adopting CSR programs was misguided, at best. But there are some strong business incentives that have either pushed or pulled companies onto the CSR bandwagon. For example, companies confronted with boycott threats, as Nike was in the 1990s, or with the threat of high-profile lawsuits, as McDonald's is over obesity concerns, may see CSR as a strategy for presenting a friendlier face to the public.

Once launched, CSR initiatives may provoke changes in basic practices inside some companies. Nike is now considered by many to be the global leader when it comes to improving labor standards in developing-country factories. The company now leads the way in transparency, too. When faced with a lawsuit over accusations of sweatshop labor, Nike chose to face its critics head-on and this year published on its Web site a full list of its factories with their audited social reports. And Nike is not alone. A plethora of other brands have developed their own unique strategies to confront the activists, with varying degrees of success.

But no one could reasonably argue that these types of changes add up to a wholesale change in capitalism as we know it, nor that they are likely to do so anytime soon.

MARKET FAILURE

One problem here is that CSR as a concept simplifies some rather complex arguments and fails to acknowledge that ultimately, trade-offs must be made

For wealth-making organizations, how separate should social responsibilities be from economic responsibilities?

between the financial health of the company and ethical outcomes. And when they are made, profit undoubtedly wins over principles.

CSR strategies may work under certain conditions, but they are highly vulnerable to market failures, including such things as imperfect information, externalities, and free riders. Most importantly, there is often a wide chasm between what's good for a company and what's good for society as a whole. The reasons for this can be captured under what I'll argue are the four key myths of CSR.

Myth #1: The Market can Deliver both Short-Term Financial Returns and Long-Term Social Benefits

One assumption behind CSR is that business outcomes and social objectives can become more or less aligned. The rarely expressed reasoning behind this assumption goes back to the basic assumptions of free-market capitalism: People are rational actors who are motivated to maximize their self-interest. Since wealth, stable societies, and healthy environments are all in individuals' self-interest, individuals will ultimately invest, consume, and build companies in both profitable and socially responsible ways. In other words, the market will ultimately balance itself.

Yet, there is little if any empirical evidence that the market behaves in this way. In fact, it would be difficult to prove that incentives like protecting natural assets, ensuring an educated labor force for the future, or making voluntary contributions to local community groups actually help companies improve their bottom line. While there are pockets of success stories where business drivers can be aligned with social objectives, such as Cisco's Networking Academies, which are dedicated to developing a labor pool for the future, they only provide a patchwork approach to improving the public good.

In any case, such investments are particularly unlikely to pay off in the two- to four-year time horizon that public companies, through demands of the stock market, often seem to require. As we all know, whenever a company issues a "profits warning," the markets downgrade its share price. Consequently, investments in things like the environment or social causes become a luxury and are often placed on the sacrificial chopping block when the going gets rough.

Meanwhile, we have seen an abject failure of companies to invest in things that may have a longer-term benefit, like health and safety systems. BP was fined a record $1.42 million for health and safety offenses in Alaska in 2004, for example, even as Lord John Browne, chief executive of BP, was establishing himself as a leading advocate for CSR, and the company was winning various awards for its programs.

At the same time, class-action lawsuits may be brought against Wal-Mart over accusations of poor labor practices, yet the world's largest and most successful company is rewarded by investors for driving down its costs and therefore its prices. The market, quite frankly, adores Wal-Mart. Meanwhile, a competitor outlet, Costco, which offers health insurance and other benefits to its employees, is being pressured by its shareholders to cut those benefits to be more competitive with Wal-Mart.[3]

CSR can hardly be expected to deliver when the short-term demands of the stock market provide disincentives for doing so. When shareholder interests dominate the corporate machine, outcomes may become even less aligned to the public good. As Marjorie Kelly writes in her book, "The Divine Right of Capital": "It is inaccurate to speak of stockholders as investors, for more truthfully they are extractors."[4]

Myth #2: The Ethical Consumer Will Drive Change

Though there is a small market that is proactively rewarding ethical business, for most consumers ethics are a relative thing. In fact, most surveys show that consumers are more concerned about things like price, taste, or sell-by date than ethics.[5] Wal-Mart's success certainly is a case in point.

In the United Kingdom, ethical consumerism data show that although most consumers are concerned about environmental or social issues, with 83 percent of consumers *intending* to act ethically on a regular basis, only 18 percent of people act ethically occasionally, while fewer than 5 percent of consumers show consistent ethical and green purchasing behaviors.[6]

In the United States, since 1990, Roper ASW has tracked consumer environmental attitudes and propensity to buy environmentally oriented products, and it categorizes consumers into five "shades of green": True-Blue Greens, Greenback Greens, Sprouts, Grousers, and Basic Browns. True-Blue Greens are the "greenest" consumers, those "most likely to walk their environmental talk," and represent about 9 percent of the population. The least environmentally involved are the "Basic Browns," who believe "individual actions (such as buying green products or recycling) can't make a difference" and represent about 33 percent of the population.[7]

Joel Makower, co-author of "The Green Consumer Guide," has traced data on ethical consumerism since the early 1990s, and says that, in spite of the overhyped claims, there has been little variation in the behavior of ethical consumers over the years, as evidenced by the Roper ASW data. "The truth is, the gap between green consciousness and green consumerism is huge," he states.[8]

Take, for example, the growth of gas-guzzling sport-utility vehicles. Even with the steep rise in fuel prices, consumers are still having a love affair with them, as sales rose by almost 8 percent in 2004. These data show that threats of climate change, which may affect future generations more than our own, are hardly an incentive for consumers to alter their behavior.[9]

Myth #3: There will be a Competitive "Race To The Top" Over Ethics Amongst Businesses

A further myth of CSR is that competitive pressure amongst companies will actually lead to more companies competing over ethics, as highlighted by an increasing number of awards schemes for good companies, like the Business Ethics Awards, or *Fortune*'s annual "Best Companies to Work For" competitions.

Companies are naturally keen to be aligned with CSR schemes because they offer good PR. But in some cases businesses may be able to capitalize on well-intentioned efforts, say by signing the U.N. Global Compact, without necessarily having to actually change their behavior. The U.S.-based Corporate Watch has found several cases of "green washing" by companies, and has noted how various corporations use the United Nations to their public relations advantage, such as posing their CEOs for photographs with Secretary-General Kofi Annan.[10]

Meanwhile, companies fight to get a coveted place on the SRI indices such as the Dow Jones Sustainability Indexes. But all such schemes to reward good corporate behavior leave us carrying a new risk that by promoting the "race to the top" idea, we tend to reward the "best of the baddies." British American Tobacco, for example, won a UNEP/Sustainability reporting award for its annual social report in 2004.[11] Nonetheless, a skeptic might question why a tobacco company, given the massive damage its products inflict, should be rewarded for its otherwise socially responsible behavior.

While companies are vying to be seen as socially responsible to the outside world, they also become more effective at hiding socially irresponsible behavior, such as lobbying activities or tax avoidance measures. Corporate income taxes in the United States fell from 4.1 percent of GDP in 1960 to just 1.5 percent of GDP in 2001.[12] In effect, this limits governments' ability to provide public services like education. Of course, in the end, this is just the type of PR opportunity a business can capitalize on. Adopting or contributing to schools is now a common CSR initiative by leading companies, such as Cisco Systems or European supermarket chain Tesco.

Myth #4: In the Global Economy, Countries will Compete to Have the Best Ethical Practices

CSR has risen in popularity with the increase in reliance on developing economies. It is generally assumed that market liberalization of these economies will lead to better protection of human and environmental rights, through greater integration of oppressive regimes in the global economy, and with the watchful eye of multinational corporations that are actively implementing CSR programs and policies.

Nonetheless, companies often fail to uphold voluntary standards of behavior in developing countries, arguing instead that they operate within the law of the countries in which they are working. In fact, competitive pressure for foreign investment among developing countries has actually led to governments limiting their insistence on stringent compliance with human rights or environmental standards, in order to attract investment. In Sri Lanka, for example, as competitive pressure from neighboring China has increased in textile manufacturing, garment manufacturers have been found to lobby their government to increase working hours.

In the end, most companies have limited power over the wider forces in developing countries that keep overall wage rates low. Nevertheless, for many people a job in a multinational factory may still be more desirable than being a doctor or a teacher, because the wages are higher and a worker's rights seem to be better protected.

WHAT ARE THE ALTERNATIVES TO CSR?

CSR advocates spend a considerable amount of effort developing new standards, partnership initiatives, and awards programs in an attempt to align social responsibility with a business case, yet may be failing to alter the overall landscape. Often the unintended consequences of good behavior lead to other secondary negative impacts, too. McDonald's sale of apples, meant to tackle obesity challenges, has actually led to a loss of biodiversity in apple production, as the corporation insists on uniformity and longevity in the type of apple they may buy—hardly a positive outcome for sustainability.[13]

At some point, we should be asking ourselves whether or not we've in fact been spending our efforts promoting a strategy that is more likely to lead to business as usual, rather than tackling the fundamental problems. Other strategies—from direct regulation of corporate behavior, to a more radical overhaul of the corporate institution, may be more likely to deliver the outcomes we seek.

What if mandatory regulations were imposed on non-profits to ensure that they are socially responsible?

Traditional regulatory models would impose mandatory rules on a company to ensure that it behaves in a socially responsible manner. The advantage of regulation is that it brings with it predictability, and, in many cases, innovation. Though fought stridently by business, social improvements may be more readily achieved through direct regulation than via the market alone, as some examples show in Table 1.

Other regulatory-imposed strategies have done more to alter consumer behavior than CSR efforts. Social labeling, for example, has been an extremely effective tool for changing consumer behavior in Europe. All appliances must be labeled with an energy efficiency rating, and the appliances rated as the most energy efficient now capture over 50 percent of the market. And the standards for the ratings are also continuously improving, through a combination of both research and legislation.[14]

Perhaps more profoundly, campaigners and legal scholars in Europe and the United States have started to look at the legal structure of the corporation. Currently, in Western legal systems, companies have a primary duty of care to their shareholders, and, although social actions on the part of companies are not necessarily prohibited, profit-maximizing behavior is the norm. So, companies

Table 1   Regulation or Burden?[1]

Regulation	Prediction by Business	Reality
National minimum wage	Would result in over 1 million U.K. job losses within two years	Unemployment fell by 200,000
EEC introduction of catalytic converters	The cost of the technology would be £400 to £600 per vehicle, with a fuel consumption penalty on top	Real costs of around £30 to £50 per converter; technological innovation led to smaller, cheaper cars
U.S. Clean Air Act	Would cost the U.S. $51 to $91 billion per year and result in anywhere from 20,000 to 4 million job losses	Yearly cost of $22 billion to business, but employment in areas affected up by 22 percent; the benefits arising are between $120 and $193 billion
Montreal Protocol	Opposed by industry on economic cost grounds, but no projected figures	No impact; substitute technologies may have saved costs, according to follow-up studies

[1] D. Doane, "From Red Tape to Road Signs: Redefining Regulation and Its Purpose" (London: CORE Coalition, 2004).

effectively choose financial benefit over social ones.[15] . . . While a handful of social enterprises, like Fair Trade companies, have forged a different path, they are far from dominating the market. Yet lessons from their successes are being adopted to put forward a new institutional model for larger shareholder-owned companies.

In the United Kingdom, a coalition of 130 NGOs under the aegis of the Corporate Responsibility Coalition (CORE), has presented legislation through the Parliament that argues in favor of an approach to U.K. company law that would see company directors having multiple duties of care – both to their shareholders and to other stakeholders, including communities, employees, and the environment. Under their proposals, companies would be required to consider, act, mitigate, and report on any negative impacts on other stakeholders.[16]

Across the pond, Corporation 20/20, an initiative of Business Ethics and the Tellus Institute, has proposed a new set of principles that enshrines social responsibility from the founding of a company, rather than as a nice-to-have disposable addon. The principles have been the work of a diverse group including legal scholars, activists, business, labor, and journalism, and while still at the discussion phase, such principles could ultimately be enacted into law, stimulating the types of companies that might be better able to respond to things like poverty or climate change or biodiversity. Values such as equity and democracy, mainstays of the social enterprise sector, take precedence over pure profit making, and while the company would continue to be a profit-making entity in the private realm, it would not be able to do so at a cost to society.

Paradoxical Consequences of CSR
Naomi Abasta-Vilaplana

●

As CSR spreads into the developing world, it may be inadvertently triggering new barriers to humane labor practices, according to recent reports from the field. Over the past year, evidence has emerged that at least in some cases, factory officials in charge of manufacturing consumer goods for Western markets are falsifying records in order to appear to be in compliance with the tougher labor standards demanded by their multinational corporate customers.

Such factories simultaneously face demands to enforce fair labor standards and to reach levels of productivity that could only be attained by breaking these standards. Factory managers may thus consider these ethical labor standards to be a sham in light of corporations' other message: produce at all costs.

According to a report issued last year by Oxfam,[1] this tension leads many suppliers to keep fake records and to resort to such tactics as training and bribing workers to lie about working conditions to auditors. In the May 2005 issue of Supply Management, author Emma Clarke reports that there are now even software packages that are designed to help factory managers in China keep double books.

As Oxfam found, "[Suppliers] have to make compromises somewhere, and the factory managers know that so long as they do not indulge in gross abuses of human rights such as using child labor or forced labor, fulfilling the order according to the requirements of time, cost, and quality is the greater priority." And so unless the internal purchasing practices of large corporations are reassessed, excessive working hours, forced overtime, and harassment of workers who attempt to form unions may continue to be the norm.

[1] Oxfam GB, Clean Clothes Campaign, and Global Unions, "Play Fair at the Olympics," March 2004.

Corporation 20/20 Draft Principles[1]

1. The purpose of the corporation is to harness private interests in service of the public interest.
2. Corporations shall accrue fair profits for shareholders, but not at the expense of the legitimate interests of other stakeholders.
3. Corporations shall operate sustainably, helping to meet the needs of the present generation without compromising the ability of future generations to meet theirs.
4. Corporations shall distribute their wealth equitably among those who contribute to its creation.

[1] See www.corporation2020.org

     5. Corporations shall be governed in a manner that is participatory, transparent, and accountable.

Of course, we are a long way from having any of these ideas adopted on a large scale, certainly not when the CSR movement is winning the public relations game with both governments and the public, lulling us into a false sense of security. There is room for markets to bring about some change through CSR, but the market alone is unlikely to bring with it the progressive outcomes its proponents would hope for. While the *Economist* argument was half correct —that CSR can be little more than a public relations device—it fails to recognize that it is the institution of the corporation itself that may be at the heart of the problem. CSR, in the end, is a placebo, leaving us with immense and mounting challenges in globalization for the foreseeable future.

END NOTES

1. N. Klein, *No Logo: Taking Aim at the Branding Bullies* (United Kingdom: Harper Collins, 2001).
2. Co-operative Bank, 2004 Ethical Purchasing Index, http://www.co-operative-bank.co.uk/servlet/Satellite?cid=1077610044424&pagename=CoopBank%2FPage%2FtplPageStandard&c=Page.
3. A. Zimmerman, "Costco's Dilemma: Be Kind to Its Workers, or Wall Street," *Wall Street Journal*, March 26, 2004.
4. M. Kelly, *The Divine Right of Capital: Dethroning the Corporate Aristocracy* (San Francisco: Berrett-Koehler, 2003).
5. U.K. Institute of Grocery Distributors, 2003.
6. "Who Are the Ethical Consumers?" Co-operative Bank, 2000.
7. Green Gauge Report 2002, Roper ASW, as related by Edwin Stafford.
8. http://makower.typepad.com/joel_makower/2005/06/ideal_bite_keep.html.
9. http://money.cnn.com/2004/05/17/pf/autos/suvs_gas/.
10. "Greenwash + 10: The U.N.'s Global Compact, Corporate Accountability, and the Johannesburg Earth Summit," Corporate Watch, January 2002.
11. "The Global Reporters 2004 Survey of Corporate Sustainability Reporting," SustainAbility, UNEP, and Standard & Poor's.
12. J. Miller, "Double Taxation Double Speak: Why Repealing Tax Dividends Is Unfair," *Dollars & Sense*, March/April 2003.
13. G. Younge, "McDonald's Grabs a Piece of the Apple Pie: 'Healthy' Menu Changes Threaten the Health of Biodiversity in Apples," *The Guardian*, April 7, 2005.
14. Ethical Purchasing Index, 2004.
15. E. Elhauge, "Sacrificing Corporate Profits in the Public Interest," *New York University Law Review* 80, 2005.
16. See www.corporate-responsibility.org.

The Dangers of Weasel Words: "Corporate Social Reponsibility" as a Banner for Left-Wing Politics

T. E. Bostock

For at least a decade and a half, company directors and managers have had to confront a world-wide movement, made up of a curiously various collection of interests—ranging at one end from many of the world's largest multi-national enterprises, apostles by their actions if not by their words for capitalism, to extreme environmentalists, to whom capitalism is the root of all evil, at the other—all parading, apparently collectively, under the banner of Corporate Social Responsibility (C.S.R.). Not surprisingly, there appears to be no general agreement on what C.S.R. actually means or entails. Yet it is a movement that company directors and managers cannot ignore; but how are they to come to grips with it? What does it mean? What does it imply? As a start, we should, perhaps, first remind ourselves of the essential purpose of the limited company.

WHY LIMITED COMPANIES EXIST

A limited company exists to pursue a business with the object of generating as high a return as business exigencies permit for its shareholders, who have contributed the capital without which the company would not exist at all. They are encouraged to contribute that capital by the risk-limiting principle of limited liability.

In pursuing that object, the company will also generate wealth for its employees, lenders, suppliers and other parties in meeting the demands of its customers. Ultimate responsibility for the success or otherwise of the company's business lies with its directors, who can be seen as stewards for the capital-providing shareholders. The extensive fiduciary and other duties imposed on directors under the general law, and increasingly enlarged or supplemented by statute, are in general owed to the company as representing the general body of its shareholders.

It is important to keep in mind that the shareholders, far from being in any position of privilege, are the most at risk should the company fail. In its liquidation, all that they are entitled to is such of the company's wealth, if any, as remains after the company's liabilities to its creditors, be they employees, creditors, suppliers or other outside parties have been met. While the company remains in operation, the shareholders' return depends entirely on the profits earned by the company: no profits, no dividends.

It follows that the company's business, under the stewardship of its directors, should be directed towards maximizing the return to its shareholders. That is the basis of company law as we know it. In pursuing that objective, the company must comply with its obligations to outside parties whether assumed by contract or imposed by law. That is not to say that the company may not impose upon itself obligations, such as for employee benefits and occupational health and product safety over and above those imposed by law; but in doing so, the law requires its directors to be satisfied that it is in the interests of the company and its shareholders.

The importance of corporate profitability cannot be over-emphasised: on it depends the well-being not only of the outside parties mentioned but also of its shareholders, whose number includes indirectly a vast number of superannuation fund members and life and general insurance policyholders, not to mention the community generally through the generation of tax revenue. The limited liability company is the instrument of converting the savings of a given community into the capital that generates the corporate investment that secures the general well-being of that community as nothing else can.

From your perspective, which is more important— social responsibility or profitability?

CORPORATE SOCIAL RESPONSIBILITY—WHAT DOES IT MEAN?

The threshold problem with C.S.R. is working out what exactly it means. The difficulty lies with the word social which, as F.A. Hayek memorably observed, "can be used to describe almost any action as publicly desirable and has at the same time the effect of depriving any terms with which it is combined of clear meaning": the perfect example of a weasel word, sucking out from the word it qualifies any real meaning, just as a weasel sucks out the contents of an egg. The problem would perhaps not matter if all that C.S.R. were intended and understood to mean was that a company's operations should be conducted in accordance with the requirements of law, and beyond those requirements where it is in the interests of shareholders to do so.

That, however, does not appear to be the intention of the promoters of C.S.R. For example, the World Council for Sustainable Development (W.B.C.S.D.), an influential body whose 175 members include many of the largest multinational enterprises, and a significant proponent of C.S.R., defines C.S.R. as business' commitment to contribute to sustainable economic development, working with employees, their families, the local community, and society at large to improve their quality of life, an example of defining a meaningless term in meaningless terms, the word sustainable being as much a weasel word as social. And share-holders are notable for their absence of mention.

As W.B.C.S.D. itself acknowledges, "C.S.R. means very different things to different people, depending on a range of local factors, including culture, religion, and governmental or legal conditions. There can be no universal stan-dard." Seen in that light, C.S.R. is scarcely a sure foundation on which compa-ny directors and managers could develop corporate policy or legislators could develop corporate law. Perhaps the essential meaninglessness of C.S.R. is the cement that keeps together the strange coalition of its advocates. If that were all that there were to it, C.S.R. would come quickly to be seen as no more than a passing fad. That, however, is not all that there is to it. Whatever C.S.R. is supposed to mean, we should be alert to what it is seen to imply.

IMPLICATIONS OF C.S.R.

The principal implication is that company directors and managers should di-rect their company to operate in the interests of parties other than shareholders beyond the requirements of law, whether or not to do so is in the interests of its shareholders. That implication arises from attaching to those other parties the misleading label of stakeholders: misleading in so far as it suggests that those other parties have as legitimate a claim on the company's ultimate wealth, after the company's legal obligations to them have been met, as shareholders.

What flows from that implication is that company directors and managers would face the insoluble dilemma of defining and weighing the interests of the various "stakeholders" and judging whose are to be preferred to others, and how they are to be variously weighed against the interests of shareholders. The touchstone that seems to be emerging to guide them through the dilemma is the notion of "society's" or "community" expectations. On examination, the no-tion seems worse than useless: society's is a cognate of the weasel word social, and community in this context is itself another weasel word, sucking out any real meaning from the word expectations.

The fact is that the application of those weasel words is a matter of politics, not business; and if C.S.R. takes hold, we shall surely find the operations of companies increasingly directed not by the directors and managers as stew-ards for the capital-contributing shareholders in accordance with their general duties to the company, but by them towards the requirements of the State in its ever-changing assessment of community expectations. Company direc-tors and managers will, inevitably, find themselves beholden in the conduct of their company's business not to the company and its shareholders, with all the consequent benefits to outside parties and to the community generally, but to the State and its politicians and bureaucrats, just as they became in National Socialist Germany. In the meantime, the countless citizens whose welfare depends on corporate profitability will find their welfare diminishing as the process proceeds.

HOW HAS IT ALL COME ABOUT?

As noted, prominent among the members of the W.B.C.S.D., and also no doubt other like bodies, are leading multi-national enterprises. For all the great benefits they bring to the world at large, and to the advancement of less developed countries in particular, multi-national enterprises—for all their undoubted contribution to advancement of less-developed countries—have for years laboured under attack from bodies purporting to represent the various interests of labour, women, children, consumers, the environment and other special interests, almost all of which bodies are imbued with what Ludwig von Mises called the anti-capitalist mentality. C.S.R., and at least the pretence of implementing its nostrums, are seen by its corporate proponents as a means of appeasing sectional activists; and by sectional activists as a means of quarrying more and more from the corporate sector. On both sides, the interests of a company's shareholders are seen as expendable in favour of outside sectional interests.

Corporate advocates of C.S.R., in seeking to appease sectional interest groups, seem not to be aware of, or to be content to ignore, three fairly obvious points. First, the single issue activist body is concerned solely about the supposed interest it purports to represent, and not about the interests of the community at large. Secondly, the wish-list of the single issue activist body can never be satisfied: satisfy one wish, and another bobs up. Thirdly, it has regrettably to be said that leaders in the corporate sector have on the whole been less than whole-hearted in reminding the public generally of how much it owes for its welfare to free market capitalism in general, and to the limited company in particular. Those of their number who seek to live by weasel words run the risk of dying by them.

At the other end of the spectrum of the C.S.R. coalition, for those imbued with the anti-capitalist mentality, at a time when the failure of socialist regimes—particularly Marxist régimes—has become generally recognised, C.S.R. can be seen as a means of knee-capping capitalism, in much the same way—albeit unperceived—as the German National *Socialists* (the latter half of their label needs emphasis) did, and under slogans like C.S.R.

CONCLUSION

Were C.S.R. intended to mean no more than that company directors and managers should meet their duties under the law, and do what they reasonably can to ensure that their company does likewise, it could be seen as merely creating the unnecessary confusion that comes from, to borrow from a great English judge, well-meaning sloppiness of thought.

That, however, does not seem to be what proponents of C.S.R. for the most part have in mind. The essential meaninglessness of the expression C.S.R. has proved remarkably successful as a cloak under which to smuggle into the uncritical consciousness of businesspeople, lawyers (academic and practising), politicians, bureaucrats and the public generally, ideas that are potentially at least fundamentally subversive of the institution of the limited company as it has evolved in the English-speaking world over the last 150 years. Once we grasp the essential meaninglessness of C.S.R., we are in a surer position to defend an institution to which, above all others, we owe the highest standard of living in all history.

ISSUE SUMMARY

G ood citizenship is about accountability and protection. When applied to a person, good citizenship is a matter of living right with others and caring for the environment. But applied to an organization, being a good citizen has implications of a larger magnitude. Corporate citizenship becomes a matter of justifying activities to the public, not simply answering to stockholders or a board.

Three decades ago, economist Milton Friedman (1970) argued that a company had a three-fold obligation: making a profit, paying taxes, and providing jobs. It is interesting to compare the scope of that obligation three decades ago with what many people expect of organizations now. Today's three-fold obligation implies that a company's goals and benchmarks are more than financial; they are social and environmental as well. A company that accepts this obligation has a "triple bottom line," an alternative term for CSR. For many organizations, Friedman's concept of the bottom line is no longer adequate to account for increasing expectations.

Clearly there is a divided opinion on whether all organizations are obligated to a bottom line that incorporates social responsibility. To a certain extent, non-governmental organizations are of the opinion that corporate action on social issues (such as AIDS, poverty, global warming) is the duty of all. Stockholders, customers, and employees, on the other hand, typically demand that companies concentrate on the financial bottom line and maximize return. The pressure is heavy on organizational leaders. In today's economy, financial return and social obligation are melding in new ways and leaders are caught in the search for ways to compromise between investor needs and social needs. We are learning that the compromise is more subtle—strong fiscal performance and citizenship are more interrelated than we thought.

This closing of the gap between fiscal return and corporate social policies is seen most clearly in multinational organizations, whose business is worldwide. Essentially, these corporations cannot afford *not* to be good neighbors with others—their work is too public to go unscrutinized. Paying attention to societal issues will cost these groups money (for example, using costly technology to reduce emission of greenhouse gases or stopping forest degradation in Africa) but they have determined that goodwill and health of the organization outweighs immediate costs.

For organizational leaders, at the heart of the myriad issues around corporate social responsibility is a deceptively simple question: What is the highest business mission of the organization?

ISSUE HIGHLIGHTS

- Corporate social responsibility has moved from a fringe activity to a priority for many organizations; for some, CSR is a mantra.
- CSR encompasses a limitless variety of philanthropic, charitable, and consumer-driven organizational activities.
- Some see CSR as a new business mission.
- One perspective claims that the pressure for organizations to be socially responsible is the result of "excess profit" due to globalization.
- For many investors, profit comes before social responsibility.
- For some corporations, social responsibility is a matter of enlightened self interest.
- Americans' expectations of corporate citizenship are at an all-time high and many believe corporations are still not fulfilling these expectations.

CRITICAL THINKING

For businesses and nonprofits alike, making a better world comes with a price tag, and the cost is not in dollars alone. The cost can be in terms of governance, community partnerships, environmental protection, or investor relationships. If CSR—like citizenship—is about accountability and protection, the question becomes how many bottom lines are sufficient.

NGOs and other organizations are making the argument that "wealthier is healthier." For these groups, the barriers between wealth-making and health-supporting are false. In response, corporations are taking the position that the private sector needs to increase its responsibility for addressing societal ills. To a certain extent, the issues of corporate social responsibility center around "noblesse oblige"—to whom much is given, much is required. The question is whether the concept of noble obligation is fair for today's wealth-making organizations.

ADDITIONAL READING RESOURCES

Matthew Bishop et al., An apology for capitalism? The Stockholm Network, 2004.

Milton Friedman, The social responsibility of business is to increase its profits. *New York Times Magazine*, September 13, 1970.

From awareness to action: 2005 annual review. *World Business Council for Sustainable Development*. Available at http://www.wbcsd.org/DocRoot/FajVUwhVkUtHso6dDE0G/ar2005.pdf

The good company. *The Economist*, January 22, 2005. (Note: The entire issue is dedicated to CSR.)

David Henderson, The role of business in the modern world. *Institute of Economic Affairs*, July 2004.

Michael E. Porter & Mark R. Kramer, The competitive advantage of corporate philanthropy. *Harvard Business Review*, December 2002.

For more information check these sites:

www.csr-asia.com
www.csreurope.org
www.csrwire.com

What Does It Take for an Organization to Act Ethically?

INTRODUCTION

It is disheartening to learn that ethical misconduct in the workplace is on the rise, despite the attention being paid to formal ethics programs and codes these days. This is the disturbing discovery in the latest survey of American workers by the Ethics Resource Center. And a second national survey reaches the same conclusion—that ethical misconduct is increasing. The author of "Ethical Culture: Most Important Barrier to Ethical Misconduct" points to this key finding as an indication that while compliance programs are being stepped up, workplace culture is being ignored. The first reading is a summary of results of two similar surveys of employees across the nation. It sets the stage for readings that present different perspectives on the question of what it takes for an organization to act ethically. It could take enforcing an ethics code or it could take a performance-based approach or it could take a values-based approach— judge for yourself what it will take to make an organization ethical.

"Putting Teeth in Corporate Ethics Codes" is an analysis of how organizations are enforcing their codes of ethics. As an outcome of the Sarbanes-Oxley Act, companies are requiring employees to read and sign codes. Moreover, today's codes are not simple statements; they typically contain an outline of sanctions for code violations. Once an employee signs a code and is informed of the sanctions, enforcement does not end there. The trend is for organizations to require ethics training that directly relates to practice and key decision-making points. Even with all of these strategies in place, the executives and consultants interviewed for this article admit that enforcement does not prevent ethical lapses in conduct.

The author of the third reading believes compliance strategies and sanctions are not effective in dealing with poor ethics. Dean Bottorff, a Fellow of the American Society for Quality, proposes that organizational ethics is a quality issue that can be improved by a performance-based approach. In "Advancing from Compliance to Performance," Bottorff defines an approach he calls ethics quality (EQ) and demonstrates how it improves consensus and accuracy in decision making. As with all logic-based or scientific processes in organizations (such as finance, marketing, quality), EQ follows a sequence of reasoning steps. The goals of the process are to improve ethical reasoning and assist in

65

early detection of problem areas. Essentially, Bottorff regards organizational ethics as a quality process that embeds ethics in performance.

In the final reading, "Creating an Ethical Culture," David Gebler presents the case for values-based ethics programs. While such programs may include a code of ethics, they are much broader in concept than mere compliance. To Gebler, compliance is a shallow approach that is typically generated top down and leads to a quick-fix mentality. He believes that the critical factor in a values-based approach is a culture that promotes ethical behavior. But generating an ethical culture can be an enormous undertaking. As Gebler says: "to truly develop an ethical culture, the organization must be aware of how its managers deal with issues up and down the line and how the values they demonstrate impact desired behaviors." To assist an organization in reaching this level of awareness, Gebler describes a model for categorizing values that can be used to assess strengths and weaknesses. And based on that understanding, an organization can take steps to correct areas of ethical weakness.

SOURCES

Curtis C. Verschoor, Ethical culture: Most important barrier to ethical misconduct. *Strategic Finance*, December 2005.

Amey Stone, Putting teeth in corporate ethics codes. *Business Week Online*, February 19, 2004.

Dean L. Bottorff, Advancing from compliance to performance. *Quality Progress*, April 2006.

David Gebler, Creating an ethical culture. *Strategic Finance*, May 2006.

Ethical Culture: Most Important Barrier to Ethical Misconduct

Curtis C. Verschoor

T he Ethics Resource Center (ERC), a nonprofit U.S. organization devoted to the advancement of organizational ethics, has released the results of its 2005 National Business Ethics Survey (NBES) of more than 3,000 American workers. The findings show that more than half of U.S. employees have observed at least one example of workplace ethical misconduct in the past year, and 36% have observed two or more. This represents a slight increase from the results of the 2003 survey. During the same period, willingness to report observed misconduct at work to management declined to 55%, a decrease of 10 percentage points since 2003.

Should an organization's ethics program attempt to clarify or to inculcate ethical values or neither?

The increase in misconduct and decline in reporting occurred despite the fact that workers are more aware of formal ethics and compliance programs in their organizations. The NBES survey measures workplace ethics, implementation of formal ethics programs and their impact, and factors that pose risks of misconduct. Types of misconduct employees observed most include:

- 21% observed abusive or intimidating behavior toward employees.
- 19% observed lying to employees, customers, vendors, or the public.
- 18% observed a situation that placed employee interests over organizational interests.
- 16% observed violations of safety regulations.
- 16% observed misreporting of actual time worked.

On the positive side, implementation of five of six elements of the model formal ethics and compliance program set forth by the U.S. Sentencing Commission has increased since 2004, with the presence of written standards of business conduct up 19 percentage points. The survey also showed that 69% of employees reported their organization has ethics training, up 14 percentage points since 2003, and 65% indicated their organizations have a place where they can seek ethics advice. The only element of the model program to show a decrease in compliance since 2003 was the percentage of employees who said their supervisors evaluate ethical conduct as a part of their job performance, which was down to 69% from 74%.

Noting the divergence between increases in formal program participation and decreases in positive outcomes, ERC President Patricia Harned observed that "organizations, especially for-profit companies, have invested significant resources in ethics and compliance programs," yet ERC isn't seeing a lot of change in the direct impact they are having. She believes that "organizations need to evaluate what will work most effectively, including a closer look at the role workplace culture plays."

Perhaps the most important finding in the 2005 NBES research is the significance of the ethical culture in organizations as a determinant of observed ethical behavior and the readiness of employees to report misconduct they see to a higher authority. The study found that employees in organizations with a weak ethical culture reported a much higher level of observed ethical violations than those with a strong ethical culture (70% compared to 34%). Those employees in organizations with a strong ethical culture were also much more likely to report misconduct to higher-ups than those in weak-culture organizations (79% compared to 48%).

"Creating a strong ethical environment should be a top priority of all companies," Harned concluded. "This data shows, for example, that management needs to lead by example to set the right tone throughout the organization."

The NBES survey report points out that outcomes are most positive when ethical cultures are strong—defined as having accountability for actions and the display of certain ethics-related actions at various levels in an organization. The report notes that actions of leaders and peers significantly influence employees' ethics, concluding that "where cultures are strong, it is in part because a formal ethics and compliance program is in place." Even further, the report says, "Formal ethics and compliance programs are likely to be an essential element in the maintenance of a strong culture. . . . While culture matters in making an impact, formal programs are still essential to creating a culture."

The final finding of the NBES report describes the impact of employees' exposure to risk of misconduct. Risk factors include:

- Employee exposure to circumstances that invite misconduct.
- Employee recognition of those situations as misconduct.
- Pressure to compromise the standards of the organization.
- Preparedness of employees to respond to these situations.

The report indicates that one-third of all employees encounter a situation at work that they think invites ethical misconduct. Of those people, 74% observed at least one act of misconduct. Among employees who felt pressured to compromise the standards of their organizations, 94% observed at least one instance of ethical misconduct.

To summarize the NBES findings, the positive outcomes of lower observed wrongdoing and greater likelihood of reporting violations should they occur is associated with a superior ethical culture in an organization, and the presence of a formal ethics and compliance program has less impact than the strength of the ethical culture.

Another survey of employee perceptions of ethical misconduct was issued at about the same time as the NBES report. This research was sponsored by the Hudson Highland Group (HHG), an international staffing provider, and is based on a national poll of 2,099 U.S. workers. The results and conclusions of the HHG survey mirror those from the NBES. The HHG survey states that nearly one-third of U.S. workers have witnessed co-workers engaging in ethical misconduct, yet only half (52%) of those witnessing unethical or illegal acts reported it to anyone in authority. Despite this prevalence of wrongdoing, 78% of U.S. workers state that their companies clearly communicate what they consider unethical and ethical behavior in the workplace.

According to David Rhind, HHG North American counsel, encouraging employees to do the right thing when they seem to know what that is requires fostering better ethics in the workplace. Rhind states, "Even with clear ethics policies in place, companies must create a culture of integrity throughout the organization by providing both the means and the mandate to report concerns." He adds, "When senior executives lead by example, employees are more likely to follow suit."

Additional conclusions suggested by the findings of these two independent studies include:

- Companies need to increase their recognition of the importance of the tone at the top. Senior management and the board of directors must engage in hands-on efforts to cultivate a climate of ethical behavior by their actions. The ethics-related duties of boards of directors of all companies—private as well as public and nonprofit as well as for-profit—are clearly set forth in the U.S. Sentencing Guidelines.
- Actions of managers at all levels speak much louder than all the words contained in a formal ethics and compliance program. For example, employees need to understand that "gaming" of an incentive compensation system won't be tolerated and that violators will be punished.

How strong is the ethical culture in your organization?

ARTICLE 3.2

Putting Teeth in Corporate Ethics Codes

Amey Stone

C lark Consulting (CLK), a compensation and benefit consulting firm, has had a corporate code of ethics in place for years. But following the 2002 passage of the Sarbanes-Oxley law reforming corporate governance, Chief Executive Tom Wamberg revised it, redistributed it, and started referring to it in weekly newsletters distributed to all employees. It wasn't long before the code was put to the test.

Earlier this year, Wamberg learned that one of his senior consultants was bragging to other employees about how he had "fired" a particularly demanding client. Wamberg was outraged. Rule No. 1 of the code is that clients come first. "For us, that was a cardinal sin," says Wamberg, who dismissed that consultant, citing the code.

Now he sees the benefits of having a public statement in place and sticking to it. "If you don't have something to stand up to and look to, you could easily give a slap on the wrist and say, 'Don't do it again,'" says Wamberg.

"Sanctions" section • Well, not so easily anymore. In part due to new regulatory requirements (including a new Nasdaq rule that goes into effect May 4, requiring listed companies to distribute a code to all employees)—and also because of so many high-profile cases recently where corporate malfeasance has brought down major businesses—chief executives are doing their best to turn the code of ethics into a document with real teeth.

"There's a whole spectrum of activities that can make this thing come alive," says Dan DiFilippo, who leads PricewaterhouseCoopers' governance and compliance practice. Companies are rewriting the codes, making them much more detailed and specific. German software giant SAP (SAP) has a 14-page code with sections that describe conduct with customers, vendors, and competitors, as well as stock-trading rules.

Businesses are adding enforcement measures, including guidelines for employees to follow if they see violations. A "sanctions" section in SAP's code explains that any act "in opposition to this Code of Conduct is subject to internal review, and can result in consequences that affect employment, and could possibly lead to external investigation, civil law proceedings, or criminal charges."

Signatures required • No longer just published in an employee handbook, the codes are being posted on corporate Web sites and around offices. Companies now want the statement to be visible to people outside, like regulators, vendors, and customers—as well as employees.

70

"It always was part of our DNA," says Harold Tinkler, chief ethics and compliance officer at accounting firm Deloitte & Touche, which is finalizing a new, more detailed code. "But in today's world, the public at large wants to see it demonstrated." According to a recent survey by New York-based research firm Governance Metrix, which rates companies on their compliance efforts, 51% of U.S. concerns disclose a code of ethics, although 32% allow a waiver in some cases.

Perhaps most notably, businesses are increasingly requiring all employees to read and sign the ethics statement. This measure is an apparent extension of the Sarbanes-Oxley rule that CEOs and CFOs certify the accuracy of company financials. "They're pushing that requirement down the ranks," says Kirk Jordan, a compliance attorney who's vice-president for research at Integrity Interactive, which provides Web-based ethics and compliance training programs. Usually the sign-off is a condition of employment—and sometimes a condition of getting a bonus or a raise.

Tech backup • Another new trend: Companies are adding more training around their codes of ethics. Jordan says the new focus is on providing guidance for senior managers, rather than assuming they understand the issues. At software concern Hyperion Solutions, CEO Jeff Rodek trains managers to distinguish between employees who underperform—who should be given several chances to improve—and workers who violate the ethics code, where "it can be one strike, you're out," he says. "It's important that people know the difference."

One goal of the training is to bring ethics into play during key decision-making points. Some outfits are making research into ethical issues a part of the due diligence on another company during an acquisition, says PWC's DiFilippo. Deloitte & Touche will ask managers to explore ethical issues with the engagement team before starting each new audit, says Tinkler.

Technology is increasingly involved in all these pursuits. Integrity Interactive's code-of-ethics training course includes a testing component. All employees must continue training until they score 100% on a test.

How much good? • Last November ACL Services, which makes software used in internal audits, launched a new "Continuous Controls Monitoring" solution, which flags possible code-of-conduct violations, like purchasing from a vendor that charges more than the standard price (that might mean the employee is getting some sort of kickback). "Actively testing for controls begins to create a culture of accountability and ethics," says Harald Will, ACL's president and CEO.

It's still unclear how much good a code of conduct can do in preventing ethical lapses. Even though accounting firm Arthur Andersen had a strong ethics program in place, it didn't survive the fallout of having signed off on failed energy giant Enron's books. The program clearly didn't do much good when the firm's Houston office should have raised questions about a major clients' activities.

"It's during difficult decisions that someone's ethics are put to the test," says William Henrich, vice-chairman of turnaround consulting firm Getzler Henrich & Associates and a former partner at Arthur Andersen. "At that point, whether or not they signed a piece of paper doesn't make a difference."

From the top • Many consultants on business-risk issues say a company needs to take more important measures than a statement to prevent ethical lapses from harming it. "A code of ethics is an easy thing to redo," says Michael Chagares, who leads consulting firm Marsh's business-risk practice. "The question is how you get a real change in behavior."

More important than emphasizing the code is making sure the board has independent members and that a system of checks and balances on management is in place throughout the company. It's also essential that the business has mechanisms in place that lets problems come to the surface, Chagares says.

Even if a code of ethics is just a starting point, it certainly doesn't hurt, consultants and chief executives agree. And it has the most power if it appears to come straight from the top. Wamberg says he worries that people at his company pay only lip service to standing by the corporate code of ethics. "That's why I just pound it in," he says. When it comes to ethics statements, employees can expect more pounding in the months to come.

What are some pros and cons of establishing a public statement on ethics (or a code of conduct)?

Advancing from Compliance to Performance

Dean L. Bottorff

One of the great lessons of our post Enron economy is that poor ethics has finally been recognized as a leading killer of organizations.

It has been a long road, resulting in a lot of bad outcomes for a lot of people. But after decades of commanding little respect, poor ethics has finally joined ranks with other controllable factors, including quality, culture and leadership, that can either give life to an organization through excellence or take it away through dysfunction.

Over the last 50 years we have learned volumes about the nature of poor ethics in organizations—what causes it and how it can be prevented. The problem is we are not fully applying what we know.

From the economics of quality we know it is much cheaper to prevent failure than to let it happen, catch it and then try to fix it.[1]

If organizations would practice ethics as the logic based discipline and quality problem it is, they would achieve higher levels of accuracy, repeatability and performance. This, in turn, would result in better moral and economic outcomes for all involved, including themselves. I call this performance oriented approach to organizational ethics Ethics Quality (EQ).

EQ DEFINED

EQ occurs when two conditions are met:

1. Sound ethical reasoning (right thinking, or ensuring supporting arguments are fallacy free) is applied as controllable process inputs. The outputs result in intents, means and ends that are good for all involved.
2. This process of right inputs and good outputs becomes repeatable and is integrated throughout the organization.

Three attributes of EQ differentiate it from prevailing policy and compliance approaches:

1. EQ is a process capability driven by scientific methods. It applies universal principles of logic and ethical reasoning in decision making so organizations can determine, with high assurance, what is right or wrong and good or bad for themselves and others.
2. EQ is an integrator of compliance and gray zone ethics management (clear-cut policies and standards either do not fit well or do not exist) approaches, making each more effective.

73

3. EQ is a culture and performance booster by removing process constraints, improving consensus and accuracy in decisions and improving teamwork in execution.

Ethics may seem like one of those soft disciplines that has no scientific backbone, but this could not be further from the truth. The field of philosophy regards ethics as a normative science.

When ethics is practiced systematically in an organization, such as with EQ, it becomes a social science discipline just as are quality, finance, marketing and other management fields.

In 50 Words Or Less

- Ethics is logic based discipline and a quality problem.
- Applying compliance tools in a poor ethical culture is a misapplication of compliance.
- There are proven ways to improve ethical intents, means and outcomes for all involved and benefit performance and compliance in the process.

SEQUENCE OF REASONING STEPS

All scientific disciplines follow a sequence of reasoning steps related to the scientific method, and so must ethics. An example of a five-step roadmap that can improve ethical reasoning and economic outcomes in any organization follows:

1. Identifying the moral issues.
2. Transforming wrong thinking to right thinking.
3. Refining viable alternatives.
4. Validating and following through.
5. Renorming.

Identifying the problem • Identify a moral issue or moral aspect of a problem that warrants deeper examination. Many problems in organizational life actually are two interrelated problems:

1. The factual business problem at hand such as low sales or process errors.
2. A moral problem connected to the business one, such as how much pre-sales disclosure to provide, how to avoid competition, whether to punish or reward a whistle-blower or how to assign process performance responsibility.

According to Nobel laureate Herbert Simon, actual decision making in organizations is rarely driven by hard facts alone. Instead, most decisions are made under a cloud of informational uncertainty and moral constraints, requiring a rational integration of value and fact at the beginning of the decision process.[2]

Table 1   Common Forms of Wrong Thinking

- **False dilemma:** When only two possible a lternatives are considered when in fact there are many. This is also called false dichotomy or black and white thinking.

- **Begging the question:** When premises directly or indirectly presume the conclusion is true. This is also called circular reasoning.

- **Part to whole/whole to part:** The false presumption that what is true among parts is equally true to the group as a whole or that what is true applies equally to the parts.

- **Complex question or cause:** When two unrelated points are falsely presumed to be naturally related and are combined into an oversimplified single proposition or when the cause identified is falsely presumed to be the exclusive cause when it is only a part of a larger set of causes. This is also called oversimplification fallacy.

- **Regression fallacy:** When a trend is presumed beyond the relevant range of underlying data or evidence.

- **Contradiction:** When incompatible statements are falsely presumed to be true at the same time.

- **Hasty generalization:** when a leaping or sweeping claim is made from a limited sample of evidence.

- **False or weak analogy:** When two thoughts being compared as similar are not sufficiently similar to support a claim.

- **Guilt by association:** When an argument is made to reject a claim because others who are disliked accept the claim or because the person making the argument is merely affiliated with unfavorable groups.

- **Anonymous authority and ambiguous collective:** When the authority or parties in question are deliberately not named or are commingled and generalized together in such broad terms it becomes impossible to identify them to support the claim.

- **Fallacious rhetoric used to manipulate and persuade illegitimately (irrelevant appeals and attacks)**

   Appeal to force: Using a threat of force to support a claim instead of considering the claim's merits.

   Attack the person: Attacking a person's character to support a claim instead of considering the claim's merits.

   Bandwagon: Using the threat of rejection by your peers to support a claim instead of considering the claim's merits.

   Wishful thinking: Seeking to avoid negative consequences instead of considering the claim's merits.

   Name calling: Using mockery to psychologically damage the opponent instead of considering the claim's merits.

   Hostile humor: Launching humor at the expense of the opponent instead of considering the claim's merits.

(continued)

Table 1   (*continued*)

Appeal to false authority: Turning to an expert claim because of a person's credibility or notoriety in other matters when the person is not qualified on the matter at issue.

Prejudicial language: Attaching either complimentary or uncomplimentary characterizations to a claim to influence its credibility instead of considering the claim's merits directly.

Poisoning the well: Attempting to discredit a person by presenting unfavorable information (true or false) about the person to discredit claims he or she may make in the future.

- **Using diversionary tactics:**

Red herring: Introducing an irrelevant topic as relevant to divert attention away from the main argument.

Straw man: Transforming the main argument into a distorted version, making it more vulnerable to attack.

Changing the subject: Ceasing to discuss a claim because unrelated subjects have been introduced for discussion.

Burden of proof fallacy: Shifting the true burden of proof (which usually lies with the challenger) to the wrong side to support a claim.

Definitional distortion: Intentionally distorting a true definitional by using too many or too few clarifying terms or by making the definition too complex to be understood.

The Greek philosophers considered initial awareness to be the most important step in ethical reasoning because without this step agents (people involved in the situation) are likely to follow existing patterns of thinking and behavior, making deeper examination or change unlikely.[3]

Transforming wrong thinking to right thinking • This step ensures supporting arguments are fallacy free by identifying forms of wrong thinking (see Table 1) and transforming them to right thinking.

Transforming is considered the blocking and tackling of ethics management. Transforming is where most poor ethics get their start and where we have the best opportunity to prevent the illusions, deceptions and falsehoods that cause the preponderance of poor ethics in organizations.[4]

For more than two millennia philosophers have told us people are highly gullible to common fallacies. Yet, no matter how plausible these fallacies may sound or how creatively they are applied, they are as false as a three-dollar bill and are completely incapable of supporting any argument.

Table 1 lists some of the most common fallacies in organizational life. Naturally, all need to be rejected as reasons for doing anything and replaced by logical arguments using universal ethical principles, some of which are illustrated in Table 2.

Refining of viable alternatives • This step requires agents to logically balance duty and consequential ethical theories and to use universal ethical principles to find the best possible alternative.[5]

Table 2   Universal Ethical Principles for Organizations

Duty Based Principles	Outcome Based Principles
Higher principles:	*Higher principles:*
• **The Golden Rule:** Do unto others as you would have them do unto you.	• **Greatest good for the most.**
• **Categorical imperative:** Act as if you could will the action to be universally applied by everyone.	• **Virtue:** Do your intents, means and ends reflect the kind of person or group you wish to be?
Competing principles (must choose which take priority):	*Complementary principles:*
• **Not harming:** Not allowing harm to come to others who depend on you.	• **Time horizons:** What are the short- and long-term outcomes?
• **Fidelity:** Keeping promises and confidences and fostering honest dealings.	• **Inclusiveness:** Who is affected, included and excluded from the planned outcomes? Are all affected parties included and considered?
• **Justice:** Recongnizing people commensurately for their merits; avoiding unjust treatment, scapegoating or taking unfair advantage of people.	• **Proportionality:** Do the expected good outcomes outweigh the expected bad ones?
• **Helping others:** Helping others improve and have a better life.	• **Calculus:** Have ideas been examined, facts researched, alternatives considered and outcomes reasonably estimated?
• **Helping self:** Helping yourself improve and have a better life.	• **Win-win:** Is someone clearly better off, while most are as well off and nobody is worse off?
	• **System:** Will the act contribute to or at least not harm the system as a whole the act operates within?

Requirements of this step include identifying alternatives that meet the highest duty and the greatest good for the situation, solving false dilemmas, calculating true dilemma trade-offs and refining viable alternatives into higher utility options until a single best alternative supports a decision.

Validating and following through • This step monitors actual outcomes, validates that they met expectations or conducts follow-through with changed reasoning and corrective action until the needed outcomes are ensured.

Renorming • This step is the control phase that attempts to formalize the best practices discovered in steps one to four. Renorming seeks repeatability.

MORE THAN A FEW BAD APPLES

Compliance programs seek to catch a few bad apples so the rest of the good apples can operate ethically. The problem with this assumption is instead of a few bad people causing most of the trouble, the situation frequently involves many good people working together as an operating culture collectively perpetuating a few bad ethics with devastating effect. In such cases the bad apples are not people at all but rather a few bad forms of ethics or wrong thinking.

Applying compliance tools when the culture is perpetuating poor ethical processes is a misapplication of compliance ethics. Compliance tools are to ethics management as the control phase of define, measure, analyze, improve and control is to Six Sigma.

Six Sigma Black Belts would never consider applying the control step exclusively to the exclusion of the other steps, nor should people manage their ethics this way. Compliance approaches presume the underlying ethics are basically good and all that is needed is some monitoring and the occasional removal of bad apples to ensure good ethics.

It is important to note Enron and WorldCom had extensive ethics compliance programs, and you can see where this got them. Compliance ethics are akin to inspection programs. They can only catch what is nonconforming by definition. And what if conforming behavior is unethical?

Also, if you have too much nonconformance you need more than just inspection to improve the situation. As W. Edwards Deming said, "You cannot inspect quality into a process or product."[6]

To improve ethics, root causes of unethical reasoning must be identified, transformed, refined, validated and renormed according to their natural logical sequence as they occur.

TWO FACES OF ETHICS MANAGEMENT

Ethics management is a system with two integral parts:

1. **Basic compliance**. Some issues are clear-cut, such as not breaking the law or crossing a clear line of moral conduct. For these, compliance programs can play an effective role by showing where the lines are, but they can never be the exclusive basis for ethical performance. For every clear-cut issue there usually are many that are not so visible and need to be examined and managed.

2. **Gray zone issues**. The preponderance of ethical problems in organizations arise in a gray zone in which clear-cut policies and standards either do not fit well or do not exist. Here the issues can be mixtures of both good and bad. Decisions can be skewed by incomplete information. Behaviors can be driven by conflicting requirements, rewards, motives and complex trade-offs in a competitive, dynamic environment. Most poor ethics in organizations are born and incubated here, and it is here ethics management as a preventive discipline needs to be practiced.

Table 3   Preconditions of Poor Ethics in Organization

Preconditions	Process Level	System Level
Attitudes	**Abuse of power:** Manifested in the attitude that more power is authorized than actually is and extra privileges or entitlements exist more for some than for others.	**Leadership by poor example:** Making poor behavior likely because leaders exemplify it.
	Managerial counter norms: When managers use deceptive mentalities as tools:	**Rewarding poor ethics:** Encouraging poor ethics tacitly or overtly with rewards.
	• **False pretexts:** When a false reason is given for doing something or a guise of dialogue and shared decision making is created when a decision has already been made and the true purpose of the dialogue is to manipulate and secure buy-in.	**Punishing principled dissent:** Not protecting whistle blowers and dissenting views.
	• **Persuasion mentality:** Believing anything is true as long as you can convince people it is true.	**Bottom-line mentality:** Accomplishing an objective in an unethical way because management supports it and the ends justify the means.
	• **Public relations mentality:** Putting on false airs. It is more important to appear ethical than to be ethical.	**Short-term mentality:** Securing short-term strategies and outcomes at the expense of long-term benefits.
	• **Labeling mentality:** Arbitrarily labeling a person or an idea to limit merit and consideration.	**False benefit mentality:** Trying to tell stakeholders an action makes them better off, knowing full well the action actually makes them worse off.
	• **Puffing mentality:** Exaggerating a claim beyond the supporting evidence to get approval or buy in.	**Letting the foxes guard the henhouse:** Seeking to reduce legitimate checks and balances to benefit a few at the expense of the many.
	• **Selective truthfulness:** Providing only favorable portions of the truth.	
	• **False win-win:** Two parties arriving at a solution in which both win but at the moral exclusion of another rightful party.	
	• **Permitting falsehoods to stand:** Knowing an argument is false but avoiding the revealing of this because the falsehood promotes a valued position or objective.	
Pressure	**Setting unrealistic goals:** Pushing people beyond their actual process capabilities in a manner that encourages "do whatever it take" thinking.	**Bad policy:** Putting people into bad positions, forcing them to choose between bad ethical alternatives.
	Directing others to be unethical: Directing subordinates to be unethical due to time	**Lacking guidance channels:** Not offering channels for workers to access for guidance on ethical issues.

(continued)

Table 3   (*continued*)

Preconditions	Process Level	System Level
	or resource constraints when better alternatives are available.	
Opportunity	**Preventing examination:** Controlling agendas and communications to dampen opportunities for dialogue and deeper examination of ethical issues.	**Insufficient checks and balances:** Not instituting cross functional checks and balances to ensure against major ethical failures.
	Overdelegation: Favoring management styles with excessive delegation and with too little oversight and examination of decisions and practices.	**Insufficient information sharing:** Allowing functions to operate as kingdoms and constrain interactions by impeding information flow.

An essential principle of organizational ethics is that compliance and gray zone ethics need to be managed together as a system. Compliance needs to be relevant to the actual gray zone issues the organization faces, and improvements in gray zone ethics need to be supported by new norms and standards on the compliance side.

Compliance issues provide valuable signals of gray zone problems, and solving gray zone problems becomes a rationale for creating new norms and standards.

INTO THE GRAY ZONE

Gray zone ethics are what ultimately defines the moral maturity of the organization. It not only accounts for the majority of poor ethics in organizations but also can account for more than half of the cost of poor quality.

Gray zone ethics can account for failed change management efforts and entire quality journey missteps. It can impede product development and marketing execution and can be causes of dysfunction in operating cultures, leadership and governance, reaching out and affecting all functional areas and stakeholders.

Unless identified and resolved, gray zone issues can proliferate and impact process performance at every level and emerge as causes for future high impact compliance failures.

Poor ethics is often preconditioned by three factors: attitudes, pressure and opportunity.[7] These three factors can be manifested at the process or system level of the firm, as demonstrated in Table 3.

Many logical errors, which frequently underlie ethical errors, are caused by accident, ignorance or cognitive failure[8,9] or by carelessness, mental laziness or paying insufficient attention to the situation you are in.[10,11] Ambiguous language, manipulative rhetoric and unconstructive dialogue are also causes of poor ethics.[12]

Table 4   Organizational Culture Study

Five Main Factors Groups	32 Subfactors
Leadership	• Comfort. • Difficulty. • Readiness. • Management style.
Ethical wrong thinking	• Abuse of power. • Heavy handedness. • Double standards. • Whatever it takes. • False pretexts. • Might makes right. • Don't get caught. • Convincing = truth. • Rationalizing. • Others do it, too. • Ends justify means. • Ethical in appearance only. • Lack of openness.
Process capability	• Sufficient resources. • Performance feedback. • Waste. • Firefighting. • Routine stability. • Obstacles. • Teamwork. • Root cause focus.
Risk-reward perception	• Negative experiences. • Job security. • Monetary rewards. • Nonmonetary rewards. • Intrinsic rewards.
Satisfaction	• Job satisfaction. • Desire to stay with the organization.

While many of these cultural factors may be identical for non-profits and for-profits, which ones could affect non-profits more?

Many actions are daily routines and may never get examined for quality unless someone brings a potential problem out into the open for discussion. For this reason, the ability to detect and initiate dialogue on potential problems sooner rather than later is pivotal to preventing poor ethics in the gray zone.

It is an unfortunate fact that many organizations discourage rather than encourage early detection only to have to deal with the problems later, after they have grown larger and more expensive to correct.

IMPROVING PERFORMANCE THROUGH THOUGHTFUL CONSENSUS

According to the philosopher W.D. Ross, "Ethical behavior is that which is morally accepted by a consensus of thoughtful and knowing people."[13]

Consensus about the goodness or badness of things is not only achievable but is considered essential to the ethical reasoning process. This consensus approach should not be confused with the notion that majority opinion is necessarily right, because majority opinion can be and often is on the wrong side of ethics. The distinction is one of being thoughtful and knowing, which suggests a shared awareness of ethical reasoning principles and the facts of a situation.

The recognition of good or bad ethical behavior in organizations often deals with complex questions involving many parties and necessitating a thoughtful and knowing consensus for conclusions to be drawn with high assurance.

Once a thoughtful and knowing consensus starts to jell, new knowledge is added to the group's collective consciousness, enabling a more accurate consensus or synthesis to emerge around what the true situation is and what ought to be done.

Promoting adherence to four requirements can accelerate this jelling process:

- Agents must raise fallacy free arguments.[14]
- Agents must share a similar understanding of moral principles, the facts of the situation and the expected outcomes.
- Agents must be willing and able to engage in constructive dialogue using fair and honest rhetoric.[15,16]
- Agents must be reasonably objective and willing to change their views as facts and sound reasoning dictate.[17]

Once this consensus principle is understood, you can witness its application everywhere—in jury deliberations and structured group discussion methodologies, including failure mode and effects analysis (FMEA).

In FMEA, it is common for initial risk mode scores to show low consensus (high variations) but later improve dramatically—with lower variations—after training teams to better meet these four requirements.

IMPROVING PERFORMANCE THROUGH THE OPERATING CULTURE

Poor ethics leaves negative footprints on several cultural factors that correlate strongly with performance. One of these factors is a group's focus on root causes. Culture generally—which is a major influencer of ethics in organizations—and root cause focus specifically—which is an important performance factor in quality—become powerful allies in ethics management by providing a window to observe and prevent ethical wrong thinking.

Table 5   Correlations Between Main Factor Groups

	Less Ethical Wrong Thinking	Leader- ship	Process Capa- bility	Perceived Risk- reward	Satis- faction
Less ethical wrong thinking	1.000	.315*	.491*	.535*	.407*
Leadership	.315*	1.000	.320*	.412*	.292*
Process capability	.491*	.320*	1.000	.617*	.440*
Perceived risk-reward	.535*	.412*	.617*	1.000	.579*
Satisfaction	.407*	.292*	.440*	.579*	1.000

Notes: Pearson correlations in SPSS 9.0; Asterisks denote significance (2-tailed) to the 0.01 level; Data = ordinal; N = 498.

Table 6   Organizational Culture Regression Analysis

Dependent Variable	Predictor Factors	Significance	Adjusted R^2
Root cause focus	**Ethical wrong thinking:**		
	• Lack of openness .501	.000	
	• Double standards .151	.000	.411
	• False pretexts .116	.001	
Root cause focus	**Perceived risks-rewards:**		
	• Negative experiences .247	.000	
	• Intrinsic rewards .224	.000	.308
	• Nonmonetary rewards .185	.000	
	• Monetary rewards .161	.000	

Notes: Regression analysis in SPSS 9.0; N = 498.

A few years ago I conducted a survey of 498 employees from 35 departments of organizations throughout North America. The companies varied by size and industry, and the departments ranged from operations, production and engineering to sales, accounting and information systems.

My objective was to explore the inherent relationships I believed existed between certain culture performance factors and common forms of ethical wrong thinking. There were 32 subfactors clustered into five main groups, with one of the groups representing ethical wrong thinking (see Table 4). Analysis of the data revealed the following:

- The original four groups correlated strongly as predicted by previous studies,[18] and the fifth group, less ethical wrong thinking, correlated significantly with the other four factor groups (see Table 5).
- Regression analysis on root cause focus (see Table 6) found three forms of ethical wrong thinking—lack of openness, double standards and false pretexts—explained 41% of the variation in root cause focus, while four perceived risk-reward factors—negative experiences, intrinsic rewards, monetary rewards and nonmonetary rewards—explained 30% of the variation.

Table 7   Organizational Culture Factor Analysis

Wrong thinking was a leading cause of variation in the model.

Factor groupings	Principal components analysis (PCA) [common + unique variation] Rotated component coefficients >.500	Total model variation explained by PCA: 58.41% Percentage of variation explained by factor groups
1. Wrong thinking	Convincing = truth .760 Others do it, too .738 Whatever it takes .715 Double standards .686 Ends justify means .671 Might makes right .614	14.35%
2. Satisfaction, commitment and cooperation	Job satisfaction .789 Job security .701 Intrinsic rewards .615 Performance measures .570 Teamwork .565	13.05%
3. Dissatisfaction and retention	Negative experiences .764 Desire to stay/leave .556 Nonmonetary rewards .549 Lack of openness .523	10.81%
4. Bottom-line improvement	Waste .782 Monetary rewards .756 Readiness .568	8.45%
5. Process capability and control	Routine .741 Resources .554	6.74%
6. Leadership	Management style .744	4.95%

Notes: Extraction method: PCA in SPSS 9.0; Varimax rotated solutions; EganV > 1; N = 498.

- Principal component analysis (see Table 7 ...) revealed the leading factor cluster explaining the most variation in the model was wrong thinking.

Common sense and experience should also tell us wrong thinking will hurt decisions and performance.

In consulting projects involving many of the surveyed departments, I noticed that after subsequent training to prevent wrong thinking, many documented problems shrank or, in some instances, disappeared altogether.

Furthermore, these improvements consistently enabled groups to solve problems faster, making Six Sigma or other fast paced methodologies more attractive to them. In all cases, it was not a few bad people causing the problems but rather a few forms of wrong thinking holding the groups back.

IMPROVING THE VALUE OF THE FIRM

The pursuit of profit growth is one of the few universal constants in business organizations. However, profit can be pursued for many reasons and by many means, not all ethical. Here are two ethics inspired thoughts that provide a powerful framework that can help any organization improve profits, ethics and sustainability at the same time:

1. Profit is never an end in itself but a means to a higher end to reward all stakeholders commensurately for their cooperation and service to best ensure the future sustainability and prosperity of the enterprise.
2. Treating people right is not just a means to an end but a worthy end in itself, creating intrinsic value for the enterprise and all who interact with it.

GETTING STARTED

A single group, team or department can justify doing its own high performance ethics program, but the program's benefits are best extended to the entire enterprise. Initially any group will need:

- Executive overview training to secure upper management's moral and economic support.
- An ethics committee to serve as ethics champions and trusted intermediaries to open dialogue channels to enable ethical issues to get examined and as a formal renorming authority.
- Training for employees, especially for improvement team members at the beginning of their projects, so they are ready to transform wrong thinking to right thinking.
- Recognition and rewards for employees who contribute to the overall effectiveness of the ethics system.

BEYOND COMPLIANCE

Most organizations want to improve intents, means and outcomes for all involved and benefit themselves in the process. They just need to learn the proven ways to do it and apply these methods in a sustainable way.

Organizations can continue to invest resources in compliance programs with diminishing or negative returns, or they can turn a cost center into a profit center by redirecting some of the compliance resources to the ethics performance concept.

Whether their motives are noble, pragmatic or perhaps a little of both, a more preventive approach to organizational ethics promises to be a positive and rewarding step in the right direction.

Note

The feedback and data in Tables 4, 5, 6 and 7 were derived from an organizational culture study conducted by Ethics Quality Inc.

REFERENCES

1. Philip B. Crosby, *Quality Without Tears*, McGraw Hill Book Co., 1984, chapter 7.
2. H.A. Simon, *Administrative Behavior*, fourth edition, Free Press, 1997, p. 6.
3. Julian Marias, *History of Philosophy*, Dover Publishing, 1981, pp. 38–41.
4. Immanuel Kant, *Critique of Pure Reason*, 1929; unabridged edition, translated by Norman Kemp Smith, St. Martins Press, 1965.
5. Jonathan Dancy, *A Companion to Ethics*, edited by Peter Singer, Blackwell Publishers, 1993, chapters 18 and 36, both citing excerpts from W.D. Ross, *The Right and The Good*, Clarendon Press, 1930, chapters 1 and 2.
6. W.E. Deming, *Out of the Crisis*, MIT Press, 1986.
7. R.R. Sims, *The Challenge of Ethical Behavior in Organizations*: *Business Ethics 95/96*, seventh edition, pp. 210–217, reprinted from *Journal of Business Ethics*, July 1992.
8. *Protagoras and Plato*, translated by Benjamin Jowett, Project Gutenberg, e-text 1999, Socrates Dialogue With Protagoras, www.gutenberg.org/dirs/etext99/prtgs10.txt.
9. Plato, "Plato's Shorter Ethical Works," *Stanford Encyclopedia of Philosophy*, The Instrumentality of Virtue, the Unity of Virtue, the Impossibility of Acrasia, Protagoras, http://plato.stanford.edu/ entries/plato-ethics-shorter/#5.
10. B.M. Patten, *Truth, Knowledge or Just Plain Bull*, Prometheus Books, 2004, p. 19.
11. D.Q. McLnery, *Being Logical: A Guide to Good Thinking*, Random House, 2005, chapter 1.
12. Aristotle, Rhetoric, book 1, chapter 1 (Rhetoric needs to be fair, honest and with good moral intent), compiled by Lee Honeycutt, Iowa State University, www.public.iastate.edu/~honeyl/ Rhetoric/index.html (case sensitive), based on translations by W. Rhys Roberts, "Notes on Aristotle's Rhetoric," *American Journal of Philology*, vol. 45, 1924.
13. W.D. Ross, *The Right and The Good*, edited, with introduction by Philip Stratton-Lake, Oxford Press, reprint of the original 1930 edition.
14. Kant, *Critique of Pure Reason*, see reference 4.
15. Ross, *The Right and the Good*, see reference 13.
16. Aristotle, Rhetoric, see reference 12.
17. John Rawls, *Theory of Justice*, revised edition, Harvard University Press, 1999, pp. 10–19.
18. A.R. Cohen, *Effective Behavior in Organizations*, sixth edition, Irwin, 1995, p. 94.

Creating an Ethical Culture

David Gebler

While the fate of former Enron leaders Kenneth Lay and Jeffrey Skilling is being determined in what has been labeled the "Trial of the Century," former WorldCom managers are in jail for pulling off one of the largest frauds in history.

Yes, criminal activity definitely took place in these companies and in dozens more that have been in the news in recent years, but what's really important is to take stock of the nature of many of the perpetrators.

Some quotes from former WorldCom executives paint a different picture of corporate criminals than we came to know in other eras:

> "I'm sorry for the hurt that has been caused by my cowardly behavior."
> —*Scott Sullivan, CFO*
> "Faced with a decision that required strong moral courage, I took the easy way out. . . .There are no words to describe my shame."
> —*Buford Yates, director of general accounting*
> "At the time I consider the single most critical character-defining moment of my life, I failed. It's something I'll take with me the rest of my life."
> —*David Myers, controller*

These are the statements of good people gone bad. But probably most disturbing was the conviction of Betty Vinson, the senior manager in the accounting department who booked billions of dollars in false expenses. At her sentencing, U.S. District Judge Barbara Jones noted that Vinson was among the lowest-ranking members of the conspiracy that led to the $11 billion fraud that sank the telecommunications company in 2002. Still, she said, "Had Ms. Vinson refused to do what she was asked, it's possible this conspiracy might have been nipped in the bud."

Judge Jones added that although Ms. Vinson "was among the least culpable members of the conspiracy" and acted under extreme pressure, "that does not excuse what she did."

Vinson said she improperly covered up expenses by drawing down reserve accounts—some completely unrelated to the expenses—and by moving expenses off income statements and listing them as assets on the balance sheet.

Also the company's former director of corporate reporting, Vinson testified at Bernie Ebbers's trial that, in choosing which accounts to alter, "I just really pulled some out of the air. I used some spreadsheets." She said she repeatedly brought her concerns to colleagues and supervisors, once describing the entries to a coworker as "just crazy." In spring 2002, she noted, she told one boss she would no longer make the entries. "I said that I thought the entries were just being made to make the income statement look like Scott wanted it to look."

Standing before the judge at her sentencing, Vinson said: "I never expected to be here, and I certainly won't do anything like this again." She was sentenced to five months in prison and five months of house arrest.

PRESSURE REIGNS

While the judge correctly said that her lack of culpability didn't excuse her actions, we must carefully note that Betty Vinson, as well as many of her codefendants, didn't start out as criminals seeking to defraud the organization. Under typical antifraud screening tools, she and others like her wouldn't have raised any red flags as being potential committers of corporate fraud.

Scott Sullivan was a powerful leader with a well-known reputation for integrity. If any of us were in Betty Vinson's shoes, could we say with 100% confidence that we would say "no" to the CFO if he asked us to do something and promised that he would take full responsibility for any fallout from the actions we were going to take?

Today's white-collar criminals are more likely to be those among us who are unable to withstand the blistering pressures placed on managers to meet higher and tougher goals. In this environment, companies looking to protect themselves from corporate fraud must take a hard look at their own culture. Does it promote ethical behavior, or does it emphasize something else?

In most companies, "ethics" programs are really no more than compliance programs with a veneer of "do the right thing" messaging to create an apparent link to the company's values. To be effective, they have to go deeper than outlining steps to take to report misconduct. Organizations must understand what causes misconduct in the first place.

We can't forget that Enron had a Code of Ethics. And it wasn't as if World-Com lacked extensive internal controls. But both had cultures where engaging in unethical conduct was tacitly condoned, if not encouraged.

BUILDING THE RIGHT CULTURE

Now the focus has shifted toward looking at what is going on inside organizations that's either keeping people from doing the right thing or, just as importantly, keeping people from doing something about misconduct they observe. If an organization wants to reduce the risk of unethical conduct, it must focus more effort on building the right culture than on building a compliance infrastructure.

The Ethics Resource Center's 2005 National Business Ethics Survey (NBES) clearly confirms this trend toward recognizing the role of corporate culture. Based on interviews with more than 3,000 employees and managers in the U.S., the survey disclosed that, despite the increase in the number of ethics and compliance program elements being implemented, desired outcomes, such as reduced levels of observed misconduct, haven't changed since 1994. Even more striking is the revelation that, although formal ethics and compliance programs have some impact, organizational culture has the greatest influence in determining program outcomes.

The Securities & Exchange Commission (SEC) and the Department of Justice have also been watching these trends. Stephen Cutler, the recently retired SEC director of the Division of Enforcement, was matter of fact about the importance of looking at culture when it came to decisions of whether or not to bring an action. "We're trying to induce companies to address matters of tone and culture…. What we're asking of that CEO, CFO, or General Counsel goes beyond what a perp walk or an enforcement action against another company executive might impel her to do. We're hoping that if she sees that a failure of corporate culture can result in a fine that significantly exceeds the proverbial 'cost of doing business,' and reflects a failure on her watch—and a failure on terms that everyone can understand: the company's bottom line—she may have a little more incentive to pay attention to the environment in which her company's employees do their jobs."

What can leaders do to reduce the risk of unethical conduct in the workplace?

MEASURING SUCCESS

Only lagging companies still measure the success of their ethics and compliance programs just by tallying the percentage of employees who have certified that they read the Code of Conduct and attended ethics and compliance training. The true indicator of success is whether the company has made significant progress in achieving key program outcomes. The National Business Ethics Survey listed four key outcomes that help determine the success of a program:

- Reduced misconduct observed by employees,
- Reduced pressure to engage in unethical conduct,
- Increased willingness of employees to report misconduct, and
- Greater satisfaction with organizational response to reports of misconduct.

What's going to move these outcomes in the right direction? Establishing the right culture.

Most compliance programs are generated from "corporate" and disseminated down through the organization. As such, measurement of the success of the program is often based on criteria important to the corporate office: how many employees certified the Code of Conduct, how many employees went through the training, or how many calls the hotline received.

Culture is different—and is measured differently. An organization's culture isn't something that's created by senior leadership and then rolled out.

A culture is an objective picture of the organization, for better or worse. It's the sum total of all the collective values and behaviors of all employees, managers, and leaders. By definition, it can only be measured by criteria that reflect the individual values of all employees, so understanding cultural vulnerabilities that can lead to ethics issues requires knowledge of what motivates employees in the organization. Leadership must know how the myriad human behaviors and interactions fit together like puzzle pieces to create a whole picture. An organization moves toward an ethical culture only if it understands the full range of values and behaviors needed to meet its ethical goals. The "full-spectrum" organization is one that creates a positive sense of engagement and purpose that drives ethical behavior.

Why is understanding the culture so important in determining the success of a compliance program? Here's an example: Most organizations have a policy that prohibits retaliation against those who bring forward concerns or claims. But creating a culture where employees feel safe enough to admit mistakes and to raise uncomfortable issues requires more than a policy and "Code training." To truly develop an ethical culture, the organization must be aware of how its managers deal with these issues up and down the line and how the values they demonstrate impact desired behaviors. The organization must understand the pressures its people are under and how they react to those pressures. And it must know how its managers communicate and whether employees have a sense of accountability and purpose.

CATEGORIZING VALUES

Determining whether an organization has the capabilities to put such a culture in place requires careful examination. Do employees and managers demonstrate values such as respect? Do employees feel accountable for their actions and feel that they have a stake in the success of the organization?

How does an organization make such a determination? One approach is to categorize different types of values in a way that lends itself to determining specific strengths and weaknesses that can be assessed and then corrected or enhanced.

The Culture Risk Assessment model presented in Figure 1 has been adapted from the Cultural Transformation Tools® developed by Richard Barrett & Associates. Such tools provide a comprehensive framework for measuring cultures by mapping values. More than 1,000 organizations in 24 countries have used this technique in the past six years. In fact, the international management consulting firm McKinsey & Co. has adopted it as its method of choice for mapping corporate cultures and measuring progress toward achieving culture change.

The model is based on the principle, substantiated through practice, that all values can be assigned to one of seven categories:

Figure 1   Seven Levels of an Ethical Organization

SUSTAINABILITY	7	Resilience to withstand integrity challenges
SOCIAL RESPONSIBILITY	6	Strategic alliances with external stakeholders
ALIGNMENT	5	Shared values guide decision making
ACCOUNTABILITY	4	Responsibilty and initiative
SYSTEMS AND PROCESSES	3	Compliance systems and processes
COMMUNICATION	2	Relationships that support the organization
FINANCIAL STABILITY	1	Pursuit of profit and stability

© Working Values, Ltd. Based on Cultural Transformation Tools © Richard Barrett & Associates

Levels 1, 2, and 3—The Organization's Basic Needs

Does the organization support values that enable it to run smoothly and effectively? From an ethics perspective, is the environment one in which employees feel physically and emotionally safe to report unethical behavior and to do the right thing?

Level 1—Financial stability • Every organization needs to make financial stability a primary concern. Companies that are consumed with just surviving struggle to focus enough attention on how they conduct themselves. This may, in fact, create a negative cycle that makes survival much more difficult. Managers may exercise excessive control, so employees may be working in an environment of fear.

In these circumstances, unethical or even illegal conduct can be rationalized. When asked to conform to regulations, organizations do the minimum with an attitude of begrudging compliance.

Organizations with challenges at this level need to be confident that managers know and stand within clear ethical boundaries.

Level 2—Communication • Without good relationships with employees, customers, and suppliers, integrity is compromised. The critical issue at this level is to create a sense of loyalty and belonging among employees and a sense of caring and connection between the organization and its customers.

The most critical link in the chain is between employees and their direct supervisors. If direct supervisors can't effectively reinforce messages coming from senior leadership, those messages might be diluted and confused by the time they reach line employees. When faced with conflicting messages, employees will usually choose to follow the lead of their direct supervisor over the words of the CEO that have been conveyed through an impersonal communication channel. Disconnects in how local managers "manage" these messages often mean that employees can face tremendous pressure in following the lead established by leadership.

Fears about belonging and lack of respect lead to fragmentation, dissension, and disloyalty. When leaders meet behind closed doors or fail to communicate openly, employees suspect the worst. Cliques form, and gossip becomes rife. When leaders are more focused on their own success, rather than the success of the organization, they begin to compete with each other.

Level 3—Systems and processes • At this level, the organization is focused on becoming the best it can be through the adoption of best practices and a focus on quality, productivity, and efficiency.

Level 3 organizations have succeeded in implementing strong internal controls and have enacted clear standards of conduct. Those that succeed at this level are the ones that see internal controls as an opportunity to create better, more efficient processes. But even those that have successfully deployed business processes and practices need to be alert to potentially limiting aspects of being too focused on processes. All organizations need to be alert to resorting to a "check-the-box" attitude that assumes compliance comes naturally from just implementing standards and procedures. Being efficient all too often leads to bureaucracy and inconsistent application of the rules. When this goes badly, employees lose respect for the system and resort to self-help to get things done. This can lead to shortcuts and, in the worst case, engaging in unethical conduct under the guise of doing what it takes to succeed.

Level 4—Accountability

The focus of the fourth level is on creating an environment in which employees and managers begin to take responsibility for their own actions. They want to be held accountable, not micromanaged and supervised every moment of every day. For an ethics and compliance program to be successful, all employees must feel that they have a personal responsibility for the integrity of the organization. Everyone must feel that his or her voice is being heard. This requires managers and leaders to admit that they don't have all the answers and invite employee participation.

Levels 5, 6, and 7—Common Good

Does the organization support values that create a collective sense of belonging where employees feel that they have a stake in the success of the ethics program?

Level 5—Alignment • The critical issue at this level is developing a shared vision of the future and a shared set of values. The shared vision clarifies the intentions of the organization and gives employees a unifying purpose and direction. The shared values provide guidance for making decisions.

The organization develops the ability to align decision making around a set of shared values. The values and behaviors must be reflected in all of the organization's processes and systems, with appropriate consequences for those who aren't willing to walk the talk. A precondition for success at this level is building a climate of trust.

Level 6—Social responsibility • At this level, the organization is able to use its relationships with stakeholders to sustain itself through crises and change. Employees and customers see that the organization is making a difference in the world through its products and services, its involvement in the local community, or its willingness to fight for causes that improve humanity. They must feel that the company cares about them and their future. Companies operating at this level go the extra mile to make sure they are being responsible citizens. They support and encourage employees' activities in the community by providing time off for volunteer work and/or making a financial contribution to the charities that employees are involved in.

Level 7—Sustainability • To be successful at Level 7, organizations must embrace the highest ethical standards in all their interactions with employees, suppliers, customers, shareholders, and the community. They must always consider the long-term impact of their decisions and actions.

Employee values are distributed across all seven levels. Through surveys, organizations learn which values employees bring to the workplace and which values are missing. Organizations don't operate from any one level of values: They tend to be clustered around three or four levels. Most are focused on the first three: profit and growth (Level 1), customer satisfaction (Level 2), and productivity, efficiency, and quality (Level 3). The most successful organizations operate across the full spectrum with particular focus in the upper levels of consciousness—the common good—accountability, leading to learning and innovation (Level 4), alignment (Level 5), sustainability (Level 6), and social responsibility (Level 7).

How would a non-profit organization categorize these values? Would the levels change?

Some organizations have fully developed values around Levels 1, 2, and 3 but are lacking in Levels 5, 6, and 7. They may have a complete infrastructure of controls and procedures but may lack the accountability and commitment of employees and leaders to go further than what is required.

Similarly, some organizations have fully developed values around Levels 5, 6, and 7 but are deficient in Levels 1, 2, and 3. These organizations may have visionary leaders and externally focused social responsibility programs, but they may be lacking in core systems that will ensure that the higher-level commitments are embedded into day-to-day processes.

Once an organization understands its values' strengths and weaknesses, it can take specific steps to correct deficient behavior.

STARTING THE PROCESS

Could a deeper understanding of values have saved WorldCom? We will never know, but if the culture had encouraged open communication and fostered trust, people like Betty Vinson might have been more willing to confront orders that they knew were wrong. Moreover, if the culture had embodied values that encouraged transparency, mid-level managers wouldn't have been asked to engage in such activity in the first place.

The significance of culture issues such as these is also being reflected in major employee surveys that highlight what causes unethical behavior. According to the NBES, "Where top management displays certain ethics-related actions, employees are 50 percentage points less likely to observe misconduct." No other factor in any ethics survey can demonstrate such a drastic influence.

So how do compliance leaders move their organizations to these new directions?

1. **The criteria for success of an ethics program must be outcomes based.** Merely checking off program elements isn't enough to change behavior.
2. **Each organization must identify the key indicators of its culture.** Only by assessing its own ethical culture can a company know what behaviors are the most influential in effecting change.
3. **The organization must gauge how all levels of employees perceive adherence to values by others within the company.** One of the surprising findings of the NBES was that managers, especially senior managers, were out of touch with how nonmanagement employees perceived their adherence to ethical behaviors. Nonmanagers are 27 percentage points less likely than senior managers to indicate that executives engage in all of the ethics-related actions outlined in the survey.
4. **Formal programs are guides to shape the culture, not vice versa.** People who are inclined to follow the rules appreciate the rules as a guide to behavior. Formal program elements need to reflect the culture in which they are deployed if they are going to be most effective in driving the company to the desired outcomes.

Culture may be new on the radar screen, but it isn't outside the scope or skills of forward-thinking finance managers and compliance professionals. Culture can be measured, and finance managers can play a leadership role in developing systematic approaches to move companies in the right direction.

ISSUE SUMMARY

——●

Judging from the attention being given to ethics in the workplace, ethical conduct is no longer regarded as a personal issue for each worker to deal with alone. Ethics is taking a prominent place alongside quality, finance, and governance as an essential system of an organization. And judging from the increase in resources on organizational ethics available in print and online, many people believe that ethics needs standards, programs, measures, and methodologies similar to all other essential operations. But will all of this ensure that ethics becomes part of the DNA of an organization? Some say ethics is not truly a corporate matter; it is a matter of individual conscience and no amount of structure or enforcement can make ethics corporate.

The position statement on corporate governance of the Society of Corporate Secretaries and Governance Professionals ends by taking this stand: "that ethics, integrity and independence cannot be legislated and that many governance practice prescriptions tend to elevate form and appearance over substance." Some organizations are beginning to reach the same conclusion— that ethics cannot be legislated. The challenge for these organizations is to determine what approach will work. It comes down to whether an organization believes ethics is a matter of values, performance, or compliance.

It would be logical to conclude that compliance is the least desirable approach. Yet if many people believe that ethics cannot be enforced, why do so many organizations have codes of ethics? After all, a code is only a guide for ethics, not a guarantor. Most codes are intended to be general and are geared toward minimum expectations. Seen from this perspective, codes serve as external control mechanisms. They have a useful, but limited role.

Organizations must go beyond code compliance if they want ethics to be integrated into all aspects of the organization and that brings us back to the best approach. Given the rise in misconduct, evidently compliance is not working, but neither is simply leading by example. Regardless of the approach, it is clear that without a formal program, misconduct is more likely to occur. Based on key findings of the National Business Ethics Survey, the Ethics Resource Center has concluded: "While culture matters in making an impact, formal programs are still essential to creating a culture."

And what about organizations in the nonprofit sector? Are organizations whose mission is driven by ethical principles more ethical than for-profits? Just because a nonprofit exists for charity or service and is prohibited from enriching its members or employees, that does not mean daily practice is faultless. Most ethical issues of a 501(c) are identical to corporations whose scandals are lead stories on the nightly news. For any organization, honesty, conflict of interest, and justice are concepts with ethical implications. Unless a nonprofit has found effective ways to embed values in practice and procedure, eventually it too will have to deal with employees who act unethically.

ISSUE HIGHLIGHTS

- National studies reveal ethical misconduct is on the rise, despite increasing reliance on formal ethics programs.
- Organizational culture plays a significant role in ethical behavior.
- Codes of ethics are becoming more prevalent.
- Compliance with ethics statements is being enforced as an extension of the Sarbanes-Oxley Act.
- Formal ethics programs are essential to improving conduct.
- The ethical quality approach is performance oriented and emphasizes better moral outcomes.
- The values-based approach centers on an organization's understanding of its values.
- A significant factor in ethical behavior is the organization's culture.
- The best approach to creating an organizational culture remains unclear.

CRITICAL THINKING

Some people claim that it is impossible to establish principles or codes of ethics for organizations. They point out that there is no set of universal ethical principles that would apply to all cultures, faiths, and societies. Judging by the proliferation of business ethics centers and think tanks, they are right. Each center has created its own framework for how to think about ethics in the workplace.

What is missing is a universal guide to ethical decision making that could be applied in situations with implications. Such principles could not be religious or absolutes, if they are to serve across cultures and faiths. Nor could they be completely laissez-faire, providing no better guidance than "live and let live." Universal principles would need to be compelling enough to guide conscience and to encourage dialogue.

Several groups are attempting to create sets of principles to guide organizations. One group is Crossroads Programs, Inc. They have crafted principles that may seem simple or obvious at first, but are proving to stand the tests of time and universality. The principles are in three categories: personal, professional, and global. All of the principles flow from the central idea of concern for the well-being of others, an ethical concept that appears in all faiths and cultures. It is important to note that the group points out the principles can only provide guidance—there is no magic formula. And they acknowledge that at times principles will collide with other principles.

As a follow-through to the readings, review the principles at the University of British Columbia Centre for Applied Ethics site: www.ethics.ubc.ca/papers/invited/colero.html This site also contains a "Corporate Integrity Checkup" that is useful for establishing a baseline for the organization.

ADDITIONAL READING RESOURCES

Knight Kiplinger, Who's watching the watchdog? *Ethics Today Online*, December 2005. http://www.ethics.org/today/et_v3n80505.html#kk

National Business Ethics Survey: How employees view ethics in their organizations 1994–2005. *Ethics Resource Center*, Washington, D.C., 2005.

Position statement on corporate governance. *Society of Corporate Secretaries and Governance Professionals*. Available at http://www.governanceprofessionals.org/ascsposition.shtml

Joseph Weber, Calling the ethics cops. *Business Week Online,* February 13, 2006.

For more information check these sites:

www.crossroadsprograms.com
www.ephilanthropy.org
www.ethics.org
www.theecoa.org

ISSUE 4

Does Organizational Culture Link to Success or Profitability?

INTRODUCTION

The question for this issue—does culture matter?—leads to another question—does culture matter to whom or for what? Organizational scientists would say it matters to productivity. Sociologists would say it matters to the individuals. Consumer or watchdog organizations would say it matters to the public. And new research is proving that culture definitely matters to the success or failure of any organizational improvement initiative. Whether the initiative is TQM, quality circles, or statistical process control, experts are saying that culture plays a role previously unrecognized.

Some regard a weak organizational culture as the cauldron for ethical lapses, low performance, and failure to succeed. Is the culture of some organizations so powerful that it has such dire consequences? Conversely, is a strong culture the breeding ground for ethical steadiness, excellent performance, or success?

The problem with culture is that it is difficult to quantify. In this era of "accountability equals quantifiability," that makes culture the elephant in the room. Granted, many improvement initiatives are holistic efforts and one would assume all have the potential to be culture changers. However, it is apparent that cultural "best practices" continue to be elusive and no particular initiative is large enough to encompass culture. In fact, it is distressing to learn that new research shows if culture is left undisturbed, most initiatives are doomed. "Although the tools and techniques may be present and the change strategy is implemented with vigor, many efforts to improve organizational performance fail because the fundamental culture of the organization—values, ways of thinking, managerial styles, paradigms, approaches to problem solving—remain the same" (Cameron & Quinn, p. 11).

One of the most analyzed organizational cultures is Wal-Mart. Some view their fundamental culture as a cauldron for crime and greed. Criticism and accusations have been so vicious that Wal-Mart has undertaken a cultural overhaul. As extraordinarily successful as the corporation has been, Wal-Mart has decided to make organizational culture a priority. Wal-Mart.com now features several pages on corporate culture, with explanations of their beliefs (respect the individual, service to customers, and strive for excellence) and rules (sundown rule, ten-foot rule, Sam Walton's personal set of ten rules). With a stronger focus on beliefs and rules, it appears that Wal-Mart is learning that the best way to refute their reputation as ruthless competitor is to be transparent about efforts to create a positive, distinctive culture.

What could possibly be wrong with a positive workplace culture?—nothing, unless positivism is a cover for fear and anxiety. This is precisely what Susan Davidson found when she investigated corporate culture in America. In "The Irresolute American" Davidson brings the sociological perspective of organizational culture by focusing on the behavior of employees in the organization. Her survey of foreign executives working in the United States is a reality check on an interesting paradox—American workers' reputation for being honest and forthright in the workplace is simply untrue. Professionals from other places around the world find that Americans live in fear at work and the result is often deferential treatment. The reason: "The outward egalitarianism of American manners is deceptive. Within a business organization there is a well-defined and rigorously observed hierarchy." Evidently, command-and-control leadership is more prevalent than Americans would like to believe.

"Leading by Leveraging Culture" takes an unexpected perspective by placing culture at the center of the equation of organizational success. Rather than strategy formulation, culture is a better predictor of success. The authors assert that culture is a leadership tool, yet it cannot be directly manipulated: "The irony of leadership through culture is that the less formal direction you give employees about how to execute strategy, the more ownership they take over their actions and the better they perform." Strong culture consists of two variables, high levels of agreement among employees about what is valued and intensity about these values. How to get to the point of high levels of agreement is a matter for leaders to consider. The authors outline three tools for leaders to leverage culture.

A passive-aggressive organization is not a rarity—in fact, many organizations suffer this syndrome, according to the authors of the final reading. "The Passive-Aggressive Organization" points to a cluster of factors that identify an organization as passive-aggressive. When the term "passive-aggressive" is applied to an organization, a cluster of behavioral dynamics can appear: procrastination, resentment, pessimism, sabotage. As with a passive-aggressive individual, it may not be apparent at first that an organization is passive-aggressive. Only over time, as a pattern of subtle resistance or obstruction becomes obvious, is the behavior understood to be harmful or dysfunctional. Interestingly, such an organization can be conflict-free, friendly, pleasant work environments and still be intransigent.

Does a passive-aggressive organization imply that the employees are all passive-aggressive or is something else occurring? Neilson, Pasternack, and Van Nuys contend that flawed processes and policies are the root cause, not an inordinate number of hostile people. Turnaround is difficult, but not impossible when what's "broken" is not people but processes and policies. The authors end with an ominous warning that what is broken must be fixed: "It's only a matter of time before the diseased elements of a passive-aggressive organization overwhelm the healthy ones and drive the organization into financial distress." Culture does matter; it can handicap an organization to the point of its demise or it can propel an organization to amazing performance.

SOURCES

Anne D'Innocenzio, Wal-Mart tries to modify corporate culture. *ABCNews. com*, April 16, 2006.

Susan Davidson, The irresolute American. *Executive Action*, May 2006.

Jennifer A. Chatman & Sandra Eunyoung Cha, Leading by leveraging culture. *California Management Review*, Summer 2003.

Gary L. Neilson, Bruce A. Pasternack, & Karen E. Van Nuys, The passive-aggressive organization. *Harvard Business Review*, October 2005.

Wal-Mart Tries to Modify Corporate Culture

Anne D'Innocenzio

After years of accusations that it caused the demise of thousands of smaller merchants, Wal-Mart Stores Inc. is undertaking an unusual strategy: helping competing local establishments stay in business. Wal-Mart recasting itself as a friendly neighbor? It's the latest course change by the world's largest merchant as it tries to modify its corporate culture—and the perception that it's a ruthless competitor obsessed with maintaining its dominance of the retail industry.

Wal-Mart's proposal to help rival small businesses, from bakeries to hardware stores, focuses on blighted urban markets where the retailer plans to open 50 stores within the next two years. The efforts will range from giving those businesses financial grants to producing free radio ads that will be broadcast on its stores' radio network.

The image makeover extends to Wal-Mart's selling floor as well. In recent months, for example, it has embraced organic products from baby clothes to fish caught in ecologically friendly ways.

And the company, which has long been shrouded in secrecy, is trying to appear more transparent. Late last year, it sponsored a debate among a group of economists about whether Wal-Mart is good or bad for the economy. And it's holding its second annual media conference starting Tuesday near its Bentonville, Ark., headquarters, to share information about the company, from its plans to improve its stores to updates on its employee health care proposals.

The changes are Wal-Mart's response to critics, particularly union-backed groups, who have long argued that the company has exploited the business model of folksy founder Sam Walton, putting profits before its own employees and towns and cities where it does business.

"The notion that Sam Walton cared about its workers, and the community, those positive aspects have gone," said Chris Kofinis, spokesman for WakeUp-WalMart.com, a campaign group funded by the United Food and Commercial Workers. He described the recently announced moves as a series of public relations stunts.

Analysts say that although Wal-Mart is used to succeeding, it has no guarantees in this endeavor, especially since its core business model—built around offering incredibly low prices—won't change.

"The culture remains frugal and very focused on costs and price . . . It is going to be very hard to change the culture of the company," said Charles Fishman, author of "The Wal-Mart Effect," a book on the company's impact on the national economy. "Their image of themselves is powerfully fixed, and our image as shoppers is very powerfully fixed."

In fact, as part of its ongoing cost-cutting campaign, Wal-Mart plans to become more reliant on part-time workers, which currently account for about 20 percent of its work force.

Some analysts say Wal-Mart actually won't be fixated in the future on offering the cheapest prices, but will try instead to offer the best value in different merchandise categories. A few years ago, customers would not have imagined Wal-Mart selling $5,000 diamond rings or $2,000 plasma TVs, but the retailer is now offering attractive deals in more upscale products.

"I think that Wal-Mart has come to the realization that it cannot be focused on low-prices alone," said C. Britt Beemer, chairman of America's Research Group. "They need a broader offering."

Wal-Mart, whose officials declined to be interviewed, has a lot at stake. Its stock has fallen 20 percent over the past two years, and is now trading at about $45. And the company is finding it harder to sustain profit growth in the high teens as in previous years as it struggles with higher expenses. For the year ended Jan. 31, Wal-Mart said net sales were up 9.5 percent to $312.4 billion and net income rose 9.4 percent to $11.2 billion, or $2.68 per share.

Wal-Mart has also had very public legal problems, from child labor law violations to charges of gender discrimination. It's also fighting legislation aimed at making the company more generous with its health care benefits; the legislation was in response to charges that many Wal-Mart employees have had to turn to state Medicaid programs for health care.

Meanwhile, the discounter also faces very vocal opposition to some of its store openings and suffered embarrassing revelations that former top executive Tom Coughlin stole money from the company.

That's why some critics look at some of Wal-Mart's recent generous overtures with skepticism. Kofinis questioned Wal-Mart's expansion plans for the inner city. He wondered about Wal-Mart's real intent behind its proposals for local businesses and store expansion in urban markets.

Opponents have also questioned the company's recently announced improvement of health care benefits for part-time workers, which includes shortening the waiting time to be on the company's health plan. Opponents say that move is undermined by Wal-Mart's much less publicized plan to rely on more part-time workers, who are less expensive than full-time workers to keep as they don't enjoy the same level of benefits.

Kofinis believes a larger percentage of part-time workers—JPMorgan's Charles Grom estimates it could be up to 40 percent over the next 12 to 18 months—will lead to an unhealthy environment at Wal-Mart.

"You are basically creating a turnstile environment, that is based on exploitation and one that minimizes building positive relationships with the company," Kofinis said.

Wal-Mart has established several Web sites to inform the public of its true culture (forwalmart. com, paidcritics.com, walmartfacts.com). Judging from current postings on these sites, what is your analysis of corporate efforts to influence public perception? What do these efforts reveal about the resilience or intransigence of organizational culture?

The Irresolute American

Susan Davidson

A merican executives are aggressive, competitive, straight-talking, and don't mince words when they say, "You're fired!" At least that's how they come across in the global marketplace. So it's no wonder that foreign professionals who relocate to work in the United States expect to speak their mind with the likes of The Donald (Real Estate tycoon Donald Trump). Instead, they are stunned to walk into the office and find a covey of corporate cubicle drones obediently carrying out the orders of the autocratic boss.

Welcome to corporate America, where you're invited to check your straight-shooter outside the company door. After surveying a broad spectrum of foreign executives from 26 countries who live and work in the United States, I discovered that they are shocked—and ultimately frustrated—that the bold face Americans put on in the marketplace is quite different than the one we have in the workplace. Why the split personality? Because, foreigners say, Americans work in fear—of confrontation, of retaliation, of litigation.

"A LOT OF FLUFF"

Certainly foreigners can't be blamed for arriving at Los Angeles' LAX or New Yorks' JFK airport with expectations of, come Monday morning, meeting a posse of no-nonsense co-workers—especially if they've read up on their co-workers-to-be.

In *Global Smarts: The Art of Communicating and Deal Making Anywhere in the World*, Sheida Hodge writes that "speaking one's mind is generally considered a virtue in American corporate culture." Trainer Craig Storti's *Americans at Work: A Guide to the Can-Do People!* characterizes American directness as "straight talk" and a "badge of honor" in a country where "the right to say what you think, to anyone anytime, is the ultimate expression of individual liberty."

In *Mind Your Manners: Managing Business Cultures in the New Global Europe*, U.K. consultant John Mole cautions readers: "Business discussions [in America] may be forthright to the point of being brusque. Bluntness is preferred to subtlety." And Esther Wanning's *Culture Shock! USA: A Survival Guide to Customs and Etiquette* notes that American managers prefer initiative to deference: "Managers encourage ideas from subordinates, and subordinates may contradict their superiors."

But while foreigners concede that Americans speak their minds outside of the office, they do not do so in the workplace. Indeed, the vast majority of foreigners surveyed say Americans are obsessed with being politically correct at work. They claim Americans deliberately withhold honest opinions because they fear embarrassment, disagreement, and negative consequences. In *Americans at Work*, Storti supports this charge, calling it the "new national norm." When this overweening sensitivity is coupled with the concerted effort Americans make to avoid being negative, Storti adds that "it is no wonder the American reputation for straight talk has taken such a hit in recent years."

"People are afraid to say honestly what's on their mind," says a Finnish HR specialist who relocated to the United States with Delta Air Lines. "People aren't as straightforward as they are in Europe." A Delta sales coordinator from Colombia adds that she learned that honesty is not the best policy at work. "You are a troublemaker if you disagree with others by giving your honest opinion," she says. "And if your boss is not your friend, he or she will talk about you behind your back with co-workers."

Americans' careful choice of words at work adds up to "a lot of fluff," complains a Swedish consultant for a small IT firm. And an Australian IT consultant for SAP goes even further, saying that the constant caution and concern about being sensitive is sometimes debilitating, in that you feel as if "you're dancing around landmines all the time."

Not only are Americans cautious about what they won't say, foreigners are quick to point out, we are equally careful about putting a positive spin on what we will say. If you don't say that something is great or that there's been dramatic improvement, says a French project manager at Hewlett-Packard, then you leave people with the impression that they are doing a poor job.

Indeed, foreign professionals find it particularly frustrating to give and receive honest feedback at work because of American sensitivity about being perceived as negative. After relocating from Paris to Atlanta, Guy Harari, the Brazilian president of the North American division of France-based Adisseo, a manufacturer of livestock-feed additives, says he was surprised to learn that his American team found his straightforward management style unduly harsh. "Americans are educated not to offend people," he says. "I focus more on the things that need to improve. Here, it's difficult to give feedback as average." In fact, one German executive at a real-estate investment firm was shocked to learn that, after giving a co-worker honest feedback, he had been promptly nicknamed "the Terminator."

"BUT IT'S YOUR JOB!"

Of course, American's desire to put a positive spin on things isn't all negative. At least they get high marks from our foreign counterparts for using positive reinforcement to motivate employees and teams. A French project manager concedes that he enjoys receiving frequent tokens of appreciation: kind words, pizza, tickets to ballgames. Likewise, an Indonesian engineer appreciates being recognized for good work, something he'd never experienced in his home country.

Americans' positive approach to motivating employees spills over into fostering good teamwork as well. Compared to many other countries, foreigners say, U.S. teams show more cooperation and respect for each other and work hard to keep the peace. Says an Australian IT specialist with IBM: "I do like the American team spirit. It's rah-rah, like being forced to sing camp songs, but I really enjoy it."

Yet the "rah-rah" American approach to recognizing employee efforts can become excessive. All the kudos, high-fives, and trophies lose their sincerity and meaning when doled out in daily doses. A German customer-service-center VP says, "For every small thing, I have to tell an employee, 'Thank you, thank you.' But it's his job!" A British executive with a staffing-services firm recalls receiving a salesman-of-the-month plaque, which had no value to him. "Instead," he says, "just tell me that I'm doing a wonderful job."

Culturally, Americans have come to expect a certain level of recognition. When it's sincere, foreign business persons are intrigued and delighted with its emotional appeal. When it's overdone, they at once are suspicious and cynical. Either way, positive reinforcement is the salve that Americans rely on to soothe psyches and bolster performance, accentuate the positive and eliminate the negative.

If U.S. workers are adept at doling out praise, we are equally skilled at dodging direct conflict. Non-Americans are baffled by the American practice of either avoiding face-to-face confrontation altogether or taking cover in offices to fire off e-mails, letters, and voicemails to deal with disputes, discipline, and disagreements rather than speak to co-workers in person.

"Americans will have e-mail wars that will go on for months and months with a lot of malice at times," observes the Australian marketing-communications director for the U.S. office of Brambles, a multinational consultancy based in Australia. "If I have a problem with something, the first thing I'll do is talk to somebody, and it's usually resolved there and then. But Americans are really uncomfortable with that." When we avoid talking out differences early on and head-on, problems only tend to simmer, say foreigners.

If Davidson's findings are right—American workers are skilled at dodging conflict—the result is endless disputing and disagreement. What is the leader's role in helping employees face conflict?

"BECAUSE I AM THE CFO"

One thing becomes readily apparent to foreign professionals working in the United States: When it comes to our corporate empires, all men and women are not created equal. In *Mind Your Manners*, John Mole astutely observes: "The outward egalitarianism of American manners is deceptive. Within a business organization there is a well-defined and rigorously observed hierarchy." America's corporate ladders are built from the top down, and non-Americans are keenly aware of the deferential treatment Americans grant to those on the higher rungs. So while Americans may kick ass in the marketplace, in the workplace the subordinates kiss up and the bosses kick down.

Which means that not only are Americans cautious about what they say and how they say it—they are timid about to whom we say it. As subordinates, they transform themselves into risk-averse order-takers who temper their comments, shy away from conflict, and readily defer to their bosses' power and authority. And as bosses, Americans may talk about empowerment, problem-solving, and risk-taking, but they know they can pull rank anytime.

"One thing that is striking in the United States is the importance of the boss. He drives the decisions," says the French marketing director of the U.S. division of Royal Philips Electronics. The Frenchman points out the surprising similarity between the "top-down hierarchy" of U.S. corporations and those of his native country, adding that, "Americans are sensitive to who calls the shots and try to sense which direction the wind is blowing."

While being able to refer to colleagues by their first names makes some foreigners feel more comfortable, many are surprised to find a stark contrast between Americans' superficial first-name, business-casual informality and a leadership style seen as hierarchical and autocratic. Scandinavian executives, in particular, see a distinct difference between the command-and-control leadership style of many U.S.-based companies and the more inclusive, matrix style found in their own organizations, where anyone can talk openly to anyone about anything. In many U.S. workplaces, lower-ranking employees offer feedback only if it appears to confirm a decision that they believe has already been made. "If an American CEO says something is a good idea, then people nod and say yes, whether they agree or not," says Marjon de Groot, a former Dutch director of product marketing for Philips. Another Dutchman at Philips, a former senior VP of marketing, agrees: "Dutch feedback enriches the decision. You don't get that kind of feedback in the United States."

Several foreign professionals argue that corporate America's excessive respect for rank and need to please people in power stifles employee creativity and buy-in. The result is that lower-level employees become order-takers who "execute without questioning," as a German IBM manager puts it. "In Europe, people would expect the boss to lead the team to work together to build the direction," says Adisseo's Guy Harari. "Here, they expect the boss to have the answers."

"People worry to the point where they're in meetings and won't say anything because their boss is there," says a British IT developer. A French VP of staffing firm Randstad North America adds that "employees don't challenge or debate the CEO or other executives."

Several foreigners point out that American bosses themselves reinforce a culture of deference where titles often trump talent and initiative. "On a couple of occasions, I've seen people go off on their own and do something only to be swatted back into place," says a repatriated Australian sales manager. A German IT programmer recalls an American executive telling a lower-level employee that he could not be spoken to in a certain manner "because I am the CFO." In corporate America, democracy gets checked at the door.

"PHENOMENAL WASTE OF MONEY"

The fear of losing their jobs also keeps Americans from speaking their minds, foreigners say. "In Europe, I can quit today and be assured income for at least one year to become stable," says a Congolese engineer who had previously worked in Germany for several years. "If you don't have savings in the United States, you can't survive a job loss. You can lose everything, including your lifestyle."

Many other Western countries have generous unemployment benefits and labor laws that protect workers from termination at will. Says a Swedish project manager working for a Swedish woodworking company in the United States: "Because of how the United States employs people, you can walk away the same day or get fired the same day. In Europe you're in a contract where you have more job security. You've got one month's notice before you're fired, which gives people greater security to discuss things with their boss." A Dutch manager adds that because of the continuous threat of being fired, employees without executives' golden parachutes "don't want to take risks that will endanger their careers, so they do not express their opinions—especially not toward their boss."

Coupled with the prospect of job loss with little or no financial safety net, foreigners cite Americas litigious society, which prompts both employees and employers to dilute and document their words and actions. "This is a big difference between America and the rest of the world," says Chris Sundell, the Finnish CEO of UFI Filters USA, a U.S.-based distributorship for an Italian manufacturer. "Frivolous lawsuits don't exist elsewhere." An Australian manager goes even further, claiming, "You may see someone not being let go because it's too dangerous to do it."

A British staffing-services executive claims that "actions are based on the presumption that the person might sue me," which has everyone walking on eggshells rather than making decisions in the best interest of the business. He concludes: "It's a phenomenal waste of money."

MARKETPLACE AND WORKPLACE BEHAVIORS DIFFER

"A lot of my thoughts on American culture were driven by movies—get 'em!" says an Australian sales manager who transferred to the United States with Switzerland-based Holcim, a construction-supplies company. "I came here thinking I'd be challenged. I scratch my head and wonder how America got to be the biggest and best in the world."

The answer lies in the fact that the marketplace demands different behaviors (or actions) than the workplace. Whereas the former rewards boldness, the latter rewards (or "calls for") compliance. In the marketplace, customers have many choices and companies face pressures to meet short-term revenue goals.

As a result, competition for business is fierce and requires bold action, fast response, and the ability to stand out from the pack. By contrast, success in the workplace requires a much different type of behavior: fitting in, following rules and policies, and carrying out the tasks delegated by bosses.

Yet even with the surprises and disappointments that American corporate life brings, the United States more than lives up to its reputation as the land of opportunity. "There's unbelievable opportunity here if you're willing to work hard and go above and beyond what's called for," says an Australian who came to the United States nine years ago with PricewaterhouseCoopers. "The market is so big, and you have the potential to shine here."

Most foreign businesspeople admire the "can-do" spirit of Americans whom they describe as people "on the go." Compared to workers in their own countries, Americans are able to arrive at decisions quickly, spring into action, and "make things happen." So it seems that if the task is tough, Americans take charge. If the talk is tough, we take cover. For all of our superpower successes, Americans still have a craving to be liked, recognized—and employed.

Leading by Leveraging Culture

Jennifer A. Chatman and Sandra Eunyoung Cha

We occasionally get calls from prospective clients who, having heard that we consult with organizations to improve their cultures, ask us, "Come on down to our organization and get us a better one." Perhaps they are thinking that, somehow, after we have worked our culture magic, employees will be singing and dancing in their cubicles. Although this is a nice image, simply trying to make employees happy misses the power of leveraging culture. The problem is that organizational culture has become faddish; and, as such, it has been over-applied and under-specified. Our goal here is to precisely clarify why culture is powerful and to provide specific criteria for developing a strong, strategically relevant culture that is likely to enhance an organization's performance over the long haul.

We will not claim that by simply managing culture, leaders will be assured of organizational success, or that by neglecting culture, they will be doomed to failure. Leveraging culture is but one of a number of key leadership tools. We *will* claim, however, that by actively managing culture, an organization will be more likely to deliver on its strategic objectives over the long run.

WHY IS ORGANIZATIONAL CULTURE POWERFUL?

Focusing People Intensely on Strategy Execution

A 1999 *Fortune* magazine article highlighting pathbreaking research by Ram Charan and Geoffrey Colvin began with a provocative title: "Why CEOs Fail."[1] The definitive answer had been found, and it was notoriously simple:

CEOs failed when they were unable to fully execute their strategy. This was an amazing conclusion because it stood in contrast to what industrial economists have been telling us for years—that firms with well formulated and hard-to-imitate business strategies emerge as the winners.[2] Charan and Colvin's article suggested that firms whose strategies were merely reasonable but were executed fully could be the most successful.

This shifts the focus from strategy formulation to strategy *execution*—and culture is all about execution. Consider the often-cited example of Southwest Airlines, a company with a transparent, almost simple, strategy: high volume along with short and convenient flights using only fuel-efficient 737s, culminating in low costs and the ability to offer customers low-priced tickets. As a result, Southwest has been the only U.S. airline to be profitable for 28 consecutive years.[3] One key to Southwest's success is its remarkably short turnaround time, 15 minutes versus competitors' average of 35 minutes.[4] Planes don't sit long at the jet way. Instead, employees across functional lines band together to get the planes out quickly. This results in an average plane utilization of around 12 hours at Southwest versus the industry average of closer to 9 hours. Southwest's success hinges not on how brilliant, unique, or opaque their strategy is, but on the alignment between their culture and strategy, on how clearly employees understand the culture and how intensely they feel about it.

Culture is a system of shared values (defining what is important) and norms (defining appropriate attitudes and behaviors).[5] Strong cultures enhance organizational performance in two ways. First, they improve performance by energizing employees—appealing to their higher ideals and values and rallying them around a set of meaningful, unified goals. Such ideals excite employee commitment and effort because they are inherently engaging[6] and fill voids in identity and meaning.[7] Second, strong cultures boost performance by shaping and coordinating employees' behavior. Stated values and norms focus employees' attention on organizational priorities that then guide their behavior and decision making. They do so without impinging, as formal control systems do, on the autonomy necessary for excellent performance under changing conditions.[8]

An effective culture is closely related to business strategy. Indeed, a culture cannot be crafted until an organization has first developed its business strategy. The first criterion for using culture as a leadership tool is that it must be *strategically relevant.*

Formal Versus Social Control: The Power of Shared Norms

Norms—legitimate, socially shared standards against which the appropriateness of behavior can be evaluated—are the psychological bases of culture.[9] Norms influence how members perceive and interact with one another, approach decisions, and solve problems.[10] Norms are distinct from rules, which are formal, codified directives. The concept of norms also implies social control—that is, norms act as positive or negative means of ensuring conformity and applying sanctions to deviant behavior.[11]

Roethlisberger and Dickson's classic research showed that group norms shaped employee's behavior more powerfully than either monetary rewards or physical work environments.[12] Employees at Western Electric's Hawthorne Plant developed norms that dictated the acceptable amount of work each employee should complete. Unfortunately, this constrained many employees' productivity. Just as those who worked too little, those who worked *too much* were shunned by other members of the work unit. As a result, few employees deviated from the norm. We are so influenced by other's expectations, specifically their expectations that we uphold shared social norms, that we are willing and likely to *alter our behavior* in their presence—that is, to do something different than we would do if we were alone. We assimilate because the consequences of violating strong norms—at best, embarrassment, and, at worst, exclusion or alienation from the social group—threaten our ability to survive in an interdependent world. . . .

Think back to the last time you had a peak consumer experience—when you were "wowed" by someone or an organization. What impressed you? When we ask people this question, they typically talk about how someone went above and beyond the call of duty to solve *their specific problem.* Formal rules are useful for standardizing performance and avoiding having to relearn things each time. However, they are only useful for addressing situations that are *predictable and regular.*[13] In contrast, outstanding service is determined, in customer's eyes, by how organizations deal with situations that are nearly impossible to anticipate, unique to a particular person, and difficult to solve.

The irony of leadership through culture is that the less formal direction you give employees about how to execute strategy, the more ownership they take over their actions and the better they perform. New employees at Nordstrom are told simply to "use your good judgment in all situations."[14] At Southwest, they are encouraged to "do what it takes to make the Customer happy."[15] Employees have to be freed up from rules in order to deliver fully on strategic objectives; they have to understand the ultimate strategic goals and the norms through which they can be successfully achieved, and they must *care* about reaching those goals and what their coworkers will think of them if they don't. Strong norms increase members' clarity about priorities and expectations as well as their bonds with one another. Unlike formal rules, policies, and procedures, culture empowers employees to think and act on their own in pursuit of strategic objectives, increasing their commitment to those goals.[16] . . .

What Makes Culture Strong?

Strong cultures are based on two characteristics, high levels of agreement among employees about what's valued and high levels of intensity about these values. If both are high, a strong culture exists; and if both are low, the culture is not strong at all. Some organizations are characterized by high levels of intensity but low levels of agreement, or what could be called "warring factions."[17] Such intensity exists within many high-tech firms, but groups disagree about priorities. For example, marketing groups typically focus on customer-driven product features while engineering groups focus on elegant product designs. More common, however, are organizations in which members agree about what's important, but they don't much care and, as such, are unwilling to go the extra mile (e.g., take a risk, stay late) to deliver on strategic objectives or to sanction others for a failure to uphold those norms. These are called "vacuous" cultures and their prevalence probably reflects the faddish nature of organizational culture and the lip service such organizations pay to it.[18] Most organizations are aware of the importance of managing culture, but in

What are the characteristics of a strong organizational culture that promote success?

their attempt to jump on the culture bandwagon they are unable to develop the clarity, consistency, and comprehensiveness that encourage employees to care intensely about executing strategic objectives.

Though strong organizational cultures have long been touted as critical to bottom-line performance in large organizations,[19] newer evidence from a unique sample suggests that developing a strong, strategically relevant culture may be best accomplished when an organization is young. In a longitudinal study of 173 young high-technology companies, founders' initial model of the employment relation dramatically influenced their firms' later success.[20] Firms that switched models as they aged were less successful. Firms that were built around the commitment model, which emphasizes a strong culture and hiring based on culture fit, stood out from those founded on the engineering or bureaucracy models by completing initial public stock offerings sooner.[21]

Emphasizing Innovation

The final criterion for using culture as a leadership tool involves the content of organizational culture. Though organizational norms revolve around many dimensions,[22] only one appears to be universally applicable across organizations regardless of their size, industry, or age and that is innovation.[23] In a comprehensive longitudinal study of 207 large firms over an 11-year period, Kotter and Heskett found that firms that developed a strong, strategically appropriate culture performed effectively over the long run only if their culture also contained norms and values that promoted innovation and change.[24]

Most creativity research has focused on hiring creative people, but innovation may depend more on whether cultural norms support risk-taking and change.[25] Consider the following study. Outside observers were asked to evaluate the intelligence of product development team members engaged in meetings in which one member was pitching a product idea to the other members. Guess whose intelligence was rated the lowest by the outside observers time and again? It was the person pitching the product idea. Why would this be the case? Imagine what team members are saying—things like: "Didn't you think of . . . ?" and "We already tried. . . ." The product pitcher is responding with phrases such as "Um, I'm not sure" and "I don't know." Not only are critical skills valued more than creative skills, but also creativity and wisdom are inversely related in people's minds.[26] Expressing a creative idea is, therefore, risky—since a person suggesting one can end up being perceived as unintelligent.[27] The lesson for organizations is clear: employees may refrain from generating creative ideas because the cost of expressing them is too high. Managers can bet on their employees having creative ideas in their head—about how to do their jobs better, improve a system, or develop a new product. The question is: Are they willing to say their ideas out loud?

Establishing these norms and promoting innovation may require thinking unconventionally and adopting some "weird" ideas such as "ignore people who have solved the exact problem you face" and "find some happy people and get them to fight."[28] Three times a year, executives at Walt Disney Company host a "Gong Show" in which everyone in the company—including secretaries, janitors, and mailroom staff—gets to pitch movie ideas to the top executives.[29] Structured brainstorming groups can also create an environment where publicly raising creative ideas is not only. acceptable, but also rewarded socially. At IDEO, one of the most successful product development companies in history, brainstorming sessions take on the character of a "status auction" where the more creative the idea, the higher the bid.[30]

Leaders also promote innovation by creating a shared belief that team members are safe to take interpersonal risks. When employees feel psychologically safe, they engage in learning behavior—they ask questions, seek feedback, experiment, reflect on results, and discuss errors or unexpected outcomes openly.[31] Leaders create these norms by influencing the way creative ideas and errors are handled, which, in turn, leads to shared perceptions of how consequential it is to make a mistake. These perceptions influence employees' willingness to report mistakes and ultimately can feed into a more lasting culture of fear or of openness that will influence employees' ability to identify and discuss problems and develop new ideas.[32] . . .

LEADERSHIP TOOLS TO MANAGE AND CHANGE ORGANIZATIONAL CULTURE

These three criteria for using culture as a leadership tool are supported by substantial empirical and applied evidence.[33] The question, however, is how can leaders develop, manage, and change their culture to meet these criteria and promote extraordinary performance? There are three key managerial tools for leveraging culture for performance.[34]

Tool #1: Recruiting and Selecting People for Culture Fit

Selection is the process of choosing new members (for organizations) and choosing to join a particular organization (for job candidates). Our approach to selection contrasts with typical approaches by emphasizing person-culture fit in addition to person-job fit.[35] This requires anticipating whether the culture a firm emphasizes will be rewarding for potential recruits.

First, consider General Electric's description of desirable candidates, who "stimulate and relish change and are not frightened or paralyzed by it, see change as an opportunity, not a threat," and "have a passion for excellence, hating bureaucracy and all the nonsense that comes with it." Note the intensity of the language, which does not focus on which computer programs people know or their geographic preferences, but rather their thirst for challenge and change. These are qualities that differentiate between people who are, and are not, successful at GE. Firms often get caught focusing exclusively on hiring

Person-mission fit relies on a mission statement. Does person-culture fit rely on a culture statement?

people whose skills fit their entry-level jobs, and yet, if a person is successful, he or she will hold multiple jobs within the firm. These jobs are linked by the organizational culture. Therefore, it makes sense to hire people who will fit the culture, possibly even trading off some immediate skills necessary for the specific entry job for better culture fit. People can learn new skills; establishing culture fit is much harder.

Second, be mindful of recruiter characteristics.[36] A fundamental theory in psychology is the "similarity-attraction effect." [37] We are attracted to people who are similar to ourselves. Why? Well, most of us like ourselves, think we're doing a pretty good job, and wouldn't mind having lunch with ourselves now and then. Therefore, when you ask us to recruit new members, we are likely to pick people just like us. The message is simple but important: Be careful which people you send out to do your recruiting because you will get more of them back.

Third, consider the selection process in light of the organizational culture. How, for example, did Cisco Systems ensure high culture fit despite facing Silicon Valley's brutally competitive labor market in the late 1990s, hiring an average of 1000 new employees through small acquisitions and individual recruiting *every month*? First, they developed culturally consistent selection criteria targeting candidates who were frugal, enthusiastic about the future of the Internet, smart, and not obsessed with status.[38] Second, they conducted benchmarking studies and focus groups so that the selection process was maximally effective in getting the people they wanted. [39] Third, they targeted "passive applicants," people who are satisfied in their current jobs and not job hunting but who might be lured to Cisco, and developed a convenient web site for them to learn about Cisco. Noticing that they were getting over 500,000 hits per month during work hours, Cisco made sure that the web site was fast and easy to use; for example, the initial application took 5 minutes to complete. Applicants who pressed a "friends@Cisco" hot key got a call from a current Cisco employee at a comparable level within 24 hours.[40] These discussions typically focused on the hard-to-convey culturally relevant information that, because of the similarity of the source to the candidate, provided credible information about what it is really like to work at Cisco. Cisco aggressively pursued and won desired candidates by constructing a comprehensive, culturally relevant selection process.

Tool #2: Managing Culture through Socialization and Training

Socialization is the process by which an individual comes to understand the values, abilities, expected behaviors, and social knowledge that are essential for assuming an organization role and participating as an organization member. Socialization and selection processes are somewhat substitutable. [41] In tight labor markets, firms need to rely more on socializing people once they join, and, conversely, when labor is more freely available and firms can be highly selective, they will not need to invest as much in socialization practices. Much is known about effective socialization practices.[42] Two key aspects of socialization are ensuring that employees acquire cultural knowledge and that they bond with one another. . . .

Tool #3: Managing Culture through the Reward System

Culture is an organization's informal reward system and needs to be intricately connected to formal rewards. At CompUSA, the largest retailer and reseller of personal computer related products and services in the United States, CEO James Halpin has created "a cross between a college fraternity and a military boot camp."[43] The company's strategic focus on revenue is extremely salient, sometimes encompassed in rather uncomfortable practices. For example, regional sales managers attending quarterly meetings are assigned a seat at the U-shaped table according to their store sales, with those with the lowest sales being assigned to the tables nearest the front because, as Halpin says, "they have to listen to everything we've got to say."[44] Name badges include a person's name and their stores' "shrink number," or inventory losses due to theft or accounting errors. On the positive reinforcement side, when employees make large commissions—such as when a young employee made $50,000 in commission in one month—Halpin travels to their store to deliver the cash to them personally, in front of customers and other employees. Though these specific rewards (and punishments) may be inappropriate for some organizations, the lesson is that rewards need to be clear, consistent, and comprehensive—the focus on generating revenues at CompUSA is simply impossible for employees to miss. . . .

THE THREE C'S OF CULTURE

Organizational culture can be a powerful force that clarifies what's important and coordinates members' efforts without the costs and inefficiencies of close supervision. Culture also identifies an organization's distinctive competence to external constituencies. Managing culture requires creating a context in which people are encouraged and empowered to express creative ideas and do their very best. Selection, socialization, and rewards should be used as opportunities to convey what's important to organizational members. Organizational cultures that are strategically relevant, strong, and emphasize innovation and change are most effective. Three levers exist for forming, strengthening, and changing culture, how organizations: recruit and select; socialize, orient, and train; and reward and lead people. Paradoxically, the very strength of cultural values can also be a leader's downfall. However, leaders who embrace cultural values when threatening events occur can avoid this risk. Culture "works" when it is clear, consistent, and comprehensive.

One thing is guaranteed: A culture will form in an organization, a department, and a work group. The question is whether the culture that forms is one that helps or hinders the organization's ability to execute its strategic objectives. Organizational culture is too important to leave to chance; organizations must use their culture to fully execute their strategy and inspire innovation. It is a leader's primary role to develop and maintain an effective culture.

NOTES

1. Ram Charan and Geoffrey Colvin, "Why CEOs Fail," *Fortune*, June 21, 1999, pp. 68–78.
2. E.g., M.E. Porter, *Competitive Strategy*: *Techniques for Analyzing Industries and Competitors* (New York, NY: Free Press, 1980).
3. J.R. Laing, "Nothing but Blue Skies," *Barron's*, July 2, 2001, pp. 25–29.
4. C. O' Reilly and J. Pfeffer, "Southwest Airlines: Using Human Resources for Competitive Advantage (A)," HR-IA, Graduate School of Business, Stanford University, 1995.
5. R.E. Walton, "Establishing and Maintaining High Commitment Work Systems," in J.R. Kimberly, R.H. Miles, and Associates. eds., *The Organizational Life Cycle: Issues in the Creation, Transformation, and Decline of Organizations* (San Francisco, CA: Jossey-Bass, 1980), pp. 208–290.
6. C. O' Reilly and J. Chatman, "Cultures as Social Control: Corporations, Cults, and Commitment," in L. Cummings and B. Staw, eds., *Research in Organizational Behavior,* Vol. 18 (Greenwich, CT: JAI Press, 1996), pp. 157–200, at 166.
7. R.F. Baumeister, "The Self," in D.T. Gilbert, S.T. Fiske, and G. Lindzey, eds., *The Handbook of Social Psychology,* 4th ed. (New York, NY: McGraw-Hill, 1998), pp. 680–740.
8. M.L. Tushman and C.A. O' Reilly, Winning *Through Innovation: A Practical Guide to Leading Organizational Change and Renewal* (Boston, MA: Harvard Business School Press, 1997).
9. A. Birenbaum and E. Sagarin, *Norms and Human Behavior* (New York, NY: Praeger, 1976).
10. K.L. Bettenhausen and J.K. Murnighan, "The Development of an Intragroup Norm and the Effects of Interpersonal and Structural Challenges," *Administrative Science Quarterly,* 36/1 (March 1991): 20–35, at 21.
11. E.g., O' Reilly and Chatman, op. cit.
12. F.J. Roethlisberger and W. J. Dickson (with H.A. Wright), *Management and the Worker: An Account of a Research Program conducted by the Western Electric Company, Hawthorne Works. Chicago* (Cambridge: MA, Harvard University Press, 1939).
13. C. O' Reilly, "Corporations, Culture, and Commitment: Motivation and Social Control in Organizations," *California Management Review,* 31/4 (Summer 1989): 9–25.

14. R. Spector and P.D. McCarthy, *The Nordstrom Way* (New York, NY: John Wiley & Sons, 1995), p. 16.

15. O' Reilly and Pfeffer, op. cit., p. 7.

16. O' Reilly and Chatman, op. cit.

17. O' Reilly, op. cit.

18. Ibid.

19. E.g., J. C. Collins and J.I. Porras, *Built to Last: Successful Habits of Visionary Companies* (New York, NY: Harper Business, 1994).

20. E.g., J. N. Baron, M. T. Hannan, and M. D. Burton, "Labor Pains: Change in Organizational Models and Employee Turnover in Young, High-Tech Firms," *American Journal of Sociology,* 106 (2001): 960–1012.

21. M. T. Hannan, M. D. Burton, and J. N. Baron, "Inertia and Change in the Early Years: Employment Relations in Young, High Technology Firms," *Industrial and Corporate Change,* 5 (1996): 503–537.

22. E.g., J. A. Chatman and K. A. Jehn, "Assessing the Relationship between Industry Characteristics and Organizational Culture: How Different Can you Be?" *Academy of Management Journal,* 37 (1994): 522–553.

23. D. Caldwell and C. A. O' Reilly, "Norms Supporting Innovation in Groups: An Exploratory Study," working paper, University of Santa Clara, Santa Clara, CA, 1995.

24. J. P. Kotter and J. L. Heskett, *Corporate Culture and Performance* (New York, NY: Free Press, 1992).

25. T.M. Amabile, Motivating Creativity in Organizations: On Doing What you Love and Loving What you Do," *California Management Review,* 40/1 (Fall 1997): 39–58.

26. R. J. Sternberg, I. A. O'Hara, and T.I. Lubart, "Creativity as Investment," *California Management Review,* 40/1, (Fall 1997): 8–21.

27. T.M. Amabile, "Brilliant but Cruel: Perceptions of Negative Evaluators," *Journal of Experimental Social Psychology,* 19 (1983): 146–156.

28. R. I. Sutton, "The Weird Rules of Creativity," *Harvard Business Review,* 79/8 (September 2001): 94-103, at 97,

29. S. Wetlaufer, "Common Sense and Conflict: An Interview with Disney's Michael Eisner," *Harvard Business Review,* 78/1 (January/February 2000): 114.

30. A. Hargadon and R. I. Sutton, "Building an Innovation Factory," *Harvard Business Review,* 78/3 (May/June 2000): 157–168.

31. A. Edmondson, "Psychological Safety and Learning Behavior in Work Teams," *Administrative Science Quarterly*, 44 (1999): 350–383.

32. A.C. Edmondson, "Learning from Mistakes Is Easier Said than Done: Group and Organizational Influences on the Detection and Correction of Human Error," *The Journal of Applied Behavioral Science,* 32 (1996): 5–28.

33. E.g., Kotter and Heskett, op. cit.

34. For greater detail on these three tools, see J. A. Chatman, "Matching People and Organizations: Selection and Socialization in Public Accounting Firms," *Administrative Science Quarterly,* 36 (1991): 459–484; O' Reilly (1989), op, cit.; O' Reilly and Chatman, op. cit.; Tushman and O' Reilly, op. cit.

35. Chatman, op. cit.

36. M. L. Connerley and S. L. Rynes, "The Influence of Recruiter Characteristics and Organizational Recruitment Support on Perceived Recruiter Effectiveness: Views from Applicants and Recruiters," *Human Relations,* 50 (1997): 1563–1586.

37. E. g., E. Berscheid and H. T. Reis, "Attraction and Close Relationships," in D. T. Gilbert, S. T. Fiske, and G. Lindzey, eds., *The Handbook of Social Psychology,* 4th ed. (New York, NY: McGraw-Hill, 1998) pp. 193–281.

38. C. O' Reilly, "Cisco Systems: The Acquisition of Technology Is the Acquisition of People," Case # HR-10, Graduate School of Business, Stanford University, 1998.

39. B. Beck, "Cisco Systems," class presentation, Haas School of Business, Berkeley, CA, March 2000.

40. O' Reilly (1998), op. cit.

41. Chatman, op. cit.

42. E.g., J. Pfeffer, *The Human Equation: Building Profits by Putting People First* (Boston, MA: Harvard Business School Press, 1998).

43. S. Puffer, "CompUSA's CEO James Halpin on Technology, Rewards, and Commitment," *Academy of Management Executive,* 13 (1999): 29–36, at 29.

44. Ibid., p. 33.

The Passive–Aggressive Organization

Gary L. Neilson, Bruce A. Pasternack, and Karen E. Van Nuys

Healthy companies are hard to mistake. Their managers have access to good, timely information, the authority to make informed decisions, and the incentives to make them on behalf of the organization, which promptly and capably carries them out. A good term for the healthiest of such organizations is "resilient," since they can react nimbly to challenges and recover quickly from those they cannot dodge. Unfortunately, most companies are not resilient. In fact, fewer than one in five of the approximately 30,000 individuals who responded to a global online survey Booz Allen Hamilton conducted describe their organizations that way.[1] The largest number—over one-quarter—say they suffer from the cluster of pathologies we place under the label "passive-aggressive.'' The category takes its name from the organization's quiet but tenacious resistance, in every way but openly, to corporate directives.

In passive-aggressive organizations, people pay those directives lip service, putting in only enough effort to appear compliant. Employees feel free to do as they see fit because there are hardly ever unpleasant consequences, and the directives themselves are often misguided and thus seem worthy of defiance. Making matters worse, senior management has left unclear where accountability actually lies, in effect absolving managers of final responsibility for anything they do. Those with initiative must wait interminably for a go-ahead, and their actions when finally taken are accompanied by a chorus of second-guessing, a poor but understandable substitute for the satisfaction of accomplishing the task at hand. (See the exhibit "What Kind of Company Is Yours?")

When employees' healthy impulses—to learn, to share, to achieve—are not encouraged, other harmful but adaptive conduct gradually takes over. It is no wonder that action of any kind becomes scarce and that erstwhile doers find safety in resisting unpromising efforts. The absence of confrontation at such places is only a disguise for intransigence.

As a general rule, companies that are not healthy suffer from either too much control at the top or not enough. Either can cripple performance: in the former case, by failing to devolve authority, share information, and reward constructive decision making; in the latter, by allowing individuals and business units to work at cross-purposes or do little. The passive-aggressive corporation, due to the peculiarities of its evolution, can exhibit the drawbacks of both too much control and not enough.

In such organizations, people with authority lack the information to exercise it wisely or the incentives to serve the company's strategy and interests or the personnel that will carry out their directives. Conversely, people with the incentives and information necessary to make good decisions lack the authority to execute them or oversee their execution by others. As a result, many in senior positions operate under the false impression that they control things they actually do not. At the same time, many think they cannot control what they actually can.

Of course, there is no such thing as a pure exemplar of the passive-aggressive corporation, any more than there is a firm somewhere that has never suffered from the syndrome. Even high-performing organizations harbor pockets of resistance, while semiautonomous pockets of excellence lift up poorly performing ones. These areas of excellence can be the levers by which good managers show to the rest of the firm that action is possible. Nonetheless, we've found that the passive-aggressive organization is the hardest to change of the seven types we studied because such companies have generally had more time than the others to accumulate and institutionalize dysfunctions, and their people are the most cynical about reform attempts.

Before bursting into full flower, passive-aggressive organizations are dotted with frustrated world-beaters who cannot understand why their most promising projects can't gain traction. After a couple of years, such individuals either quit or become demoralized into ineffectuality by the thanklessness and futility of effort. Still, it would be wrong to say that organizations displaying passive-aggressive behaviour must have lots of passive-aggressive people in them. The passive-aggressive organization is not one where bad outcomes can be attributed to the hostile or perverse intentions individuals bring to the job. It is, in fact, a place where mostly well-intentioned people are the victims of flawed processes and policies.

To some venerable observers, the employees of such companies bear a passing resemblance to the "organization man" of 1950s sociology and literary fiction. In the postwar era, when U.S. corporations dominated their domestic markets and enjoyed stable market shares, personal initiative and risk taking were understandably seen as disruptive rather than opportunity seeking. But what may have been innocuous and even suitable behavior for its time can, in today's world of global markets and unfettered competition, bring a company to the brink of failure. Indeed, some of the companies today that find security and comfort in inertia are the very ones that dominated markets 50 years ago.

Our conception of the passive-aggressive company and the other six organizational types in our seven-part schema grew out of our decades of experience advising firms in a wide variety of industries and locations on organizational issues. Over and over, we saw certain classic behavioral patterns occur, which, we began to notice, correlated with certain objective features of those companies, such as size and age. To explain the emergence of these patterns, we postulated the existence of a limited number of underlying forces in every organization. After isolating what we determined to be the four most basic ones, we studied how each operated and interacted with the others to shape the seven organizational types. As we came to understand what made each type of organization function well or poorly, we were able to refine our definitions. When we tested the soundness of our schema in the online survey, we found that the organizational portraits the responses painted corresponded closely to the seven types we had identified.

THE SLIDE INTO PASSIVE-AGGRESSIVENESS

Most passive-aggressive organizations don't start out full of entrenched resistance. Problems develop gradually as a company grows, through a series of well-intended but badly implemented organizational changes layered one upon another. Passive-aggressive organizations are, therefore, most commonly large, complex enterprises whose seeds of resistance were often sown when they were much smaller.

While each organization takes a unique path, we have seen a particular development pattern recur. A company is founded on a healthy core business. The large amount of cash it throws off finances a series of acquisitions, increasing organizational complexity and confusion. As it grows beyond about $1 billion in revenues, the firm becomes too large and complex to be run effectively by a small, hands-on senior team. So it begins to experiment with decentralization in ways that are ill planned, because it is inexperienced at integration or growing too quickly, and halfhearted, because the founders have trouble genuinely letting go. To regain control, the founders add layers of managers to oversee the line managers whose performance has disappointed them. The additional layers make it difficult for people in the organization to understand who bears responsibility for specific results. Some managers become reluctant to make decisions, and others won't own up to the ones they've made, inviting colleagues to second-guess or overturn them. An already passive-aggressive organization grows increasingly so as its people become more certain of the acceptability of such conduct. Resistance becomes entrenched, and failure to deliver on commitments becomes chronic. . . .

Regardless of how they arrived where they are, passive-aggressive organizations are usually the sum of a series of ad hoc decisions or events that made sense in the moment but have the effect of gradually blurring decision rights. Over time such shotgun arrangements outlive their individual rationales, and the organization loses all vestiges of a coherent overall plan.

What Kind of Company Is Yours? Of the seven major organizational types we've observed, the healthiest is the resilient organization, which as its name implies is the most flexible and adaptable. Our online survey shows, unfortunately, that the most common is the far-from-healthy passive-aggressive type, in which lines of authority are unclear, merit is not rewarded, and people have learned to smile, nod, and do just enough to get by.

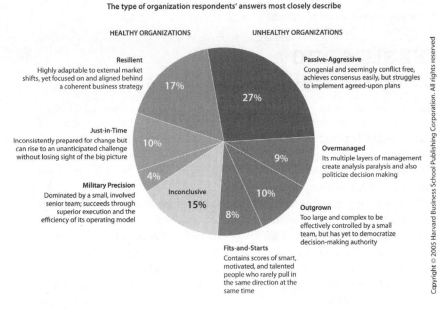

The type of organization respondents' answers most closely describe

HEALTHY ORGANIZATIONS   UNHEALTHY ORGANIZATIONS

Resilient
Highly adaptable to external market shifts, yet focused on and aligned behind a coherent business strategy — 17%

Passive-Aggressive
Congenial and seemingly conflict free, achieves consensus easily, but struggles to implement agreed-upon plans — 27%

Just-in-Time
Inconsistently prepared for change but can rise to an unanticipated challenge without losing sight of the big picture — 10%

Overmanaged
Its multiple layers of management create analysis paralysis and also politicize decision making — 9%

Military Precision
Dominated by a small, involved senior team; succeeds through superior execution and the efficiency of its operating model — 4%

Inconclusive 15%

10%

8%

Outgrown
Too large and complex to be effectively controlled by a small team, but has yet to democratize decision-making authority

Fits-and-Starts
Contains scores of smart, motivated, and talented people who rarely pull in the same direction at the same time

Source: Org DNA data set, 30,000 observations; Booz Allen analysis

THE ANATOMY OF THE ORGANIZATION

In all unhealthy organizations, dysfunction is rooted in a fundamental misalignment of four basic building blocks of the organization: incentives or, more broadly speaking, motivators; decision rights; information; and organizational structure. In passive-aggressive organizations, the misalignments generally involve complicated interactions among all four, which together conspire to freeze initiative.

Ineffective motivators • We define "motivators" to include not just financial compensation but all the factors, explicit and implicit, that affect anything an employee cares about: whether her office has a window, whether he is promoted to a position with greater visibility or a larger number of direct reports, whether she receives a company car or is invited to important meetings

Diagnosing the Passive-Aggressive Organization. People working in passive-aggressive organizations feel strongly that they don't know which decisions they're responsible for, that no decision is ever final, that good information is hard to obtain, and that the quality of their work is not being accurately appraised. People in resilient organizations feel the opposite.

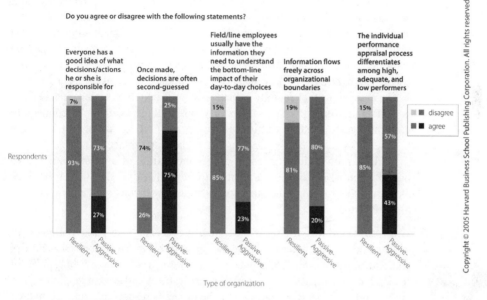

Do you agree or disagree with the following statements?

Source: Org DNA data set, 30,000 observations; Booz Allen analysis

or foreign off-sites. Far surpassing these in influence is some tangible evidence of the impact of one's efforts.

Passive-aggressive organizations are exceptionally poor at providing that evidence, often failing to judge and reward individuals according to their business value to the organization—or even to distinguish better performance from worse. Fifty-seven percent of respondents working at passive-aggressive companies agreed that in their organizations the individual appraisal process fails to differentiate among high, adequate, and low performers. Yet only 15% of respondents from resilient companies agreed with that statement. (See the exhibit "Diagnosing the Passive-Aggressive Organization.") In some cases, the rewards given to certain job titles seem incommensurate with those functions' overall contribution to the firm. People who expect their efforts to go unrecognized or to be inadequately valued put in just enough effort to stay out of trouble, since they have no reason to believe that any extra effort or initiative will lead to additional rewards or superior results.

What's more, incentive systems communicate to the organization as a whole what really matters to upper management. Corporate may send out countless memos about its strategy, mission, and goals, but its true values are embodied in what it is willing to pay for and otherwise recognize, which is one reason that the annual e-mail describing how bonuses will be calculated is the one everybody not only reads but remembers.

Within passive-aggressive firms, privileges and pecking order often loom larger than the realities of the marketplace. Such firms' very size and wealth can insulate employees from competitive pressures, which register as mere symbols—the share price or numbers on a P&L statement—not as forces that will affect the company's success. So, for example, a manager may be rewarded for the number of market studies his department prepared in the past fiscal year, regardless of how many of those studies served as the basis for marketing campaigns that actually enhanced sales. The job of senior management is to remind everyone else of the reality behind those symbols by connecting each manager's standing within the firm—size of office, size of bonus, access to superiors—to the firm's standing within the marketplace.

Still, as profoundly in need of proper motivation as a passive-aggressive organization is, it would be a mistake to think that tinkering with incentives alone, without regard to the other forces at play, will coax such a company out of its doldrums.

Unclear decision rights • . . . Nearly everyone in a passive-aggressive organization is unsure about where the limits of his or her own responsibilities end and those of other colleagues begin. In our online survey, only 27% of respondents from passive-aggressive organizations agreed that "everyone has a good idea of what decisions/actions he or she is responsible for," compared with 93% at resilient organizations.

What are some of the reasons "decision rights" are unclear?

Vaguely defined roles give their occupants "plausible deniability" when things go badly. The problem can always be said to be the responsibility of the next person, who can likewise shift blame elsewhere. Meanwhile, conscientious employees may hang back for fear of intruding on someone else's turf.

As a consequence, authority becomes fragmented. When everyone has a say in making a decision, everyone thinks he has the right to stymie or reverse it after it has been made. In passive-aggressive organizations, 75% of respondents believe that "once made, decisions are often second-guessed," versus just 26% in resilient organizations. And second-guessing that occurs in the middle of the decision-making process can bring it to a halt. . . .

Of course, it is never possible to specify every decision right a priori. Opportunities and challenges will appear as matters unfold, and any attempt to give a complete accounting of all decisions that can be foreseen would take too long and be too complex to be useful. But in healthy organizations, decisions do not go unmade because no one has been designated to make them. Most of the time, someone will jump in and get the job done. In such places, people take the initiative because they know their efforts will be rewarded. . . .

The wrong information • Employees of a passive-aggressive organization are often more interested in learning about what goes on inside their company than about the competitive realities that affect the firm's long-term survival. For example, though never officially, brand managers at one software company were judged on the elaborateness of their forecast presentations. However, forecasts and results differed on average by as much as 25% in that volatile industry, suggesting that spending so much time on documents intended for internal consumption was diverting brand managers from more productive pursuits.

In another case, employees noticed that executives who received frequent promotions spent a lot of their time in meetings at headquarters. Wanting to get ahead, they started seeking invitations to those meetings themselves, whether or not they had anything to contribute. They failed to realize that the high performers were called into meetings because they had important market insights others sought. In a passive-aggressive organization, rituals and routines, even modes of dress, become fetishized, as though they contain the secret to the firm's past successes.

When in possession of information or knowledge of genuine value, employees of passive-aggressive organizations are reluctant to share it, since doing so frequently benefits the recipient more than the sharer. For example, many departments use acronyms and terms of art to abbreviate the information they use internally. When sharing that information with a new department, they neglect to explain what their shorthand means, if not out of a desire to hoard the information for their own benefit then because spending the time required to translate it will not be rewarded.

Finally, in an organization already rife with meddling, many managers find that providing information gives the recipients a pretext to interfere. All these factors explain why only 20% of surveyed individuals in passive-aggressive organizations agree that "information flows freely across organizational boundaries." By contrast, that figure is 81% at resilient organizations.

Misleading structure • Because individuals in passive-aggressive companies often lack clear measures of how they add value, they may instead rely on the organization chart as a map of relative status—focusing on how many direct reports they have, how many levels away from the CEO they are, or whether their immediate supervisor is a favorite. Ironically, the org chart rarely conveys much information about how work gets done in these firms because decision rights are unclear or often reside in unexpected places.

CURING THE PATIENT

Passive-aggressive organizations are, by definition, uniquely resistant to change and are therefore uniquely difficult to rehabilitate. To begin with, it's hard to discern their actual condition from beneath the accretions of earlier failed fixes. What's more, the remedy is bound to be complicated and taxing. Analysis may reveal the need for greater centralization in some areas (to support products that rely on the same basic technology or production process, for instance) and greater decentralization in others (perhaps to serve a market requiring significant product tailoring).

The first order of business is the greatest challenge of all: getting a passive-aggressive organization's attention. A long history of seeing corporate initiatives ignored and then fade away makes employees almost hopelessly jaded. Many people have become so hard-bitten that only a significant business threat can rouse them to action. But because such organizations are also so inward gazing, such a threat remains invisible until it's almost too late. . . .

In addition to these catalysts, elements of successful programs to fix passive-aggressive organizations include the following:

Bring in new blood • Outsiders often lead the change in passive-aggressive organizations, for several reasons. First, they send an unmistakable signal to the troops that "things are so badly broken we can't fix them ourselves anymore." Second, outsiders bring new standards they expect the organization to meet; they haven't been worn down by the old habit of making excuses. And third, they often find it easier than incumbents to treat the organization more like a business than a family.

John Thompson was one such outsider when he became CEO of software security firm Symantec in April 1999 after 28 years at IBM. He says of Symantec: "This was a company that had lost its way, and it needed somebody who was not connected to the people or processes or strategy to ask the tough questions and be prepared to act on the answers. The former CEO, Gordon Eubanks, did a terrific job of building the company from nothing. The raw material, the raw attributes, were there. I just brought a different set of eyes, a different set of lenses."

Nevertheless, outsiders like Thompson have certain handicaps. If they alienate middle management by going too fast, they can aggravate its natural tendency to display resistance in classic passive-aggressive fashion. Successful newcomers retain enough senior members of the old guard to enlist the organization's loyalty while purging those who are unlikely ever to get on board.

Because of these hazards, a homegrown CEO who is capable of grasping the urgency of the situation can sometimes be the safer choice. But the message he or she sends that a new day has arrived must be unequivocal.

Leave no building block unturned • Passive-aggressive organizations are so fundamentally misaligned that the best way to get their attention is by changing everything at once, so that the magnitude of the problem, and of the effort that will be required to fix it, cannot be denied.

Soon after he arrived at Symantec, Thompson spun off several businesses and product lines, changed the management team, reassigned decision rights, and revised all the incentive systems—in short, "changed almost everything about the company." Thompson explains: "We chopped up all of the old signal paths. It's like what goes on in Florida when the hurricanes hit, one after another. The power lines are down; they're just crackling there on the ground. And somebody's got to reconnect them. We decided to seize the opportunity to reconnect them a different way."

Make decisions, and make them stick • Clarifying and articulating decision rights is often the first order of business in fixing a passive-aggressive organization, where decisions have been made, unmade, overturned, and second-guessed so many times that no one really knows who truly decides what any more. In many cases, decision-making authority has become lodged where it doesn't belong. When Thompson took over at Symantec, "the product manager was king. And the regional managers were even more autonomous." Regions were known to redesign packaging and sit on inventory they didn't want to sell.

"We had many people who could say no, but few people who could say yes and make it stick," Thompson explains. So one of the first things he did when he arrived was firmly establish, once and for all, what the respective roles of the regional and product managers should be. "We told the regions, 'Your job is execution. You're going to do what you're told to do. You're not a business unit. You are the sales engine of the company. Your job is to sell what we build, not to decide whether or not you want to sell it and then design your own company campaign around it.'"

Once decision rights are clarified, they must be respected. If they are, people in the organization begin to count on one another and to trust that what is planned will be done.

Early in his tenure, Thompson realized the company could save money by providing computer cables free only to customers who requested them instead of putting them in every box of software. At a meeting on cost reduction, everyone, including the executive responsible, agreed it should be done. But weeks later, the boxes still contained the cables. "We don't make decisions but once," Thompson told the executive. "If you've got a disagreement or a point of view, bring it up when we're going through the discussion. Don't hold back and give me this smiley kind of benign agreement. Go back and get it fixed. We're not shipping cables any more. And if you can't communicate that, I will.

"That was the shot heard around the world," Thompson says. "There was this epiphany, 'Wow, this guy's serious.'"

Spread the word—and the data • No organization can make good decisions without having access to the relevant information. But to know what's relevant, people must be clear about which issues deserve the highest priority. This is not just a matter of sending out a memo or two.

At 7-Eleven, for example, bright and early every Monday morning, the eight members of the executive committee and invited guests convene to discuss strategic issues and survey the week that was and the week coming up. They arrive knowing which of the 2,500 products in the 7-Eleven inventory are moving and which are not in its 5,800 stores across the United States and Canada. By 11 AM the senior executive team has determined the week's priorities and begins relaying them to all executives down to the vice president level. During the first half of this two-hour national video conference, division VPs go over the updated forecast for the month and the quarter. At noon, department heads, product directors, category managers, and sales and marketing managers discuss issues at the store level that need to be bumped up to headquarters.

On Tuesdays at 11:15 AM, 7-Eleven's nearly 800 field consultants—each of whom oversees a group of stores—are debriefed in another videoconference. The call covers case studies, new merchandising issues, featured products, findings in test markets—everything the field consultants need to educate store owners and associates about that week's priorities. When these consultants head into the field after the call, they know exactly what news to deliver to the stores because they've heard it directly from the top. Clearly, the care in setting and keeping to priorities is paying off: As of July 2005, 7-Eleven had reported 35 consecutive quarters of same-store sales growth.

Match motivators to contribution • When Thompson arrived at Symantec, any executive who was promoted to vice president automatically was given a BMW. Senior management's bonuses were paid quarterly and were heavily skewed toward cash rather than stock. "So if the stock didn't do well, they didn't care," Thompson explains. "We [now] have a stock option plan that is broad based but not universal. One of the things we recognized early on was that if we were going to grow at the rate that we were growing, we had to be more selective in who we gave options to so as not to dilute the value of our stock. And so the first thing we did was identify a range of employees who were valuable to the company but didn't need equity to come to work, and we focused their compensation around cash bonuses. Then we increased the equity we gave to the engineers and other people that were critical to our long-term success." By paying the two groups differently, the new compensation scheme recognizes their distinctive importance.

"We changed the alignment throughout the organization," says Thompson. "Now everyone gets paid based upon revenue production as well as profit generation. My view was, 'Most of you don't have anything to do with profit. But all of you have something to do with revenue, so let's rebalance our incentives to reflect that reality.'"

It's only a matter of time before the diseased elements of a passive-aggressive organization overwhelm the healthy ones and drive the organization into financial distress. In fact, our research confirms a link between organizational health and profitability. Respondents who identify their organizations as resilient report better than average profitability nearly twice as often as respondents in passive-aggressive organizations (see the exhibit "Where There's Health, There Are Profits").

A full transformation of a passive-aggressive organization is impossible without the engagement of senior management. But even those in the middle of the organization can make a difference within their own scope of influence. Large organizations are made up of many small overlapping units. Even if

Where There's Health, There Are Profits.   In our survey, more than half the respondents from resilient organizations characterized their companies as being more profitable than the average for their industry. But less than a third of the people from passive-aggressive companies said theirs was.

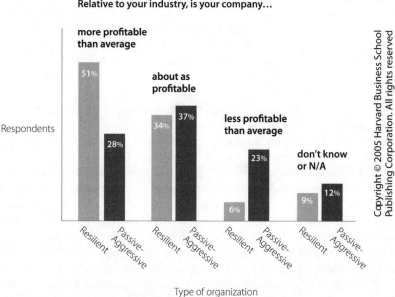

Relative to your industry, is your company...

more profitable than average — Resilient 51%, Passive-Aggressive 28%

about as profitable — Resilient 34%, Passive-Aggressive 37%

less profitable than average — Resilient 6%, Passive-Aggressive 23%

don't know or N/A — Resilient 9%, Passive-Aggressive 12%

Respondents

Type of organization

Source: Org DNA data set, 30,000 observations; Booz Allen analysis

they are not entirely independent, most of us can make changes in ours. If you are a brand manager in a passive-aggressive company, for instance, you can make it clear to your team that delivering on promises matters. Then find an opportunity to prove it—not a public hanging, but some signal that things have changed. When, say, your market researchers report in the staff meeting that the focus groups have to be postponed for two weeks, express disappointment that the team contract hasn't been followed. Make the point in the staff meeting so that everyone gets the message.

When such a message is delivered clearly and consistently, it sinks in. Slowly, your division can become a source of initiative in a sea of lassitude. You may not change the whole company overnight, but you just might begin to set a new tone.

NOTE

1. In addition to the approximately 30,000 responses to our Web site (orgdna.com), our research also includes about 20,000 responses to the same survey given in the course of client engagements.

ISSUE SUMMARY

Getting a handle on organizational culture is particularly complex because so many aspects are invisible, thus difficult to discern. Characteristics of culture like norms, assumptions, and unwritten rules are implicit and carried in people's minds. Retirees and job changes take the unwritten aspects of culture with them. For organizations with frequent turnover, this only exacerbates the difficulty of passing culture along. There are consequences of such gaps in cultural memory. A sort of cultural meltdown can occur when no one is making sure the expectations continue to be translated and norms restated.

It is not that culture doesn't matter; it is simply difficult to quantify. And once quantified, those characteristics are even more difficult for individuals to address and change. The balanced scorecard strategy may be helpful here—if it includes factors other than progress on joint objectives.

Still, there is a pervasive tendency to regard culture as a given, thus impervious to alteration or overhaul. If culture is intransigent, why call for its reform, which many experts are doing these days? Largely it is because so many organizations abandon so many well-conceived improvement initiatives. Quality initiatives are costly, labor intensive, and risky. If Americans live in fear at work—fear of intimidation, of confrontation, of litigation—and none of these fears are addressed, it becomes more apparent why improvement initiatives fail.

Positivism and risk aversion are part of many organizational cultures. These characteristics, along with others, are what critics are pointing to as the "bold face" of American organizational culture. For some organizations, striving for a close alignment and compatibility of culture and improvement initiatives is the key to performance and success.

ISSUE HIGHLIGHTS

- A corporation with a reputation for ruthless competition can attempt to recast its culture by being more transparent and responsive to critics.
- A corporation attempting to change its culture must recognize that its core business model will be affected.
- Massive culture-changing will inevitably result in public skepticism and questioning the organizations' true intent of change.
- Around the world, American organizations have the reputation for cultural virtues such as speaking one's mind, open exchange of ideas, and initiative, yet in many organizations the culture is not that open and honest.
- One perspective on organizational culture involves intentional efforts to socialize and train employees, a preventive measure.

- Another perspective claims the majority of organizations fall in the category of passive-aggressive, an unhealthy condition that is resistant to change.
- Rehabilitation of passive-aggressive organizations requires use of systematic steps and often complete realignment throughout the organization.

CRITICAL THINKING

Culture is a complex social system. It consists of processes, patterns, and events. The tendency is for leaders to focus on the events themselves; however, a systems approach requires taking a "balcony view." Looking at the processes and patterns rather than the events per se, is what Peter Senge refers to as personal mastery of the situation: "continually clarifying and deepening our personal vision, of focusing our energies, of developing patience, and of seeing reality objectively" (1990, p. 7). When leaders have clarified the big picture, they can then form a mental image of the culture: "Mental models are deeply ingrained assumptions, generalizations, or even pictures or images that influence how we understand the world and how we take action" (p. 8).

Any participant in an organization can reach this stage in systems thinking yet still not influence the culture, but leaders take the next step by sharing their mental model: "If any one idea about leadership has inspired organizations for thousands of years, it's the capacity to hold a shared picture of the future we seek to create" (p. 9).

For Senge, shared vision is necessary to culture change, but it is not sufficient. The way to change a culture is through a group approach: "Team learning is vital because teams, not individuals, are the fundamental learning unit in modern organizations" (p. 10). It is a simple strategy, but tremendously ignored—through dialogue shared understandings emerge and the culture is changed.

ADDITIONAL READING RESOURCES

Kim S. Cameron & Robert E. Quinn, *Diagnosing and Changing Organizational Culture: Based on the Competing Values Framework.* John Wiley & Sons, 2006.

James L. Gibson, John M. Ivancevich, Jamies H. Donnelly, Jr., & Robert Konopaske, Organizational culture. *Organizations: Behavior, Structure, Processes.* McGraw-Hill, 2003.

John P. Kotter & James L. Heskett, *Corporate Culture and Performance.* Simon & Schuster, 1992.

Peter Senge, *The Fifth Discipline.* Doubleday, 1990.

For more on improvement of organizational culture, visit these sites:

http://cqmextra.cqm.org/cqmjournal.nsf/reprints/rp09100
http://www.novalearning.com/html/institutional_formation.htm
http://www.strategic-organizational-change.com

ISSUE 5

How Can Leaders Capitalize on Diversity in the Workplace?

INTRODUCTION

Employee diversity is a fact of life in organizations. The range of differences among employees in a particular workplace can be quite amazing. Employees can vary by age, gender, national origin, physical appearance, race, religion, sexual orientation, to name a few factors. Whether these differences are considered a given, a goal, a problem, or a strength depends on the organization. For decades, workforce diversity was a matter of assimilation. Through the years initiatives and programs were created to cope with increasing diversity, mainly to ensure that employees adapted. Compliance became the measure of workforce diversity. Now however, instead of attempting to homogenize employees, there is another way for leaders to handle workplace diversity. Diversity is no longer ignored; in fact, it is in the spotlight. Today the focus is on leveraging or capitalizing on diversity. Diversity can be used strategically to create a more effective organization. Some regard diversity as good business; others regard it as good values. This is not to abandon diversity programs— they are still needed; however, they are not the same as in past decades. When diversity programs are regarded as a way of asset mapping, diversity is viewed as a resource, not an impediment.

Workplace diversity should be regarded as a vital resource for competitive advantage, according to the author of the first reading, "Workplace Diversity: Leveraging the Power of Difference for Competitive Advantage." Nancy Lockwood, a consultant with the Society for Human Resource Management, makes the case that workplace diversity initiatives have shifted away from a focus on antidiscrimination compliance. This is largely due to a broadening of the range of diversity characteristics. No longer is diversity limited to gender and race; it includes factors that are less visible like culture, religion, and socioeconomics. Today's focus is more about inclusion and corporate learning, with diversity prominent in goals and objectives. Workplace diversity is now considered an organizational asset with tremendous bearing on effectiveness and competitiveness. In fact, Lockwood contends that the business case for diversity means making managers accountable for results of diversity. Clearly the role of leaders in managing human capital is vastly different from earlier decades.

It is one thing to declare the advantages of diversity in the workplace by incorporating diversity in the mission and goals of an organization. It is quite another to take action by implementing specific strategies to leverage diversity. Joseph Coates, the author of the second reading, goes a step farther than simply making the case for workplace diversity by advocating for a radically different approach to diversity initiatives. He maintains that traditional diversity programs have forced people into diversity "boxes." Instead, Coates establishes the general principle of treating employees as unique individuals, which enables managers to view each person as a resource for the company. In "An Increasingly Diverse Workforce Makes Traditional Diversity Programs Passé," Coates provides specific examples of how organizations can overhaul their diversity programs. Rather than viewing certain employees as having diversity problems to be treated, organizations should establish systematic ways to take advantage of the range of abilities and potential of each person.

The final reading is about how organizations handle a workforce that includes four generations. "Managing Generation Y" contributes much to our understanding of diversity in terms of age of workers. Author Susan Eisner believes that "intergenerational differences may become a foremost aspect of diversity in the U.S. workplace." If so, what do leaders need to know about these four generations, typically called Traditionalists, Baby Boomers, Generation X, and Generation Y? According to Eisner strategies are needed that are intentionally intergenerational. While age differences should be built into strategies, age stereotypes need to be avoided. Of particular value to leaders is a summary table defining the four generations at work.

According to Lockwood, the emerging paradigm of workplace diversity is for companies to "promote equal opportunity and value cultural differences." For organizations to achieve this, they are turning to other organizations for help. DiversityInc is one such group. Their goal is ambitious: "a prosperous world that continuously leverages all human capital through expanded opportunity and elimination of bias to increase economic and societal well being." The increasing number of support groups with similar missions, ready to assist organizations and corporations, shows that we have moved very far from the days of diversity as assimilation and compliance.

SOURCES

Nancy R. Lockwood, Workplace diversity: Leveraging the power of difference for competitive advantage. *The Society for Human Resource Management,* 2005.

Joseph Coates, An increasingly diverse workforce makes traditional diversity programs passé. *Employment Relations Today,* Spring 2006.

Susan P. Eisner, Managing Generation Y. *SAM Advanced Management Journal,* Autumn 2005.

ARTICLE 5.1

Workplace Diversity: Leveraging the Power of Difference for Competitive Advantage

Nancy R. Lockwood

Workplace diversity has taken on a new face. Today, workplace diversity is no longer just about anti-discrimination compliance. Workplace diversity now focuses on inclusion and the impact on the bottom line. Leveraging workplace diversity is increasingly seen as a vital strategic resource for competitive advantage. More companies are linking workplace diversity to their strategic goals and objectives—and holding management accountable for results. Thus, HR plays a key role in diversity management and leadership to create and empower an organizational culture that fosters a respectful, inclusive, knowledge-based environment where each employee has the opportunity to learn, grow and meaningfully contribute to the organization's success.

"Diversity represents a company's fundamental attitude that it not only respects and values the individuality of its employees but also understands how to tap the potentially significant contributions inherent in diversity."[1]

—Alexandra Groess
Allianz Group's International Diversity Project

WORKPLACE DIVERSITY—AN EVOLUTION

From compliance to inclusion, the concept of workplace diversity is evolving. Coming from an organizational viewpoint, this article explores the changing perception of workplace diversity, elements of an inclusive corporate culture, the business case and HR's leadership role to maximize the benefits of a diverse workforce in a changing marketplace. While a broad range of issues is covered, it should be noted that "one size does not fit all," as organizations are in different stages of development regarding workplace diversity. In addition, workplace diversity is not strictly a U.S. concept: a brief discussion on the drivers of workplace diversity in the European Union is presented.

Diversity Defined Today

As predicted in the landmark study *Workforce 2020,* rapid technological change, globalization, the demand for skills and education, an aging workforce and greater ethnic diversification in the labor market have forever changed the employment landscape.[2] The definition of diversity extends well beyond the traditional view that once focused primarily on gender and race and reflects the broader perspective of workplace diversity today.

> "A broad definition of diversity ranges from personality and work style to all of the visible dimensions such as race, age, ethnicity or gender, to secondary influences such as religion, socioeconomics and education, to work diversities such as management and union, functional level and classification or proximity/ distance to headquarters."[3]

Integration and Learning: A New Paradigm for Managing Diversity

Diversity in the United States has evolved since the 1960s. As illustrated in Figure 1, diversity was first based on the assimilation approach, with everyone being part of the "melting pot." Compliance (e.g., affirmative action, equal employment opportunity) is important in diversity, and key legislation has been an effective tool for change (e.g., Title VII of the Civil Rights Act of 1964, Age Discrimination in Employment Act of 1967, Americans with Disabilities Act of 1990). Today, however, the impetus behind workplace diversity is that of *inclusion and the business case:* embracing and leveraging differences for the benefit of the organization. The collaboration of cultures, ideas and different perspectives is now considered an organizational asset—bringing forth greater creativity and innovation—with the result that many companies are increasingly focusing on corporate diversity initiatives to improve organizational performance.[4]

In what ways can collaboration of cultures be an organizational asset?

Diversity initiatives do not always meet expectations. The traditional schools of thought behind many diversity interventions are: 1) assimilation, based on the idea that "we're all the same" (promoting equal opportunity); and 2) differentiation, from the philosophy "we celebrate differences." Today, groundbreaking research goes beyond the historical framework of workplace diversity. The emerging paradigm is *integration and learning.* That is, companies

Figure 1   Evolution of Approaches to Workplace Diversity

Approach:	assimilation	➡	legal	➡	valuing diversity	➡	managing diversity
Basis:	melting pot myth	➡	EED/AA	➡	differences as assets	➡	multicultural corporate cultures

Source: Carr-Ruffino, N. (1999). *Diversity success strategies.* Boston: Butterworth-Heinemann.

promote equal opportunity and value cultural differences, using the talents of all employees to gain diverse work perspectives. To achieve this level of diversity management, however, organizational leaders must have a clear understanding of how they define diversity as well as what exactly the organization does with the experiences of being a diverse workforce.[5]

An Inclusive Corporate Culture

The concept of inclusion is increasingly important in the discussion of workplace diversity. In many ways, this evolution reflects societal values in the workplace. For example, two beliefs commonly held by Americans are that everyone deserves a chance (equal opportunity, sometimes referred to as the "level playing field") and that all people should be treated with dignity and respect.[6] The values of equality, respect and opportunity for all represent the cornerstone of workplace diversity. Inclusiveness is thus a win-win dynamic: it generates opportunities for growth, flexibility and adaptation in the marketplace for both the employee and the organization.

THE BUSINESS CASE FOR WORKPLACE DIVERSITY

Increasingly, the case for workplace diversity as a business imperative is gaining recognition by leaders in the business world. At a symposium sponsored by The Conference Board regarding diversity in the workplace, for example, 400 executives agreed that "diversity programs help to ensure the creation, management, valuing and leveraging of a diverse workforce that will lead to organizational effectiveness and sustained competitiveness."[7]

One of the major drivers behind the business case is the demographic changes that directly affect the labor pool and available talent (see Figure 2). These changes are significant. In an organization, human capital and workforce relationships are the backbone of success. The flow of information between colleagues, work teams, customers and suppliers, for example, depends on the quality of relationships and talent in the workplace.[8] Consequently, workplace

Figure 2   Demographic Trends Transforming the Workforce

- **Greater diversity in the labor pool:** By 2008, women and minorities will represent 70% of the new labor force entrants, and by 2010, 34% of the U.S. workforce will be non-Caucasian.

- **An aging workforce:** By 2010, the U.S. workforce will have an increase of 29% in the 45–64 age group, a 14% increase in the 65+ age group and a 1% decline in the 18–44 age group.

- **Globalization:** In the next decade, 75% of new workers will likely be from Asia, while North America and Europe will have 3% of the world's new labor force.

Source: Hewitt Associates. (2004, February). *Preparing the workforce of tomorrow.* Retrieved March 21, 2005, from www.hewitt.com.

diversity is increasingly viewed as an essential success factor to be competitive in today's marketplace,

Advantages

Six key reasons to tie workplace diversity to organizational strategic goals and objectives are: 1) greater adaptability and flexibility in a rapidly changing marketplace; 2) attracting and retaining the best talent; 3) reducing costs associated with turnover, absenteeism and low productivity; 4) return on investment (ROI) from various initiatives, policies and practices; 5) gaining and keeping greater/new market share (locally and globally) with an expanded diverse customer base; and 6) increased sales and profits.

Workplace diversity can be viewed as having both direct and indirect links to the bottom line. In business, the preferred equation for success is a single action that directly impacts financial performance. Workplace diversity, however, is a complex phenomenon. Consequently, the link of workplace diversity to financial success is not always immediately apparent, nor is it always linear. . . .

SENIOR MANAGEMENT'S ROLE

Visibility, communication and accountability are key to achieving a competitive diverse workforce. A recent study on what makes and breaks diversity initiatives found three critical points of leadership: 1) accountability; 2) a passion for diversity; and 3) sustained involvement. Visible commitment throughout the organization is important: adding diversity on the agenda at executive meetings and company conferences, appointing diversity candidates to top positions, and assigning clear roles and responsibilities to the senior management team regarding diversity management. Accountability creates sustained involvement—that is, holding managers accountable to deliver diversity results. Participation in diversity councils is recommended as a development path for senior leadership.[9]

However, simply placing women and/or minorities in high-profile positions, for example, is insufficient. Rather, the more effective approach is to hold management accountable for results. Consequently, to get middle management and employee buy-in, top management must establish clear implementation and reporting requirements. At DuPont, for example, senior management ensures accountability for diversity management by integrating diversity into the overall business performance evaluation process, including developing cost and profit objectives as well as how compensation is determined. The company also uses targeted career development initiatives to help diverse people fill key work assignments, thus supporting advancement and addressing glass ceiling issues. The Quaker Oats Company aims to keep diversity management simple by using two key tools: 1) the diversity progress menu; and 2) the diversity accountability guidelines. The company's goal is to supply managers with a best practices list that offers flexibility tied to individual business cultures as well as performance.[7] Nine of the top 50 companies on the 2004 Diversity Inc Top 50 Companies for Diversity list tie diversity to managers' compensation. For example, CitiGroup measures its managers' attempts to attract talent and develop a diverse workforce. At Verizon Communications, 5% of bonuses for directors and above are related to diversity.[10] Simple daily actions also communicate commitment to workplace diversity: the CEO greets employees in their native language, and the supervisor takes time to understand direct reports with different cultural values and viewpoints.[8]

Diversity Management and the Board of Directors

Increasingly, the business case for diversity focuses on the board of directors. The impetus to change the board composition is a direct result of the trend toward corporate governance and diversity of the workforce, customer base and other stakeholders. Organizations want a wider range of leadership skills, work styles, perspectives and expertise, as well as increased representation of women and minorities among board directors.[11] There is positive evidence of change. For example, in the Fortune 500 in 2003, women held 14% of board seats (up from 10% in 1995), and 54 companies had 25% or more women on boards of directors (up from 11% in 1995).[12] Finally, change in board composition is also occurring at an international level, as global organizations expand the cultural diversity of their boards with expertise in international business from other countries."[13]

MANAGING DIVERSITY: HR CHALLENGES AND OPPORTUNITIES

With the changing marketplace and an increasingly diverse labor pool, HR leaders are dealing with a myriad of factors regarding diversity management. Broadly speaking, workplace diversity challenges can be considered within three interrelated categories: attracting and retaining talent, greater diversity among employees and training.

Attracting and Retaining Talent

Competition for talent is growing—from competition abroad, lower education levels of U.S. workers compared with other countries, U.S. immigration challenges and fear of terrorism in the United States.[14] Further, with the retirement of the baby boom generation (those born from 1944 to 1960) in the next 10 years, a key concern is retention of older workers. Organizations are in different stages of preparation regarding this likely loss of talent. As of 2003, 35% were just becoming aware of the issue, 35% did not know if their organizations were ready, 23% were beginning to examine policies, and 4% had proposed specific changes. Many HR leaders are looking for ways to attract and retain older workers. Benefits and workplace programs, such as reward initiatives and flexible work arrangements (e.g., part-time work, phased retirement), are key tools that offer attractive options to older workers.[15]

The skill shortage, however, will hit some industries harder and sooner than others. The nuclear power industry, for example, faces replacing as much as 50% of its workforce. The talent crunch will also strike the expanding service industry: sales positions in the United States, for example, are expected to increase by 25%, yet many in today's sales force are aged 55 or older.[16]

A recent study notes most firms are not paying close attention to retention and promotion strategies. For example, top minority talent is seeking leadership opportunities; yet companies indicate they have difficulty attracting talent for executive leadership (42%) and professional and technical skills (42%).[17] In corporate America, the "revolving door syndrome" is particularly evident for women and minorities. To retain women and minorities, HR professionals should re-evaluate their organization regarding talent, mentoring, career development and succession planning. Strategic initiatives, such as mentoring, on-boarding and "listening" forums, are additional tactics to address minority retention.[18]

Greater Diversity Among Employees

The term "diversity" has typically referred to women and minorities. Today, however, employers are beginning to formally acknowledge other employees as well (e.g., ethnic groups, people with disabilities and self-identified gay, lesbian and bisexual persons). Some firms encourage a welcoming and inclusive environment for all employees by creating diversity network groups. Kraft Foods uses employee councils to build employee development. Through nine employee councils (African-American Council, Hispanic Council, Asian-American Council, Rainbow Council, Women in Sales Council, Black Sales Council, Hispanic/Asian Sales Council, Women in Operations and African-Americans in Operations), Kraft takes an active role in mentoring and supporting its diverse workforce. For example, the company builds relationships with universities to bring in talent through internships and internally sponsors career days focusing on leadership competencies.[10]

Different groups have different needs, and they want their needs recognized and met. Acknowledgment of different needs yields greater employee satisfaction, employer loyalty and, in turn, lower turnover and greater productivity. As a result, more organizations offer programs to address issues such as work/life balance and demands for more flexibility with telecommuting, adoption support, flexible health and dependent care spending accounts, elder care and domestic partner benefits.[19]

Within workplace diversity, one of the least discussed minority groups is people with disabilities. This group is a source of under-represented talent in the workplace. One study reveals that in the majority of companies, individuals with disabilities comprise less than 10% of their total workforce. The study recommends top management lead by example and hire qualified individuals with disabilities on their staff. Through training and focus groups, HR leaders can improve sensitivity toward employees with disabilities.[20]

Training

Within the context of workplace diversity, training plays a key role in retaining talent. The role of training is to promote workplace harmony, learn about others' values, improve cross-cultural communication and develop leadership skills. Awareness training raises understanding of diversity concerns by uncovering hidden assumptions and biases, heightening sensitivity to diversity in the workplace and fostering individual and group sharing. Skill-based diversity training improves morale, productivity and creativity through effective intercuitural communication.[21] Leadership development, team building and mentoring programs are also examples of organizational training that promotes growth and collaboration. An overlooked area regarding retention is cross-cultural competence within the organization, often a missed opportunity to address minority retention concerns.[18]

Finally, working in a diverse organization requires diversity competencies for everyone, including HR (see Figure 3). Yet not all HR professionals are experts in diversity. A survey notes that only about one-third of companies think their HR staff has the skills to serve a diverse U.S. workforce and only 22% believe HR has the skills to serve a global workforce.[22] HR professionals best qualified to deal with workplace diversity have experience in areas such as team building, change management, conflict resolution and cross-cultural communication.

ALIGNING THE DIVERSITY PROCESS WITH STRATEGIC BUSINESS GOALS

The organization that best utilizes the full potential of all employees intentionally and thoughtfully aligns workplace diversity with strategic business goals by following these steps:

Define diversity • Clarify the role of workplace diversity in the organization, including leadership roles and expectations for diversity initiatives. In vision and mission statements, highlight the importance of diversity (for example, is the organization's philosophy on inclusion clearly stated?). Place the vision and mission statements on the company Web site as a public statement of the organization's commitment to workplace diversity. Communicate commitment by allocating the necessary resources—staff, budgets and time—to move the diversity process forward.[23]

Establish accountability • With senior management, HR diversity leaders should develop challenging yet realistic goals for diversity interventions. Demonstrate organizational commitment: 1) appoint senior executives to diversity

Figure 3   HR Competencies for Diversity Management

- Active/nonjudgmental listening.
- Willingness to challenge one's own concepts about diversity.
- Collaboration skills.
- Experience with conflict resolution and change management.
- Sensitivity toward terms labeling groups regarding diversity.
- Ability to identify diversity issues and understand related tensions.
- Intercultural team building.
- Ability to express respect and appreciation.
- Openness to learning about others who are different.
- Ability to educate others on how to build diverse people skills.
- Ability to provide appropriate responses.

Source: Adapted from Carr-Ruffino, N. (1999). *Diversity success strategies.* Boston: Butterworth-Heinemann.

In addition to these accountability measures, what other strategies can leaders use to deliver diversity results?

task forces for succession planning, education and training initiatives; 2) recruit diversity candidates for senior leadership positions; and 3) establish diversity goals and objectives for all leadership levels in the performance management process and reward programs. Demonstrate commitment to workplace diversity by developing solutions when problems are identified through employee attitude surveys, focus groups, etc.[24]

Develop a diversity scorecard • Often overlooked, the scorecard is an important tool to manage diversity. The scorecard includes financial and non-financial recognition of diversity ROI initiatives as well as relevant feedback (e.g., change management lessons). When developing the diversity scorecard, include measures aligned with the organization's strategic business goals. When determining measures, keep in mind four themes: 1) key deliverables that leverage the role of diversity in the organization's overall strategy; 2) utilization of diversity in the development of a high-performance work environment; 3) ways in which the corporate culture is aligned with the organization's strategy; and 4) the efficiency of the diversity deliverables.

STUDIES ON WORKPLACE DIVERSITY AND THE BOTTOM LINE

Several studies link workplace diversity and company performance. The study results run the gamut from identifying critical success factors for diversity initiatives that impact organizational effectiveness to connecting gender and diversity with financial performance.

The "Makes and Breaks" of Diversity Initiatives[9]

This study found that successful initiatives that leverage diversity to enhance organizational effectiveness share certain characteristics and approaches. Specifically, successful workplace diversity initiatives hinge on committed leadership, goals/targets of measures of effectiveness, strong diversity professionals, employee involvement and ties to performance evaluation, as well as data to identify, quantify and communicate progress and challenges.

Diversity Practices That Work[25]

Companies with diversity practices collectively generated 18% greater productivity than the U.S. economy overall. The results of this study suggest that, at a minimum, diversity progress may enhance productivity through effective good leadership and management practices. Key factors that had the greatest impact on overall perceived effectiveness of diversity initiatives were: 1) a track record of recruiting diverse people; 2) management that is accountable for diversity progress and holds others accountable; 3) leaders who demonstrate commitment to diversity; 4) rewarding people who contribute in the area of diversity; and 5) training and education to increase awareness and help employees understand how diversity can impact business results.

The Effects of Diversity on Business Performance[26]

This study looks at the effects of racial and gender diversity on organizational performance. A key finding reveals that racial diversity has a positive effect on overall performance in companies that use diversity as a resource for innovation and learning. Further, the study results suggest that the best performance outcomes occur when diversity is found across entire organizational units.

Connecting Corporate Performance and Gender Diversity[27]

Based on an examination of 353 Fortune 500 companies, this study connects gender diversity and financial performance. (The study does not, however, demonstrate causation.) The key findings show that the group of companies with the highest representation of women on their top management teams experienced better financial performance than the group with the lowest women's representation: that is, 35% higher return on equity and 34% higher total return to shareholders. The study results suggest there is a business case for gender diversity (e.g., recruiting, developing and advancing women)—specifically, organizations that focus on diversity are in a stronger position to tap the educated and skilled talent in the marketplace. This is important because women comprise 47% of the U.S. paid labor force and hold 46% of management positions. In addition, women earn more than half of all bachelor's and master's degrees in the United States (57% and 59%, respectively) and nearly half of all doctorates and law degrees (45% and 47%, respectively).

GLOBAL DIVERSITY—THE EUROPEAN UNION

Focus on gender equality and anti-discrimination by the European Union (EU) offers a unique example of workplace diversity outside of the United States. With the addition of 10 member states in May 2004, the European Union—with 25 member states in 2005 and nearly 500 million people—is one of the largest economic forces in the world. Through legislation (called Directives) under the Social Policy Agenda, the EU is establishing significant social, economic and political change. The goal is to be "the most competitive and dynamic knowledge-based economy in the world capable of sustainable economic growth with more and better jobs and greater social cohesion." To achieve the necessary economic and social renewal, the Commission of the European Communities developed a five-year action plan (2000–2005) that focused on investing in people and combating social exclusion.[28] In 2000, with the introduction of the EU Article 13 Race and Employment Directives (to be effective by 2006), the EU put in place measures designed to enforce the right to be treated equally.[29]

1. The Racial Equality Directive 2000/43/EC prohibits discrimination on the grounds of a personal racial or ethnic origin.
2. The Employment Equality Directive 2000/78/EC prohibits discrimination on the grounds of religion or belief, disability, age or sexual orientation.

However, the establishment of a Directive does not guarantee immediate results or even substantial progress. While EU Directives require member states to meet the minimum legislative standards, more work is needed to achieve workforce diversity. For example, a recent report notes that while gender employment and education gaps are closing, the gender gap in the EU remains almost unchanged.[30]

Drivers and Benefits of Diversity in Europe

In Europe, there is a growing recognition of the benefits of workplace diversity for both the society and the economy. To remain competitive, however, there are a host of issues to address, from racial and ethnic diversity and new roles of women to work/life balance and an aging population coupled with declining birthrates. A recent study notes that a third of the top European companies are gaining competitive advantage from diversity management. These progressive organizations, rather than seeing diversity as a regulatory response that requires anti-discrimination and equal opportunity policies, view diversity management as a vehicle to develop an engaged, motivated and heterogeneous workforce to develop creative business solutions in the global marketplace.[31]

Another study notes the three most often mentioned benefits of workplace diversity by European companies are: 1) improved team effectiveness and cooperation; 2) improved productivity; and 3) improved customer markets with broader access to labor markets. Other drivers considered moderately beneficial are improved employer image, more openness to change, improved morale and commitment, ease of entry into new markets and enhanced effectiveness of complex organization. Overall, the most important shifts in workplace diversity are in the areas of gender and ethnic diversity. For example, as women obtain higher professional degrees and qualifications and earn more money in the marketplace, they are increasingly viewed as important in the workplace. Ethnic minorities are seen as a growing workforce as well as customer base.[32]

ENHANCING COMPETITIVE ADVANTAGE THROUGH DIVERSITY MANAGEMENT: RECOMMENDATIONS FOR HR

- Assess. Conduct a top-to-bottom critical assessment of all company policies and programs. Determine if there are biases that create potential challenges for diverse employees. Review diversity initiative results (e.g., recruitment of top talent, retention strategies, succession planning, career development goals) to determine if the workplace is structured to exclude certain employee groups. Determine where changes in organizational culture, policies and programs need to be made.
- Capitalize. Promote diversity initiatives to the top agendas of senior management by capitalizing on reputation as a diversity management consultant.
- Dialogue. Develop and maintain continuous dialogue with the CEO and senior management regarding diversity as a business strategy.
- Discover. Through focus groups, confidential employee surveys and exit interviews, determine how diversity initiatives are viewed and gather feedback for improvement.
- Network. Network with other HR professionals to learn different approaches to diversity management, challenges encountered and recommended best practices.
- Learn. To best utilize a diverse workforce, profit from lessons learned.

Resources: Diversity in the European Union

- European Council on Work-Life & Diversity: www.conference-board.org/pdf_free/councils/353.pdf
- European Disability Forum: www.edf-feph.org

- European Monitoring Centre on Racism and Xenophobia (EUMC): www.eumc.eu.int/eumc/lndex.php
- European Women's Lobby: www.womenlobby.org
- For Diversity/Against Discrimination: www.stopKliscrimination.info
- International Labour Organization—The Gender Toolkit: www.ilo.org/public/english/bureau/gender/newsite2002/about/defin.htm
- Discover. Through focus groups, confidential employee surveys and exit interviews, determine how diversity initiatives are viewed and gather feedback for improvement.
- Network. Network with other HR professionals to learn different approaches to diversity management, challenges encountered and recommended best practices.
- Learn. To best utilize a diverse workforce, profit from lessons learned.

IN CLOSING

There is no "best way" to manage diversity. The identification, selection and purpose of diversity initiatives and their development and implementation differ from company to company. The likelihood of success is dependent on business needs and workforce issues as well as situational factors, such as the organizational culture and workplace environment. Ultimately, the strength of commitment by the CEO, senior management and HR leadership will determine whether the organization successfully leverages workplace diversity for competitive advantage.

NOTES

1. Murray, S. (2003). *Diversity makes a difference*. Retrieved February 22, 2005, from www.allianzgroup.com.
2. Judy, R. W., & D'Amico, C. (1997). *Workforce 2020: Work and workers in the 21st century*. Indianapolis, IN: Hudson Institute.
3. SHRM Glossary of Human Resource Terms, www.shrm.org/hrresources/hrglossary_published/d.asp.
4. Jayne, M. E. A., & Dipboye, R. L. (2004, Winter). Leveraging diversity to improve business performance: Research findings and recommendations for organizations. *Human Resource Management, 43*, 4, 409–424.
5. Thomas, D. A., & Ely, R. J. (2002). *Making differences matter: A new paradigm tor managing diversity*. Retrieved March 15, 2005, from Harvard Business Online, www.hbsp.harvard.edu.
6. Gardenswartz, L., Rowe, A., Digh, D., & Bennett, M. F. (2003). *The global diversity desk reference: Managing an international workforce*. San Francisco: John Wiley & Sons, Inc.
7. Hart, M. A. (1997). *Managing diversity for sustained competitiveness*. New York: The Conference Board.

8. Carr-Ruffino, N. (1999). *Diversity success strategies.* Boston: Butterworth-Heinemann.

9. Matton, J. N., & Hernandez, C. M. (2004, August). A new study identifies the "makes and breaks" of diversity initiatives. *Journal of Organizational Excellence, 23,* 4, 47–58.

10. Cole, Y. (2004, June/July). Top 10 companies for diversity. *DiversityInc Top, 3,* 3, 56–96,

11. Business for Social Responsibility. *Board diversity.* Retrieved March 4, 2005, from www.bsr.org.

12. Catalyst. (2003). 2003 *Catalyst census of women board of directors.* Retrieved March 7, 2005, from www.catalystwomen.org/knowledge/titles/files/fact/Snapshot%202004.pdf.

13. The Conference Board. (1999). *Board diversity in U.S. corporations.* New York: Author.

14. Richard, O. C., & Johnson, N. B. (2001, Summer). Understanding the impact of human resource diversity practices on firm performance. *Journal of Managerial issues.* 13, 2, 177–196.

15. Collison, J. (2003, June). *SHRM/NOWCC/CED older workers survey.* Alexandria, VA: Society for Human Resource Management.

16. Towers Perrin HR Services. (2004, October). *The coming talent crisis: Is your organization ready?* Retrieved March 21, 2005, from www.towers.com.

17. Hewitt Associates. (n.d.). *The workforce is changing: Is your organization?* Retrieved March 21, 2005, from www.hewitt.com.

18. Hewitt Associates. (2004, February). *Preparing the workforce of tomorrow.* Retrieved February 10, 2005, from www.hewitt.com.

19. Burke. M. E. (2004, June). *SHRM 2004 benefits survey report.* Alexandria, VA: Society for Human Resource Management.

20. Lengnick-Hall, M. L., Gaunt, Ph., & Collison, J. (2003, April). *Employer incentives for hiring individuals with disabilities.* Alexandria, VA: Society for Human Resource Management.

21. Grant, B. Z., & Kleiner, B. H. (1997). Managing diversity in the work place. *Equal Opportunities International, 16,* 3, 26–33.

22. See Ref. 18

23. Hubbard, E. E. (2004). *The diversity scorecard: Evaluating the impact of diversity on organizational performance.* Burlington, MA: Elsevier Butterworth-Heinemann.

24. See Ref. 23

25. National Urban League. (2004, June). *Diversity practices that work: The American worker speaks.* New York: Author.

26. Kochan, T., Bezrukova, K., Ely, R., Jackson, S., Joshi, A., Jen, K., et al. (2002, October). *The effects of diversity on business performance; Report of the Diversity Research Network.* Building Opportunities for

Leadership Development Initiative, Alfred P. Sloan Foundation and the Society for Human Resource Management.

27. Catalyst. (2004). *Connecting corporate performance and gender diversity*. New York: Author.

28. European Commission. (2000, June 28). *Communication from the Commission to the Council, the European Parliament, the Economic and Social Committee and the Committee of the Regions: Social policy agenda*, Brussels: Author.

29. European Commission. (2004). *Equality and nondiscrimination—annual report 2004*. Brussels: Author.

30. European Commission. (2005). *Report from the Commission to the Council, the European Parliament, the European Economic and Social Committee and the Committee of the Regions on equality between men and women*, 2005. Brussels: Author.

31. Singh, V., & Point, S. (2004, August). Promoting diversity management: New challenges and new responses by top companies across Europe. *Management Focus* [Cranfield School of Management, www.cranfield. ac.uk/som/research/centres/cdwbl].

32. Simons, G. F. (2002). *EuroDiversity: A business guide to managing difference*. Woburn, MA: Elsevier Science.

An Increasingly Diverse Workforce Makes Traditional Diversity Programs Passé

Joseph Coates

For 40 years, Federal Legislation has expanded to affirm and establish workplace access and fair treatment rights for blacks and other minorities, women, the aged, the disabled, and a wide range of other people with special or unusual characteristics. As these rights grew, early resistance—based on anticipated high cost and inconvenience—has faded. The demonstrable work capabilities of these diverse people are today unequivocally clear. The old view of diversity as an imposed cost of doing business is history, at least in forward-thinking firms. The endless differences in knowledge, skills, experiences, special abilities, culture, and linguistic talent, to name a few, are all now widely seen as assets to be respected and drawn on as needed. Diversity is so great as to be beyond any inventory. Social and business changes have blasted the concept wide open. To paraphrase the Army's slogan that each soldier is "an army of one," each employee is a total diversity of one.

To illustrate the point about total diversity, I made an arbitrary list of obvious categories: race, religion, ethnicity, national origin, age, level of education, gender, demographic location, urban/suburban/rural background, height, weight, occupation, income, and so on. Then I estimated the percentage of the population I fit into with regard to each of those categories. For example, I am white, which would make me fit about 85 percent of the population; based on age category, I'd fit in with about 10 percent of the population. In putting these scores together, I found that by using just eight of these measures, I became 1 person in 300 million, which is the total population in the United States. It is clear that some of us might end up being 1 in 200 million, and still others might end up being 1 in a billion. The point is that each of us is an individual, and our individuality is spread over a substantial number of factors or variables that make us who we are.

The problem for human resources departments is that as they have addressed one or another element of diversity—race, gender, physical condition, and so on—they have followed the usual practice of bureaucracy when faced with a new issue. That is, they form a unit, set up an activity, and treat the characteristic as if it were a distinct problem, seeming to overlook the more important fact that each of us is unique. Rather than forcing us into boxes where they can do generic activities for Box A, another set for Box B, a third set for Box C, and so on, they should recognize that everyone in the organization should have access to the array of activities from Boxes A–Z. In general, diversity programs are either mechanisms for maximizing the reward structure or ways to better fit, prepare, train, and select the person for specific jobs. By recognizing that each of us is an individual and making these activities available to all, we can educate, reward, and train everyone according to his or her own and the firm's needs.

As a general principle, every change planned or unplanned, within or connected to the firm has ripple effects, most of which will affect the workforce. Those ripple effects may involve new talents, new hires, schedules, benefits, compensation, training, the organization of work, new goals and forms of management, and just about anything else. The challenge for senior management is to leverage the ripple effects of the widespread diversity within their enterprises by recognizing the uniqueness of each employee.

Would you agree with this author that each individual is diverse; therefore, diversity programs are passé?

HARNESSING DIVERSITY TO ENHANCE THE ORGANIZATION

The single most important flaw of diversity programs is that they categorize people into diversity boxes, concentrating on the label on the box—e.g., black, female, handicapped—and deemphasizing the range of abilities and the potential that each person has. It would be better to treat each person as a unique individual; unfortunately, this is difficult and uncongenial for the large corporation to do. In the examples that follow, we examine a variety of situations that today's HR departments commonly handle by forcing people into a diversity box and see how a different approach to diversity can yield better solutions for individual employees, to the benefit of all.

Transforming the Disabled Employee into a New Product Designer

Companies that have accommodated disabled employees can reap unexpected benefits by simply changing their perspective. For the company that sells products or services, disabled employees may be able to coach company designers on the needs and limitations of the physically disadvantaged consumer.

Wouldn't it be great if car companies and food packagers, for example, surveyed and learned from their own disabled workers? Furthermore, if we assume that 5 percent of workers have relatives with disabilities, treating every employee as an individual resource may help the company capture their observations and experience and expand its ability to serve the market of the disabled.

Companies that have incorporated the disabled into the workforce are being rewarded in another way as well: disabled employees are usually more reliable workers than their peers.

Minority Workers as Litmus Testers for Your Foreign Operations

When companies open facilities in foreign countries, they face two universal issues—an alien language and unanticipated customs. The common U.S. business mistake is the belief that people everywhere are just like us, except that they wear funny hats and don't speak English. Companies that have hired employees from other nationalities and cultures will find that these employees can alert management to the differences they will encounter abroad, even if they cannot state them in scholarly language or technical jargon. More generally, by treating everyone as a resource, the company will likely find some number of its employees who have personal experience in almost any country of new interest. Find them and use them. They will give you directly useful insights, raise uncertainties you had not considered, and even allay some anxieties.

As an example, a few years ago, a U.S. multinational decided on Geneva as its new European headquarters. It began a sensibly slow but steady move of personnel. Only in the midst of this process did management discover that the available housing was unsuited to U.S. customs and budgets. An early internal reconnoiter within the company could have helped avoid the problem. This example shows the shortcomings of the established approach to diversity as boxes for troublesome people. Management could easily have put out a general notice asking if anybody had lived in Geneva, or was familiar with the size, structure, and organization of dwellings and how they might fit U.S. employees like themselves. When diversity is seen as something positive, management is more likely to recognize that it already has information it urgently needs.

Managing Employees from Dual-Income Households with Dependents

Employees from dual-income families with dependents make up a rapidly growing category of diversity across all employees that presents management with special challenges. Whether they are caring for children or aged parents, workers face inevitable and mandatory needs that simply trump work responsibilities—sickness and doctor visits, school events, and the like—and require greater flexibility at work. At the same time, having two sources of income gives each of them—if they have handled their finances wisely—unprecedented independence. Companies that fail to provide the needed flexibility risk demoralizing their staff; as family tension increases, so does vituperative hostility toward the employer. After complaining, requesting, or suggesting and still getting no satisfactory response, valuable employees may quit.

In response, more companies are allowing these families to balance the demands of work and personal life through flexible scheduling, telecommuting, or job sharing. These solutions are facilitated by technologies that can connect employees to the enterprise from home or any remote site. Work at home has been widely appreciated by those doing it. It gives employees an hour or more of free time by eliminating travel and offers flexibility in arranging the day and its often complex obligations.

You can recognize employees as individuals by offering this benefit of flexibility to everyone, not just those who have been categorized as telecommuters. Companies that do so will find themselves rewarded with increased employee loyalty and the improved productivity that happy employees provide.

Managing the Minority Worker for Upward Mobility

Many minority employees (more so in earlier times) were hired into an employment *cul de sac*—low-income jobs with only one or two steps up possible. That's deadly for morale and murderous on company reputation. One of the highest-priority expectations of most minority hires is the opportunity for upward mobility and the appropriate internal training and experience to earn the rise up. If there ever was an HR situation begging the boss to put himself or herself in the employee's shoes, this is it. Unfortunately, upward mobility remains just a hope for most low-income minorities.

Undereducated minority workers are all too often exploited, underpaid, and overworked in U.S. businesses. The worst practices are usually in overseas facilities run by suppliers whose workplaces are sweatshops. But even domestically, we have some of those worst practices. It has been national news for a couple of years that Wal-Mart has engaged in questionable practices, taking advantage of either immigrant minority or relatively poor domestic workers. Aside from wage adjustment, educational programs could go far in both opening up those workers to new opportunities and higher expectations and making them more useful to their current employers.

One of the near-universals in workers' hopes and expectations is that with hard work and experience they will enjoy continual increases in income over their working lives. To not provide that fair wage and route to upward mobility is to populate your workplace with alienated and even hostile employees. That doesn't seem to make much strategic sense for any company.

Companies that understand the total diversity of the workforce will recognize this desire for opportunity among many of their lower-income employees. By creating training and educational programs and making them available to all employees, these companies can improve their future competitive advantage.

It is worth noting that today's low-paid worker becomes tomorrow's consumer of your products. The fast-food industry provides a powerful example of this. Some incredibly large percentage of Americans under 50 will have worked in their teens for a fast-food chain. Ten or 15 years after holding those jobs, they are likely to be married and have children, therefore becoming part of a new generation of the chain's customers—assuming it was a good youthful experience.

Now run the reel for an immigrant whose early job was scut work in a big company. Ten or 15 years later, he or she is likely to be a comfortable member of the middle or working class. Will their menial-work employer be able to sell its product or service to the former low man on the totem pole? The implications of how you treat members of a category of workers—in this case, all young people doing unskilled work—can be subtle and last well into the future.

To generalize further, every worker or former worker is a social megaphone potentially shouting out good, bad, or indifferent information about your firm as a place to work. If he or she is angry with you, that broadcast may include anecdotes that, whether true or false, will hurt your reputation and damage your drawing power.

Differing Career Orientations Among Female Employees

Catherine Hakim of the London School of Economics has published a study in her book *Work-Lifestyle Choices in the 21st Century* (Oxford University Press, 2001) in which she divides women in the American, British and Dutch workforces into three groups. One group, containing 20 percent of the sample, is fundamentally home-oriented. A second 20 percent are primarily work-oriented. The remaining 60 percent she calls adaptive. They want to pursue both work and domestic goals and to have the best of both worlds.

While Hakim's numbers may be open to some minor challenges, the main point for management is crystal clear. Plan for all three groups, and do your best to determine who fits each pattern so you can motivate and reward them effectively. You can take this a step further and understand that male employees also have differing life goals, with work being of varying personal importance. Your company will get the most from each employee by recognizing this.

COMPENSATION PACKAGES FOR THE DIVERSE WORKFORCE

The foolishness of the diversity box is nicely illustrated by the usual corporate reward system, which runs counter to what we know from decades of research on rewards. Ideally, the reward should closely follow the act, the event, or the situation that merits the award. Second, it should reflect some attention to personality, personal characteristics, or something idiosyncratic about the individual.

Instead, what we find are rewards that are generally distributed by formula and given out at a fixed time of the year to everybody or almost everybody in the company. We basically have turned our back on what science has shown to be the best way to reward, and instead treat people like a slot machine: put in the Christmastime annual award coins and expect them to deliver what is ordered all year. Treating people like robots does work—to robotize them.

But monetary rewards are not the only coinage to lure and hold good people, and an understanding of the diversity in the workforce can help the company offer workers the benefits that really matter to them. For example, in the trucking industry, the lures for new drivers may be in the quality of the cab and its amenities, free telephone cards, permission to bring the driver's spouse along, and many other things to make the long, hard drive more pleasant. Why not give the same benefits for the sales force on the road?

WHAT EVERYONE WANTS

The emphasis on diversity in this article is not meant to imply there are no universal workforce desires and needs. Quite the contrary—there are four near-universals that are often shaped by diverse personal situations:

1. The desire to move up in skills, jobs, and often in responsibility.
2. The desire to do socially significant work. Ask yourself whom you would rather have working in your company—the person who, in response to the question, "What do you do?" says, "I tighten nut 7396z," or the one who says, "I make cars." It is a fair assumption that the latter worker is the more productive one whose high morale reflects management's good practices in developing its relationship with its workforce.
3. The desire to be compensated according to points one and two above. Here compensation includes what is usually called benefits.
4. Job stability. Few people today really expect their employment to be permanent. But they may reasonably expect management to be honest, forthright, and timely in informing the employees about the business, its work problems, and plans.

THE CHALLENGES OF MANAGING FOR UNIVERSAL DIVERSITY

Diversity in the firm has implications for at least three groups: senior managers, the human resources department, and frontline managers.

Senior Management

There are several factors that keep senior management in many U.S. companies from responding to the changes in the twenty-first century workforce and taking advantage of the benefits of diversity. One key problem is that most of the basic changes challenge their core assumptions about managing a successful organization. It is understandable that senior managers, being older on average than their workforce, tend to see the organizational structure and policies and practices of the environment in which they grew to power as still applicable to company success.

In addition, executives themselves are a diverse group. Those who see any change as likely to be risky will take a conservative approach to business and be wary of any new plans, programs, or policies relating to the workforce. Others suffer some degree of social isolation from the sweeping changes taking place within their own organization, among their successful competitors, and in other industries. For too many of them, diversity is only a surface activity to ensure compliance with legal requirements about workforce composition; they fail to see that diversity is universal and has advantages they should be promoting.

Other executives are aware of social changes and want to act but are constrained by superiors who see matters differently, while still others are only responding to fear of the potential negative social and moral ramifications of not having a diversity initiative. A relatively small number of executives are proactively pushing diversity initiatives because they know or believe that it improves the bottom line. Microsoft, for example, prizes the intellectual capital of its employees that has been essential to company success.

HR Departments

Many HR departments, in the past 15 years or so, have incorporated three big changes. The first two concern the outsourcing of records management and the pushing down into lower levels of operations responsibility for dealing with workers on HR issues. The third change, resulting from the first two, leaves HR more latitude for developing strategic inputs into corporate planning. These are the departments that are best positioned to take advantage of the benefits of a total diversity approach. Firms that have not adopted these new policies have left their HR departments with all the traditional functions and relatively little time to analyze and innovate with regard to the expanding diversity of the workforce and other strategic issues.

There are two primary diversity-related changes that HR should promote. First is the rewards program. The second is a focus on linking work to the employee's personal life in the areas described earlier. This work-life focus can show up in many ways, but perhaps the key now is flexibility. In so many of the areas discussed earlier—dealing with families with dependents, male or female workers seeking to enhance their personal lives, or minority workers making time for training and education; facilitating communication with and among workers who come from different national, geographic, and demographic backgrounds who often speak different languages; or developing compensation packages that address the full spectrum of employees' concerns—flexibility is a chronic and sometimes critical need. HR departments that use the reward structure and flexibility to solve the challenges of diversity can go a long way toward reversing the widely recognized decline in worker loyalty to the corporation.

Frontline Managers

The frontline manager confronts many types of diversity issues every day:

- Age differences between a younger manager and older subordinates, or the spread of ages within a team, can be troublesome for managers, because we tend psychologically to link authority to age.
- Employees have different personal preferences with regard to time, work, benefits, compensation—just about everything—that can create conflicts managers must resolve.
- Evoking from the workers critical knowledge, which they may not even see as important, or if they do, are reluctant to give out, requires attention to rewards.
- Contrary to the widespread notion that everyone wants a degree of self-direction, some workers need and want detailed descriptions of what they are to do. Managers must determine the optimal amount of direction for each employee.
- The need for training must be a subject of continual attention, especially if the work itself is changing.

Flexible, adaptive management goes against the grain of tradition; this has left many long-time managers ill equipped to do their current job. Put differently, managing diversity requires common sense that traditionally trained managers are still unaccustomed to providing. Frontline managers should receive training in interpersonal skills and in sensitivity to the individual characteristics of each worker, not to his or her diversity box. That will reward the company with far more effective supervision.

SHARING KNOWLEDGE IN THE DIVERSE COMPANY

In the culture of U.S. business, it is often taken as a mark of incompetence to ask for help, especially broadly outside one's immediate range of responsibility. There is also widespread uncertainty, even fear, that responding to a question from someone in the company who is unknown to you amounts to a giveaway of the special knowledge that is the basis for your employment.

Knowledge management has been a hot new thing in U.S. business for over a decade. It is the generalized response to an observation made by an executive at Hewlett Packard that "if HP knew what HP knows, profits would triple." Tons of money and myriad consultants have tried to meet the need implicit in that statement by offering computer systems to inventory staff knowledge and experience and to reorganize in order to channel the effective flow of inquiries and replies. All of that misses two core points: (1) the open flow of information from the total diversity of staff experience and knowledge requires a new and appropriate reward structure and (2) the open exchange of information must become an all-embracing practice beginning at the top.

MOVING BEYOND CATEGORIES

In the general business press as well as professional HR journals, there is a growing awareness of universal diversity as a positive factor, one with the potential to boost a company's bottom line. Two sections of advertorials demonstrate the increasing attention to diversity in the business sector. (An advertorial is a paid article in a newspaper or magazine often written in the style and matching the format of the publication.) The Boston Globe (October 17, 2004) ran an advertising supplement of 16 pages made up of eight advertorials and numerous display ads. The bylined articles covered aging, ethnicity, race, gender, health care, the young worker, and the disabled, as well as other topics. The second example is a 14-page piece by the Society for Human Resource Management published in the October 18, 2004, edition of Fortune magazine. It covered similar topics and offered a good bit of quantitative information.

Given that the dynamics and factors of diversity are complex, and "hard" measures are difficult to establish, how can the business case for diversity be made more robust?

Harnessing the diversity of the firm for productivity and profit requires that management keep two facts in mind. First, people are all different from each other. Second, successful management must be based on understanding specific individual differences.

Managing diversity is now a cost-effectiveness business issue, not an issue of fairness or of satisfying seemingly arbitrary government regulations. It calls for an uncommon degree of common sense, flexibility, fellowship, and HR experimentation. Try it. You cannot lose.

Managing Generation Y

Susan P. Eisner

INTRODUCTION

With the entry of Generation Y to the working world, the workforce for the first time contains four generations: *Traditionalists* (also called Veterans, Silents, or Greatest Generation; 75 million born before 1945; 10% of the workforce), *Baby Boomers* (80 million born 1945–1964, 45% of the workforce), *Generation X* (46 million born 1965–1980, 30% of the workforce), and *Generation Y* also called Echo Boomers, Millenials, Internet Generation, or Nexters; 76 million born after 1980; 15% of the workforce) (Paul, 2004; Francis-Smith, 2004; Johns, 2003; Martin and Tulgan, 2004; Raines, 2002). Despite some variations in the way the literature names these generations and classifies start and end dates, there is general descriptive consensus among academics and practitioners regarding these generations.

More important, there appears to be agreement that this confluence of generations has immediate consequences for managers. Over the next 10 years, the U.S. population older than 65 will increase by 26%, those 40–54 will fall by 5%, and those 25–30 will increase by 6% (Connelly, 2003). By 2006, two experienced workers will leave the workforce for every one who enters it (Piktialis, 2004). Already, nearly 60% of HR professionals in large companies report conflict between younger and older workers (Work Ethic Primary Conflict, 2004), and cite impending labor shortages as increasing the value of every employee (Southard and Lewis, 2004; Dealing With Your New Generation Mix, 2004). Against this backdrop, intergenerational differences may become a foremost aspect of diversity in the U.S. workplace. . . .

FOUR GENERATIONS AT WORK

The literature is remarkably consistent in its descriptions of the four generations now in today's workforce. On the whole, it describes the coexistence of age-diverse workers in a transitioning workplace once characterized by long-term, mutually loyal, employer–employee relations that produced work through command and control management. That workforce is moving toward a 21st century workplace characterized by free agency. There, workers no longer expect long-term rewards, but instead negotiate each new job seeking the best overall working environment including opportunities for training and work-life balance (Connelly, 2003; Tulgan, 2004).

The most senior generation at work today is frequently termed Traditionalists. Children of Depression and World Wars, Traditionalists were socialized through scarcity and hardship. They tend to value family and patriotism, have had a parent at home to raise children, prefer consistency, and use a top-down management style. They are inclined to inform on a need-to-know basis, be satisfied by a job well done, remain with one company over time, and have amassed wisdom and experience (Allen, 2004). Traditionalists are likely to be loyal and self-sacrificing employees who prefer a traditional, hierarchical management structure (Francis-Smith, 2004). When in command, they tend to take charge. When in doubt, they tend to do what is right (Martin and Tulgan, 2004).

The Traditionalists' children were socialized in the 1950s and 1960s feeling prosperous, safe, and that anything was possible. The largest generation in history, these Baby Boomers believe in growth, change, and expansion. Their numbers alone made them competitive. Baby Boomers tend to want it all and seek it by working long hours, showing loyalty, and being ruthless if necessary; many do not plan to retire. They are likely to respect authority, but want to be viewed and treated as equals (Allen, 2004). Baby Boomers tended to be the center of their parent's attention and redefined many social norms, especially family, in which their generation increased divorce rates. They tend to be driven to succeed and to measure that success materially. Like their parents, they are inclined to lack technological skills but to be social beings; networking works well for them in career building (Johns, 2003). Baby Boomers tend to be optimistic and confident and to value free expression and social reform (Francis-Smith, 2004).

In the workplace, Baby Boomers tend to seek consensus, dislike authoritarianism and laziness, and micro-manage others (Francis-Smith, 2004). They have paid their dues and proactively climbed the corporate ladder making new rules along the way. But now they tend to find themselves reactive in an era of downsizing and reengineering. The sink-or-swim survival mode they are accustomed to becomes more difficult as they reach a life stage in which keeping up a nonstop pace becomes an ever-greater challenge (Martin and Tulgan, 2004).

Gen X is the child of the workaholic Baby Boomer. Socialized as latchkey kids in a downsizing work world where technology was booming, Gen X tends to lack the social skills of its parents but to have strong technical ability (Johns, 2003). It is likely to be self-reliant, individualistic, distrustful of corporations, lacking in loyalty, and intent on balancing work and personal life. Independent, entrepreneurial Gen X lives on the edge and embraces change; it produced the 1990's dot-com stars. Gen X tends to be outcome-focused, and seeks specific and constructive feedback (Allen, 2004). It is skeptical but loves freedom and room to grow (Francis-Smith, 2004).

At work, Gen X is not likely to prioritize long-term employment with a single company or value long hours. It tends to respond well to competent leadership and to be educated and technically skilled enough to move into management more quickly (Francis-Smith, 2004). Gen X is likely to value developing skills more than gaining in job title and to not take well to micromanaging. Reflecting its lack of social skills, Gen X tends to be reluctant to network and is attracted more by ads and recruitment (Johns, 2003). It pioneered the free-agent workforce and believes security comes with keeping skills current. This generation is likely to find a way to get things done smartly, fast, and best even if it means bending the rules. It tends to respond well to a coaching management style that provides prompt feedback and credit for results achieved (Martin and Tulgan, 2004).

Gen Y is the most recent cohort to enter the workforce. Far larger than the generation before it, much of Gen Y was raised in a time of economic expansion and prosperity. But Gen Y is coming of age in an era of economic uncertainty and violence. Though it is the most affluent generation (Allen, 2004), some 16% of Gen Y grew up or is growing up in poverty (Raines, 2002). In its post-Columbine, post-9/11, 24-hour media world, this latest generation has seen more at an earlier age than prior generations have seen (Sujansky, 2004). It is not surprising that Gen Y reflects some values held by Traditionalists. Like that "greatest generation," Gen Y tends to have a strong sense of morality, to be patriotic, willing to fight for freedom, is sociable, and values home and family. But Gen Y's large size, level of education, and technical skill position it to echo the Baby Boomers' impact on business and society (Allen, 2004).

Having worked throughout high school while continuing to live with parents in a 24/7 digitally connected and globalizing world, Gen Y is the most technically literate, educated, and ethnically diverse generation in history and tends to have more discretionary income. It tends to want intellectual challenge, needs to succeed, seeks those who will further its professional development, strives to make a difference, and measures its own success. Meeting personal goals is likely to matter to Gen Y, as is performing meaningful work that betters the world and working with committed co-workers with shared values. Making a lot of money tends to be less important to Gen Y than contributing to society, parenting well, and enjoying a full and balanced life (Allen, 2004).

Gen Y was socialized in a digital world. It is more than technically literate; it is continually wired, plugged in, and connected to digitally streaming information, entertainment, and contacts. It has so mastered technology that multitasking is a habit it takes into the workplace, where it tends to instant message its contacts while doing work (Lewis, 2003). A recent study found Gen Y consuming 31 hours of media (through multi-tasting) within a 24-hour period (Weiss, 2003).

Gen Y has been told it can do anything and tends to believe it (Martin, 2004). It has lived with strong social stressors ranging from pressure to excel in school to parental divorce and one-parent homes. It is accustomed to being active in family decisions and is likely to expect to contribute to decisions in employer organizations (Johns, 2003). Overall, Gen Y is inclined to be positive, polite, curious, energetic, and respectful of its parents and grandparents (Francis-Smith, 2004).

In the workplace, Gen Y tends to favor an inclusive style of management, dislike slowness, and desire immediate feedback about performance (Francis-Smith, 2004). It is a truly global generation, socially conscious and volunteer-minded and positioned to be the most demanding generation. If treated professionally, it is likely to act professionally. Gen Y is likely to perform best when its abilities are identified and matched with challenging work that pushes it fully. Speed, customization, and interactivity—two-way nonpassive engagement—are likely to help keep Gen Y focused (Martin and Tulgan, 2004). Technically able, highly informed and confident, but lacking direction, Gen Y is more likely to "rock the boat" than any prior generation (Johns, 2003). . . .

GEN Y: OPPORTUNITY AND CHALLENGE

Gen Y has been deeply affected by several trends of the 1990s and 2000s: a renewed focus on children, family, scheduled and structured lives, multiculturalism, terrorism, heroism, patriotism, parent advocacy, and globalization. Coincidentally, Gen Y has been socialized with several core messages: be smart—you are special, leave no one behind, connect 24/7, achieve now, and serve your community (Raines, 2002). It tends to ignore traditional media and advertising channels, play video games, and watch DVDs rather than listed TV programming. Those in Gen Y tend to live with their parents before college, plan to return to their parents' home after college, and are less at home in the real world than in the virtual world—in which they spend more than six hours a day online. One-third of 21-year olds are not Caucasian. A similar number is being raised by single parents, and three-quarters have working mothers. Perhaps reflecting 9/11/01, Gen Y tends to want to connect with its parents rather than rebel. As consumers, Gen Y is likely to be independent and not brand loyal. Traditional at home, it tends to be nontraditional and sophisticated in the marketplace (Weiss, 2003).

Gen Y's entrance into the workplace would seem to present many opportunities in today's ever-more competitive organizations in which high-performing workers are an asset, and demographic shifts point to impending labor shortages. Gen Y workers would seem to be a timely addition. They tend to be goal-oriented (Southard and Lewis, 2004) and interested in self-development and improvement (Dealing With Your New Generational Mix, 2004). They are likely to have high expectations of personal and financial success, feel that hard work pays off, and have a get-it-done result-producing attitude (Breaux, 2003). They are inclined to plunge into work they find interesting and important even when they know little about it (Lewis, 2003).

Some of Gen Y's characteristics may make it easier to manage than Gen X. Gen Y tends to value teamwork and fairness and is likely to be more positive than Gen X on a range of workplace issues including work-life balance, performance reviews, and availability of supervisors (What You Need to Know, 2003). Moreover, Gen Y descriptors include attributes predictive of high performance. Gen Y workers are inclined to be sociable, hopeful, talented, collaborative, inclusive, and civic-minded. In addition to being well educated and technically savvy, they tend to be open-minded, achievement-oriented, and able to work on parallel tasks (Raines, 2002). Cautiously optimistic and enthusiastic about the future, Gen Y is likely to have a solid work ethic and entrepreneurial bent. At the same time, it tends to acknowledge and admire authority, especially Traditionalists. Strength, cooperation, energy, conformity, virtue, and duty tend to be among Gen Y's values (Pekala, 2001).

A recent Work and Education survey by the Gallup Organization also suggests that Gen Y will not be harder to manage than workers from other generations. Like workers in the 30–49 and 50+ age groups, Gen Y has a strong sense of company loyalty, is at least as satisfied with supervisors as are older workers, is as content as the others with the amount of praise received, and is as satisfied as the others with amount of vacation time and work flexibility or hours required. Additionally, Gen Y feels no more workplace stress than the other workers and is as satisfied as the others with retirement and health benefits (Saad, 2003).

At the same time, Gen Y's entrance to the workforce seems to present some challenges. Although Gen Y workers tend to be more positive than Gen X about working in general, Gen Y tends to be less satisfied than Gen X with their jobs and employers. The survey described earlier in this paper pinpoints several dimensions of that dissatisfaction. Further, Gen Y is more open than Gen X to leaving for something better (What You Need to Know, 2003). Gen Y is likely to equate job satisfaction with a positive work climate, flexibility, and the opportunity to learn and grow more than any prior generation. Compared with other generations, Gen Y tends to have less respect for rank and more respect for ability and accomplishment. It is likely to trade more pay for work it feels is meaningful at a company where it feels appreciated (Alati, 2004). Gen Y tends to value respect and wants to earn it. Acknowledgement and freedom to perform as it finds best tend to matter to Gen Y, too (Dealing With Your New Generational Mix, 2004).

Additionally, Gen Y workers are likely to dislike menial work, lack skills for dealing with difficult people, and be impatient (Raines, 2002). Less than half of this youngest generation describe themselves as confident or prepared to enter the workforce. Their strong technical skills are not matched by strong soft skills such as listening, communicating, independent thinking, being a team player, and managing time (Pekala, 2001). Mercer Human Resource Consultant's 2002 People at Work Survey found Gen Y rating employers lower than other employees do on being treated fairly, getting necessary cooperation from others, and having opportunity to do interesting and meaningful work (The Next Generation, 2003).

Moreover, Gen Y workers tend to look for instant gratification rather than long-term investments of time and effort (Southard and Lewis, 2004). In addition to demanding immediate rewards, they are likely to prefer special projects rather than "dues-paying chores." They often prefer being given time off to receiving money; putting in face time tends to puts them off. Accustomed to coming, going, and staying as needed, and being involved when present, Gen Y workers tend to be constant negotiators and questioners. As one author describes it, "The forty hour workweek doesn't apply . . . (and) 'how' meetings become 'why' meetings" (Lewis, 2003). Intergenerational management expert Bruce Tulgan describes the resulting challenges of Gen Y workers this way: "Gen Y'ers are like X'ers on steroids . . . They are the most high-maintenance generation to ever enter the work force" (Breaux, 2003).

RECOMMENDATIONS: MANAGEMENT STRATEGIES

Presenting both challenges and opportunities, Gen Y is entering the workforce in ever-increasing numbers. What management strategies are likely to be most effective for achieving high performance in today's intergenerational workplace? Experts suggest that managers apply messages and strategies deliberately tailored to the characteristics of each of the four generations. They recommend identifying and addressing the motivational needs of each generation, and training each generation mindful of its learning styles. Age stereotypes should be avoided, and age differences should be built into diversity training. Team building should include intergenerational pairing based on complimentary strengths. Open and ongoing discussions for discussing intergenerational needs should become corporate culture norms (Piktialis, 2004).

What strategies should resonate with Traditionalists? Members of this longest-working generation should respond well to being told that their experience is respected and important to the company and that their perseverance is valued and will be rewarded. They should be encouraged to share their knowledge of what has and has not worked in the past. They are likely to welcome training that is offered in formats consistent with their more traditional learning style (Kogan, 2001). Also, Traditionalists should be encouraged to respectfully assert their authority and demonstrate their track records. Engaging them as teachers is recommended. Rehiring them as part-time team leaders and coaches when they retire is also suggested (Martin and Tulgan, 2004).

On the other hand, Baby Boomers should respond well to being told that they are important to the organization's success, are valued for their unique and important contributions, and are needed. They should be provided feedback with sensitivity. Change should be presented to them in a way that minimizes conflict (Kogan, 2001). What's more, Baby Boomers should be encouraged to become facilitating coaches rather than authoritarian figures dictating expectations and methods. They should be offered flexibility, authority, and respect. Additionally, Baby Boomers should be challenged to keep on growing (Martin and Tulgan, 2004).

For its part, independent Gen X should respond well to being told to do things its own way, with minimal rules and bureaucracy. This first techno-savvy generation should be provided with current hardware and software (Kogan, 2001). Its growth-oriented nature should be managed with a coaching style. At the same time, this outcome-focused generation should be asked to learn just-in-time for each new assignment (Martin and Tulgan, 2004).

The newest entrants to the workplace, the Gen Y group, are largely uncharted territory for many managers. Gen Y workers tend to have unbridled energy, endless enthusiasm, and the skills and experience of those much older. They too, then, should be managed with a coaching style (Sujansky, 2002). Gen Y should respond well to being told that it will be working with other bright and creative people, and that the boss is over 60. Hearing that, together with peers, they can turn the company around, and that they can be heroes at the company, should also resonate with Gen Y workers (Kogan, 2001). Flexibility and voice, access to co-workers and company information through technology, and project-centered work are recommended (Allen, 2004). Expectations should be explained to Gen Y from the outset, including the big picture and how they fit into it. Gen Y should be given a sense of belonging (Hansford, 2002).

Leaders would do well to model expected behavior for Gen Y workers and interact with them, creating a sense of enjoyment and challenge. Candid talk without hype and with a sense of humor should help reach Gen Y. Movement toward cultural openness and transparency is recommended, as is investment in programs encouraging teamwork and flexibility. At the same time, roles and responsibilities should be defined and written for Gen Y. Task lists and time-lines should suggest how and when to reach goals (Dealing With Your New Generation Mix, 2004).

Job conditions that cannot be attained should not be promised, as doing so will leave Gen Y feeling disappointed and betrayed. Instead, Gen Y workers should be given the chance to contribute to a greater good and to work for a socially responsible company (Loughlin and Barling, 2001).

Spaces, processes, and practices tailored to Gen Y should be well worth the cost. Office spaces set up to facilitate the exchange of ideas with others are recommended. Goal accomplishment in Gen Y team projects should be evaluated as a whole. Reverse mentor programs in which Gen Y's technical skills can be recognized and shared are also suggested (Raines, 2002).

Furthermore, it is advisable to meet the high expectations of Gen Y workers with respect and positivism (Raines, 2002). Digital-based training programs should resonate with Gen Y, for whom work and play are blended and achievement and winning matter. Training for Gen Y workers should focus on strategic areas and not be trivial. Optimally, it will engage them experientially, allow for practice, and provide a valued pay-off at the end (Salopek, 2003).

Some companies are tackling the challenges of recruiting and retaining Gen Y using innovative strategies tailored to Gen Y characteristics. These techniques include providing on-site leadership academies, creating formal mentoring programs to maximize Gen Y access, and giving early chances to do meaningful work. To better reach Gen Y, some are streamlining the recruitment process and providing longer vacations after shorter service. For similar reasons, some are building comprehensive intranet sites, allowing conversion of unused administrative leave into cash, and permitting conversion of health benefits into deferred compensation accounts (Southard and Lewis, 2004).

Some companies are literally going where Gen Y workers are, connecting with them through the media and locations such as Internet cafes and video game stores. Or they recruit Gen Y through on-site career-day seminars in which ranking personnel share their own success stores. Some companies are using their Gen Y employees as the first outreachers to peer Gen Y candidates in an effort to quicken the pace of recruitment. In this way, the companies aim to both engage their Gen Y employees more fully and to create a workplace ally for the Gen Y candidate (Employing Generation Why, 2004).

WIDER HORIZONS?

A 2001 article by Loughlin and Barling provides solid foundation for understanding the context within which today's intergenerational workforce operates. It reports that almost 80% of North American high school students worked part-time for pay before graduating from high school. Coinciding with this unprecedented rate of employment is the conclusion Gen Y has drawn from their parents' work experience. Gen Y workers tend to distrust long-term job security and seek immediate payoffs from employers as a result. Many have developed a work-to-live rather than live-to-work mindset that spills over into valuing the quality of the work environment as well as work-life balance. Moreover, an increasing number of jobs awaiting Gen Y are "non-standard;" 30% of North American and European jobs are temporary, part-time, or contract. Under-employment is an additional reality. Some 75% of the labor force in most industrial countries is doing little more than simple, repetitive tasks. The level of skilled jobs available is far less than the skill levels of the employable population (Loughlin and Barling, 2001).

In 2003, intergenerational expert Bruce Tulgan reported the results of a comprehensive 10-year study that interviewed more than 10,000 people and studied management practices of more than 700 companies to explore the contemporary U.S. workplace. The study found generational shifts amounting to significant and lasting workplace changes. Tulgan states, "Between 1993 and 2003, a profound revolution has taken place in the values and norms of the U.S. workforce; the impact has been felt throughout the world . . . the new economy is a far cry from dot-coms with magical business models, and rather has created a very challenging environment for most workers today" (Tulgan, 2004).

In that study, Tulgan identified several core dimensions of the workplace transformation. First, work has become more demanding. Second, the employer–employee relationship has become less hierarchical and more

Table 1   Summary (1) — Four Generations at Work

	Traditionalists *75 million born pre-1945; 10% of workforce*	**Baby Boomers** *80 million born 1945–1964; 45% of workforce*	**Generation X** *46 million born 1965–1980; 30% of workforce*	**Generation Y** *76 million born post-1980; 15% of workforce*
Formative Events	Great depression World war	Post-war prosperity Largest generation	Globalization Downsizing Technology boom	Prosperity/uncertainty Violence/terrorism Outsourcing/under-employment
Socialization	Scarcity/hardship Parent at home	Prosperous/safe Anything is possible Parent's focal point	Latchkey kids	Strong social pressure Structured life/live at home Nontraditional families Active role in family Fallout from work Nonstandard word Multiculturalism
Imprint Made	Greatest generation Dual incomes	Free generation Redefined norms Civil rights	Me generation Dot.com stars Free agency	We generation Wired/switch/populist Work at early age/worldly
Pattern	Stay with company	Loyal Workalcoholic Sink or swim	Live on edge Embrace change Devalue long hours Job hop Will find a way	Expect to make decisions Need to achieve/self-reliant Curious/energetic/question Distrust job security Dislike face time/menial job
Qualities	Loyal Self-sacrificing	Pro-growth/change Competitive Optimistic/confident Paid dues/climbed Want it all	Independent Individualistic Distrust companies Lack loyalty Entrepreneurial	Large size/diverse/loyal Skilled/energetic Polite/positive/leave none Socially conscious/hopeful Sophisticated/demanding
Value	Family Patriotism	Success/materially Free expression Reform Equity	Skill more than title Work-life balance	Heroism/patriot/virtue/duty Elderly/family/home/time Service/respect more than $ Work to live; shared norms

transactional. Third, employers have moved away from long-term employment relationships. Fourth, employees have less confidence in long-term rewards and greater expectations for short-term rewards. Fifth, immediate supervisors have become the most important people in the workplace. Sixth, supervising employees now requires more time and skill at the very time when there are fewer managers (Tulgan, 2004).

Tulgan's study depicts a 21st century workplace in which traditional career paths and management techniques, long-term employment, and cookie cutter approaches to employee relations are disappearing. What replaces them? Employees take responsibility for their own success and failure. Employees make their own way by attaining and marketing cutting edge skills that they

Table 2   Summary (2) — Four Generations at Work

	Generation 1	Generation 2	Generation 3	Generation 4
Assets	Wisdom Experience Perseverance	Social skills	Technology skills Education Fast track to manage	Educated/experienced Sociable/technical/perform Work ethic/multitask
Lack	Technology skills	Technology skills	Social skills	Direction/focus/confidence Interpersonal/soft skills
Style	Top-down Directive Inform as needed Take charge Do what's right	Respect authority Network Micro-manage Proactive Work hard	Skeptical Reluctant to network Outcome-focused Achieve well/fast Bend rules as need	Get done/produce/negotiate Plunge right in/fast-paced Open and civic minded Blend work and play Measure own success
Strategy for	Respect experience Share past lessons Reward staying Teach to assert Match learning style Use as teachers Rehire to coach/lead	Give important roles Value contributions Show respect Minimize conflict Sensitize feedback Be flexible Challenge to grow Have coach/facilitate	Recruit traditionally/ad Manage by coach Don't micro-manage Reduce rules/layers Allow innovation Update technology Feedback quickly Specify and help Credit for results Train just in time	Treat fairly/professionally Give meaningful/fun work Challenge intellectually Meet growth/personal goals Model expected behavior Manage inclusively/belong Provide importance/voice Have positive/open environ Don't over-promise/hype Assign projects/teams/tasks Allow freedom to try/access Focus by speed/target/win Train strategically/digitally Clarify big picture/timeline Specify roles/responsibilities Use to reverse mentor Streamline/target recruiting

leverage through networking into career opportunity. Managers are pressured to hire the best person for every opening. Managers aggressively push each person to unleash the highest productivity (Tulgan, 2004).

The result? Tulgan's study projects an inevitable push-pull between the employer's need to squeeze the employee and the employee's need for quality of work life. To resolve this, the employee is likely to become more assertive about exacting short-term transactions in return for meeting the employer's goals. Tulgan describes that transforming 21st century workplace this way: "Managers will have to discard traditional authority, rules, and red tape, and become highly engaged in one-on-one negotiation and coaching with employees to drive productivity, quality, and innovation" (Tulgan, 2004).

To older workers, that description may seem like a brave new world in which the culture shock is unpalatable and even incomprehensible. But younger workers may have a leg up. The following summary of this paper shows that, to Gen Y, the workplace Tulgan describes seems very much like the one it expects to enter. . . .

Because the managerial implication of Gen Y's entrance to the contemporary workplace is still largely uncharted territory, it may be helpful to present some recurring comments from such discussions. First, some say that generational labels tend to be determined by marketers, and should not be allowed to create differences between people that might otherwise not exist. A second point some raise is that managers should be careful not to oversimplify workplace differences, but should see intergenerational differences as one of several aspects of diversity. A third set of comments contemplates the consequences of management failure to manage intergenerational realities and projects the resulting possibility of further erosion of psychological contract between manager and employee. This is a particularly interesting line of thought given the free agent, quality of work life, and inclusive mindset of newer entrants to the workplace. If these workers are alienated by managerial strategies that do not resonate with them, will managers be able to retain them, let alone unleash their potential? The relevance of that question is underscored by a final line of comment, expressed repeatedly by those of Gen Y: Will managers recognize intergenerational workplace factors and begin to use responsive strategies that optimize this aspect of diversity?

What strategies should a leader consider in successfully dealing with age diversity?

REFERENCES

Alati, D. (2004, May). Retention race. Incentive, 178(5), 6.

Allen, P. (2004, September). Welcoming Y. Benefits Canada, 28(9), 51(3).

Breaux, J. (2003, November 19). Face of American workplaces is changes, human resource professionals say. *Knight Ridder/Tribune Business News.*

Connelly, J. (2003, October 28). Youthful attitudes, sobering realities. *The New York Times.*

Dealing with your new generation mix. (2004, August). *Accounting Office Management & Administrative Report*, 4(8), 5–7+ (4).

Employing generation why? (2002). *Workforce Management*. Retrieved on November 2, 2004, from http:// www.workforce.com

Francis-Smith, J. (2004, August 26). Surviving and thriving in the multi-generational workplace. *Journal Record*, 1.

Hansford, D. (2002, June). Insights into managing an age-diverse work-force. *Workspan*, *45*(6), 48–54.

Johns, K. (2003, April 11). Managing generational diversity in the work-force. *Trends & Tidbits*. Retrieved on October 10, 2004, from http:// www.workindex.com

Kogan, M. (2001, September 1). Talkin' 'bout four generations. Govexec. Retrieved on October 29, 2004, from http:www.govexec.com

Lewis, K. R. (2003, November 3). Managing multiple generations in the workplace can be a challenge. *Newhouse News Service*.

Loughlin, C., and Barling, J. (2001, November). Young workers' work values, attitudes, and behaviours. *Journal of Occupational and Organizational Psychology*, 74(4), 543–558.

Martin, C., and Tulgan, B. (n.d.) Managing the generation mix—part II. *Top Echelon, Employers*. Retrieved on October 29, 2004, from Pekala, N. (2001, November/December). Conquering the generational divide. *Journal of Property Management*, 66(6), 30–38.

Piktialis, D. (2004, August). Bridging generational divides to increase inno-vation, creativity, and productivity. *Workspan*, 47(8), 26–41.

Raines, C. (2002). Managing millenials. *Generations At Work*. Retrieved on October 29, 2004, from http:// www.generationsatwork.com

Saad, L. (2003, October 14). Are young employees harder to manage? *The Gallup Organization*. Retrieved on February 11, 2005, from The Gallup Brain database.

Salopek, J. (2003, June). Going native: cross the generation gap by learning to speak. T+D, 57(6), 17 (3).

Southard, G., and Lewis, J. (2004, April). Building a workplace that recog-nizes generational diversity. Public Management, 86(3), 8(5).

Sujansky, J. (2002, May). The critical care and feeding of generation Y. *Workforce*, 81(5), 15.

Sujansky, J. (2004, April). Leading a multi-generational workforce. *Occu-pational Health and Safety*, 73(4), 16–18.

Thtulgan, B. (2004, Winter). Trends point to a dramatic generational shift in the future workforce. Employment Relations Today, 30(4), 23–31.

Weiss, M. J. (2003, September 1). To be about to be (Generation Y). *American Demographics*, 25(7).

Work ethic primary conflict among different generations. (2004, August 25). *PR Newswire*.

ISSUE SUMMARY

The discussion of workplace diversity is not complete without attention to its impact on return-on-investment (ROI). Any organization desiring to achieve diversity goals must pay attention to the bottom line. However, even in this age of sophisticated measures, the calculus of diversity ROI is difficult to identify. Some organizations invest considerable time and effort devising causal equations that link diversity factors with performance and productivity. Certifications in diversity ROI are available for professionals who are charged with calculating the impact of diversity on the bottom line. The approach of diversity analysts is to isolate, measure, and track diversity-related data to explain the effects of diversity.

Others believe causal models are inappropriate, given the improbability of converting diversity factors into dollars and cents. This diversity-ROI calculation uses the costs and benefits of the diversity initiative as the metric, instead of conducting an audit of diversity factors in the workforce.

Regardless of the metric used, it is clear that the return on investment of diversity needs to be known. Any organization should know whether its commitment is more than mission/vision statements. It takes more than words to make diversity integral to an organization's goals and success. For some it takes more than goodwill or "doing the right thing." Today it takes metrics.

ISSUE HIGHLIGHTS

- Workplace diversity has evolved from assimilation to valuing and managing diversity.
- Organizations that value cultural differences use the unique talents of every employee to increase effectiveness and competitiveness.
- Today, workplace diversity is viewed as a business imperative.
- Traditional diversity training programs are no longer adequate for handling diverse employees.
- "Harnessing" diversity is predicated on an understanding of specific individual differences.
- The presence of four generations in the workforce has definite consequences for leaders of organizations.

CRITICAL THINKING

Diversity of the workforce is a good thing for organizations, but are leaders convinced of that? When times are good economically, diversity programs thrive. However, studies show that when times are bad, diversity programs are the first to be reduced or cut. The issue for leaders, as cited by Nancy

Lockwood in the first reading, is "sustained involvement." For diversity to be on the agenda in good times, but off again in an economic downturn is an indication that diversity is not being sustained.

The problem could well be that leaders are not applying systems thinking to the diversity question. For leaders to capitalize on diversity, any initiative must be related to the organization's vision of the future and shaped through group dialogue. Some believe that an initiative fails if it does not have force of an imperative:

> The imperative must be developed in a rigorous manner—with the input of all the business units and functions that will need to implement the imperative. Although there are many reasons for an organization to want greater diversity, it is critical to identify the one or two key drivers that are compelling action. Failure to identify the impetus driving a need for change, results in a diffused initiative — one that is both hard to manage and lacks real accountability measures. The organizational imperative should inform the work and actions needed to achieve it like any other strategic initiative and should be clear, compelling, and strong enough that people in the organization see the direct link between organizational success and the effort. (Katz & Miller, 2004)

This leads back to the issue of diversity-ROI. It is apparent that diversity management must be more than a matter of the heart and conscience for some organizations. Using a systems approach to make the business case for diversity appears to be the best approach if organizations desire to sustain their commitment.

ADDITIONAL READING RESOURCES

The Business Case for Diversity., DiversityInc., 2006.

Judith H. Katz & Frederick A. Miller, Redefining the imperative for leveraging diversity and inclusion: A fresh look." *The CEO Refresher*, 2004.

Leo Parvis, Diversity and effective leadership in multicultural workplaces." *Journal of Environmental Health*, March 2003.

Joanne Sujansky, Leading a multi-generational workforce. *Occupational Health and Safety*, April, 2004.

Bruce Thigan, Trends point to a dramatic generational shift in the future workforce. *Employment Relations Today*, Winter 2004.

For more on diversity-ROI, visit these sites:

http://www.diversityinc.com/public/dibenchmarking.htm
http://www.diversityroi.com
http://www.hubbardnhubbardinc.com/diversity_roi.htm

How Is Globalization Affecting Organizations around the World?

INTRODUCTION

In very intriguing ways, worldwide ease of commerce and access to the Internet are shrinking time and space (Harvey, 1990). Around the world, people are able to gather information, exchange services, sell products, and network with others easier and faster than ever before. This sense of a connected, barrier-free world is a common understanding of what globalization means. When globalization is thought of as global connectivity, we use terms like global village, world citizens, and technoscapes.

Globalization can also be thought of as a growing awareness of the interdependence of the world's peoples. Interdependence, which is deeper than connectivity, has economic, political, and technological aspects that can be positive or negative. Some view the economic impact of globalization positively, and refer to the growth of free trade and better allocation of resources. Others see a negative economic impact, citing uneven distribution of labor and Third World outsourcing. Depending on the point of view, free trade either decreases the gap between rich and poor or it increases the gap. On the political side, there are claims that globalization restricts the rights of individuals in order to promote a universal capitalist agenda. And there are counter claims that, by harmonizing national laws and standards, globalization enhances human rights. Regardless of perspective, we are coming to understand that the processes of globalization are neither inevitable nor smooth.

There is no question that globalization is changing organizations and their leaders. Many aspects of organizations—from communication to partnerships to markets to services—are impacted by international interdependence. And to a certain extent, globalization affects even those organizations whose mind is not on macroeconomic issues such as import-export balance, exchange rates, and under- or overvalued currencies. Consider a community nonprofit that markets fair trade products on its Web site or a national youth organization whose partners are all international corporations.

Globalization, in terms of interconnectedness and acceleration of activity, is evident in the way organizations offer their products and services to the

171

public these days. But when one nation's corporations dominate worldwide sales or services, the rest of the world doesn't necessarily respond favorably. According to the author of the first reading, "Rebuilding Brand America: Corporate America's Role," this is exactly the situation for America. While firms have been spreading the idea of free-market capitalism around the globe, the reaction of people, particularly in the Third World, is increasingly negative. Globalization's effects are not always positive.

So what should leaders do when organizations lose their good reputation in the world? Martin believes the problem is not the message, but the brand. He is not referring to a product or service brand, but to the brand of capitalism American organizations are communicating to the world. How leaders and employees act and portray their organization has a lot to do with the outcome of globalization. To Martin, this is a matter of organizational leadership. By attending to relationship and public diplomacy, organizational leaders can gain legitimacy in the global marketplace and put a different face on capitalism.

The negative image of free-market capitalism is one impediment in the process of globalization. Another impediment is insufficient innovation. This is the focus of the second reading summarizing results of a survey conducted by The Council on Competitiveness. The council was founded on the premise that to succeed in global markets, organizations must be innovation-driven. When reading this summary, keep in mind that innovation is not limited to product development. In today's world, innovation in management, systems, leadership, and work environment are more crucial than simply improving a product. Results of the survey show that while leaders believe innovation is valuable for global competition, there are significant barriers that diminish the capacity of organizations for innovation. This gap is definitely problematic according to a recent editorial by the CEO of the council:

> In this hyper-competitive, rapidly changing environment, it is clear that firms in the United States cannot compete on low wages, commodity products, standard services, and routine science and technology development. Science and technology are not enough. Lower cost and improving quality alone won't answer the new competitive realities either, as they have become merely the baseline for entry into global markets. (Wince-Smith, 2006)

The final reading is based on the premise that the effects of globalization are so intertwined, it is impossible to point to one aspect that impacts organizations more than another. The title, "Making the Trend Your Friend," may make it sound like globalization is a simple matter, but the trends are complex and it is crucial for organizations to heed them. All ten trends are global and cover the gamut of business, social, and technological dimensions of globalization.

These readings on the connections between globalization and organizations point to accelerating forces that are technological, political, and economic. All of these forces, while unpredictable, play a significant role in how organizations function. One thing is certain, change is global. To prosper in this time, organizations and their leaders need critical skills in discerning the future, designing partnerships, and anticipating new directions.

SOURCES

Dick Martin, Rebuilding brand America: Corporate America's role. *Journal of Business Strategy*, vol. 27, no. 3, 2006.

Richard Seline, "2005 National Innovation Survey." *New Economy Strategies*, 2005.

Karen Crennan, Paul F. Nunes, & Marcia A. Halfin, Making the trend your friend. *Outlook*, 2006.

ARTICLE 6.1

Rebuilding Brand America: Corporate America's Role

Dick Martin

The world, we are told, is flat. It is also tipping, and not in America's favor. Pollsters tell us that US foreign policy—especially in the Middle East—accounts for 35 percent of anti-American feelings around the world. But that's small comfort for American businesses, which not only share plenty of blame for the balance but may be unwittingly contributing to the tilt.[1]

When communism collapsed, it seemed that free-market capitalism had become the world's reigning economic ideology; US corporations, its principle delivery vehicle. The Wall Street Journal was even moved to editorialize that "We are all capitalists now".[2] Well, we are not all happy about it.

Consider how closely American-style capitalism is identified with the current activist bugaboo, globalization. US firms account for less than a third of the sales of the top 200 companies in the world. In fact, of the top 200, Japanese firms account for almost 39 percent of total sales compared to US firms' 28 percent. But when was the last time you heard of someone marching on the local Sony office to protest globalization?

The reason may be that much of the world has a sharply different conception of "capitalism," and subsequently of a corporation's role in society, than the American model. Charles Hampden-Turner and Alfons Trompenaars asked 15,000 executives from around the world to choose one of the following as the proper goal of a corporation:

- the only real goal of a corporation is making a profit; or
- a company, besides making profit, has the goal of attaining the well-being of various stakeholders, such as employees, customers, etc.

Out of the 12 nationalities surveyed, 40 percent of American managers said the sole goal of the corporation was to make a profit, compared to less than 30 percent of their non-Anglo-Saxon counterparts.[3]

A 2003 survey by the Pew Research Center showed broad support for the "free market model" in Eastern Europe, sub-Saharan Africa, the Middle East or Asia.[4] But when the possible impacts of free market capitalism get specific—such as closing inefficient factories or laying off large numbers of people—a great deal of resistance surfaces. In India, for example, 53 percent say they favor free markets, but 78 percent oppose closing inefficient factories.

Many protests against "globalization" are rooted in the perception it is being driven by US companies trying to export a "stock ticker" capitalism that sacrifices human values on the altar of quarterly earnings expectations. Globalization not only crowds Tintin, Orangina and Wimpies off the shelves, it forces local companies to change their social contract in a race to the bottom where Deutsche Bank will be no more German than CitiGroup.

People in industrialized countries worry that American-style capitalism will eventually lead to massive layoffs and a general meaning and leaning of the workplace for those who survive. People in the third world worry about being exploited only to be discarded when American sweat-shops and natural resource companies have stripped them clean. It is not only US foreign policy that is seen as arrogant, heavy-handed and self-centered, so is American business. The "ugly American" of the 1950s was loud, boring and obnoxious. His twenty-first century descendant is all that, plus a sharp-elbowed, sanctimonious bully who patronizingly assumes that, given the chance, everyone would adopt his way of life in a heartbeat. Meanwhile, he will force it on them.

When European intellectuals complain about the pervasive influence of American culture, they are not so much bemoaning our fast food, gangster rap and movie violence as our hyper-competitive, share-price obsessed business culture. Jack Welch scares them much more than Britney Spears.

Right or wrong, these perceptions have significant implications for American businesses.

Hard-core anti-American activists have already demonstrated how they can inflame the emotions of the larger body of consumers when a potential forum (e.g. a meeting of the World Bank) meets examples of "bad behavior," either by the American government (e.g. Abu Ghraib prison) or a US-based corporation (e.g. allegations that Coke is stealing water from peasants in India). In such an environment, iconic American corporations can find themselves the target of attack if only because they have publicity value. For example, globalization protestors trashed a McDonald's restaurant in Bern, Switzerland, during the 2001 World Economic Conference being held in Davos, three hours away by train over the Alps.

Though isolated, such incidents surely reinforce attitudes with long-term consequences. We are all wired to keep our thoughts, feelings and actions in sync one way or another. Anyone who believes action follows feelings knows that the impact of negative attitudes towards America and all things American will one day be felt. Business people who believe otherwise are like the window washer who fell off the scaffolding of a skyscraper and yelled "so far so good" as he plunged by the 13th floor.

Anti-American feelings already contribute to a hostile business environment, increasing security costs in overseas facilities and making it more difficult to recruit employees outside the US as well as to win public approval for mergers, opening new facilities, etc.

The risks are significant. General Electric, for example, expects 60 percent of its growth to come from developing countries in the next decade versus about 20 percent for the past ten years. Countless American companies share similar ambitions.

The solution is not to create distance between company and country of origin (which is probably impossible in an era when information flows so freely), but to build a bridge between company and country of interest. That is why business leaders cannot look solely to the government to solve the problem.

This is not a messaging problem. It is a brand problem.

THE POWER OF BRANDS

Any cowboy with a hot iron can create a brand. In fact, brands started as a signal of ownership and evolved into a ''maker's mark'' in the world of artisans and, later, manufactured goods. Over time, the brand mark became a sign of quality and consistency. When you pass through the golden arches of a McDonald's restaurant, you assume that the burgers and fries you scarf in Bangkok will taste just like the ones you had in Boston. You expect the tables, floors and bathrooms to be clean. And you expect the time between ordering and getting your food to be relatively brief. That is your left brain at work.

But brands are most powerful when they ignite synapses on the right side of your brain. The power of the McDonald's brand rests not only in its information content, but in the emotions it evokes. Some of those feelings derive from memories of the context within which you used the brand in the past— Saturday afternoons eating Big Macs with your dad after a little league game or Friday evenings hanging out in the parking lot with your friends. Brands are not concerned so much with what you think, but with what you feel. That distinction can make all the difference. Brain scientist Donald Calne argues that the ''essential difference between emotion and reason is that while reason leads to conclusions, emotion leads to action''.[5] . . .

Brands do not stimulate considered decisions, they are visceral. The Coca-Cola Company learned that the hard way when it introduced New Coke in 1985. They re-jiggered the soft drink's famous secret formula because their own blind taste tests showed that people preferred Pepsi to Coke. Despite their marketing prowess, Coke's executives missed the key point of the tests—they were blind. When people knew which brown, fizzy liquid was Coke, most said it tasted better. Their taste buds were overwhelmed by the symbology surrounding Coke, the feelings of refreshment it evoked, maybe even the warm memories of small town parades and patriotism. Researchers at the Baylor School of Medicine have even been able to track the phenomenon on brain scans (McClure et al., 2004). Coke's brand has insinuated itself into people's nervous system so deeply that when people see the Coke label their dorsolateral prefrontal cortex and hippocampus light up like a Christmas tree. Both of these areas are implicated in modifying behavior based on emotion and affect. Your taste buds may say you prefer Pepsi, but your hippocampus overrules them.

A brand exists not in ads or on the store shelves, but in a consumer's head. It sums up the consumer's ideas and feelings about a particular product based on everything she has read, seen, heard and, most importantly, experienced—not all of which is under a brand's control. As van Ham (2001) observed in *Foreign Affairs* magazine, for global consumers "brands and states often merge." Thus Mercedes evokes German engineering precision; Hermes scarves, French *élan* and style; Sony consumer electronics, Japanese ingenuity and compactness.

But that synergy only works when it is accurate and salient. The German people really do have a long history of engineering achievement, and it is obviously relevant to the manufacture of automobiles. Mercedes is smart to link itself to that heritage and to reinforce it in its communications from the exact machining of its three-pointed star logo to the dominant use of silver in its sales brochures and showrooms. Finally, the car itself delivers on the implicit promise. Audi's efforts to make the same connections were undermined by its refusal to accept responsibility for accelerator problems in the early 1990s. And the house of Chanel understandably does nothing to play up the German roots of its star designer, Karl Lagerfeld.

The question at hand is what aspects of brand America are salient to American brands. The five top brands in the 2005 study conducted by the Interbrand consultancy are US-based. They range from Coke and Microsoft, in first and second positions respectively, to industrial giants IBM, GE and Intel in third, fourth and fifth places. From the perspective of a global customer, the only thing those companies have in common is their "American personality."

The USA's brand manager-in-chief, George W. Bush, has been outspoken on the attributes he would associate with brand America—opportunity, democracy, freedom. Anti-Americans have been just as vociferous—America stands for exploitation, corruption, and hyper-materialism. Bush believes Americans are a "God-fearing" people. But to paraphrase Tolstoy, friends of the US are all alike, anti-Americans are all anti-American in their own way. Europeans are put off by the ostentatious religiosity of many American leaders; Muslims consider Americans materialistic, irreligious hypocrites. But one attribute seems to run from the intellectual salons of Europe through the *madrassa* of the Islamic world. Harvard Business School dean John Quelch first identified its emergence as a "consumer lifestyle with broad international appeal that is grounded in a rejection of American capitalism".[6] The point of salience between brand America and corporate America is our brand of capitalism.

That does not mean US companies need to abandon their values when operating overseas. But they should consider precisely how they express them. They need a global brand development plan to ensure a stable environment within which to do business. Successful US-based global brands follow three best practices: they sink deep roots wherever they do business, they share their customers' cares and they share their dreams.

SINK ROOTS, DO NOT JUST SPREAD BRANCHES

Thanks to an influential article in the *Harvard Business Review* by B-school professor Ted Levitt (Levitt, 1983), a generation of MBAs was brought up thinking that the world was morphing into one global market for standardized products. Levitt may have been ahead of time by a century or two.

For example, MTV looks like the very exemplar of a Levittian global brand. And indeed it entered Europe in 1987 with pan-regional, advertiser-supported English programming. Within a few years, however, MTV discovered that the sum was smaller than its parts—there were far more local ad buys than pan-European. There simply were not many advertisers who offered the same product across Europe. Further, while young people shared many common attitudes and musical tastes, there were also sharp differences from country to country. When local competitors began to exploit these differences, MTV quickly changed business models.

Does the mantra "think global, act local" describe this best practice?

Today, MTV Europe is in 41 countries with multiple languages and formats and nearly 50 percent local programming. In all, MTV runs 80 distinct music programming services in Canada, Asia, Europe, Australia, Latin America, the Caribbean and Africa. It tailors its channels to local cultural tastes with a mixture of national, regional and international artists, along with locally produced and globally shared programming.

Successful global companies adopt a local face and adapt to local culture.

When Proctor & Gamble entered the Chinese market in the late 1980s, one of their first steps was to recruit the top students at the 25 leading Chinese universities. They hired about 200 students a year in the early years and today P&G is a net exporter of talent from China to other countries, meaning that there are more Chinese P&G people abroad than P&G people from other countries in China.

Hiring local managers sends a signal that a company has come to stay. But it also ensures the company understands and respects local culture. In addition to hiring and developing local managers, P&G dispatches hundreds of researchers to live with Chinese families and observe how they approach everyday tasks from changing the baby to brushing their teeth. The resulting knowledge plays in everything from the names of products to their formulas. For example, P&G's brands in China have distinctly Chinese names. "Pampers," for example, is translated into three Chinese characters meaning "help," "baby's," and "comfort." And P&G formulates products using local flavors, colors, and textures. A jasmine-flavored Crest toothpaste, for example, builds on the Chinese belief that tea is good at controlling bad breath. . . .

"We don't act local; we are local," said Walt Riker, a spokesman at McDonald's. Indeed, when McDonald's French restaurants came under attack as a symbol of American culinary and cultural imperialism, the local managers ran ads in French newspapers making fun of Americans and their food choices.

One depicted a beefy American cowboy and said that although McDonald's was born in the US, its food was made in France, by French suppliers using French products. . . .

Of course, effective brand management means ensuring that a customer's experience is consistent with a company's brand values, even if the way those values are expressed varies from market to market. McDonald's core values of quality, service and cleanliness are broad enough to include wine, where that is an expected—not just accepted—menu item. But their values of food, family and fun are incompatible with gambling even if plenty of other Las Vegas fast-food restaurants have slot machines near the indoor playground.

Localization is not abdication. In fact, it requires an even deeper under-standing of a company's core values and business processes than operating in its home territory. Training and performance reviews are essential to ensure that a company does not lose its soul when it ventures into global markets. McDonald's famous Hamburger University teaches in 28 languages because restaurant managers from around the world are expected to cycle through. They also leave with an operating manual that is six inches thick.

Part of the secret to global success is knowing when to be local.

SHARE YOUR CUSTOMERS' CARES

According to the *Harvard Business Review*, consumers outside the Anglo-Saxon world hold global brands to even higher standards of social responsi-bility than local brands. They do not demand that the corner gas station try to solve the global warming problem, but they expect the giant oil companies "to address social problems linked to what they sell and how they do business" (Holt et al., 2004).

These consumers accurately see multi-national companies as the most powerful institutions on the planet. They expect more than "philanthropy" or "charity" from them. John D. Rockefeller may have softened his image by dispensing shiny new dimes to street urchins, but benevolent paternalism is not enough. And enlightened self-interest, especially if it is designed to co-opt efforts to regulate their behavior, also falls short. Global consumers expect global companies to be active at the intersection of society's needs and the company's unique capabilities.

Management guru Peter Drucker cautioned companies not to get sucked into social causes far removed from their area of expertise. But he also exhorted them to be active at the intersection of their specific competence and society's needs. "Corporations are in the community," he argued. "They cannot retreat into isolation when the world around them goes to pieces" (Drucker, 1989). For example, at the beginning of the twentieth century, Sears Roebuck realized that its mail-order business depended more on what farmers could afford to buy than on what it was trying to sell. But farmers of the time were dirt-poor, isolated and ignorant of modern agricultural techniques. So Sears invented the farm agent to introduce new methods. It financed the program for ten years until it was so successful the government took it over. By then, farm families had sufficient purchasing power to buy from the Sears Roebuck catalog, eventually making Sears the world's largest, most profitable retailer. . . .

Corporate social responsibility is not what the vice president of being nice is supposed to do. It only works when it fits a company's competence and is a targeted extension of its business, not a distraction. Then it is the source of real competitive advantage.

A global company's best partner in that kind of social responsibility can be the very non-governmental organizations (NGOs) that were once little more than stiff-necked, tree-hugging critics. Lester Salamon, founding director of John Hopkins Institute for Policy Studies, claims that the role of NGOs in the twenty-first century will be as significant as the role of the nation state in the twentieth. More than 2,000 NGOs have consultative status with the UN. And an annual survey by the Edelman public relations agency has consistently shown public confidence in NGOs outpacing that of governments, businesses and the media.

Of course, corporations and NGOs do not always see eye-to-eye. Like a good exercise coach, one of an NGO's functions in life is to push companies and governments to go further than they would if left at their own comfort levels. But the largest NGOs also understand the limits of a purely adversarial relationship. Randall Hayes founder of the Rainforest Action Network explained it well in a talk to other activists:

> If you [as an NGO] are not talking to business, you are just preaching to the choir. Real change . . . is going to come from the business sector; we can't depend on government regulation to solve our problems.

Further, companies have long entered new markets with partners who know the lay of the land. Today, when the landscape includes social and political issues as foreign to corporate managers as the indigenous language, those partners are likely to include non-governmental organizations. The UK's Sir Anthony Hurd remembers that one of his deputies seemed to surround herself with NGOs, and not just for defensive reasons. Hurd explained:

> If you want to know about the Sudan, you don't go to the Foreign Office anymore. You go to the Church of England or to Oxfam. They actually do have a much wider experience of information than the representatives of government in dealing with that country.

In addition to providing intelligence on the new market, they also bring perspectives that can help avoid missteps. . . .

SHARE YOUR CUSTOMERS' DREAMS

Ever since the first man or woman drew on a cave wall, one of the ways we have made sense of the world is by telling stories. Brands serve the same function. They are the stories that run through people's minds as they wheel their cart up and down the supermarket aisles or examine a business card. They drive awareness, consideration, trial and purchase. The clarity, consistency and credibility of a company's brand story is what sets it apart from its competitors.

The most successful global brands tell stories that are so evocative of their customers' values, hopes and aspirations that they rise to the level of "myths." The popular definition of "myth" today is a "tall tale." But it actually has a deeper psychological meaning. King Arthur, the Knights of the Round Table and Camelot may not have existed, but the Arthurian legend tells us a lot about the world-view of the people who embraced the story and kept it alive through retelling.

What is the leader's role in ensuring that the company's brand story is clear, consistent, and compelling?

Similarly, a simple pair of denim blue jeans—Levi's—took on mythic quality. First, in America as a retelling of gold rush stories, then in post-war Europe as a symbol of the youthful, fun-loving country of its liberators. By the 1980s, a pair of used Levi's were so packed with meaning that they were a form of currency in parts of Eastern Europe for traveling Americans.

Myths have held tribes together for millennia. Starbucks is more than a cup of coffee. It is a total experience. You order in an idiosyncratic language where "tall" means "small," "grande" means "medium" and "venti" means "large." A "barista" makes the coffee fresh for you right across the counter. You can take your cup to a comfortable chair or sofa, and if you pass someone on the street carrying the familiar cup in a safety liner you know they are members of the same club, what many brand experts call a "coffee house" community.

The American dream was one of the strongest myths of the twentieth century, but it is no longer the wellspring of all brand myths, if it ever was. Parts of the American dream are clearly still relevant around the world. Mothers and fathers everywhere want their children to be better off than they were. Opportunity and freedom combine to feed the Horatio Alger myth. And who can argue that "the pursuit of happiness" is not universal?. . . .

Even Europe, with which so many Americans share a cultural and genetic heritage, has sharply different values. Americans value individual autonomy; Europeans consider themselves interdependent. Americans seek personal wealth; Europeans tend to emphasize the quality of their lives. Americans focus on economic growth as a measure of progress; Europeans are more concerned with sustainable development. Americans brag about how hard they work; Europeans covet their leisure. Americans are by and large religious; Europeans are ostentatiously secular.

The homogenized global market that Levitt predicted has yet to gel. What we have instead is more of a stew. That does not mean American brands need to travel incognito. On the contrary, based on surveys of 3,300 consumers in 41 countries, Research International/USA concluded that "consumers expect global brands to tell their myths from the particular places that are associated with the brand" (Holt et al., 1994). The richness of that stew comes from people of every nation contributing their own ingredients and mixing them with others'. . . .

Whatever its source, a successful brand myth tells customers a story that they not only find relevant and credible, but compelling. It is a story that gains credibility by unreeling in a specific place at a specific time, but it speaks to values and aspirations that are universal and timeless.

Anti-Americanism gets a lot of press these days and the Bush administration deservedly gets most of the blame for it. But there are three dangers in that. First, that US-based companies jump to the conclusion that negative attitudes towards the US have no bearing on their commercial success or failure. Second, that the business community considers it a problem to be solved by the professional politicians who caused it. And third, that those politicians try to solve it the way they solve any "campaign problem"—through better message management and discipline.

Box 1 Working with NGOs

In the mid-1990s, when ExxonMobil began planning a new oil pipeline in Chad and Cameroon, it turned to the World Bank to help the countries fund their portion of the cost. Even though the project promised to create 5,000 construction jobs and would pay billions in royalties and taxes to two of the poorest nations on earth, it took five years to win World Bank support. The reason? The World Bank now invites non-governmental organizations (NGO's) to review major projects.

According to ExxonMobil's vice president of public affairs, the NGOs "helped improve the project in several ways, but they also almost killed it".[7]

Some of the NGOs were opposed to development of any kind. Some did not think the countries should get loans until they fixed their governance and human rights problems. But others believed the economic benefits that would flow from the pipeline project were worth the risk. They not only advised ExxonMobil on pipeline routes and labor practices, they helped devise a payment system that would ensure the pipeline taxes and royalties would benefit the country's people and not line the pockets of local politicians. Sadly, once the oil revenue started flowing, Chad started spending some of it on the military as well as schools, hospitals and roads, forcing the World Bank to suspend its loans in January 2006.

Exxon/Mobil's experience in Chad was a microcosm of the evolution many NGOs have undergone. In the beginning, many NGOs were moral absolutists incapable of compromise. Obsessed with a single issue, their driving purpose was to block an action. Their default setting was for high-profile media campaigns designed to embarrass their opponents into submission. They used companies or brands as springboards to publicize their cause.

But over the years many NGOs have realized that even the most successful media campaign can only accomplish so much. It is an inherently negative strategy and most NGOs want to stand for something. As a result, many of them are increasingly willing to work with global companies to reach their goals. They can be highly effective partners. In addition to wide credibility, NGOs command impressive resources on the ground in some of the world's most hostile environments. Indeed, following the Asian Tsunami of January 2005, many corporations turned to NGOs to distribute the products they were donating to the relief effort.

But you do not find potential NGO partners in the Yellow Pages. And working with them requires special skills. First, NGOs are very jealous of the independence that is the wellspring of their credibility. Nothing about your relationship can even create the appearance of compromising the NGO's independence. Second, NGOs are totally dedicated to furthering their cause. They will not even consider working with you unless you can demonstrate that you are equally serious about it and moreover well positioned to influence activity in your sector. Finally, as Richard Edelman, the CEO of Edelman public relations, once counseled me, "No NGO will roll over. But you can do better than have the stuffing kicked out of you." So choose to partner with an organization that has a track record of constructive relationships.

As in any other partnership, both partners need to understand how the other benefits. For their part, NGOs are more inclined to trust companies that point to business goals, as opposed to fuzzy notions of corporate citizenship, as key drivers in their decision making. Peter Melchett, the former executive director of Greenpeace in the UK says "I think the key thing in relationships with NGOs is to look at the core business of what you actually do, what the products are, what the processes are. (An NGO relationship) is not something about media spin press coverage in the long-run. There may be some short-term gains. But they're going to be very short-term." Do not do it for the initial good press. If that is your sole motivation, you are almost guaranteed a world of hurt in the end.

At the very beginning of the partnership, make sure the roles, rules and even the risks of a partnership are crystal clear to all parties. Both partners need to agree to the scope of their work together, their mutual expectations, how they will make decisions, how they will evaluate progress, how they will resolve conflicts, and most importantly what success looks like. Then make sure the business manager responsible for the NGO relationship has the authority to make things happen and quick access to the highest level of the company when they do not. Finally, just as you would in any joint venture, you should have an exit plan in case the relationship sours.

But global consumers are not confused, and they do not reject everything about America. They just do not want to abandon their own values when they conflict with ours. Non-Americanism, after all, is not the same as anti-Americanism.

NOTES

1. Global Market Insite's 2004 survey of people in 20 countries found that 35 percent say ''US foreign policy is the most important factor in formulating their image of America.''
2. *Wall Street Journal editorial*, 1991.
3. Specifically, 28 percent in Italy, 27 percent in Sweden, 26 percent in The Netherlands, 25 percent in Belgium, 24 percent in Germany, 16 percent in France and just 8 percent in Japan. In the UK, 33 percent shared the US view, as did 35 percent in Australia and 33 percent in Canada (source: Charles Hampden-Turner and Alfons Trompenaars, The Seven Cultures of Capitalism, Currency/Doubleday, New York, 1993).
4. ''Views of a changing world,'' Pew Research Center for the People and the Press, June 3, 2003.
5. Quoted by several sources. Looking for original.
6. April 21, 2003, interview with Quelch in Working Knowledge published by the Harvard Business school.
7. Remarks by Ken P. Cohen, Vice President, Public Affairs, Exxon Mobil Corporation Gitelson Symposium, Columbia University, January 26, 2001.

REFERENCES

Drucker, P. (1989), *The New Realities*, Harper & Row, New York, NY.

Holt, D.B., Quelch, J.A. and Taylor, E.L. (2004), ''How global brands compete'', *Harvard Business Review*, Vol. 82, No. 9, pp. 68–76.

Levitt, T. (1983), ''The globalization of markets'', *Harvard Business Review*, Vol. 61, No. 3, pp. 92–102.

McClure, S.M., Li, J., Tomlin, D., Cypert, K.S., Montague, L.M. and Montague, P.R. (2004), ''Neural correlates of behavioral preference for culturally familiar drinks'', *Neuron*, Vol. 44, pp. 379–87.

van Ham, P. (2001), ''The rise of the brand state: the postmodern politics of image and reputation'', *Foreign Affairs*, Vol. 80, No. 5, pp. 2–6.

2005 National Innovation Survey

Richard Seline

THRIVING IN A WORLD OF CHALLENGE AND CHANGE

- American business executives are neutral to slightly positive about the innovation climate in the United States, but significantly more enthusiastic about innovation prospects globally.
- Survey respondents report that they collaborate most frequently with customers and suppliers—indicating that innovation is occurring increasingly on both sides of the cash register—and less frequently with university faculty federal labs and research centers, and private, non-profit institutions.
- When asked to rank the most valuable assets to their company's innovation capacity, survey respondents indicate that their highest priorities are access to a science and engineering talent pool, supplier and customer relations, availability of entrepreneurial managers and a communications infrastructure.
- Survey respondents identify poor communications infrastructure, inadequate science and engineering talent pool, low quality of life, and a poor K–12 educational system as the top factors that eliminate regions from a company's candidate list of prospective sites to create or relocate innovation centers.
- American business executives see their prospects for innovation growing over the next four years. Nearly half believe that innovation drives productivity gains.
- According to the survey respondents, innovation is not the principal driver of today's competitiveness. When asked to rank the factors that are most important in competing for customer sales, executives rank low price and quick delivery as the highest priorities.
- Survey respondents more frequently characterize their innovative activities as product modifications or line extensions rather than new product introductions.
- Business executives cite internal barriers to innovation as the key challenge, with competing management priorities due to finite resources as the most frequently cited barrier.

INNOVATION IS GOING GLOBAL

Why is innovation important for an organization in a globalizing world?

One of the most intriguing results of the survey is the expectation by American business executives about global innovation capacity. For U.S. regions, survey respondents are neutral to slightly positive that the resources available for innovation will improve over the next three years. For the United States as a whole, the respondents are slightly positive that innovation assets will improve. But they are much more enthusiastic about prospects for improvement in the global environment; with nearly 65 percent indicating expectations of an improvement in innovation capacity in countries around the world (see Chart 1).

This finding is consistent with the growing evidence of significant investments abroad in science and technology. China has doubled its investment in research and development (R&D) as a percentage of its gross domestic product (GDP), while more than one-third of OECD countries have increased government support for R&D by an average annual rate of over 5 percent. In fact, many countries are emulating the U.S. innovation model with considerable success. Asia now spends as much on nanotechnology as does the United States. China now ranks second in the world in annual flows of foreign direct investment. Only six of the world's 25 most competitive information technology companies are based in the United States. Foreign-owned companies and foreign inventors now account for nearly half of the patents granted in the U.S. system.[1]

HOW INNOVATION OCCURS IS CHANGING

The survey findings reinforce the conclusion of the Council on Competitiveness National Innovation Initiative (NII) that the nature of innovation—and how it occurs—is changing. The NII's report, *Innovate America: Thriving in a World of Challenge and Change*, notes:

> In the industrial model, the world was divided into "producers" and "consumers," with the former in control. But today, the center of gravity is shifting as innovation increasingly occurs on both sides of the cash register.[2]

Survey respondents are consistent across multiple questions that their networks of suppliers and customers are becoming an integral part of their innovation process. When asked which groups they collaborate with most frequently in the innovation process, over three-quarters respond that they collaborate most frequently with suppliers and customers (see Chart 2).

INNOVATION CAPACITY RESTS ON MULTIPLE PILLARS

The survey responses make clear that innovation capacity rests on many pillars, including the availability of talent, capital, infrastructure and networks. The survey sheds light on what executives most value in an innovation ecosystem.

Chart 1   Over the Next Three Years, How Do You Anticipate that the
Regional, National and Global Innovation Resources Available to Your Company Will Change?

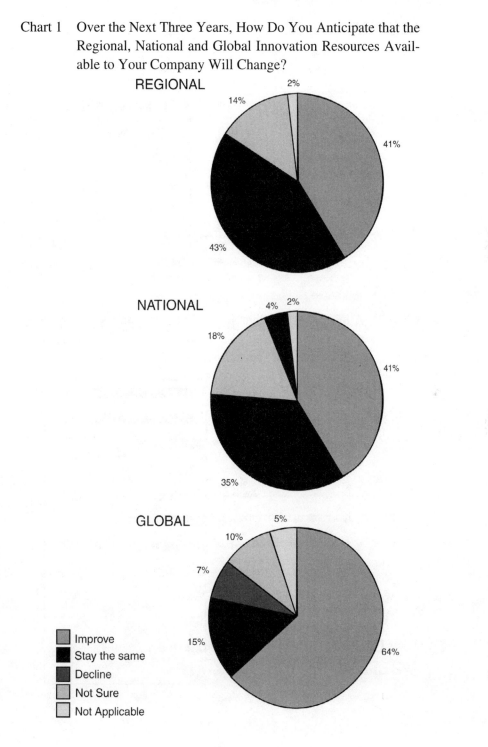

Chart 2   How Frequently Does Your Company Collaborate with the Following Groups in the Innovation Process?

% That Answered Very Frequently or Frequently

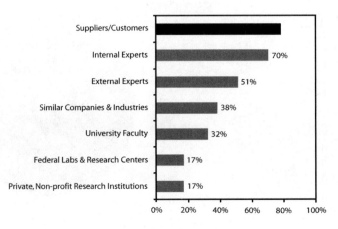

Chart 3   Allocate 100 Dollars across These Resources According to the Relative Value to Your Company's Level of Innovation over the Next 3 Years.

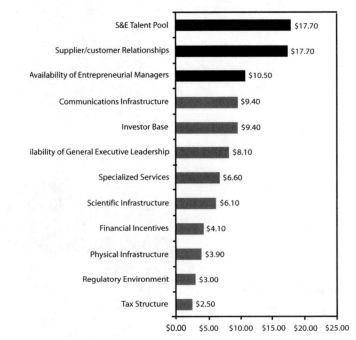

Top responses include access to a pool of scientists and engineers (S&E), a network of supplier and customer relations, the availability of entrepreneurial managers, and a robust communications infrastructure (see Chart 3).

TOP BARRIERS TO INNOVATION INVESTMENT INCLUDE INADEQUATE COMMUNICATIONS INFRASTRUCTURE AND INSUFFICIENT ACCESS TO S&E TALENT

The challenge for every region in the nation is to attract high-value investment out of a global investment stream. Increasingly, the competition for investment is not simply between regions in America, but among regions across the globe. The survey results indicate that lack of a robust communications infrastructure, quality education, and S&E talent are key barriers to attracting high-value investment (see Chart 4). The focus on talent reinforces the view of the Council's member CEOs that their most important asset are the people

Chart 4   If Your Company Were to Create or Relocate Centers of Innovation, Which of the Following Elements Would Eliminate a Prospective Location?

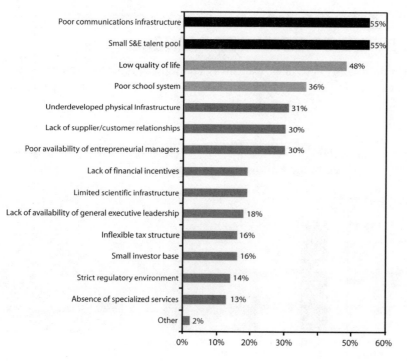

Poor communications infrastructure	55%
Small S&E talent pool	55%
Low quality of life	48%
Poor school system	36%
Underdeveloped physical Infrastructure	31%
Lack of supplier/customer relationships	30%
Poor availability of entrepreneurial managers	30%
Lack of financial incentives	
Limited scientific infrastructure	
Lack of availability of general executive leadership	18%
Inflexible tax structure	16%
Small investor base	16%
Strict regulatory environment	14%
Absence of specialized services	13%
Other	2%

who walk in the door every morning —scientists, engineers, and the rest of the skilled workforce.

Quality of life concerns also rank highly as a barrier to investment, confirming the hypothesis that attracting knowledge workers requires a new focus on a more vibrant cultural environment. The data show that many communities are losing younger, educated citizens to more attractive regions. According to a recent census report, 243 U.S. Metropolitan Areas showed a net loss in migration of young college graduates, while only 75 showed a net gain.[3] Even fewer rural areas have been able to maintain next-generation workers.[4]

U.S. EXECUTIVES TIE INNOVATION TO PRODUCTIVITY GAINS

Overall, business executives rate their innovation performance and prospects quite highly. More than half rate their innovation performance over the past three years as strong or very strong, and 66 percent see their innovation prospects over the next three years as strong or very strong. Business leaders also tend to tie innovation to productivity gains. Forty-two percent believe that innovation drives their productivity growth—a more significant factor than capital improvements (14 percent), downsizing (12 percent) or outsourcing (11 percent) (see Chart 5).

BUT INNOVATION REMAINS LOOSELY LINKED TO COMPETITIVENESS

For the majority of business executives, innovation was not the principal driver of competitiveness. When asked to rank the factors that are most important in

Chart 5   What Percentage of Your Productivity Gains Can Be Attributed to the Following:

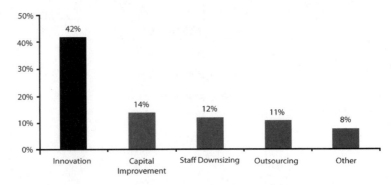

Chart 6   Please Rank the Following Factors According to How Your Company Competes for Customer Sales:

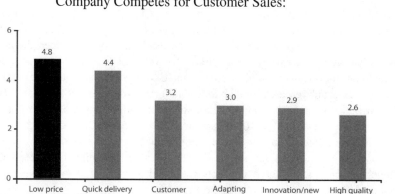

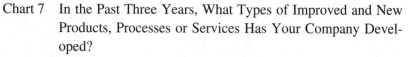

Chart 7   In the Past Three Years, What Types of Improved and New Products, Processes or Services Has Your Company Developed?

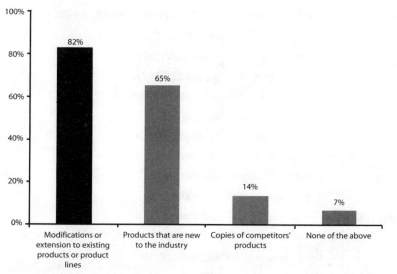

competing for customer sales, executives rank low price and quick delivery as the highest priorities. Customer service and tailoring products to customer needs are next in importance, while innovation/new technology and quality rank the lowest (see Chart 6).

Survey respondents describe their innovative activities more frequently as product modifications or product line extensions than launching products that are new to the industry or market segment (see Chart 7 . . .). These responses raise questions about the relative advantages of incremental versus radical innovation strategies. On the one hand, the recent line of iPods, peripherals and related services clearly demonstrates the value of maximizing return on investment for a generation of discovery and development. On the other hand, the "Blue Ocean" research by Kim and Mauborgne documents that new product introductions are far more profitable than line extensions. In studying the business launches of about 100 companies, they found that 86 percent of the launches were line extensions that accounted for 62 percent of total revenues but only 39 percent of total profits. By contrast, the remaining 14 percent of launches that generated new products generated 38 percent of total revenues and a whopping 61 percent of total profits.[5]

Chart 8   Currently, What Are the Greatest Challenges to Your Company's Ability to Innovate?

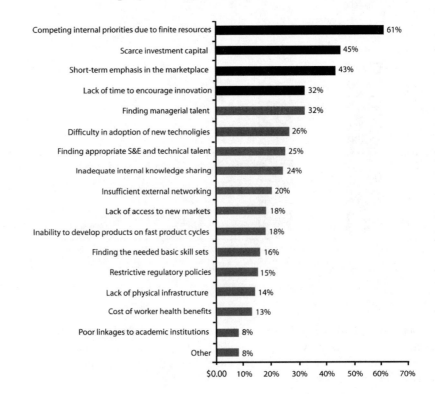

BUSINESS EXECUTIVES CITE INTERNAL BARRIERS TO INNOVATION AS KEY CHALLENGES

When asked about the greatest challenges to their company's ability to innovate, business executives report that internal factors matter as much or more than external ones. Four out of the top five challenges to innovation are linked to private sector priorities: competition of finite resources, scarce investment

Georgia Institute of Technology Survey Results[6]

Georgia Manufacturers Have Not Adopted Innovation-Based Strategies

More than half of Georgia manufacturers chose quality of service as their primary strategy in competing for customer sales. Low price was a primary strategy for just under 20 percent. Adapting to customer needs was cited by 14 percent of the manufacturers, followed by quick delivery at 12 percent and value-added services at 10 percent. Innovation/new techniques constituted a top strategy for the fewest manufacturers—at less than 8 percent.

Firms that Focus on Innovation Do Better

Average returns on sales for all Georgia manufacturers dropped from 8 percent to 5 percent between 2002 and 2005.[7] Although profit margins were similar in 2002 for firms that focused on low price and those that focused on innovation, they dropped more sharply for firms that prioritized low-price strategies. The highest profit margins were found among firms competing primarily on high quality and innovation. Low-price strategies had the lowest mean return on sales.

Firms with Innovation Strategies Pay Higher Wages

T.E. Georgia survey found that average wages, as a performance metric, can be viewed as a "return to the community" since well-paid employees also generate further economic growth through the purchase of goods and services. Average wages by strategy were around $33,000 for all groups except for value-added services (associated with an average wage of around $38,000) and innovation strategies (associated with an average wage of nearly $44,000).

capital, short-term market focus, and lack of time to encourage innovation (see Chart 8).

EXECUTIVES COLLABORATE LESS WITH UNIVERSITIES

What aspects of organizational leadership are being transformed by global processes?

Survey respondents indicate that universities and state-of-the-art research centers are not integral to their company's innovation processes. Poor linkages to academic institutions rank last as a barrier to a company's ability to innovate (see Chart 8). And survey respondents report that their companies collaborate significantly less with private, non-profit research institutions, federal labs and research centers, or university faculty in the innovation process compared to their customers and suppliers, internal or external experts, or other companies and industries (see Chart 2 . . .).

SURVEY METHODOLOGY

Respondent Type

- The survey has a total sample size of 199 senior business executives (Chairman, President, CEO, VP) from U.S. companies with $68 billion in annual sales volume. Actual sales volume averaged $345 million.

Data Collection

- The survey contains 28 questions, which took approximately 20-25 minutes to complete.
- Survey was conducted as a digital, online service.
- All of the data were collected between March 2005 and May 2005.

NOTES

1. Council on Competitiveness. *Innovate America: Thriving in a World of Challenge and Change.* 2005. p. 38.
2. *Innovate America.* p. 40.
3. U.S. Census Bureau. *Migration of the Young, Single and College-Educated: 1995–2000.* November 2003.
4. *Migration of the Young, Single and College-Educated: 1995–2000.*
5. Kim, W. Chan and Renee Mauborgne. "Blue Ocean Strategy," *Harvard Business Review.* October 1, 2004.
6. Youtie, Jan and Philip Shapira. "Innovation Strategies and Manufacturing Performance: Insights from the 2005 Georgia Manufacturing

Survey." Prepared for the Third Klein Symposium on the Management of Technology. October 12–14, 2005.

7. "Innovation Strategies and Manufacturing Performance: Insights from the 2005 Georgia Manufacturing Survey ".

ARTICLE 6.3

Making the Trend Your Friend

Karen Crennan, Paul F. Nunes, and
Marcia A. Halfin

On Wall Street, they like to say that "the trend is your friend." Most management experts feel the same way and can reliably be counted on for commentary about the most important trends affecting markets and business. Yet few of those voices are able to prescribe the specific steps organizations should take to get out in front of those trends.

Accenture recently completed a comprehensive analysis and visioning project that fills this action void. In addition to being a research-based analysis of the most important global trends—business, social and technological—it links those trends to specific actions organizations should be considering right now if, as the late Peter Drucker once wrote, they wish to create the future, not just predict it.

What makes this analysis particularly pertinent is that it has been filtered through the key insights that have emerged from a larger strategic initiative—Accenture's High Performance Business research—including consideration of the impact of each trend on the three "building blocks" of high performance: market focus and position, distinctive capabilities and performance anatomy.

This additional inquiry helped us determine the importance of each of the following 10 trends to business performance, and informed our choices of the business imperatives companies must follow to achieve or maintain high performance.

We observed that each trend dictates a slightly different configuration of these building blocks—and therein lies one of the secrets of high performance: High performers detect the implications of trends for the distinctiveness of their capabilities, the strength of their market focus and position, and the vigor of their performance anatomy. They then take action to shape their own futures while their competitors are preoccupied with imitating the high performers' current successes.

1. PERMANENT, INCREASINGLY PERVASIVE INFORMATION CONNECTIVITY

Information technology is extending not only its horizontal reach but its vertical reach—delving deeper into patterns of behavior or into operational information, enabling richer knowledge about companies, products and customers. Companies know more about their customers, but customers also know more about companies' products and services.

Imperative: Maintain Competitive Advantage by Counteracting Pricing Transparency

As customers become increasingly comfortable shopping online, they learn how easy it is to compare market prices, inventories and even production costs. As a result, pricing and discounting have been upended, with the average retail discount in the United States rising from 10 percent to 30 percent between 1967 and 1997.

Of course, companies that generally come out on top in a comparative search will welcome price transparency. Toyota Motor Corporation, for example, even provides a link from its website to the comparative pricing thus using pricing transparency to its advantage.

But most companies will be vulnerable. One way companies are responding to the threat is by using the same IT trend to create a slew of enhanced pricing and revenue optimization capabilities, including ones for revenue management, markdown management, dynamic pricing, promotion optimization and customized pricing. Beyond this approach, however, companies must learn ways to bundle products and services to create new kinds of value in the eyes of customers, so it becomes more difficult for them to make simplistic comparisons. Companies will also find value in enabling customers to reduce information overload, helping them overcome the "decision paralysis" that can result from an overabundance of purchase information.

Imperative: Create Real-Time Business and Market Insights to Change the Competitive Game

Increasingly sophisticated software and tools will enable companies to use analytics not only for better decision making but as a competitive weapon as well. The ability to derive real-time insight from predictive analytics can help a high performer dominate the game, or even change the game entirely. Amazon.com uses analytics to predict what products will be successful and to optimize the efficiency of its supply chain. Supply chain analytics also help companies such as Dell and Wal-Mart to reduce inventory and stock-outs. Harrah's Entertainment competes on the basis of analytics for customer loyalty and customer service, rather than predominantly relying on building mega-casinos, as many of its competitors do.

Imperative: Engineer the Context and Nature of Work for Optimal Performance

Permanent information connectivity is fundamentally changing the way employees, teams and businesses communicate, collaborate and interact with one another. Organizations must be proactive about designing work tasks and flows to increase productivity and to enhance the kinds of collaboration that more frequently result in innovations. For example, investment bank Dresdner

Kleinwort Wasserstein uses "wiki software," which enables workers to collaborate on Web pages, to encourage teamwork among its traders and bankers; the technology has also replaced e-mail and conference calls for tasks like pricing international bond offerings.

2. THE ASCENDANCY OF MAJOR EMERGING ECONOMIES

Competitive advantage across industries in the coming years will be determined in large part by the manner in which companies anticipate both the opportunities and the threats of four vital emerging economies: Brazil, Russia, India and, especially, China.

Imperative: Prepare to Compete in the Chinese Industry Segments that are Right for Your Business

China already is one of the largest global consumer markets. The Chinese, for example, buy 16 percent of the world's refrigerators and 33 percent of the world's air conditioners. Moreover, China's large domestic market is creating strong local companies that are expanding beyond the country's borders and vying for spots as leading global players. Haier Group, for example, has in just 22 years grown into a global brand and the world's fourth-largest whitegoods maker.

The key to proactive entry strategies in China and the other emerging economies is selecting the right segments, based on specific industry dynamics, and then managing risk accordingly. The Chinese marketplace is anything but monolithic; the country has more than 20 provinces and multiple languages and dialects. Accenture recently began discussions with a local company there about CRM services in the communications industry. The company suggested doing a "small trial"; "small," in this case, turned out to be 50 million people.

3. THE ACCELERATING PACE OF GLOBALIZATION

The pace of globalization and its effects have increased dramatically because of ubiquitous information connectivity. When major business functions, from production to sales, can be performed almost anywhere, it presents companies with unprecedented opportunities for both cost optimization and brand extension.

Imperative: Create Best-of-Breed Global Solutions for Operating Businesses with the Best Capabilities at the Lowest Possible Cost

Optimizing cost in a global labor market is about more than moving jobs to low-wage countries. Increasingly, it is about creating a global network in which every location is put to its best use, independent of its labor costs or even if the company sells or produces in the country.

Consider American appliance maker Whirlpool Corporation, which makes its microwave ovens in southern China and its washing machines in Germany. Despite Germany's relatively high labor costs, it has the necessary technology, as well as a trained workforce and a factory already tooled to the company's needs. If Whirlpool had focused its strategy only on labor costs, it would have missed the nuances of the global sourcing strategy by which it was ultimately able to expand its capacity at a very incremental investment.

Imperative: Pursue a Transformative Outsourcing Strategy

The globalization of work and the removal of global sourcing barriers will create much more flexibility in an organization's value chain, and outsourcing models will actually become a strategic means by which to fine-tune that value chain. With the new discipline of "capability sourcing," more and more of that value chain will be outsourced.

One noteworthy example is Toshiba Corporation's hiring of logistics provider UPS to administer its customer PC repair processes. Companies will continue to more easily mix off-the-shelf and customized solutions to quickly gain new benefits from outsourcing activities, which range from application and business process outsourcing, through vertical outsourcing, to partnering to offshore owned and shared assets. Such a strategy is already in place at a number of companies, including Procter & Gamble, which has pursued outsourcing solutions in the United States and Europe for a range of corporate functions such as human resources and IT.

Imperative: Enable a Brand Strategy that is Simultaneously Global and Local

Yes, a brand must have global appeal. But global marketing must be accompanied by greater product and marketing differentiation, with brands adapted to local markets. For example, although McDonald's has adopted uniform brand packaging throughout the world, during 2006 the company is including nutritional value charts on the product packaging that are designed to be visually appealing to local markets. Procter & Gamble adjusts its branding strategy depending on regional perceptions. For example, it prominently displays the company name on its packaging in Asia, but in the United States and Europe it focuses instead on its product brand names and images.

4. RAPIDLY CHANGING DEMOGRAPHICS

In both industrialized nations and emerging economies, a large percentage of the workforce will soon retire, resulting in the loss of critical knowledge and skills. Because of declining fertility rates in many developed nations, retiring workers are not being replaced fast enough, which raises the specter of global shortages of highly skilled labor. The situation is particularly troublesome in the public sector. Meanwhile, huge areas within both rich and poor nations are being hollowed out by the mass movement of populations to urban zones.

Imperative: Support Workforce Performance to Raise the Productivity of Every Employee

As the number of skilled workers declines in some industries, companies must focus on getting the most out of those who remain, on developing strength in what we call an organization's performance anatomy—the integration of elements such as leadership and strategy, people development and performance management. By taking a more comprehensive approach to talent management, companies must become effective "talent multipliers," able to increase the productivity and impact of each employee. Companies such as Yahoo are already becoming more sophisticated at developing a "talent organization"—a holistic approach to managing talent that attracts, hires, develops and retains the workers needed to achieve high performance.

Imperative: Treat Employees like a "Workforce of One"

What changes would an organization need to consider in moving from a traditional human resources approach to a "talent management" approach?

Successfully managing human capital is becoming increasingly challenging in a world where more workers are temporary; where they want to carry their learning, performance history, health care records and more between employers; and where generational differences—between Gen X and Gen Y as well as with Baby Boomers—lead to misunderstanding and resentment in the workplace. Companies must therefore create new employment value propositions, which, in turn, require different people capabilities and tools.

In addition, to counteract the effects of skills shortages, companies must both retain their best workers and ensure that each worker is supported by the organization's best knowledge and experience. For a start, companies are increasingly tailoring benefits—for example, allowing employees to choose not only individualized retirement and medical plans but also more wide-ranging and important components of their jobs, such as work hours, location and vacation days. The result is increased employee satisfaction, engagement and retention. Companies are also modifying everything from leadership styles to levels of social activism to be more fully responsive to these changes.

In terms of supporting individual performance, role-based knowledge portals, or "performance workspaces," are now supporting specific performance needs of workers. BT Retail's performance workspace for its call center employees, for example, has increased employees' confidence in their ability to perform well by 23 percent, and also produced call handling efficiencies that generated $6 million in savings.

Imperative: Focus on Offerings that Leverage or Address the Effects of Urban Congestion

The percentage of the world's population living in cities is expected to grow to 61 percent by the year 2030, up from just 30 percent in 1950 and 48 percent in 2003. Denser urban environments create many business opportunities for those companies that can think creatively outside their existing business models. One example is the development of "small box" formats by retailers such as Wal-Mart and The Home Depot.

Another recent phenomenon is the "lifestyle center," a roofless retail center in an urban setting that features primarily upscale retail stores meant to attract higher-income shoppers. The appeal is not only the quality of the merchandise but also the experience of the "good old days," when small, downtown shopping centers provided comfort and a sense of community, as well as easy access and the ability to make quick purchases.

Public-sector entities are also responding to these demographic trends with innovative thinking of their own. Several local governments in the United States have moved to implement "congestion pricing"—higher tolls on the busiest highways or during high-traffic hours, for example. They also have begun to partner with the private sector. The state of California has been an early adopter of highway privatization, and the state of Indiana recently leased one of its major highways to a Spanish-Australian consortium for several billion dollars.

5. AN INCREASINGLY COMPLEX AND FRAGILE BUSINESS ENVIRONMENT

As business solutions and services become more elegant and complex, they also become more fragile and susceptible to business failure and security risks. With ever-larger infrastructures with more components, more things can go wrong. High mobility and extended customer reach increase the possible points of attack for those seeking to breach both information and physical security.

Imperative: Secure the Business and Create Security-Based Value-Added Offerings

Security is one of the salient concerns for the 21st century, as businesses and governments look for solutions not only to protect both information and physical assets in real time but also to recover in the event of disasters. One financial services group, for example, had responded to some information security concerns during the 1991 Gulf War by developing "mirror sites" (redundant backups) for its most critical information systems. Consequently, within an hour of the 2001 terrorist attacks on the World Trade Center in New York, a mirror site in another city had already taken control of the company's mission-critical systems.

Security will also become a revenue generator for companies that develop innovative products and services to protect businesses and consumers from the effects of fraud, identity theft, computer viruses and other kinds of privacy or security violations. Products or services with embedded security features will grow in importance.

6. SHORTER TIME FRAMES FOR DECISION MAKING

How does systems thinking impact this imperative?

The increasing pace and complexity of business today means managing almost moment to moment, with an eye on both cost optimization and the quality of business performance. But many managers find themselves either unable to access the data needed to inform their decisions fast enough through their legacy IT systems, or overwhelmed by the amount of data available to them.

Imperative: Develop the Capability to Comprehensively View and Act on Business Performance in Real Time

Recent research has clearly shown that effective enterprise performance management capabilities are critical to achieving high performance, and can increase a company's ability to create value. A *Harvard Business Review* study shows that companies with best-in-class performance management processes achieved nearly 3 percent higher return on assets and just over 5 percent higher returns on equity than their competitors.

Accenture's own research has found the depth of enterprise performance management capabilities and the pervasiveness of a value-centered organization to be key predictors of high performance.

Better analytic tools are key. According to the same Accenture study, more than half of the CFOs of high-performance businesses studied considered business analytics to be one of the three most important contributors to shareholder value. Fewer than 20 percent of their lower-performing counterparts felt the same way.

7. SHRINKING WINDOWS OF PROFITABILITY

The global information network and the transparency of business operations have resulted in less opportunity for an innovative or first-mover product to maintain market dominance. The competition can more rapidly imitate or even leapfrog over products originally seen as innovative. Intellectual property rights are not protected for as long, or are violated more easily. Meanwhile, brand loyalty is declining.

Imperative: Innovate Rapidly or Die

Market dominance cannot be maintained without the continuous use of innovation to extend the value of existing products or to develop new ones. To increase revenue from new products, companies must develop the capability to introduce highly differentiated products in targeted markets more rapidly. Consider, for example, Apple Computer's aggressive rollout of new variants of iPod products, a strategy reminiscent of how pharmaceuticals companies extend the value of a blockbuster drug, even as it goes off patent, by rapidly releasing enhanced versions while dropping the price of older varieties.

Just as important is establishing an "ideas infrastructure"—a formalized process by which ideas can be captured, analyzed and transformed into innovations. For example, Kaiser Permanente encourages more innovative attitudes, making employees feel they can effect change that will lead to improved care, member loyalty and affordability. The health care company has developed what it calls Innovation Support Teams, which are charged with focusing on innovations and are also connected to operations to assist in making the innovations a reality.

Finally, bottlenecks to innovation must be removed more quickly, through a constant review of new ideas and the conscientious application of solutions to remove any barriers to such new thinking (see "Innovation unbound," *Outlook*, January 2006).

8. RAPIDLY CHANGING INDUSTRY AND MARKET BOUNDARIES

Falling trade barriers are redefining markets globally, while technology advances and other factors are blurring lines between industries like entertainment and telecommunications. Competing in evolving global markets at today's pace of innovation requires making rapid adjustments to capabilities and scale.

Imperative: Accelerate Value Through Rapid Acquisitions and Divestitures

Companies must continue to shorten the time between a merger or acquisition and when that move begins generating value. Today, most companies' approach to inorganic growth reflects the cottage industries of the 19th century. Just as new product development and R&D have been industrialized in companies in the past 25 years, the same must now occur for M&A and related capabilities. This type of approach will no longer be reserved for companies like Cisco Systems, BP and Novartis; instead, it will extend out to all companies.

Accenture research into post-merger-integration initiatives has found several common themes among companies that have been able to realize value through the industrialization of M&A activity. Among these themes are an experienced and dedicated integration team, and the careful application of programs related to cultural change and human performance. When Bank Austria and Creditanstalt merged, for example, helping employees understand and own the change and enabling them to perform in the merged environment was important to delivering value more rapidly at the new scale of the merged company.

The importance of divestitures is also now being understood better by high performers, which can more rapidly cast off pieces of the business that are underperforming or have become noncore. In Spain, for example, Telefónica has divested its stake in Eutelsat satellite operations to concentrate more on its core business.

9. A GROWING PUBLIC DEMAND FOR MORE CORPORATE TRANSPARENCY AND BETTER GOVERNANCE AND ACCOUNTABILITY

Calls for stricter accounting and reporting standards and more transparency are coming not just from regulators but from employees and shareholders as well. Shareholders are also now routinely pressing companies about their environmental records, hiring and firing practices, fair trade policies and charitable contributions. A number of online business practices have come under public scrutiny as well. Even companies less vulnerable to these possible actions will face an increasing need to conduct themselves in accordance with emerging national and global standards.

Imperative: Transform the Governance Mindset from Compliance to Value Creation

High performers will increasingly be those that see governance not merely as a set of operating restrictions but also as a means to create value. Consider

Brazil, Latin America's biggest economy. In 2000, the Brazilian stock market was suffering from slow growth in new listings.

Institutional investors met with Brazilian officials to help them explore how new approaches to corporate governance could stimulate the economy by raising investor confidence levels. BOVESPA, the São Paolo stock exchange, responded by creating a new listing segment, in which participating companies would have to meet more stringent standards of corporate governance to be listed on the exchange.

10. AN EXPLOSION OF THE LIFE SCIENCES ECONOMY

Recent discoveries, including the sequencing of the human genome, advances in information technology, and demographic trends such as aging populations throughout the industrialized world, are stimulating health spending and growth in the life sciences economy, or "bioeconomy."

Imperative: Find or Create the Linkages Between Your Offerings and Individuals' Better Health, and Exploit Them

Driving the leading edge of the health care industry, and health care spending, in the next few years will be consumer demand for "personalized medicine." As a consequence, one of the biggest trends in life sciences is "pharmacogenomics"—treatments tailored not just to individual need or disease but also to individual genetic makeup. Drugs are already available for groups of people sharing a genetic profile. Herceptin, for example, is a breast cancer drug designed for the approximately 25 percent of breast cancer sufferers who overproduce one particular gene. Another drug, Gleevec, is for the roughly 5,000 patients in the United States diagnosed each year with chronic myeloid leukemia, which means they have a genetic variation that causes an overproduction of white blood cells.

But it won't be simply the obvious players—pharmaceuticals companies and health care providers—that leverage opportunities of the bio-economy going forward. Implications extend to many industries, including insurance, agribusiness, food and consumer products. Each will find opportunity in the demand for better health and fitness that comes with the growing affluence of populations. Even telecommunications providers can benefit from this trend. Too far-fetched? With the advent of television programming delivered using Internet technologies—also called IPTV—telemedicine solutions will grow in importance. Such solutions would enable, for example, a physician to make an interactive virtual house call to consult directly with the homebound elderly. . . .

The imperatives and action steps listed here can be, we admit, daunting when taken in one dose. Yet most businesses will not feel the effects of all of these trends immediately or simultaneously. By mobilizing the appropriate executives and, most important, the best-suited program managers and change agents to address each imperative individually, companies will successfully begin the journey of evolving both their vision and their business strategy.

High performers know that the future does not come all at once. With vision, but also with rigorous planning, successful companies will embody the observation of the late historian Will Durant—that the future never just happens; it is created.

ABOUT THE RESEARCH

This article is based on several months of research and analysis of key business, economic, technology and sociopolitical trends. The initiative was led by more than 50 Accenture senior leaders, assisted by a global team of researchers and practitioners. This wide-ranging visioning program was based on consultation with internal and external experts; business journals and academic research; technology analysts; financial services and other industry-specific research studies; and data compiled by international organizations such as the United Nations, the International Monetary Fund and the World Economic Forum.

Research findings were distilled into a list of more than 30 preliminary core trends. Using scenario planning sessions and workshops, the trends were extended and prioritized according to their business importance and their impact on the three building blocks of high performance, identified by Accenture's ongoing High Performance Business initiative.

ISSUE SUMMARY

T he problem in analyzing the effects of globalization on organizations is that there are differing viewpoints as to the nature and meaning of globalization. Some call globalization a theory; others call it a force. This is how the authors of *Global Transformations* describe three major viewpoints:

> Hyperglobalists argue that we live in an increasingly global world in which states are being subject to massive economic and political processes of change. These are eroding and fragmenting nation-states and diminishing the power of politicians. In these circumstances, states are increasingly the "decision-takers" and not the "decision-makers."
>
> The skeptics strongly resist this view and believe that contemporary global circumstances are not unprecedented. In their account, while there has been an intensification of international and social activity in recent times, this has reinforced and enhanced state powers in many domains.
>
> The transformationalists argue that globalization is creating new economic, political and social circumstances which, however unevenly, are serving to transform state powers and the context in which states operate. They do not predict the outcome—indeed, they believe it is uncertain—but argue that politics is no longer, and can no longer simply be, based on nation-states. (http://www.polity.co.uk/global/whatisglobalization.asp)

These viewpoints on globalization are applicable to figuring out how organizations function in the world. Taking these viewpoints into consideration, the issue is how leaders position an organization in terms of people, structures, and processes. People may work in virtual teams, structures may cross national boundaries, and processes may be fluid. On the other hand, people may work in a central office in individual cubicles, structures may be local, and processes may be standardized. The key is to take a systems approach in shaping an organization for a globalized world. In determining the shape, leaders also grapple with those issues raised in the readings. What is the role of innovation for capacity building in the world marketplace? What do the trends say about the organization's connectivity to the rest of the globe? What is the brand of capitalism the organization is advertising to the world?

[Note: Global Transformations is a series of books and a Web site that furthers the study of globalization.]

ISSUE HIGHLIGHTS

- People around the world have differing ideas about capitalism and the role of organizations in society than the American model.
- Capitalism and globalization are closely linked in peoples' minds.
- Anti-American feelings center on negative aspects of highly competitive corporate culture.
- Successful global organizations relate closely to people in the country of interest.
- Innovation is occurring increasingly with customers and suppliers.
- While innovation is necessary for global competitiveness, it is not the principal driver.
- The accelerated pace of globalization presents new opportunities for networking and for extension of products and services.
- Global shortages of highly skilled labor means organizations need to take a more comprehensive approach to talent management.
- With global competition shrinking profitability and brand loyalty in decline, organizations need to innovate aggressively.

CRITICAL THINKING

One of the implications of the acceleration of globalization is that the nature of decision making changes for an organization. Instead of long-term planning, organizations must plan and adapt continuously. Yet, leaders of organizations in the information business are often stymied in their ability to make decisions. Their IT capability may be deficient or they are inundated with data. This is a paradox of organizations in the information age. Successful organizations must have robust analytic tools that keep up with the pace of decision making.

Another implication of globalization is the increasing flow of people across boundaries. This aspect of globalization is often accompanied by idealistic notions of a merged culture, as though global citizens are like-minded people. While community organizations are able to gain workforce diversity from other countries, they must also increase their attention to the shifts that will occur in work and culture. The formation of a local global village takes effort and intention. It means being willing to learn from others in order to develop mutual understanding, a process that takes much more time than today's pace of decision making. An organization needs to acknowledge that globalization of goods and services happens at a faster rate than globalization of a local work culture.

ADDITIONAL READING RESOURCES

David Harvey, *The Condition of Post Modernity: An Inquiry into the Origins of Cultural Change.* Blackwell, 1990.

Lester M. Salamon, Leslie Hems, & Kathryn Chinnock, *The Nonprofit Sector: For What and for Whom?* Johns Hopkins Center for Civic Society Studies, 2000.

Deborah Wince-Smith, *Out-Innovating: The New Competitiveness Imperative.* February 20, 2006. http://innovateamerica.org/hot_topics/hot_topics.asp?id=67

For more information check these sites:

www.compete.org
www.globalissues.org
http://www.polity.co.uk/global
www.theglobalist.com

UNIT 2

Operational Issues in Organizational Leadership

The readings in Unit 2 of this book focus on traditional areas of management and control—performance measures, strategic planning, systems, and functioning in the future. In each of these operational areas, the search is for better technique and efficiency, as captured in the questions, "How Can a Systems Approach Help Organizational Leaders?" "What Performance Measures Should Organizational Leaders Consider Today?" "Has Strategic Planning Been Left Behind?" and "How Will Organizations Function in the Future?" Keep in mind—it does not follow that one day the search will be over and these operations will finally be controlled. That is because the fundamental factor cutting across all four of these operations is "continuous change and uncertainty."

At heart, a systems thinker knows the importance of asking one question: How can I help you deal with reality and manage change? This is very different from the authoritative thinker who declares: I know what you need to do. Beyond the clichés and short lists that often mark change literature, the systems approach places decision making and strategy in a larger context. The readings on systems thinking provide different views on the role of systems thinking in leadership. Taken together, the readings establish a framework of theoretical knowledge and practical experience that enables leaders to become more adept systems thinkers.

Performance measures and strategic planning are essential operations and are unlikely to disappear from sight. What makes these operations problematic and issue-laden for organizational leaders is that work is changing dramatically. This is obvious in the range of perspectives presented by the authors dealing with performance. One author contends that traditional performance measures are no longer worthwhile. Another examines the performance of project teams. A third proposes a new way of measuring organizational performance.

Four readings question whether strategic planning is actually a worthwhile enterprise for organizational leaders. Each reading makes a different argument about the right approach to strategy development. One reading calls for the end to traditional strategic planning and another calls for organizations to become settings for continuous learning. Possibly strategic planning isn't the problem; it may simply be in the implementation, according to another reading. And the final reading paints a completely different approach to strategic planning—futuring.

The book ends with a very compelling issue—the organization of the future. Whether it's dramatic shifts in corporate communication, the necessity to adapt to the unknown, new ways of networking to promote innovation, or relationship-based marketing—an old idea made new again—the readings provide some valuable ideas for tomorrow's organization. The future calls for smarter, more connected organizations. Global technology, labor, and economics will demand it. But the shape of the organization is virtually unlimited.

Issue 7: How Can a Systems Approach Help Organizational Leaders?

Issue 8: What Performance Measures Should Organizational Leaders Consider Today?

Issue 9: Has Strategic Planning Been Left Behind?

Issue 10: How Will Organizations Function in the Future?

ISSUE 7

How Can a Systems Approach Help Organizational Leaders?

INTRODUCTION

Leaders of organizations are continually confronted with issues and problems—it's the nature of the job. The dilemma is how to handle a wide range of organizational issues effectively and proficiently. Because the issues are myriad, complex, and seem unrelated, leaders and their staff may not be alert to the fact that a problem in one area may be negatively affecting another area. And all the while, quality can be slipping and effectiveness lessens. To stay on top of issues, while ensuring that quality does not suffer, leaders are turning to comprehensive approaches to decision making. Over the past few decades, systems thinking has been commended as the best way to approach the full spectrum of organizational issues and problems. (Ackoff, Senge, Gharajedaghi, Haines are among the organizational experts calling for this approach to organizational learning.)

Take a moment to reflect on the fundamental meaning of systems. In biology, an organism is a dynamic, living, complex "system" with parts (literally molecules) that are constantly adjusting to each other to function as a whole. A mechanical system like an automobile or clock or computer also has adjustable parts. When "system" is applied to an organization, it means much the same thing—parts that interact or influence each other so they can function as a whole. The chief difference is, the organization can be composed of subsystems, some of which are mechanistic, others social. Today, experts are calling for a holistic, synthetic approach to the systems that exist within organizations.

Systems thinking allows leaders to see problems as part of a dynamic whole, with ramifications (both positive and negative) for the entire organization. Rather than making isolated decisions or taking tentative action, the goal is to understand the interconnectedness of processes and procedures, or personnel and stakeholders, in order to make better decisions. Systems thinking, based on a higher level of analysis than traditional cause and effect, makes it possible to gain broad understanding, but the question remains—does this approach make a real difference for an organization that is ineffective? The readings on this issue provide different perspectives on the value of systems thinking for an organization.

The first reading is a classic selection that provides a vantage point for the issue of systems thinking. Russell Ackoff, one of the pioneers in the field of systems, is considered the dean of the academic community of systems thinkers. In "On Learning and the Systems That Facilitate It," Ackoff establishes clear definitions for the content of organizational learning and argues that leaders have mistakenly relied on the wrong content for decision making. His design of a learning and adaptation system is a fundamental tool for systems thinkers.

The second reading, "Leadership and Systems Thinking," is an introduction to systems thinking as it applies to organizations. The source of this article, *Defense AT&L,* may be unique, but the author approaches the topic in clear and understandable terms. George E. Reed bases his perspective of systems thinking on theorists Peter Senge (learning systems), Daniel Aronson (financial systems), and Russell Ackoff (management systems). He has learned that concepts from each of these scholars are very useful for organizations. You might think that by relying on the experts Reed would go on to claim that systems thinking is the cure-all for dysfunctional organizations, but that would be a mistake. This is what he concludes about the value of systems thinking: "Systems thinking is no panacea. There is no checklist to work through that will guarantee someone is thinking in a way that will capture the big picture or identify root causes of difficult problems." However, Reed still believes that systems thinking is essential. Be sure to read this article to find out why.

Systems thinking and systems change have proven useful in educational organizations, as well as in business and industry. The third reading with the interesting title, "Suspending the Elephant Over the Table," explains how systems thinking can prevent administrators from confusing the parts for the whole. Similar to business, school systems are complex operations and require a broad approach to problem solving. The authors use the case of the superintendent who turned around a large school system operation through systems thinking to propose that "a systems approach may be the only way to tackle what has been called the 'toughest job in America.'"

As you consider the readings, keep in mind that systems thinking is not a specific program; it is not total quality management (TQM), the Baldrige award, or Six Sigma. Systems thinking may encompass a quality program or a variety of other tools but it is a much larger methodology—it is thinking about an organization's operation and its future systematically and holistically.

SOURCES

Russell L. Ackoff, On learning and the systems that facilitate it. *Reflections,* vol. 1, no. 1, 1996.

George E. Reed, Leadership and systems thinking. *Defense AT&L,* May–June 2006.

Nelda Cambron-McCabe & Luvern L. Cunningham, Suspending the elephant over the table. *The School Administrator,* November 2004.

On Learning and the Systems That Facilitate It

Russell L. Ackoff

INTRODUCTION

The extensive literature on learning deals almost exclusively with sociopsychological aspects of learning, that is, how to learn from others. All learning ultimately derives from experience, however, our own or others. Learning from experience is particularly important in organizations in part because of the continuous flux and turnover of personnel. My focus here is on learning from experience in an organizational context. It is meant to redress a shortage of discussion of experiential learning by and within organizations. This is *not* meant to diminish the importance of interpersonal learning within organizations.

I begin with definitions of what I believe are important distinctions between the different content of *learning: data, information, knowledge, understanding*, and *wisdom*. This is intended to rectify the bias in much of the organizational-learning literature toward consideration of information and knowledge to the exclusion of understanding and wisdom. Since there are no generally accepted definitions of these terms, I use my own, which I have found useful in many applications.

Then I distinguish between *learning* and *adaptation*; the latter can be considered a special case of the former. I have also found confusion in the literature on this distinction (for example, Haeckel & Nolan, 1996). In particular, I will deal with the very important role of *mistakes* in learning and adaptation and also with learning how to learn, what Gregory Bateson (1972) called *deutero-learning*.

Finally, I present a design of a *management learning and adaptation system* that meets the varied requirements formulated earlier in this paper.

THE VARIED CONTENT OF LEARNING

The learning literature contains very little about the *content* of learning, what is learned. In this article, I try to compensate for this deficiency. What one learns consists of either *data, information, knowledge, understanding*, or *wisdom*. Unfortunately, we tend to use *data, information*, and *knowledge* interchangeably; *understanding* as a synonym of *knowledge*, and *knowledge* all-inclusively. *Wisdom* is treated largely as mysterious and incomprehensible, even untransmittable.

Not only are the differences between the various contents of learning important, but they also form a hierarchy of increasing value, as reflected in the adage: An ounce of information is worth a pound of data; an ounce of knowledge is worth a pound of information; an ounce of understanding is worth a pound of knowledge; and an ounce of wisdom is worth a pound of understanding.

Nevertheless, most of our formal education and most computer-based systems are primarily devoted to the less important types of learning: to the acquisition, processing, and transmission of data and information. There is less effort devoted to the transmission of knowledge, practically none to the transmission of understanding, and even less to wisdom. This allocation of effort is reflected in the popular and persistent preoccupation with information in the press, on television game shows, and in such popular games as "Trivial Pursuits." How appropriate this name!

Data and Information

Data consists of symbols that represent objects, events, and/or their properties. They are products of *observation*. Observations are made either by people or by instruments, for example, thermometers, odometers, speedometers, and voltmeters. The dashboards of automobiles and airplanes are filled with such devices.

Like metallic ores, data are of little or no value until they are processed into usable forms. Data that have been processed into useful forms constitute *information*. Therefore, information also consists of symbols that represent the objects, events, and their properties. The difference between data and information is their usefulness—functional, not structural.

Information is contained in descriptions, in answers to questions that begin with such words as *who, what, where, when,* and *how many.* Information is usable in deciding *what* to do, not *how* to do it. For example, a list of the films currently playing in movie houses enables us to select one to see, but it does not tell us how to get there. Similarly, the address of a cinema tells us where it is but not how to get there. Answers to *how-to* questions constitute knowledge.

Knowledge

Knowledge is contained in instructions. Knowledge consists of *know-how,* for example, knowing how a system works or how to make it work in a desired way. It makes *maintenance* and *control* of objects, systems, and events possible. To control something is to make it work or behave *efficiently* for an intended end. The efficiency of a course of action is usually measured either by its probability of producing an intended outcome when a specified amount of resources is used or by the amount of resources required to attain a specified probability of success.

Knowledge can be obtained either from experience—for example, by trial and error—or from someone who has obtained it from experience, their own

Commentary by William J. Altier

●

As I read Russ Ackoff's article and reflected on his hierarchy of the content of the human mind—data, information, knowledge, understanding, and wisdom—my mind was quickly drawn to the current fad of more and bigger acquisitions and mergers. I recalled many comments in the business media to the effect that "So many mergers fail to deliver what they promise that there should be a presumption of failure...."

So what's the point? Going back to Dr. Ackoff's hierarchy, no doubt the executives responsible for these acquisitions and mergers go into them with considerable data, information, knowledge, and perhaps even understanding—all related to doing things right. But the question is: Do they go into them with adequate wisdom; do they do the right things?

Ackoff observes that "[g]rowth is an increase in size or number. Development is an increase in one's ability and desire to satisfy one's legitimate needs and desires and those of others." It would appear that the focus of today's merger mania is growth, not development. Perhaps that's the reason why the average life span of today's multinational corporations is between 40 and 50 years. A's Arie de Geus points out in The Living Company (1997), companies that develop themselves can live for centuries.

Many of the travails that organizations experience are, de facto, the result of a lack of wisdom on the part of those who make critical decisions. One factor behind this could be that many executives' mindsets acknowledge the roles of data, information, knowledge, and understanding but stop short of the cognizance of wisdom. It is hoped that Russ Ackoff has shattered that glass ceiling. He makes the case that wisdom—the fifth element in his hierarchy of learning—should be recognized as being at the pinnacle of organizational achievement, just as satisfying the fifth element in Maslow's hierarchy of needs—self–actualization—signifies the pinnacle of personal achievement. Ackoff suggests that "learning is least likely to occur the higher one goes in an organization"; this is precisely the stratum at which errors of omission are most likely to occur and "the decline or demise of organizations is generally more likely to derive from errors of omission."

The pinnacle of learning, wisdom, is the most critical element in successful decision making and in reducing errors of omission. The paradox is that the higher echelons of the organization do possess the decisive elements needed to acquire wisdom. As Ackoff notes. "[T]he acquisition of wisdom....is usually associated with age and experience because it is concerned with the long-run consequences of action."

> Ackoff states, "Wisdom is the ability to perceive and evaluate the long-run consequences of behavior." Clearly, this ability does not seem to be overly abundant. It is hoped that the world of management will recognize this shortcoming and make Ackoff's hierarchy of learning its mantra for tomorrow. This hierarchy, particularly its fifth element, will be a boon for those who use it as a model to remedy the void in their organizations' learning.
>
> Speaking as a management consultant, I find it ironic that big companies often pay big bucks to obtain advice dispensed by newly minted MBAs who lack the critical prerequisites for wisdom. What are they getting for what they pay? Could there be a corollary here?
>
> Ackoff has a profound message for another hierarchy—the hierarchy of management. Take heed!

or that of others. When computers are programmed and people are instructed, they are *taught* how to do something. Such teaching is *training*, not *education*. Failure to distinguish between training and education is commonplace and results in a so-called *educational system* that devotes a good deal more time to training than it does to education. The content of education should be understanding and wisdom.

Computer-based *expert systems* are systems that have had the knowledge of an expert programmed into them. They store and dispense knowledge. In addition, at least since Shannon developed his electronic maze-solving rat, computers have been programmed to acquire knowledge, to *learn*. Programs for acquiring knowledge, however, are still very limited.

Intelligence is the ability of an individual to acquire knowledge. Therefore, the proper measure of intelligence is an individual's rate of learning, the ability to acquire knowledge, not how much one knows. Expert systems that do not learn, and most do not, cannot legitimately be said to have intelligence, artificial or otherwise. Unintelligent systems, ones with no ability to learn, can possess knowledge but cannot acquire it on their own.

Management obviously requires knowledge as well as information, but information and knowledge are not enough. Understanding is also required. Management suffers more from lack of knowledge than it does from lack of information and more from lack of understanding than it does from lack of knowledge. Most managers suffer from information overload, not from either an overload of knowledge or understanding.

How does information overload often prevent leaders from doing the right things?

Understanding

Understanding is contained in explanations, answers to why questions. We do not learn how to do something by doing it correctly; in such a case, we already know how to do it. The most we can get out of doing something right is confirmation of what we already know. We can acquire knowledge, however, from doing something incorrectly but only if we can determine the cause of the error and correct it. Mistakes can be corrected by trial and error, but this is often very inefficient. A mistake that can be explained by identifying what produced it is understood. Understanding facilitates and accelerates the acquisition of knowledge.

Understanding is required in any situation to determine the relevance of data and information, understanding why the situation is what it is and how its characteristics are causally related to our objectives. On the other hand, explanations can be, and frequently are, suggested by observations. Theories, of course, embody explanations that are obtained by deductions from them.

Objects, events, or their properties may be explained by identifying their cause or producer, for example: "The boy is going to the store because his mother sent him." The behavior of an entity that can display choice may also be explained by identifying that entity's intended outcome, for example: "The boy is going to the store to buy an ice cream cone." Only purposeful entities have intentions. (A purposeful entity is one that can pursue the same end (1) in different ways in the same environment and (2) the same way in different environments.) Therefore, to say that an apple falls from a tree because it wants to get to the ground is no explanation at all, but to say that a person climbed a tree to avoid attack by an animal is.

It is possible to construct computer-based systems that explain the failures of some relatively simple mechanical systems. For example, some automobile-manufacturing companies have developed sensing devices that can be applied to their engines. The data collected are then processed by a computer to determine whether the engine is defective, and if so, what is the cause of the defect or its location. The Russians developed a number of such systems for application to heavy military vehicles.

Some computerized systems have been developed to diagnose the malfunctioning of organisms, but they are still in relative infancy. The types of malfunctioning that can be explained by computerized diagnostic systems do not involve choice, or purposefulness. As yet, we do not have the ability to program computers to determine the intentions behind, or the producers of, purposeful behavior.

Data, information, knowledge, and understanding presuppose each other. They are acquired and develop interdependently. They form a hierarchy with respect to value, but none is more fundamental than the others. Although computers have made inroads into providing data, information, knowledge, and understanding, I am aware of no computerized wisdom-generating or disseminating systems.

WISDOM

Peter Drucker once made a distinction between doing things right and doing the right thing. This distinction is the same as that between efficiency and effectiveness. Information, knowledge, and understanding contribute primarily to efficiency, but provide little assurance of effectiveness. For effectiveness, wisdom is required.

Commentary by Vincent P. Barabba

This article by Russell L. Ackoff is of inestimable value to those interested in understanding the differences between a systemic approach to learning and adaptation and the traditional ways in which we have been taught to manage the use of knowledge. The extent to which the reader can reap these rich rewards, however, is related directly to how well the reader is cognizant of Ackoff's other contributions—particularly related to systems thinking and idealized design. For example, Ackoff, along with Drucker and others, has made significant contributions to illustrating the change that has taken place as we have moved from an industrial-age, mechanistic approach toward a knowledge-age, organismic approach to systems thinking.

The systems thinking approach to knowledge use starts out with the belief that in any enterprise striving to meet its full measure of success, the parts that make up the enterprise, by themselves, are of little value outside their interaction with all the other parts. Familiarity with the writings of Ackoff has led me to believe that concepts such as knowledge management and data warehousing—based on taking an inventory of what is known—are ideas whose value is passing. From a systems thinking perspective, these concepts are replaced by decision support systems that pump a free flow of contextual data, information, knowledge, understanding, and wisdom (as precisely defined by Ackoff in this article) into a series of networked dialogs that take place continuously across the functions within the firm, as well as between the enterprise and its extended alliances, which include the ultimate consumers of its products and services.

A distinction between two metaphors helps illustrate the importance of these differences. The industrial-age mechanistic mind-set encouraged us to think about managing business as if it were made up of replaceable parts—like pieces in a jigsaw puzzle. The metaphor fit reasonably well for that era. When you start a puzzle, you know how many pieces you are supposed to have, and chances are good that they are all there. Each of the parts will interact with only a small portion of the other parts. If you have trouble deciding how to put the pieces together, you have a picture on the box to remind you that there is a single solution to the problem. Finally, though some puzzles are more complex than others, the underlying process of putting them together is always the same.

However, today's business challenges are more complex than this. We operate in a world of complex problems compounded by an accelerating rate of change. It is an environment that consists of constantly changing processes, relationships, and interacting components—more like a DNA molecule than a jigsaw puzzle. Depending on how the pieces come together, we can end up with a different final result than we had any reason to expect. We cannot always know up front exactly what we are creating.

Trying to "manage" this complexity is not necessarily the best approach. In many circumstances, that sort of thinking implies there is a single right way—a correct outcome or a predictable framework—and if we could only get all that we know to fit into that framework, we would come out with the "right" answers.

I believe that many of the current purveyors of knowledge management techniques and practices are anchored in the industrial-age way of thinking, based primarily on the predictable world of the make-and-sell business design. With that mental model, we are encouraged to believe that we can manage knowledge in the same way that we manage the more predictable aspects of our enterprises. These purveyors of knowledge management also bring up the issue of establishing a value for our intellectual assets. I am certainly not opposed to the need to justify expenditures for collecting and using information. I am also not negating the value of the tools that provide the proper information to those who make value-adding decisions for our public and private enterprises. What I *am* concerned about is that the attempt to establish such value forces us to try to separate the components of a system and assign value to them independently when, as Ackoff has stated elsewhere, "a system is a whole that cannot be divided into independent parts."

The experience of beginning to implement the learning and adaptation system here at General Motors leads me to believe that it is of great potential value. For it to work well, however, the enterprise needs to create an environment that stresses the interdependence of information users and providers.

My advice to the readers of this article is to read also, at a minimum, "Our Changing Concepts of the World," the first chapter in Ackoff's book *Creating the Corporate Future,* or, if the reader is truly serious, the recently published *Ackoff's Best*. In that way, readers will increase their chances of gleaning insight from the incredible amount of knowledge, understanding, and wisdom developed by this very thoughtful man, an important portion of which is presented in the article reprinted here.

Wisdom is the ability to perceive and evaluate the long-run consequences of behavior. It is normally associated with a willingness to make short-run sacrifices for the sake of long-run gains.

What one does is clearly the product of the information, knowledge, and understanding one has. The value of information, knowledge, and understanding is *instrumental*; it lies in their ability to facilitate the pursuit of ends— desired outcomes, objectives, and goals. Although one must be aware of the end that is being pursued in order to determine the efficiency of a means for pursuing it, one needs not be aware of the value of that end. Therefore, one can talk about the efficiency of immoral as well as moral acts—for example, the relative efficiency of different ways of breaking the law or harming another.

On the other hand, the effectiveness of behavior necessarily takes the value of its outcome(s) into account. Effectiveness in the pursuit of an end is the product of the efficiency of that pursuit and the value of that end. Therefore, the inefficient pursuit of a valuable end may be more effective than the very efficient pursuit of a negatively valued objective.

Put another way, it is usually better to do the right thing wrong than it is to do the wrong thing right. When one does the wrong thing right, one's error is reinforced, and this encourages further improvement in the pursuit of the wrong end. For example, improving the quality of the current automobile, which is destroying the quality of life in an increasing number of cities, is a conspicuous example of doing the wrong thing *righter and righter*, hence making things *wronger and wronger*. On the other hand, when one does the right thing wrong, identification and diagnosis of the error can lead to improved pursuit of the right end.

Wisdom is normative as well as instrumental. The difference between efficiency and effectiveness, which differentiates wisdom from understanding, knowledge, and information, is also reflected in the difference between *growth* and *development*. *Growth* is an increase in size or number. *Development* is an increase in one's ability and desire to satisfy one's legitimate needs and desires and those of others. A legitimate need or desire is one the satisfaction of which does not reduce the chances of others satisfying their legitimate needs or desires.

Although growth and development can effect each other, they can also occur independently of each other: An entity can grow without developing (for example, a rubbish heap), and a person can continue to develop long after he or she has stopped growing. *Standard of living* is an index of growth; *quality of life* is an index of development. One can grow without wisdom but one cannot develop without it. Growth and increases in standard of living do not necessarily entail increases in the value of what is obtained; but development and increases in quality of life do.

One who seeks to increase wisdom must be concerned with the value of outcomes (long-run as well as short-run) but value to whom? One person's behavior usually effects others. Then, ideally, all our behavior should serve the legitimate needs and desires of all those it effects, its *stakeholders*. This means that effective decisions must be value-full, not value-free. Objectivity, which is usually defined as the absence of value considerations in decision making, is antithetical to effectiveness, hence wisdom. Objectivity is better taken to be value-full, not value-free, that is, as a property of decisions that make them valuable to all they effect, whatever their legitimate values.

Evaluation of outcomes is a product of *judgment*. As yet we do not know how to program the process of making value judgments. In fact, this appears unprogrammable. On the other hand, the determination of efficiency can often be programmed because, among other things, the efficiency of an act is independent of the actor. This is not so for effectiveness. The value of the outcome of an act is never independent of the actor and is seldom the same for two actors even when they act in the same way in the same environment. It may not even be the same for the same actor in different environments or in the same environment at different times. In contrast, the efficiency of an act in a specified environment is constant.

Values are very personal matters. Therefore, wisdom-generating systems are ones that are very likely to continue to require human participation. It may well be that wisdom, which is essential to the effective pursuit of all ends, is a characteristic of humans that ultimately differentiates them from machines and other organisms.

LEARNING AND ADAPTATION

To learn is to acquire information, knowledge, understanding, or wisdom. Systems that facilitate learning, computer-based or otherwise, can be called learning support systems. The varieties of learning—acquisition of information, knowledge, understanding, or wisdom—can, but need not, take place independently of each other.

Individuals acquire information when their range of possible choices increases over time. To inform someone serves to increase his or her probability of making one or more choices. For example, telling someone that it is raining outside is likely to increase the probability of his or her carrying an umbrella.

Individuals acquire knowledge when their efficiency increases over time. Such increases can take place under constant conditions, as in successive tries at hitting a target with rifle shots. The acquisition of knowledge (learning) can also take place when the conditions effecting the efficiency of one's choice change—for example, a strong cross-wind arises or a distracting noise interferes with shooting. Under such conditions new learning is required to maintain, let alone to increase, efficiency. Such learning is called *adaptation*.

To adapt is to change oneself or one's environment so as to maintain or increase efficiency/effectiveness when changes of internal or external conditions, if they are not responded to, result in decreased efficiency/effectiveness. Therefore, adaptation is learning under changing conditions.

As has been noted above, one does not learn from doing something right, but one can, but does not necessarily, learn from doing something wrong, by making a mistake. In order to learn from mistakes, they must first be detected—this requires information. Then their cause or source must be identified—this requires understanding. Finally, successful corrective action must be taken—this requires knowledge.

Therefore, *a complete learning system* is one that detects errors, diagnoses them, and prescribes corrective action and these activities require information, knowledge, and understanding. The values served by such a system are those of the individuals served by the system, hence reflect their wisdom, or lack of it.

It should be noted that in most organizations mistakes tend to be concealed even from those who make them. The likelihood of such concealment increases with rank or status—the higher the rank, the greater the claim to omniscience. This implies that learning is least likely to occur the higher one goes in an organization.

There are two kinds of mistakes: *errors of commission*, doing something that should not have been done, and *errors of omission*, not doing something that should have been done. Those organizations that reveal mistakes generally reveal only errors of commission, not those of omission. Errors of omission include lost opportunities. Unfortunately, the decline or demise of organizations is generally more likely to derive from errors of omission than from errors of commission. It is much harder to correct errors of omission; these, like Clementine, are usually "lost and gone forever."

In order to accelerate learning, decisions must be made and monitored that will improve the ability to learn continuously. *Learning how to learn* is called *deutero-learning*. Such learning occurs when we identify and correct mistakes made in trying to correct mistakes. Because of the accelerating rate of change in our environment and its increasing complexity, much of what we know becomes obsolete in less and less time. Therefore, learning how to learn is much more important than what we learn.

Most learning by adults and organizations involves replacement of something thought to be known by something new; that is, much learning presupposes *unlearning*. Nevertheless, the literature on organizational learning has virtually ignored the unlearning process until recently when Peters (1994) and Hamel and Prahalad (1994, p. 59), among others, gave it a little attention. The system described below not only facilitates learning (including adaptation), but it also facilitates learning how to learn, and unlearning.

Only entities that can display choice can learn and unlearn, that is, only *purposeful* individuals or systems. Learning and unlearning can only take place in the context of decision making. Therefore, systems that support decision making should facilitate rapid and effective learning and unlearning and, of course, the acquisition and development of information, knowledge, and understanding. In addition, a *learning support system* should facilitate the following aspects of decision making.

Figure 1   Management Learning & Adaptation System.

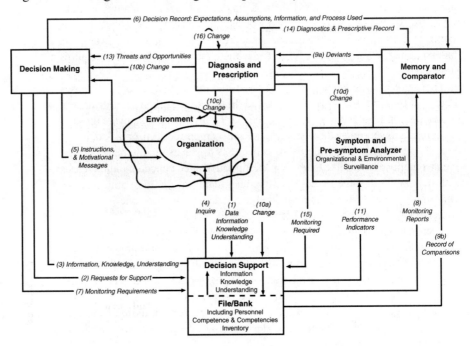

- Identification and formulation of problems
- Making decisions—that is, selecting a course of action
- Implementing the decisions made
- Controlling implementation of the decisions, their effects and the assumptions on which they are based
- Provide the information required to carry out these functions.

THE DESIGN

The design illustrated in figure 1 is meant to be treated as a theme around which each organization should write its own variation, one suited to the uniqueness of its structure, business, and environment. No two of its applications have ever been exactly the same. For example, its application in the North American organization of General Motors is very different from its application in one of the divisions of DuPont. It should be noted that the apparent complexity of the design derives from the not-so-apparent complexity of the processes of learning and adaptation. All the functions contained in the model are usually carried out in the mind of an individual who learns from experience, most of them, of course, unconsciously.

Numbers and letters in parentheses below refer to Figure 1. The boxes shown in Figure 1 represent functions, not individuals or groups. As will be seen, they may be performed by individuals or groups or even by computers and related technologies.

Since the support of learning should be continuous, a description of it can begin at any point, but it is easiest to follow if we begin with the generation of *data, information, knowledge*, and *understanding* (1) about the behavior of the organization being managed and its environment. These inputs are received by the *decision support* function.

In another article (Ackoff, 1967), I argued that management suffers more from an overabundance of irrelevant information than from a shortage of relevant information. Therefore, I suggested that a management support system should *filter* incoming messages for relevance and *condense* them to minimize the times required to acquire their content. That these two functions have received relatively little attention in the learning literature is, in my opinion, a serious deficiency.

Data must be processed to convert them into information, knowledge, or understanding; therefore, data processing is a necessary part of the *decision support* function. Information, knowledge, or understanding is transmitted to the *decision-making* function in response to its *request for support* (2).

When the decision makers receive the information, knowledge, or understanding with which they are provided, they do not always find it useful. They may find it unreadable, incomprehensible, doubt its validity, or question its completeness. Therefore, the receipt of information often leads them to additional requests (2). Such requests require two additional capabilities of the decision support function. This subsystem must be able to generate new data—that is, *inquire* (4) into the organization and its environment so that the additional data, information, knowledge, or understanding (1) required can be obtained. It must also have the ability to reuse data, information, knowledge, or understanding previously received or generated. This means that it must be able to store data in retrievable form. A data-storage facility is a *file/bank* whether it resides in a drawer or in a computer. It is a part of the decision support function.

Once the new or old data have been processed to provide the information believed to be responsive to the request received from the decision-making function, it is transmitted back to them. This request-fulfillment cycle may continue until the decision makers either have all the information, knowledge, or understanding they want or have run out of time and must make a decision with whatever they have. In some cases, they may believe that the time and cost of further inquiry is not likely to be justified by the improvement or increase of information, knowledge, or understanding they believe is possible.

The output of a decision to do something is a message that is either *instructive* or *motivational* (5) and is addressed to those in the organization whose responsibility it will be to carry out the instructions or whose motivation is the target. An instruction is a message to others or to oneself that is intended to increase or maintain the *efficiency* of the organization. A motivational message is one intended to effect the organization's, or some of its (internal or

Compare Ackoff's design for a learning and adaptation system to a SWOT (strengths, weaknesses, opportunities, threats) analysis. What are essential differences between the two approaches?

Figure 2   An Example of a Decision Record.

Decision Record   Issue Identification No.: _____

Prepared by.: _____

Description of issue: _____

_____

_____

_____

Outcome (check one):

_____ No decision   _____ Decision to do nothing

_____ Decision to do something (Describe): _____

_____

_____

_____

Documents pro: _____

_____

_____

Documents con: _____

_____

_____

Expected consequences or effects, and when they are expected: _____

_____

_____

Assumptions on which expectations are based: _____

_____

_____

Information used: _____

_____

_____

Who participated in dealing with the issue? _____

_____

Who is responsible for implementation (if anyone)? _____

_____

_____

Implementation plan: _____

_____

_____

Observations on the decision-making process: _____

_____

_____

Expected consequences or effects, and when they are expected: _____

_____

_____

Upfront learnings, if any, from dealing with this issue: _____

_____

_____

_____

_____

Additional comments: _____

_____

_____

_____

_____

_____

_____

external) stakeholders' values, hence the organization's *effectiveness*. A decision, of course, may be to do nothing as well as to do something. In this case, no instructions are required but a decision record (6) is.

Every decision has only one of two possible purposes: to make something happen that otherwise wouldn't or to keep something from happening that otherwise would. In addition, there is always a time by which the effect of the decision is expected. Therefore, to control a decision, its expected effects and the expected times of their realizations should be made explicit and recorded. All this is equally true of decisions involving the implementation of a decision. If, for example, a decision has been made to build a new factory, there are expectations about when it should be completed, what it should cost, and so forth. Implementation decisions should be separately recorded and tracked. In addition to the expected effects and when they are expected, for each decision a record should be kept of the information, the assumptions on which the expectations are based, and the process by which the decision was reached, by whom, and when.

All this should be recorded in the *decision record* (6) that should be stored in an inactive *memory and comparator*. (An example of a decision record that has been used is shown in Figure 2.) There is more on the comparator below. Because human memories are inclined to modify their content, especially forecasts and expectations, over time, it is important that the memory employed be completely inactive. Inactive storage of information may be the only thing a computer can do that a human cannot do.

A version of the decision record (6), *monitoring requirements* (7), should be sent to the decision support function, which has responsibility for checking the validity of the expectations, assumptions, and information used in making the decision and for its implementation. When obtained, information about the validity of the expected effects, the relevant assumptions, and the information used should be sent to the memory and comparator in the form of a monitoring report (8). Then, using the information on the decision record (6) stored in the memory and the monitoring reports (8), a comparison should be made of the actual and expected effects and the assumptions and relevant occurrences.

When the comparator finds no significant difference between expectations and assumptions and the performance actually observed and reported in the monitoring report (8), nothing need be done other than to enter a *record of comparisons* (9b) in the memory for future reference. This record preserves what is known or believed. Therefore, it should be stored in an easily retrievable form, for example, by the use of key words. If a significant difference is found, however, it is reported as a *deviant* (9a) to the *diagnosis and prescription* function.

Such deviations indicate that something has gone wrong. A diagnosis is required to determine what is wrong and what should be done about it. The purpose of the diagnosis is to find what is responsible for the deviations and to prescribe corrective action. In other words, the diagnostic function consists of explaining the mistake, and therefore, producing *understanding* of it.

There are only a few possible sources of error, each of which requires a different type of corrective action.

1. The information, knowledge, or understanding (3) used in making the original decision was in error, and therefore the decision support function requires *change* (10a) so that it will not repeat that type of error. The information used in decision making can also come from the symptom and presymptom analyzer that is described below. Therefore, it too may require change (10d).

2. The decision making may have been faulty. In such a case, a change (10b) in this subsystem should be made.

3. The decision may have been correct, but it was not implemented properly. In such a case changes (10c) are required for either the behavior of those in the organization who were responsible for the implementation or the communication, instructions and motivational messages (5), to them.

4. The environment may have changed in a way that was not anticipated. In such cases, what is needed is a better way of either anticipating such changes, decreasing sensitivity to them, or reducing their likelihood. Such changes involve changes (10a, 10b, or 10c) in either the decision support function, the decision-making function, or the organization.

Through these types of corrective actions, the diagnosis and prescription function assures both learning and adaptation.

Now consider how threats and opportunities that are not related to previous decisions are identified and formulated. A *symptom* indicates the presence of a threat or an opportunity. It is one of a range of values of a variable that usually occurs when something is exceptionally right or wrong but seldom when things are normal. For example, a fever is an abnormally high body temperature that is seldom associated with good health but frequently associated with illness.

Variables used as symptoms are properties of the behavior of the organization or its environment. Such variables can also be used dynamically as presymptoms or omens: indicators of future opportunities or problems. A presymptom is nonrandom, normal behavior, for example, a trend, a (statistical) run, or a cycle. Therefore, a trend of rising body temperature, each of which is separately within the normal range, is a predictor of a coming fever. There are many statistical tests for non-randomness, hence presymptoms, but the naked eye and common sense can identify many of them.

A complete *management learning and adaptation system* regularly obtains information on a number of internal and external *performance indicators* (11), some of whose values are revealed as *symptoms and presymptoms* (12) by the *symptom and presymptom analyzer*.

When symptoms and presymptoms (12) are found, they are sent to the diagnosis and prescription function. Once a diagnosis is obtained, the *threats and opportunities* (13) revealed are reported to the decision-making function.

Whenever the diagnosis and prescription function prescribes a change, a diagnostic and prescriptive record (14) of it should be prepared. This record is sent to the memory and comparator where its content can be compared with the facts supplied by the decision support function in response to the *monitoring required* (15) issued by the diagnosis and prescription function. Deviants (9a) are then reported to the diagnosis and prescription function where corrective action should be taken. Such corrective action may involve change (16) of the diagnosis and prescription function or making any of the types of change previously referred to. Such changes are what makes possible learning how to learn and adapt.

Finally, information on *threats and opportunities* (17) may be sent directly to the *decision-making* function by a source within the organization or its *environment*, but outside the management learning and adaptation system.

Implementation

As was noted above, the functions shown in Figure 1 may be carried out by individuals or by organizational units. In a small organization, the entire system can be carried out by one person.

All the functions except diagnosis and prescription (g) can currently be automated to some degree. This ability increases over time with the further development of computers and communication technologies.

Parts of the system can be created separately. Obviously, freestanding management information systems are commonplace, but I believe it is wrong to start by building such a system. I think it is wrong because the other parts of the learning support system are seldom added subsequently when an information subsystem is created first. The problems of maintaining such a system are so great that little energy and time are left for extending the system to other functions. In general, it is better to create a complete learning support system for part of an organization than a subsystem for the whole organization. Complete and coordinated systems are more likely to be developed by other parts of the organization than are subsystems to serve the entire organization.

If only one part of a system is to be developed separately, it should be the control subsystem--monitoring decisions made, correcting errors, and detecting changes that require attention in the organization managed or in its environment. There are several reasons for this preference. First, the payoffs come much sooner than they do from constructing an information system and are much more visible. Second, a successful control system in one part of the organization invites other parts to follow suit. Third, the successful operation of a control subsystem leads naturally to inclusion of other subfunctions. Unlike an information system, a control system does not give the impression of being self-sufficient. Finally, without the type of control described here, unlearning is not very likely, and without unlearning, learning is difficult or impossible to achieve.

What are some ways a free-standing management information system may not be able to facilitate learning?

Acquisition of Wisdom

We normally do not refer to the acquisition of wisdom as learning perhaps because it is not normally associated with schooling. It is usually associated with age and experience because it is concerned with the long-run consequences of action. Therefore, the acquisition of wisdom tends to be anything but systematic.

Because wisdom involves awareness of the *long-run consequences* of actions and their *evaluation*, it necessarily requires ethical judgments. Such judgments can only take place where choice is possible. (This is why ethics is a distinctively human concern.) Therefore, ethics necessarily requires the preservation and increase of legitimate options available to others as well as to oneself. *Legitimate options* are those that do not reduce the options available to others.

Wisdom must be directed toward the maintenance, if not the increase, of options for two reasons. First, we cannot forecast with accuracy most long-range consequences of choices made today so we must allow for possible error; second, we cannot predict with accuracy what choices we and others will value in the future. Both of these deficiencies are exacerbated by the accelerating rate of change occurring in our environments and their increasing complexity.

To assist in the acquisition of wisdom, a record should be made of the expected long-range effects of decisions, if any, and their ethical evaluations. When the actual consequences become apparent, they should be assessed ethically. The assessment process should be treated much like the diagnostic and prescriptive function in the system described above. Where an unethical consequence occurs, it should be noted and recorded in a memory so that future wrongs of this type can be avoided or made less likely.

CONCLUSION

I have tried to show how learning and adaptation—the acquisition and preservation of information, knowledge, and understanding—can be facilitated. A good deal of such a system can be computerized, but it need not be. The entire system can be installed in either a single mind or multiple units of a large organization. In addition, I suggested how the acquisition and preservation of wisdom might be initiated in a manner similar to the way information, knowledge, and understanding are treated in the management learning and adaptation system described here. The principal difference in the acquisition of wisdom lies in the amount of lapsed time between decision and evaluation of consequences. This increases the importance of acquiring it whenever and wherever it is possible to do so.

BIBLIOGRAPHY AND REFERENCES

Ackoff, R. L. "Management Misinformation Systems." *Management Science* 14, no. 4 (December 1967); B-147–B-156.

Ackoff, R. L. "From Data to Wisdom," Journal of Applied Systems Analysis 16 (1989): 3–9.

Ackoff, R. L. et al. *The SCATT Report: Designing a National Scientific and Technological Communication System* (Philadelphia: University of Pennsylvania Press, 1976).

Argyris, C. *On Organizational Learning* (Cambridge, MA: Blackwell Publishers, 1993).

Bateson, Gregory. *Steps to an Ecology of Mind* (New York: Ballantine Books, 1972).

De Geus, A. "Planning as Learning." *Harvard Business Review* 66 (1988): 70–74.

Geranmayeh, Ali. *Organizational Learning Through Interactive Planning: Design of Learning Systems for Ideal-Seeking Organizations* (Philadelphia: University of Pennsylvania Press, 1992).

Haeckel, S. H. and R. L. Nolan. "Managing By Wire: Using I/T to Transform a Business From Make-and-Sell to Sense-and-Respond" in *Competing in the Information Age: Strategic Alignment in Practice*, ed. J.N. Luftman. (New York: Oxford University Press, 1966).

Hamel, Gary, and C. K. Prahalad. *Competing for the Future* (Boston: Harvard Business School Press, 1994).

Peters, Tom. "To Forget Is Sublime," *Forbes ASAP Supplement* (April 11, 1994): 126, 128.

Sachs, Wladimir, Man Machine Design: An Inquiry into Principles of Normative Planning for Computer-Based Technical Systems. (Ph.D. dissertation, University of Pennsylvania, Philadelphia, September 1975).

Senge, P, *The Fifth Discipline* (New York: Doubleday/Currency, 1990).

Stata, R. "Organizational Learning: The Key to Management Innovation." *Sloan Management Review* 30, no. 3 (1990): 63–74

Leadership and Systems Thinking

George E. Reed

"For every problem there is a solution that is simple, neat—and wrong. This maxim has been attributed at various times to Mark Twain, H.L. Mencken, and Peter Drucker as a wake-up call to managers who mistakenly think that making a change in just one part of a complex problem will cure the ails of an entire system. Everyday management thinking too often looks for straightforward cause and effect relationships in problem solving that ignores the effect on, and feedback from, the entire system."

—Ron Zemke, writing in the February 2001 issue of *Training*

Leaders operate in the realm of bewildering uncertainty and staggering complexity. Today's problems are rarely simple and clear-cut. If they were, they would likely already have been solved by someone else. If not well considered—and sometimes even when they are—today's solutions become tomorrow's problems. Success in the contemporary operating environment requires different ways of thinking about problems and organizations. This article introduces some concepts of systems thinking and suggests that it is a framework that should be understood and applied by leaders at all levels, but especially those within the acquisition community.

It is insufficient and often counterproductive for leaders merely to act as good cogs in the machine. Leaders perform a valuable service when they discern that a venerated system or process has outlived its usefulness, or that it is operating as originally designed but against the organization's overall purpose. Sometimes we forget that systems are created by people, based on an idea about what should happen at a given point in time. A wise senior warrant officer referred to this phenomenon as a BOGSAT—a bunch of guys sitting around talking.

SYSTEMS ENDURE

Although times and circumstances may change, systems tend to endure. We seem to be better at creating new systems than changing or eliminating existing ones. Sociologist Robert K. Merton coined the term "goal displacement" to describe what happens when complying with bureaucratic processes becomes the objective rather than focusing on organizational goals and values. When that happens, systems take on a life of their own and seem immune to common sense. Thoughtless application of rules and procedures can stifle innovation, hamper adaptivity, and dash creativity. Wholesale disregard of rules and procedures, however, can be equally disastrous.

When members of an organization feel as though they must constantly fight the system by circumventing established rules and procedures, the result can be cynicism or a poor ethical climate. Because of their experience and position, leaders are invested with the authority to intervene and correct or abandon malfunctioning systems. At the very least, they can advocate for change in a way that those with less positional authority cannot. Leaders at all levels should, therefore, be alert to systems that drive human behavior inimical to organizational effectiveness. It is arguable that military organizations placing a premium on tradition and standardization are predisposed to goal displacement. We need leaders, therefore, who can see both the parts and the big picture; to this end some of the concepts of systems thinking are useful.

The Department of Defense is a large and complex social system with many interrelated parts. As with any system of this type, when changes are made to one part, many others are affected in a cascading and often unpredictable manner. Thus, organizational decisions are fraught with second- and third-order effects that result in unintended consequences. "Fire and forget" approaches are rarely sufficient and are sometimes downright harmful. Extensive planning—combined with even the best of intentions—does not guarantee success. Better prediction is not the answer, nor is it possible. There are so many interactions in complex systems that no individual can be expected to forecast the impact of even small changes that are amplified over time.

GETTING BEYOND THE MACHINE METAPHOR

In her book *Organization Theory: Modern, Symbolic, and Postmodern Perspectives*, Mary Jo Hatch provides an introduction to general systems theory that is useful in thinking about organizations. She makes a point worthy of repeating: The use of lower level models is problematic when applied to higher level systems. Thus, the language of simple machines creates blind spots when used as a metaphor for human or social systems; human systems are infinitely more complex and dynamic. In other words, it can be counterproductive to treat a complex dynamic social system like a simple machine.

Noted management scholar Russell Ackoff puts it another way. He asserts that we are in the process of leaving the machine age that had roots in the Renaissance and came into favor through the industrialization of society. In that era the machine metaphor became the predominant way of looking at organizations. The universe was envisioned by thinkers such as Isaac Newton, as having the characteristics of a big clock. The workings of the clock could be understood through the process of analysis and the analytical method.

Analysis involves taking apart something of interest, trying to understand the behavior of its parts, and then assembling the understanding of the parts into an understanding of the whole. According to Ackoff, "One simple relationship—cause and effect—was sufficient to explain all relationships." Much machine-age thinking remains with us today; however, there are alternatives.

SYSTEMS THINKING

Systems, like the human body, have parts, and the parts affect the performance of the whole. All of the parts are interdependent. The liver interacts with and affects other internal organs—the brain, heart, kidneys, etc. You can study the parts singly, but because of the interactions, it doesn't make much practical sense to stop there. Understanding of the system cannot depend on analysis alone. The key to understanding is, therefore, synthesis. The systems approach is to:

Why is analysis insufficient for understanding the system?

- Identify a system. After all, not all things are systems. Some systems are simple and predictable, while others are complex and dynamic. Most human social systems are the latter.
- Explain the behavior or properties of the whole system. This focus on the whole is the process of synthesis. Ackoff says that analysis looks into things while synthesis looks out of things.
- Explain the behavior or properties of the thing to be explained in terms of the role(s) or function(s) of the whole.

The systems thinker retains focus on the system as a whole, and the analysis in step three (the third bullet) is always in terms of the overall purpose of the system. Borrowing Ackoff's approach and using the example of a contemporary defense issue might help clarify what is admittedly abstract at first glance.

Consider the Institute for Defense Analyses report *Transforming DoD Management: the Systems Approach*. The authors of this study suggested an alternative approach to Service-based readiness reporting, one that considered the entire defense transportation system. One section of the report suggests that knowing the status of equipment, training, and manning of transportation units is helpful but insufficient to determine the readiness of a system that includes elements such as airfields, road networks, ships, and ports. The defense transportation system includes elements of all Services and even some commercial entities. It only makes sense, therefore, to assess readiness of these elements as part of a larger system that has an identifiable purpose—to move personnel and materiel to the right place at the right time. In this example you can clearly see the approach recommended by Ackoff.

THE PROBLEM OF BUSYNESS

Few would disagree, in principle, that senior leaders should see not only the parts, but also the big picture. So why don't we do more of it? One reason is because we are so darned busy. Immersed in the myriad details of daily existence, it is easy to lose sight of the bigger picture. While it may be important to orient on values, goals, and objectives, the urgent often displaces the important. Fighting off the alligators inevitably takes precedence over draining the swamp.

The problem of busyness can be compounded by senior leaders who are overscheduled and uneducated in systems thinking. It seems as though military officers today work excessive hours as a matter of pride. A cursory examination of the calendar of most contemporary officers, especially flag officers, will indicate an abusive pace. Consider as an alternative the example of one of America's greatest soldier-statesmen, Gen. George C. Marshall. Even at the height of World War II, Marshall typically rode a horse in the morning for exercise, came home for lunch and visited with his wife, went to bed early, and regularly took retreats to rejuvenate. To what extent are such pauses for reflection and renewal valued today? Simple cause and effect thinking combined with a culture of busyness can result in decision makers who rapid-fire short-term solutions at long-term problems without taking time to think about the actual impact of those solutions.

A common symptom of this phenomenon can be seen in leaders who unrealistically demand simplicity and certainty in a complex and uncertain environment. The drive for simplicity can lead to the need for excessive assumptions. Few contemporary issues of significance can be understood, much less solved, in a two-page point paper or a PowerPoint® slide. We might also ask whether speed and decisiveness in decision making, so valued at the tactical level, work to the detriment of good decisions at the strategic level. Absent some discipline and techniques to do otherwise, it is very hard to find time for reflection and thoughtful decision making.

> Most people expect learning to just happen without their taking the time for thought and reflection, which true learning requires. In the past, with slower communication systems, we often had a few weeks to ponder and rethink a decision. Today we're accustomed to e-mails, faxes, overnight letters, and cell phones, and have come to believe that an immediate response is more important than a thoughtful one.
> — Steven Robbins, writing in *Harvard Business School Working Knowledge* in May 2003.

INTERRELATIONSHIPS, NOT THINGS

Peter Senge submits, in *The Fifth Discipline*, that systems thinking provides just the type of discipline and toolset needed to encourage the seeing of "interrelationships rather than things, for seeing patterns of change rather than static 'snapshots.'" Senge argues that this shift of mind is necessary to deal with the complexities of dynamic social systems.

He suggests that we think in terms of feedback loops as a substitute for simple cause and effect relationships.

As an example, systems scholar Daniel Aronson suggests that we imagine a farmer who determines that an insect infestation is eating his crop. The conventional approach is to apply a pesticide designed to kill the insect. Our example at this point depicts the lowest level of the thinking hierarchy—reaction. In response to the appearance of insects, the farmer applies a pesticide because he assumes that what has worked in the past will work in this instance. As additional insects appear, the farmer applies more pesticide. While the farmer's goal is to produce a crop, his activity is increasingly consumed by recurring applications of the chemical. He is surely busy, but he may not necessarily be productive. A systems thinker might step back from the problem, take a broader view, and consider what is happening over time.

For example, he might think about whether there are any patterns that appear over weeks or months and attempt to depict what is actually occurring. Recognizing the pattern of a system over time is a higher-order level of thinking. The systems thinker might notice that insect infestation did decrease after applying pesticide, but only for a short time. Insects that were eating the crop were actually controlling a second species of insect not affected by the pesticide. Elimination of the first species resulted in a growth explosion in the second that caused even more damage than the first. The obvious solution caused unintended consequences that worsened the situation.

An accomplished systems thinker would model the above example using a series of feedback and reinforcing loops. The specifics of the modeling technique are less important at this point than the observation that systems thinking tends to see things in terms of loops and patterns aided by constant assessment of what *is* happening, rather than flow charts and reliance on what *should be* happening. At the highest level of thinking, the farmer would try to identify root causes or possible points of intervention suggested by these observations.

THE IMPORTANCE OF CONTINUOUS ASSESSMENT

In *Why Smart Executives Fail*, Sydney Finkelstein examined over 50 of the world's most notorious business failures. His analysis indicated that in almost every case, the failures were not attributable to stupidity or lack of attention. To the contrary, the leaders of well-known corporations such as Samsung Motors, WorldCom, and Enron were exceptionally bright, energetic, and deeply involved in the operation of their businesses. Up to the point of massive corporate failure, they were all extremely successful, and in almost every case, there were some in the organization who vainly raised objections to the course that eventually proved disastrous. In most instances, the executives failed to see or accept what was actually happening. In some cases, they were blinded by their own prior successes; in other cases they inexplicably held tenaciously to a vision, despite plenty of evidence that the chosen strategic direction was ill-advised. The systems thinker's pragmatic focus on determining what is actually happening serves as a preventative to self-delusional wishful thinking. Wishful thinking is no substitute for a realistic appraisal. In the language of systems thinking, the executives were trapped by their own faulty mental models.

The continuous assessment process that is characteristic of systems thinking is essential in a volatile, rapidly changing environment. It takes time and good habits of critical reflection to engage in this kind of learning, both for individuals and organizations.

A systemic approach to failure is more likely to result in effective long-term solutions. Imagine for a moment if the incidents of abuse at Abu Ghraib were chalked up merely to ineffective leadership or just miscreant behavior by some thugs on the night shift. If other factors contributed to the problem, after relieving the chain of command for cause and prosecuting the abusers, the members of the replacement chain of command might have found themselves in an equally untenable situation. While inspired leadership can make a difference under the worst of conditions, we might ask just how heroic we expect our leaders to be on a regular basis. When a system is so obviously stacked against our leaders, there is a moral imperative to change the system.

Systems thinking is no panacea. There is no checklist to work through that will guarantee someone is thinking in a way that will capture the big picture or identify root causes of difficult problems. There are some concepts and approaches embedded in the systems thinking literature, however, that can be very helpful when considering why a situation seems to be immune to intervention, or why a problem thought to be solved has returned with a vengeance. Here are some of the concepts:

Systems thinkers step back from the problem, take a broader view, and consider what is happening over time. This is a different approach from the rapid fire decision making that many leaders do. What are the signs that a situation calls for systems thinking?

- Focus on the purpose for which a system was created over the processes and procedures of the system.
- Simple cause-and-effect relationships are insufficient to understand or explain a complex social system. Patterns over time and feedback loops are a better way to think about the dynamics of complex systems.
- Think in terms of synthesis over analysis; the whole over the parts.
- Busyness and excessive focus on short term gains interferes with our ability to use a systems approach.
- Leaders must see what is actually happening over what they want to see happen.
- Thinking about systems and their dynamics suggests alternative approaches and attunes leaders to important aspects of organizational behavior, especially in military organizations that value tradition and standardization.

Suspending the Elephant Over the Table

Nelda Cambron-McCabe and Luvern L. Cunningham

Peter Negroni, former superintendent in Springfield, Mass., believes Ron Heifetz's insights about the importance of taking the long view helped save his career in school administration. Negroni was on a quick fix, my-way-or-the-highway approach to school reform in 1994 but sensed he was in trouble.

Brutal and ongoing contretemps around his efforts to close the achievement gap had left him with few allies in the schools or community and feeling increasingly isolated from union leaders and significant elements on the governing school committee.

"I was taking fire from all sides and wondering when the cavalry would arrive," says Negroni, now vice president of the College Board in New York City.

Critics derided him as a brash outsider, a know-it-all from New York who didn't understand how things were done in aging New England industrial towns. Then a candidate for the school committee won election with 17,000 votes. "She'd run a campaign demanding my head," recalls Negroni wryly. "It turned out to be a pretty popular platform."

Angry about the election result, Negroni sensed that a backlash threatened the progress he had made in Springfield. People no longer cared that he'd led successful battles for school levies, imposed order on the structural chaos in the schools or saved money and improved programs for recent immigrants. All of that was greeted with disinterest.

What critics focused on was the loss of privilege for Springfield's well-to-do. It was all vaguely reactionary and racist, worried Negroni, a man who wears his heart on his sleeve, suffers fools lightly and remembers how painful it was to listen to Irish cops in New York spit racial epithets at him and his teen-age buddies from Puerto Rico.

Then epiphany struck. "Who does this new board member represent?" asked Heifetz at a meeting Negroni attended of the Danforth Foundation's Forum for the American School Superintendent. "Those 17,000 voters? They stand for something. What's precious to them? What are you threatening?"

SACRED TEXTS

All of us like quick fixes, even though in education, as elsewhere, they rarely work well, according to Heifetz, a lecturer in public policy at Harvard's

Kennedy School of Government, and Peter Senge, senior lecturer in management at the Massachusetts Institute of Technology. Taking time to do it right may be a persuasive theory around the ivied quadrangles of Cambridge, but do superintendents enjoy the luxury of a time-consuming systems approach? With the notorious amount of heat mounting under their chairs, can they afford to acknowledge they don't have all the answers—and sometimes aren't sure about the questions?

It's daunting, but a systems approach may be the only way to tackle what has been called the "toughest job in America." That's the consensus of skilled current and former practitioners of the high-wire act of serving as a school superintendent.

Concepts of systems change can improve learning while making the job doable, according to nearly 200 superintendents who helped us develop *The Superintendent's Fieldbook* through the decade-long Danforth Foundation's Forum for the American School Superintendent. Rosa Smith, formerly the superintendent in Columbus, Ohio, and Les Omotani, who has taken the systems approach from West Des Moines, Iowa, to his new assignment in leading the Hewlett-Woodmere district on Long Island, speak of Senge's *Fifth Discipline* and Heifetz's *Leadership Without Easy Answers* as akin to sacred texts.

Tim Lucas, former superintendent in Ho-Ho-Kus, N.J., says the same about using systems thinking. Lucas, now a professor of school practice at Lehigh University, even helped write *Schools That Learn,* a book applying Senge's systems ideas to schools with one of the authors of this article.

THINK SYSTEMS

"It's not personal." That's what Heifetz reminds us to keep in mind as we struggle to survive, according to Smith, president of the Schott Foundation in Cambridge, Mass. Adds Negroni: "What I realized is that it had nothing to do with me. Sure, my new board member opposed what I stood for, but she wasn't reactionary. She represented an important constituency—voters worried about change. What was happening with their kids? Their community? Their jobs?"

Leaders in education or other fields who confuse themselves with the changes their communities are moving through are asking for trouble, and they will probably get it. Taking resistance personally, they are unable to distinguish their role from themselves.

"I was a real Lone Ranger," says Negroni, who was Springfield's superintendent from 1989 to 2000. "I even found myself lecturing the school committee, announcing that unless my proposals were adopted, they'd need to find someone else."

Omotani finds nothing unusual in Negroni's story. To state the obvious, says Omotani, who moved into the Hewlett-Woodmere superintendency in June, there's a lot involved in turning around a big school district. "We need to think systems, not programs," he says, noting that public discussions of schools isolate discrete issues like standards or assessment. "That promotes a quick-fix mentality—what is often called 'single-loop' thinking. What Senge and Heifetz encourage is in-depth, 'double-loop' thinking that attacks core assumptions, not their manifestations."

At West Des Moines, where he worked for nine years, Omotani learned the value of a systems approach that can be thought of as a dynamic triangle or arrowhead aimed at improving outcomes for kids. This triangle, which guided the overall work of the Danforth Superintendents' Forum, consists of seven related entities that we call the commonplaces of school leadership: leadership itself, at the base, interlocked with governance, standards and assessment, race and class, school principals, out-of-school support for learning and community engagement.

"Heifetz and Senge ask us to keep all this complexity in front of us," says Omotani. "In *The Superintendent's Fieldbook,* my wife, Barbara, referred to this process as suspending the elephant over the table so that we don't mistake the parts for the whole."

In West Des Moines, Omotani reports, the systems approach paid big dividends. The community agreed on a long-term vision for the schools and got behind school goals. "What did it give us?" Omotani asks. "Most importantly, we created a shared vision-driven school system and community around educating children. This was a living, breathing statement that mattered—not just a plaque on the wall."

Omotani points with pride to the community's numerous accomplishments that include an exemplary freshman high school now beginning its 10th year, a new Title I elementary school implementing an "artful" approach to learning, innovative summer intervention programs and initiation of a youth leadership forum that reflects the significant voice of West Des Moines's students.

ADAPTIVE CHANGE

The easy challenges are technical, says Lucas, who left school administration in 2003 for higher education. For officials outside education, they might involve locating oil or figuring out where to run a highway. In education, technical issues may involve balancing a budget or commissioning architectural plans for a new school. "Technical issues require expertise, which is available. Single-loop thinking is ideally suited to solving technical problems," Lucas says.

The tough challenges are adaptive, requiring transformation of existing structures and practices. They turn on what to do after the wells run dry, communities refuse to let highways cut them in half, voters demand services but balk at the costs, and schools have to be closed in one part of town and built in another.

"Expertise can't resolve these dilemmas, which involve emotions and the loss of inherited ways of doing things," says Lucas. "Communities have to coalesce around solutions that require deep-rooted change and double-loop thinking."

The distinction between technical, single-loop thinking and adaptive, double-loop problem solving appeals to Omotani, a Canadian whose earlier career was spent at the district and provincial levels in Alberta. "I can monitor the technical stuff, sometimes from afar, but with the difficult issues, I need to be deeply engaged in creating a space for the schools and community to tackle tough problems. These always involve changes around things that go to the heart of what people believe and value."

Here's where the leader's skills are sorely tested. What isn't negotiable? What will the community go to the mat over? Leaders can't afford to play games with the things the community holds dear.

It's very hard leadership work. Too frequently, leaders prefer to fall back on old ways of doing things, in the process becoming "one-trick, single-loop ponies."

TURNING WORK OVER

In Springfield, Negroni found himself reinvigorated by Heifetz's question. Determined to stop hectoring the school committee and abusing union officials, he set about transforming his style. When you're trained in command-and-control, acknowledges Negroni, the formula of "I'm OK. You're OK" does not spring readily to the lips.

But he now found himself worrying about the deep-rooted systems and transformational approaches encouraged by Senge and Heifetz. "I stopped saying, 'This is what I want,' and began asking, 'What do you think we need?'" Negroni remembers. "I went from being the Lone Ranger to being the Lead Learner."

Modeling that behavior in the school district, he started visiting individual schools five days a week, encouraging other administrators and school principals to do the same. "All of us needed to become part of a learning community," he says. "I couldn't do the community's learning for it."

What are some reasons leaders have trouble turning over work to others?

The results speak volumes: "These initial efforts at community engagement and learning changed the way we interacted in Springfield," Negroni says. "We engaged parents, businesses, religious groups and social service agencies so that we could all define an explicit covenant with one another. That covenant, which was most visible in our curriculum, then drove our common enterprise." Negroni credits improved student performance directly to the new relationships within the schools and community. These relationships also enabled the district to build or renovate 12 school buildings that led to a building boom in the city.

"Giving the work back" is what Heifetz calls this style. Community members have to do the work themselves; leaders can't do it for them. Still the approach has to be thoughtful. Unless handled deftly, the act of turning the work over can blow up in the leader's face.

That's a lesson that some Danforth Forum superintendents learned the hard way. In one school system, a savage public dispute broke out around a proposed photo exhibit of gay families at an elementary school. The superintendent, determined to push the decision back to the people who were most affected by it, turned the work over to the principal, teachers and parents.

After a raucous public gathering degenerated into a homophobic shouting match, the group agreed on ground rules for the exhibit that satisfied the central office but seemed acceptable to few of the ideologues inside or around the school. Within a year, the principal had transferred, and the assistant superintendent who represented the central office on the issue had left the system, followed shortly by the superintendent.

Turning the work over to others requires leaders to create a process or "holding environment" where they can regulate and contain the stress of working through difficult issues. According to Heifetz, leaders who expect to survive transformational change have to gauge the rate at which the community can handle the work.

LEADERS' LONELINESS

After decades in schools, including a stint as superintendent in Beloit, Wis., Rosa Smith arrived for her new assignment in Columbus, Ohio, determined to push back at the sense of isolation that envelops many school leaders.

Smith was attracted to the ideas Heifetz advances to help leaders stay alive. "You need to 'get up on the balcony' with some trusted friends," Smith says. "On the balcony you can see the patterns on the floor, who's dancing with whom and how partners change as the music changes."

Before assuming her new role in Columbus, Smith convened a two-day meeting involving several district employees and about 10 outside experts, including prominent superintendents and a few university professors. Spending a half-day on briefings about district challenges, she spent the remaining time with the experts figuring out how to proceed with a systemic approach.

"Was it worth it? You bet!" says Smith, who moved into her foundation post in 2001. "Would I do it again? I have. When I started at Schott Roundation, I convened another 'balcony' group, and I plan to visit with this group regularly."

MASTERING DISEQUILIBRIUM

Whether it's Heifetz talking about adaptive work or Senge advocating the five disciplines of personal mastery, mental models, shared vision, team learning and systems thinking, what leaders are really called on to do today is master disequilibrium in a complex environment.

Superintendents and other leaders have to generate some stress to make changes in a big system, according to Heifetz. The system needs to be thrown into disequilibrium. The challenge for the leader is figuring out how to parcel out sufficient stress to get people's attention without overwhelming them.

Sound like a tough order? It is. Nobody said that suspending elephants over tables was easy.

ISSUE SUMMARY

S ystems thinking is a way of thinking about an organization that takes into account all of its parts. The notion that systems thinking may be the solution to an ailing organization is of particular interest to those who are attracted to this way of thinking. Is systems thinking powerful enough to produce necessary changes to turn an ineffective organization into an effective one? That is what the readings for this issue address. One of readings sees systems thinking as a way of gaining wisdom, not just information. Another reading states that systems thinking makes sense, but is no panacea. And another claims that concepts of systems thinking make the job of administration doable. No doubt, systems thinking (even a mechanistic, Newtonian approach) is helpful, especially in situations that are conflicted or undergoing immense change. By thinking systems, members of an organization are able to view the parts in a holistic manner, not merely as cause and effect or points in time. An organization is not a simple machine and as one of the authors states, it would be "counterproductive" to analyze the performance of a complex entity using linear thinking. Yet it is fairly clear that the power of systems thinking extends only so far if the quest is limited to data and information. After all, organizational systems are mental models created by people and the only way the power of a mental model can be seen is in positive change, growth, and results. It takes courageous action to move an organization from being ineffective to effective and action is a matter of will and determination.

Leaders who ask difficult questions, who regard organizational systems as open, and who make every effort to keep processes transparent are likely to rely on systems thinking. These leaders are able to get comfortable with the discovery process that systems thinking requires. They refrain from jumping to conclusions or prematurely determining strategy while they take the time to understand what is in the system. Brenda Barker Scott, industrial relations professor at Queen's University, points out that diagnosis is vital: ". . . taking time in the diagnosis phase lets you uncover what is going on—and that knowledge yields both the best solutions, and just as important, the energy for change. Deep diagnosis ensures that people will be committed to solving big issues and doing whatever it takes to make change happen. Having a solid appreciation and understanding of *what is* naturally enables people to make good decisions about *what can be*."

The perspectives presented in the readings make us aware of how important it is to understand the unit of functioning that people have in mind when they think systems—is it one department or all departments, one group of employees or all stakeholders, the organization as an isolated entity or the organization and its surrounding environment? How to scan the organizational environment to include all units of functioning will continue to be a challenge, particularly as systems thinking is influenced by the sciences of complexity and quantum physics.

ISSUE HIGHLIGHTS

- Systems thinking provides a useful framework for making decisions in today's complex organizations.
- The systems approach enables leaders to identify problems within larger systems rather than arrive at answers solely on the basis of cause and effect.
- Interrelationships, patterns, and feedback loops are more effective than reliance on simple flowcharts.
- The emerging perspective, "quantum thinking," moves beyond systems thinking by providing even broader ways to conceptualize and deal with complexity in organizations.

CRITICAL THINKING

The traditional systems paradigm used by business and industry has been based on outmoded mechanistic thinking and leads to a search for certainty and control. In this form of systems thinking, leaders attempt to analyze the whole by looking at its parts in isolation. While borrowing into the details is necessary, it limits leaders' thinking to analysis, which naturally results in an emphasis on efficiency and outcomes.

For decades, organizations have been structured to reflect mechanistic thought; personnel are organized in hierarchies, operations are discrete, and quality is something to be controlled. But this paradigm of the world and its organizations has been changing due to the findings of twentieth-century sciences:

> Quantum physics tells us that the universe actually consists of patterns of dynamic energy, self-organizing wave patterns like so many whirlpools, the boundaries of each interlaced with those of all the others. . . . From chaos theory we learn about the famous "butterfly effect"—the world's physical systems are so interrelated that sometimes the mere flapping of a butterfly's wings in Beijing is enough to cause a tornado to form over Kansas City. (Zohar, 1997, pp. 11–12)

Only recently have we begun to recognize that these features appear in organizations, as in all of life. We are coming to understand that an organization's systems are not separate, but interwoven. The same holds true for an organization's human system; employees are interlaced with others, regardless of their position or responsibility. By implication, organizational leaders are working within a space that is full of energy, where everything is interrelated.

The question is how new systems thinking that is influenced by complexity sciences can be translated into working principles and strategies for such a space. Are there graphics other than flowcharts and decision maps that would be useful? What kind of infrastructure could leaders build to support change and potentiality in an atmosphere of ambiguity and uncertainty?

ADDITIONAL READING RESOURCES

Russell Ackoff, *Re-Creating the Corporation: A Design of Organizations for the 21st Century.* Oxford Press, 1999.

Jamshid Gharajedaghi, *Systems Thinking: Managing Chaos and Complexity: A Platform for Designing Business Architecture.* Butterworth Heinemann, 1999.

Stephen Haines, *The Complete Guide to Systems Thinking and Learning.* HRD Press, 2000.

Ralph H. Kilmann, What should the new organization look (and think) like? *Innovative Leader*, December 2001.

Brenda Barker Scott, The magic of diagnosis. *Change Management*, February 2006.

Peter Senge, *The Fifth Discipline.* Doubleday, 1990.

Margaret J.Wheatley, Leadership lessons for the real world. *Leader to Leader,* Summer 2006.

Danah Zohar, *Rewiring the Corporate Brain: Using the New Science to Rethink How We Structure and Lead Organizations.* Berrett-Koehler, 1997.

For more information check these sites:

www.acasa.upenn.edu
www.haines centre.com/essence
www.systemdynamics.org
http://systemsthinkingpress.com/pages/General_Systems_Theory
www.thinking.net/Systems_Thinking/systems_thinking.html
http://web.mit.edu/sdg/www

ISSUE 8

What Performance Measures Should Organizational Leaders Consider Today?

INTRODUCTION

Performance review is so commonplace, why should leaders bother to think about which measures make sense for today's organization? The reason: Performance is on the minds of everyone. Business and industry leaders have always been concerned about performance but the same cannot be said of other types of organizations. For decades the formula was simple: If profit was the organization's raison d'etre, performance of every facet was a high priority. If something other than profit was the organization's raison d'etre and competition was not a factor, performance was less important. Times have changed though and public demand for performance has increased. Whether the organization is a nonprofit, a corporation, a school, or agency of government, people want to know if it is efficient, reliable, effective, and high quality. Clients and customers may not be interested in the organization's internal processes, but they are definitely interested in the outcomes.

Increasingly, leaders are called on to influence an organization's performance. This may seem an obvious role for leaders; however, organizational performance measures still seem to be underappreciated:

> A change in mindset and culture is required to develop and use performance measures to improve performance. Agencies can lay the foundation for these changes by encouraging and fostering the use of performance measures. This will happen only if senior managers support and participate in the process itself.

> —(Plunkett, n.d., p. 3)

The change in mindset was influenced when the federal government enacted the first performance measurement legislation in 1993—the Government Performance Results Act. Since then, performance measurement has become a significant part of capital investment, not only for government agencies but for corporations, NGOs, and nonprofits. Business and industry's move to adopt performance-based budgeting and balanced score card approaches are also signals that performance measures deserve more attention.

Of all the review processes an organization undertakes, employee performance may be the most neglected. The tools have been around for so long and are so standardized that leaders often take them for granted. But which review processes make sense today? Isn't one measure as good as another? Obviously this is not the case. As the systems approach penetrates the thinking of organizational leaders, they are beginning to question regular performance measurement. Measures must take into account whether the accomplishments of employees are achieving the organization's goals and objectives. That means the measures are not chosen until the organization's business strategies are in place and resources are identified. The best measures reflect how well the conceptual language of strategies has been translated into action steps. And those action steps, which can range over a three- to five-year period, are then interpreted into performance criteria that center on daily operations, activities, and procedures. It's a matter of linking everything together, from mission to goals to projects to accomplishments. Identifying effective performance measures at the project level and individual level happens throughout this linking process.

Leaders who practice systems thinking are beginning to realize that traditional performance review is no longer adequate. Confidence in traditional performance measurement is eroding primarily because typical measures rank individuals on an ordinal scale in relation to others. Ranking may not be a good fit with emerging organizational structures such as teams or multinational work groups. In teams or work groups, no one is a subordinate, which makes positioning individuals on an evaluative scale less appropriate. Also ranking is dubious because individuals can game the system or "rank up" without actually demonstrating the criteria on which the system is based. The first reading, "The Struggle to Measure Performance," addresses forced ranking. This process is used in as many as one-third of U.S. corporations without regard for whether it matches ways employees are currently working.

Another question leaders are asking is what to do about team evaluation. Is traditional ranking appropriate or should more wholistic measures be used for teams? The authors of the second reading respond to this question on the basis of a national survey of organizations that utilize teamwork. The findings discussed in "Project Teams: How Good Are They?" indicate that performance review of teams is woefully lacking. The practices of teams and the assessment of team members are not yet aligned, which leaves leaders wondering how to manage a project if teamwork cannot be assessed.

Also in question are performance review criteria, which have traditionally involved quality and quantity of work, efficiency and effectiveness, and timeliness. These criteria are typically measured against a set of standards. A newer way of reviewing professional performance is the 360-degree assessment, a multisource feedback system. Essentially, an employee is provided with confidential feedback from several people, including peers, administrators, perhaps clients or customers. Rather than one supervisor measuring the individual against standards, the input comes from numerous sources.

Ideally, the results of feedback are used to verify strengths and determine areas of development. In the third reading, "Assessment Alternatives: Appraising Organizational Performance," Ralph Jacobson explores some of the issues related to 360-degree feedback. Jacobson contends that there are simpler, more effective ways to provide feedback that will improve individual and organizational performance.

Performance review, once regarded as a routine practice, is increasingly seen as a thorny issue for leaders. The good practices of earlier times are no longer viable and organizations are searching to better matches between contemporary functions and structures and the assessment of employee performance.

SOURCES

Jena McGregor, The struggle to measure performance. *Business Week*, January 9, 2006.

Howard M. Guttman & Andrew Longman, Project teams: How good are they? *Quality Progress*, February 2006.

Ralph Jacobson, Assessment alternatives: Appraising organizational performance. *Chief Learning Officer*, November 2005.

The Struggle to Measure Performance

Jena McGregor

Holiday shopping, yearend deadlines, and emotional family dramas aren't the only stresses in December. 'Tis the season for companies to embark on that dreaded annual rite, the often bureaucratic and always time-consuming performance review. The process can be brutal: As many as one-third of U.S. corporations evaluate employees based on systems that pit them against their colleagues, and some even lead to the firing of low performers.

Fans say such "forced ranking" systems ensure that managers take a cold look at performance. But the practice increasingly is coming under fire. Following a string of discrimination lawsuits from employees who feel they were ranked and yanked based on age and not merely their performance, fewer companies are adopting the controversial management tool. Critics charge that it unfairly penalizes groups made up of stars and hinders collaboration and risk-taking, a growing concern for companies that are trying to innovate their way to growth. And a new study calls into question the long-term value of forced rankings. "It creates a zero-sum game, and so it tends to discourage cooperation," says Steve Kerr, a managing director at Goldman Sachs Group Inc., who heads the firm's leadership training program.

Why is performance ranking so problematic that it is leading to discrimination lawsuits by employees?

MORE FLEXIBILITY

Even General Electric Co., the most famous proponent of the practice, is trying to inject more flexibility into its system. Former Chief Executive Jack Welch required managers to divide talent into three groups—a top 20%, a middle 70%, and a bottom 10%, many of whom were shown the door. Eighteen months ago, GE launched a proactive campaign to remind managers to use more common sense in assigning rankings. "People in some locations take [distributions] so literally that judgment comes out of the practice," says Susan P. Peters, GE's vice-president for executive development.

Striking that balance between strict yardsticks and managerial judgment is something every company, from GE to Yahoo! to American Airlines, is grappling with today. But finding a substitute for a rigid grading system is not an easy task. It drives truth into a process frequently eroded by grade inflation and helps leaders identify managers who are good at finding top talent.

That's one reason GE isn't abandoning its system. But it has removed all references to the 20/70/10 split from its online performance management tool and now presents the curve as a set of guidelines. The company's 200,000 professional employees tend to fall into Welch's categories anyway, but individual groups are freer to have a somewhat higher number of "A" players or even, says Peters, no "bottom 10s." Even those low achievers are getting some kinder treatment, from a new appellation—the "less effectives"—to more specific coaching and intervention than in the past.

The changes are key for a company trying to evolve its culture from a Six Sigma powerhouse to one that also values innovation. Tempering such rigid performance metrics, says Peters, "enables individuals and organizations to be more comfortable with risk-taking and with failure." To drive that point home, the company's top 5,000 managers were evaluated for the first time this year on five traits, such as imagination and external focus, that represent the company's strategic goals.

NEW DATA

Separating stars from slackers remains a long-standing part of GE's performance-driven culture. But for most companies, especially those without such cultures, the benefits of adopting a forced ranking system are likely to dissipate over the long term.

A recent study lends hard data to that theory. Steve Scullen, an associate professor of management at Drake University in Des Moines, found that forced ranking, including the firing of the bottom 5% or 10%, results in an impressive 16% productivity improvement—but only over the first couple of years. After that, Scullen says, the gains drop off, from 6% climbs in the third and fourth years to basically zero by year 10. "It's a terrific idea for companies in trouble, done over one or two years, but to do it as a long-term solution is not going to work," says Dave Ulrich, a business professor at the University of Michigan at Ann Arbor. "Over time it gets people focused on competing with each other rather than collaborating."

One company that recently decided to dump forced rankings altogether is Chemtura, a $3 billion specialty chemicals company formed by the July merger of Crompton in Middlebury, Conn., and Great Lakes Chemical in Indianapolis.

"The system forced me to turn people who were excellent performers into people who were getting mediocre ratings," says Eric Wisnefsky, Chemtura's vice-president for corporate finance. "That demotivates them, and they'd follow up with asking: 'What could I do differently next year?' That's a very difficult question to answer when you feel that people actually met all your expectations." Chemtura's new process still assigns grades. But to better motivate employees in the middle, labels such as "satisfactory" have been upgraded to phrases such as "successful performance."

Yahoo, too, was looking for better dialogue and less demoralizing labels when it made substantial changes this year to its rating system, which compared employees' performance to an absolute standard rather than to each other. Libby Sartain, Yahoo's senior vice-president for human resources, knew that review discussions at the Sunnyvale (Calif.) tech leader frequently included the wink-wink "I wanted to put you here, but I was forced by human resources to do something different" comment that discredits so many appraisals. This year, Yahoo stripped away its performance labels, partly in hopes that reviews would center more on substance and less on explaining away a grade.

But that doesn't mean Yahoo went all Pollyanna on its employees. To do a better job of finding and showering top performers with the rewards necessary to keep them from jumping ship in talent-tight Silicon Valley, the company also instituted a "stack-ranking" system this year to determine how compensation increases are distributed. It asks managers to rank employees within each unit—a group of 20 people would be ranked 1 through 20, for example—with raises and bonuses distributed accordingly. During reviews, employees are told how their increases generally compare to those of others.

Some Yahoo managers are livid about the new system. "It's going to kill morale," laments one senior engineering manager who says he's getting a stronger message to cull his bottom performers. Yahoo says its new program doesn't automatically weed out a bottom group and was designed specifically to reward its stars.

What are some pitfalls of a merit-driven approach to performance measurement?

Indeed, what Yahoo has introduced in place of its old system shows how hard it is for companies to find ways to foster merit-driven cultures that coddle standouts while staying tough on low performers. Whether a company calls it stack ranking, forced ranking, or differentiation, "there's no magic process," says Sartain. "We just want to make sure we're making our bets and that we're investing in the people we most want to keep. That's what this is all about."

ARTICLE 8.2

Project Teams: How Good Are They?

Howard M. Guttman and Andrew Longman

Project teams have become the basic work units of the modern enterprise. The ability to complete projects on goal, on time and on budget will likely set apart winners from wannabes in the years ahead. But attaining project success is a tough challenge. In 2004, the Standish Group found 51% of the IT projects it surveyed were seriously late, over budget and off goal.[1]

The IT function is not alone in its project failures, as we all know from the "big bombs" featured in the media over the past several years. Consider these:

- **DaimlerChrysler's troubled Smart car division.** The company's missteps hobbled what should have been a car that was a perfect fit for its time.[2]
- **Huge weapons systems being developed for the Pentagon.** A Government Accountability Office review of 26 weapons systems found the total cost of these programs had increased nearly 15% over the first full-cost estimates.[3]
- **The FBI's Virtual Case File system.** The agency declared an official end to its floundering $170 million effort to overhaul its computer software and said it would take at least three and a half years to develop a new system.[4]
- **The Big Dig, a Boston public works project.** Twenty years and billions of dollars later, there are continued budget overruns, investigations of fraud and a newly opened tunnel with blocked fire exits, falling debris and leaks.[5]
- **Hurricane Katrina response.** Poor project planning and execution, from the White House to the New Orleans mayor's office, turned a natural disaster into a political, economic and human catastrophe.

These examples and countless others raise a number of key questions:

- In general, how are projects currently being managed in organizations?
- How well are individual projects led, planned and executed?
- What causes projects to veer off track?
- What is life like on the typical project team?

To answer these questions, *Quality Progress* teamed up with the consulting firms of Guttman Development Strategies and Kepner-Tregoe. In September 2005, *QP* e-mailed our survey on project team performance to about half its readership. Of the 46,828 people who received the survey, 1,905 responded,

252

for a 4% response rate. Twenty-nine percent of respondents were individual contributors, 42% were first-line and middle managers, and 15% were senior managers. Respondents represented a cross section of industries. Approximately half worked for companies with more than $200 million in revenue and 1,000 employees.

We asked both quantitative and qualitative questions. The qualitative ones asked respondents to identify the most important reasons for project success and failure in their organizations. A representative sampling of answers, called "Voices From the Workplace," is sprinkled throughout the text that follows.

PROJECT TEAMS: THE BIG PICTURE

From the quantitative responses, a somewhat conflicting picture of projects emerges. On one hand, many respondents were positive about the quality and effectiveness of their organizations' project teams. But few rated their overall project performance as excellent, and, more disturbingly, a significant number reported performance was mediocre at best. When you cut to the heart of the findings, two essential facts stand out:

1. Fewer than half (46.9%) of the projects under way in respondents' organizations always or often meet their goals.
2. Fewer than one-third (32.6%) are always or often completed on time and on budget.

Given these numbers, it's not surprising fewer than half our respondents said their organizations' financial performance was in the top third of their respective industries.

To learn more about what is working and what isn't on project teams, we drilled down, asking respondents a series of specific questions about the way projects are generally managed in their organizations. We began by probing five areas vital to an organization's project success:

1. **Project alignment and goals.** Whether the analogy is with the human anatomy, automobiles or organizations, alignment implies things are effectively lined up to achieve maximum performance. When it comes to projects, how aligned are they, across the board, with overall organization strategy? The good news is 70% of respondents reported their projects were aligned. Yet, nearly one-third reported their projects were off strategy.

    Fuzzy or unrealistic goals kill project effectiveness. While slightly more than half (54%) said their organizations' project goals were often or always clear and attainable, the remaining 46% reported this is only the case sometimes, rarely or never. This points to a significant potential problem related to goal clarity and realism.
2. **Resources and staffing.** This area has frequently been a lightning rod for organizational conflict, and survey responses affirmed it still is.

More than two-thirds of respondents said their organizations' project teams are only sometimes, rarely or never given sufficient resources to accomplish their goals. Insufficient resources was also the most common answer to the open-ended question "What is the most common reason for the failure of projects in your organization?"

More than half our respondents did not think the right people were always or often selected to lead or serve on project teams. In answer to a related question, 84% said employees rarely, if ever, were relieved of their routine job responsibilities while serving on a project team.

3. **Training and development.** Eighty percent of respondents said only sometimes, rarely or never do employees receive training in project management methodology before serving on a project team. It's probably no coincidence that 62% reported project teams throughout the organization don't often follow a standard methodology to define, plan and implement projects.

4. **Rewards and recognition.** While the drive to excel may spring from deep within, sustaining that drive over the long term requires ongoing rewards and recognition. So, are project teams receiving sufficient rewards? It seems not—58% of respondents said only sometimes, rarely or never is the successful completion of projects recognized publicly by top management.

Not many teams receive financial rewards/bonuses for the successful completion of projects, with more than 87% of respondents reporting these are given only sometimes, rarely or never. In nearly 61% of the cases, there is no link between employees' annual reviews and their performance on project teams.

5. **Senior executive team.** Because top teams exercise an almost gravitational pull on the collective psyche of an organization, we asked for an assessment of the following statement: "Our senior management team serves as a positive role model for project management." Seventy percent of respondents said this occurs sometimes, rarely or never.

What prevents leaders from serving as positive role models for project teams?

Of all the survey findings, we find this to be the most troublesome. You can have clear, specific and attainable project goals. You can embed the right project management processes and methodologies and train project teams to use them. You can tweak rewards and recognition. But unless the senior team demonstrates high performance, teams elsewhere in the organization will follow the wrong example.

Overall, the responses to this section of our survey should raise serious red flags about how organizations view and manage projects. The bottom line: While responses reveal a large number of projects are sufficiently well managed, many others are not. Though these may never show up on a future list of big bombs, continued poor performance will likely compromise the organization's competitive vitality.

PROJECT TEAMS: UP CLOSE AND PERSONAL

The survey results painted a picture not only of how organizations manage projects in general but also of the personal experiences of respondents when serving on typical project teams—as team leaders, members or facilitators. Not surprisingly, a comparison of the responses of these three groups shows a slightly more optimistic view from the team leaders. Otherwise, among all three groups, the picture that emerged was one of sharp contrasts, with many respondents reporting very good to excellent experiences and many others describing teams that needed substantial improvement.

We began by asking for an assessment of the typical team's goals and roles:

- Two-thirds answered their teams' overall goals were very clear, which is good news—except for the remaining third, who said their goals were only somewhat clear or not at all clear.
- While it's one thing to be clear about your team's overall project goals, it's quite another to be clear about the individual roles of you and the person sitting next to you on a project team. Here again, while the majority (57%) said they were clear about these roles, a significant number (42%) said they were not.

Think of project management processes as organizing principles for team performance. How many typical teams followed standardized processes during their project? Once again, there was good news and bad. Sixty-two percent of respondents said their teams had followed a visible, common project management process—but the remaining 38% said a process wasn't used or they weren't sure. Similarly, 56% said their teams had used a common process for problem solving and decision making, but 43% weren't sure or said the teams hadn't used such a methodology.

We next probed the interactions and behavior of the team members. A house divided does not allow for a high performance team. Energy gets diverted from meeting project goals to dealing with dysfunctional behavior and subterfuge, which is why we asked how well typical project teams handled this critical issue.

The good news: On a scale of one to five—with one equivalent to no tolerance for confrontation/conflicts suppressed and five meaning tensions surfaced and were confronted and resolved—about half (51.3%) gave their teams a four or five. Those teams dealt with conflict in an open manner. But that leaves nearly as many respondents (48.2%) who rated their teams' performance in this area three or lower. And, while only 8.3% reported the team spent more than half its time dealing with unresolved conflict, more than 90% said the team had spent up to half its time in this unproductive activity (62.2% up to a quarter of their time, 28% between one-quarter and one-half of their time).

One of the hallmarks of a high performing team is the degree to which its members see themselves as responsible for the success of the team as a whole, rather than being narrowly "me" focused. Here again, responses were split, with nearly 60% feeling very to highly responsible for the success of their fellow team members and the other 40% feeling no or little responsibility for others.

In terms of intrateam communication, the picture was not much better: On a scale of one to five, with one equivalent to not at all effective and five very effective, nearly 44% of respondents answered one, two or three.

The final questions in the set dealing with experience on a typical project team related to project outcomes. On the positive side, 82% of those who responded said their projects were completed, and 89% said the projects met their goals. However, 36% reported the projects were late, and 26% said they came in over budget, indicating that meeting project goals is often a costly and time consuming enterprise.

PROJECT LEADERSHIP

In today's project environment, the leader-follower paradigm seems like an antiquated relic from the past. Teams reach the highest levels of performance when members step up to assume greater responsibility for thought leadership and results. Today's project leaders are less directors and more facilitators of team performance. One of their major roles is to keep resources focused and help the team set guidelines for decision making and behavior.

How well does the typical team leader carry out this role? When we asked respondents to tell us how effective their teams' leaders were at helping teams meet their goals—on a scale of one to five, with one being not at all effective and five being very effective—42.5% gave the leader three or less. And, when asked to rate the team leader's overall project management skills on a scale of one to five, with one being poor and five excellent, nearly half gave the team leader a grade of three or less.

Our last two questions about project leadership focused on interpersonal relations. First, we asked how effective the team leader was in managing conflict among team members. With one being poor and five excellent, more than half rated their leaders' conflict management skills three or less. When asked to describe their leader's behavioral style, fewer than half of team leaders were characterized as having a healthy, assertive way of interacting. The remaining half was split nearly equally between the less effective nonassertive and aggressive styles.

Overall, responses indicate there is an across-the-board deficiency of leadership capabilities. In a significant number of cases, project leaders are lacking many of the process and behavioral skills necessary for project success.

PATHWAYS TO CHANGE

In general, survey respondents reported that, on a significant number of projects, processes are loose, informal and left to chance. In many cases, team behavior is poorly managed and less than productive.

Stepping back from the survey data, how can all projects—those that are performing badly and those that are just average—be improved? One answer: Provide more resources. After all, nearly three-quarters of respondents reported projects were under resourced sometimes, often or always. But this solution may not be realistic, given the resource constraints in most organizations. And it is certainly simplistic, in light of the array of other factors that respondents say lead to project failure. Sadly, there is no one silver bullet.

What is the leader's role in dealing with the issue of scarce resources for project teams?

Based on the survey data and our consulting experiences, moving project teams to higher levels of performance requires an integrated approach that addresses four major areas:

1. **Leadership.** Top management teams must learn to serve as role models of high performance. They must become aligned strategically, reach agreement on business goals, be clear on roles and responsibilities, determine ground rules for decision making and strive for transparency in business relationships. In addition, the organization's leaders must provide visible and meaningful support for projects throughout their organization. This includes prioritizing the organization's portfolio of projects to avoid the stop-start syndrome and project overload, providing rewards for superior performance on projects and providing team leaders and members with the requisite technical, process and interpersonal skills needed to succeed.

2. **Process discipline.** As organizations become more matrixed and project teams more cross functional in nature, there is a need to move beyond a helter-skelter project management approach. Project management has evolved into a discipline, and organizations would do well to absorb project management processes, transfer them throughout the ranks and build a knowledge management legacy system that captures lessons learned. Seat-of-the-pants problem solving and decision making on projects is not working. It is crucial for project teams to employ a common, systematic process for resolving the problem solving, decision making and planning issues that come before them.

3. **The performance system.** Think about project teams as mini performance environments that must be carefully managed. Team members must be clear on project goals and the end game, possess the right skills, receive accurate and timely feedback and be aware of the positive and negative consequences for various behaviors.

4. **Interpersonal dynamics.** Given all the performance pressure on project teams and the mounting complexity of the environments in which they operate, it is not surprising that such teams have become holding pens for unproductive behavior. Such behavior takes many forms: putting functional self interest over team accomplishments, engaging in conflict (both overt and hidden), adopting a nonassertive or aggressive style, passing the buck, playing follow the leader and hesitating to confront one another's poor performance and unacceptable behavior. To eliminate these negative behaviors, all project teams should go through the same

alignment process as the senior team and receive training in conflict management and related skills.

While many respondents report experiencing project success, almost all point to an urgent need for improvement. To begin your improvement efforts, ask yourself how your organization's responses would compare to those we received. Then, look to leadership, process discipline, the performance system and interpersonal dynamics as prime targets in which to make the changes that will propel project teams to the next level of performance.

REFERENCES

1. Frank Hayes, "Chaos Is Back," *Computer World*, Nov. 8, 2004, p. 70.
2. Mark Landler, "DaimlerChrysler To Scale Back MiniCar Unit," *The New York Times*, April 2, 2005, p. C1.
3. Tim McLaughlin, "Report Says Weapons Are Costing More Than Promised," *St. Louis Post-Dispatch*, April 1, 2005, p. A16.
4. Eric Lichtblau, "FBI Ends a Faltering Effort To Overhaul Computer Software," *The New York Times*, March 9, 2005, p. B16.
5. Eileen McNamara, "The Big Dig and Blame Games," *Boston Globe*, Dec. 17, 2003, p. B1.

Assessment Alternatives: Appraising Organizational Performance

Ralph Jacobson

Considerable corporate time and resources are devoted to providing feedback to employees. In general, the vast majority of human resources professionals use the 360-degree competency assessment process as a primary means to provide feedback to employees regarding their performance. Employees, with the support of their managers, are expected to analyze this feedback to determine their strengths and weaknesses and to develop a plan to enhance their personal productivity and effectiveness. The process has become so widespread that its power to shape positive behaviors is accepted as fact. Legions of consulting organizations are willing to assist in devising competencies and generating feedback reports. But does the considerable time and investment devoted to this feedback process actually deliver a significant return? Do the reports and discussions with managers actually improve performance?

The issues involved with the 360-degree assessment include the determination of competencies, interpretation of results and subsequent efforts to use the data to create development plans. There are simpler, more cost-effective and more powerful methods for providing feedback that are more likely to improve individual and organization performance.

VALIDITY: DETERMINING THE RIGHT COMPETENCIES

To achieve statistical validity and ensure that the targeted competencies positively impact performance, managers must first identify the most competent employees. Then, they can pinpoint the specific knowledge, skills and abilities of these individuals that account for their higher performance. Establishing the validity of this data requires rigorous collection of job-specific behaviors and comparisons between highly and less productive employees. Further, focus groups, expert panels, behavioral interviews and psychological tests are often used to confirm that the right competencies have indeed been identified.

Because validating competencies is expensive and time-consuming, most human resources professionals avoid this expense by selecting a number of competencies from pre-established lists. Alternatively, they may decide to develop a competency list through the use of focus groups of senior organizational leaders. Such lists may or may not identify the competencies that lead to outstanding performance.

SoftBrands: The Toolbox Approach to Organizational Success
Ralph Jacobson

SoftBrands is a provider of enterprise-wide software solutions focused on the hospitality and manufacturing industries. For David Gahn, vice president of the Americas for Softbrands, building the success of the organization was a new assignment. But for Randy Tofteland, SoftBrands' president, it was an unresolved challenge that had been delegated to two previous vice presidents. The U.K. division, which the organization had acquired through a merger many years ago, continued to be a drain on the corporation. Tofteland charged Gahn with the task of either quickly fixing the ailing division or divesting it.

Previously, Renee Conklin, vice president of human resources, had invested heavily in traditional types of leadership training that emphasized 360-degree competency feedback and learning about personality types. Though a few individual leaders may have found some of this knowledge personally useful, the training clearly had not impacted business results. Although the company's leaders were highly seasoned, none of them had faced such a difficult and competitive market. Developing leaders who could face challenging assignments was central to the organization's long-term success.

Leaders at SoftBrands required an alternative development process that would help them quickly improve business performance. Conklin shifted her leadership development approach to provide the top and middle management teams with toolbox training, which was specifically designed not to improve their individual leadership capabilities, but to teach the leadership groups how to address current organizational leadership challenges. The toolbox training provided specific leadership language, the leader's map and the leadership tools to address the organization's challenges.

Gahn gathered together the employees of the U.K. division. With them, he used the leadership change map and the tools to analyze the market, develop scenarios, determine the organization's critical core competencies, and identify and balance the paradoxes that stood in their way. Through this process, he was able to gain employee commitment to a new strategic scenario. Tofteland was delighted with the newly crafted strategic plan and gave the U.K. division the permission, time and the resources needed to reframe its future.

In early 2002 Terry Peterson, who was responsible for the company's service contract business, watched first-quarter revenues fall quickly.

Prior to the leadership toolbox training. Peterson would have felt compelled to cut expenses and lay off employees. This time, however, he took a different route. He pulled out the leader's map and applied the leadership tools to the task at hand. Rather than follow his usual practice of tightening up, Peterson openly shared the current business reality with the employees and invited them to participate in the process of reinventing their future.

The organizational results achieved by the use of the newly learned leadership tools were astounding. At the end of the first year, revenues of the U.K. division grew 30 percent, almost all of which fell to the bottom line. While the annual industry market growth rate for manufacturing software in the year following the training was 3 percent, the U.K. division delivered a whopping 23 percent increase in revenues. By the end of the second quarter of 2002, Peterson's contract services group had erased the shortfall of the first quarter and exceeded the yearly budget revenue forecast as a result of the five new products that had been produced with the help of the leadership tools.

These two leaders learned that powerful results can be achieved by using the right leadership tools. They learned how to effectively involve employees in the process of analyzing the competitive environment and how to put in place an infrastructure for realizing financial success. Overwhelming market challenges could have led to the worst experiences of their long careers. Instead, Peterson and Gahn successfully navigated changes that led to both organizational success and high levels of personal satisfaction.

Though it has been three years since their first and only formal leadership toolbox training, the leadership map and the tools remain central aspects of SoftBrands' leadership strategies.

ORGANIZATION-WIDE COMPETENCIES

Applying a short list of competencies to all employees or to broad job categories could simplify the feedback process, reduce the upfront expenses and support a common set of values and norms. Also, learning efforts may be more efficient when focused around a narrow set of topics. Though a short list of competencies for an entire organization can support working together more effectively, the compromised list is less likely to identify the feedback that is needed to improve specific job performance of each individual. The effectiveness of this approach is therefore significantly diminished.

Why are predetermined competencies for a 360-degree assessment not a good idea?

FOCUS ON THE JOB

Most jobs require an array of competencies, which are usually defined from the perspective of individual managers. But flatter organizational structures and greater use of cross-functional teams require groups of people to perform in ambiguous and free-flowing situations. Knowing how employees should and do perform in specific group or project situations may be more important than knowing how they perform as individual contributors. The utilization of a unique combination of skills and personalities within a larger, constantly shifting structure determines organizational performance. A competency that is viewed as effective within the context of an individual job may be ineffective in a team environment. The general competency approach may not distinguish between these two work requirements.

THE ASSESSMENT PART OF THE PROCESS

In the usual 360-degree competency assessment, co-workers and managers are given a list of competencies and a set of behavioral anchors for each to use in evaluating individual employee performance. They are then asked to check their level of agreement or the frequency with which the employee must use each competency to perform in an excellent manner. Two clear issues emerge with this method of assessment. Generally, five to eight people are asked to make the assessment. As a result of the small sample size, one or two answers will have a significant impact on the averaged score for that item. Further, because relatively few people write in the comment sections on the form to clarify and further describe the behaviors they have observed and the rationale for their ratings, it is difficult to specify the context in which they expect a particular competency to be exhibited. Thus, the numerical score is likely an insufficient indicator of the behaviors that are expected to lead to desired employee performance.

INTERPRETATION OF RESULTS

Most people are content with their performance of competencies where feedback suggests they are performing in the average to above-average ranges with respect to their peer group. However, feeling content with an average score on a critical competency may be an ineffective strategy for driving sought-after performance.

In their book "The Extraordinary Leader," authors John Zenger and Joe Folkman, Ph.D., demonstrate empirically that the best leaders possess a few truly outstanding competencies. Leaders whose competency scores fall completely in the average range are perceived to be only 34 percent effective. Those with one strength above average are perceived to be 64 percent effective. Those with three strengths above average are perceived to be 80 percent effective.

The purpose of competency assessment should be to pinpoint and develop those few critical competencies that yield extraordinary and disproportionate performance. This is a more effective development strategy than shoring up less important competencies so that they are all perceived to be in at least the average range.

DEVELOPMENT PROGRAMS

Managers are expected to work with employees to develop approaches to improve targeted competencies, but few managers have the expertise to actually develop such a plan. For example, managers have difficulty effectively differentiating those skills that can be taught from innate abilities that are less likely to be improved with development activities. Trying to improve what are viewed as innate abilities is likely to frustrate employees.

Employees are more likely to improve their performance by practicing new behaviors in a work environment that allows room for experimentation and offers specific, timely and helpful feedback. Unfortunately few managers today believe they can allow employees to focus on anything other than immediate work issues. Without management support, employees are likely to revert to old behaviors. In such situations, performance feedback will have only a momentary impact on employee performance.

FEEDBACK ALTERNATIVES

On its face, the competency assessment process appears logical and relatively easy to administer. In reality, the process falls short of the goal of improving individual and organization performance. Two alternate approaches are far more effective: providing direct feedback and using leadership tools that are simple to learn and proven to have bottom-line impact. The direct-feedback approach actively involves the employee and all critical stakeholders in the improvement process. The leader's toolbox approach skips the diagnostic assessment completely and instead provides a common language for leadership at all levels, as well as many management and leadership tools to more directly achieve bottom-line improvement.

In the traditional 360-degree competency approach, employee feedback remains confidential, presumably to encourage honest responses. Major stakeholders, such as peers and associates, have little involvement in the individual's performance improvement beyond providing the initial assessment. This limited responsibility causes several problems. First, most organizational performance requires people to work together to make things happen. Even when one person improves his or her performance, the group may not perform better. More importantly, significant behavior change takes time and encouragement. Colleagues who are accustomed to an individual's on-the-job behaviors may not notice an improvement in performance or provide the necessary encouragement to sustain the improved on-the-job behaviors.

Marshall Goldsmith and Howard Morgan studied more than 86,000 people for their article, "Leadership is a Contact Sport: The 'Follow-up Factor' in Management Development," in Strategy+Business (September 2004). They state that the most critical factor in achieving positive long-term improvement is consistent, ongoing interaction and follow-up with colleagues. Dramatic performance improvement did not result from the assessment itself, but from the mutual discussion about development priorities with co-workers over time. Individuals who did not have the benefit of ongoing dialogue "showed improvement that barely exceeded random chance." Creating direct and frequent dialogue about performance has far greater impact than simply assessing behavior.

Within the direct feedback approach, the role of human resources professionals shifts from providing assessments to teaching people how to ask for and receive feedback. They train managers and internal coaches to help employees process feedback information and to create effective development plans. In this approach, responsibility for performance improvement shifts from the human resources professionals to managers and employees. Direct feedback creates opportunities for honest dialogue between people and provides the impetus for them to work closely and effectively with one another.

Many excellent leadership tools are described in great detail in business books and articles, but few of these tools are actually adopted in practice. It is more effective to encourage leaders at all organization levels to use a common leadership language and to employ processes and tools that can be applied to a broad range of organization challenges. Teaching leaders how to develop organization and functional strategies, engage critical stakeholders and coach employees in their improvement processes will more likely lead to successful implementation of large-scale organizational change. When leaders at all levels realize they face common obstacles to success, they are then more likely to open themselves to learning and personal growth. Learning and sound leadership practices address an organization's performance needs for the long run.

When using the toolbox methodology, the role of the human resources professional shifts from delivering individual assessments to determining the leadership language and processes that will have greatest impact on the organization's success. The human resources professional works closely with senior management to create practice fields in which to apply new learning to real, ongoing business issues. Creating a direct relationship between learning and organizational performance shifts responsibility for learning, thinking and development to senior leaders, where it rightly belongs.

What are some of the strengths and weaknesses of the direct feedback approach?

SUGGESTIONS FOR THE 360-DEGREE APPROACH

If you do decide to use the competency approach, consider the following suggestions:

- Undertake the rigorous process of defining those few behaviors that truly make a difference to organization's success. Avoid selecting competencies from a pre-established list.
- Identify your organization's core organization competencies, which Gary Hamel and C.K. Prahalad define as the integration of skills, technologies and knowledge across the organization that provides disproportionate competitive advantage. Critical core competencies are difficult for competitors to emulate and are perceived by customers as delivering

significant value. The contributions of employees toward shaping the organization's core competence can then become a significant determinant of critical individual competencies.

- Rather than expecting employees to fill out a standard competency questionnaire, teach employees how to actively participate in the process of defining critical competencies. Ask them to be precise, to describe in detail the specific behaviors that support their conclusions. Tell them how to avoid such common evaluation problems as the halo and devil effects.

- Provide development opportunities that will support employees' strengths. Focus only on those areas of weakness that will make a significant difference to effective performance on the job.

ISSUE SUMMARY

———•

Performance review has always been a fundamental practice of organizations. Through the years leaders have been exposed to a vast array of procedures and forms and for the most part, they have managed the process adequately. Typically, the review process follows an annual cycle of setting performance objectives, gathering and documenting evidence of meeting objectives throughout the year, and discussing the outcome at a year-end meeting.

But traditional performance assessment is becoming problematic for leaders who attempt to align mission, strategy, and work. As organizations move away from a focus on the *activities* of work to concentrating on the *results* of work, it is inevitable that assessment of performance will also shift. This is the era of mission and goals for organizations, so it is entirely appropriate that performance review is broader than simply assessing an individual's accomplishments. From a systems perspective, this alignment makes good sense. A generic measure of performance that does not encompass organizational strategy and structure, as well as results of work will not serve an organization well. Leaders who are systems thinkers acknowledge that the employee performance process is interconnected with every aspect of organizational performance.

An intriguing question about performance review is whether it should focus on uniformity and consistency or innovation and variability. Performance review that concentrates on efficiency and goal attainment is not consistent with the conditions necessary for innovation. Reviewing individuals on a predetermined set of criteria on a prearranged schedule may be appropriate for work that does not vary or that must be done to exact standards. That is not the case for many employees today. During the course of a year, goals will change, work will vary, and roles in work teams will alter.

For organizations that value or even thrive on innovation, the performance review process must be responsive and fluid. The focus of these organizations is on behaviors that demonstrate risk-taking, creativeness, experimentation, and challenge-seeking. The paradox is that "smart" objectives of normal performance appraisal—specific, measurable, achievable, results oriented, time framed—may not be so smart. Employees meeting smart objectives will demonstrate behaviors that are more conforming, predictable, and goal directed. These are not the behaviors needed by many organizations today in an era when innovation and creativity are critical to survival. An organization's capacity to innovate depends on the ability of leaders to shape the right performance review process.

ISSUE HIGHLIGHTS

- Many organizations use a performance review process that evaluates employees as compared to their colleagues.
- Some organizations are finding the forced rankings are counter to strategies such as teamwork, collaboration, and risk-taking.
- In an attempt to make the review process more flexible, performance criteria are including terms like "innovation," "imagination," and "external focus."
- Organizations are conflicted about the effectiveness of project teams.
- A national study concludes that few project teams rate their performance as excellent and many projects are not on time or on budget.
- Project success depends largely on the team leader.
- The majority of human resources professionals use the 360-degree competency assessment process.
- Some organizations are questioning the effectiveness of 360-degree assessments for improving performance.
- Direct feedback is a simpler, more effective approach to performance review.

CRITICAL THINKING

Today's organizations face constant change. Whether due to internal reorganization, a merger or acquisition, or a falling stock market, change is the new status quo for organizations. It is not only the pace of change but the size of change that will affect the success of organizations. If change is sequential or limited in scope, the functioning of an organization remains stable. However, at times an organization faces complex change. This is a time when every function is affected and everything must be handled quickly. Current leadership training recognizes the importance of change management and wise leaders understand that complex change is a formidable task. Usually leaders will take into account changes in structure, job responsibilities, communication, and coordination.

But what happens to performance review during times of complex change? Are employees held to the usual criteria and process or should review be changed along with every other function? The author of "Obstacles to Effective Strategy Implementation," a recent article in *Organizational Dynamics*, believes that performance criteria need to be relaxed in times of complex change. His rationale: "the only way to make a complex change work is to reduce its complexity. The need is to focus on a small subset of simultaneous tasks, activities, or programs and not hold individuals accountable for performance in other areas" (Hrebiniak, 2006, p. 28).

The problem is that many organizational leaders are unwilling to allow this kind of flexibility, in the belief that relaxed performance will prevent complex change from happening. Their thinking may be flawed though, if Hrebiniak is right. It is only by reducing the complexity in all areas of functioning that complex change will succeed.

ADDITIONAL READING RESOURCES

David L. Cleland & Lewis R. Ireland, Effective project teamwork. *Project Management: Strategic Design and Implementation*, McGraw-Hill, 2006.

Lawrence G. Hrebiniak, Obstacles to effective strategy implementation. *Organizational Dynamics*, 2006.

Lonnie Pacelli, Five simple strategies for unifying your project teams. *American Society of Mechanical Engineers.* http://www.asme.org/Communities/EarlyCareer/Five_Simple_Strategies.cfm

Patrick T. Plunkett, Eight steps to develop and use information technology performance measures effectively. Washington, D.C.: General Services Administration, n.d.

For more information check these sites:

www.baldrigeplus.com/leadership2.htm
www.boothco.com/elements.html#whatis360
www.theworkfoundation.com

ISSUE 9

Has Strategic Planning Been Left Behind?

INTRODUCTION

Historically, strategic planning has been one of the main activities of orga-nizational leaders. It is an enterprise that occupies many work hours. In its simplest form, strategic planning enables leaders to answer three questions: Where are we going? How will we get there? How do we know we've gotten there? Essentially the purpose of strategic planning is to get everyone on the same page with their answers to these three questions.

Approaches to strategic planning vary, depending on the organization's mission and purpose, size, and culture. Organizations can take a goal-oriented, issue-oriented, or program-oriented approach, with goal-oriented being the typical model. Resources for strategic planning are abundant and many orga-nizations are now able to turn to software for planning. (Googling will bring up 6,000 sources of strategic planning software.) So why ask if strategic planning has been left behind?

In truth, the answer to the question is neither yes nor no. For some organiza-tions, strategic planning for a five- to ten-year period has fallen out of favor. For others, strategic planning as top-down, general-to-specific is passé. And for still others, the three classic planning questions are no longer relevant. The problem is that many traditional strategic plans are obsolete instantly: Even as they are being circulated, the economy, the neighborhood, and the world have all changed.

Strategic planning continues to be a major activity of organizational lead-ers, but it is taking new shapes. This transformation is driven by much more than technology and resources. It is also due to an ever-increasing need for improvement and it is supported by a mindset that embraces complexity. New planning strategies are more robust, allowing organizational leaders to ask the why questions in addition to where and how. Sophisticated approaches like resource mapping, scenarios, and simulations enable leaders to do "what-if" analysis. No longer is strategic planning limited to corporations and solely about profitability, margin, and performance. Now, as never before, nonprofits have excellent resources for planning that focus on sustainability, volunteer-ism, and service. (See the Support Center for Nonprofit Management Web site for resources.)

A chronic complaint about strategic planning is that the important decisions are not in the plan. Another complaint is that strategies do not translate into performance. Mankins and Steele, the authors of the first reading, have discovered several reasons for misguided strategic plans. Chief among the reasons are bad timing and an ineffective planning process. Mankins and Steele's survey of 156 large companies shows that although many of the organizations continue to use strategic planning, the traditional process may not be worthwhile. There is a disconnect between planning and decision making, largely because leaders continually make decisions yet they plan periodically. Mankins and Steele believe strategic planning can be done right by moving to a continuous decision-oriented process.

The second reading, "The Learning Organization and Strategic Change," is based on the premise that organizational learning is not about a separate type of organization but applicable as a model of strategic change for any organization. The author explains four versions of strategic planning and shows how each is a variation of the learning process. Three of the four versions—conventional "predict and plan" focus on implementation and the readiness model—are limited in their ability to help organizations "plan and execute significant organizational change amid rapidly changing business conditions." The fourth version—continual learning organization—is a state of constant readiness and continual planning, and according to the author is the best way to introduce fundamental changes.

It's not strategic planning that's been left behind—it's the implementation according to Mike Freedman, author of the third reading. "The Genius Is in the Implementation" is a thorough discussion of the steps necessary in strategy execution. Freedman defines five phases of the strategy process and makes the point that leaders need to understand when it is appropriate to begin implementation. The keys to successful implementation involve a set of activities that will make or break the strategic plan: communicate the strategy, drive planning, align the organization, reduce complexity, and install an issue resolution system. For Freedman, creating a strategic plan is one half of the job. The other half—implementation—involves discipline and commitment to stay the course.

"You can't create the future in a structure designed to repeat the past," according to Rosabeth Moss Kanter (2002, p. 78). Kanter, along with other organizational leadership experts, has been influencing organizations to use new models for strategic planning—models that rely less on predictability and control, more on changeableness and alternatives. John Vogelsang, from the Support Center for Nonprofit Management, is also a proponent of new models for strategic planning. In "Futuring: A Complex Adaptive Systems Approach to Strategic Planning," Vogelsang presents a thorough comparison of traditional approaches and emerging approaches. Behind the newest approaches are recent theoretical constructs that are vastly different from traditional strategic concepts: chaos theory, complexity sciences, and quantum physics.

Traditional strategic planning is about actions and results—all of which lead to increased knowledge. Notice that knowing is at the end of the formula. For many organizational leaders today, this formula begins at the wrong place. Instead of actions, the process should begin with knowledge, and then move to actions and results. The assumption is that knowledge management and knowledge integration will enable organizations to deal with emerging events and opportunities, not just solutions to immediate problems. Making knowledge management a key component of strategic planning means an organization must replace traditional techniques with those that can accommodate unpredictable conditions, globalization, and an unforeseeable future (Akhter, 2003).

SOURCES

Michael C. Mankins & Richard Steele, Stop making plans: Start making decisions. *Harvard Business Review*, January 2006.

Robert W. Rowden, The learning organization and strategic change. *SAM Advanced Management Journal*, Summer 2001.

Mike Freedman, The genius is in the implementation, *Journal of Business Strategy*, March/April 2003.

John Vogelsang, Futuring: A complex adaptive systems approach to strategic planning. *Support Center for Nonprofit Management*, 2004.

Stop Making Plans: Start Making Decisions

Michael C. Mankins and Richard Steele

Is strategic planning completely useless? That was the question the CEO of a global manufacturer recently asked himself. Two years earlier, he had launched an ambitious overhaul of the company's planning process. The old approach, which required business-unit heads to make regular presentations to the firm's executive committee, had broken down entirely. The ExCom members—the CEO, COO, CFO, CTO, and head of HR—had grown tired of sitting through endless PowerPoint presentations that provided them few opportunities to challenge the business units' assumptions or influence their strategies. And the unit heads had complained that the ExCom reviews were long on exhortation but short on executable advice. Worse, the reviews led to very few worthwhile decisions.

The revamped process incorporated state-of-the-art thinking about strategic planning. To avoid information overload, it limited each business to 15 "high-impact" exhibits describing the unit's strategy. To ensure thoughtful discussions, it required that all presentations and supporting materials be distributed to the ExCom at least a week in advance. The review sessions themselves were restructured to allow ample time for give-and-take between the corporate team and the business-unit executives. And rather than force the unit heads to traipse off to headquarters for meetings, the ExCom agreed to spend an unprecedented six weeks each spring visiting all 22 units for daylong sessions. The intent was to make the strategy reviews longer, more focused, and more consequential.

It didn't work. After using the new process for two planning cycles, the CEO gathered feedback from the participants through an anonymous survey. To his dismay, the report contained a litany of complaints: "It takes too much time." "It's at too high a level." "It's disconnected from the way we run the business."And so on. Most damning of all, however, was the respondents' near-universal view that the new approach produced very few real decisions. The CEO was dumbfounded. How could the company's cutting-edge planning process still be so badly broken? More important, what should he do to make strategic planning drive more, better, and faster decisions?

Like this CEO, many executives have grown skeptical of strategic planning. Is it any wonder? Despite all the time and energy most companies put into strategic planning, the process is most often a barrier to good decision making, our research indicates. As a result, strategic planning doesn't really influence most companies' strategy.

In the following pages, we will demonstrate that the failure of most strategic planning is due to two factors: It is typically an annual process, and it is most often focused on individual business units. As such, the process is completely at odds with the way executives actually make important strategy decisions, which are neither constrained by the calendar nor defined by unit boundaries. Not surprisingly, then, senior executives routinely sidestep the planning process. They make the decisions that really shape their company's strategy and determine its future—decisions about mergers and acquisitions, product launches, corporate restructurings, and the like—outside the planning process, typically in an ad hoc fashion, without rigorous analysis or productive debate. Critical decisions are made incorrectly or not at all. More than anything else, this disconnect—between the way planning works and the way decision making happens—explains the frustration, if not outright antipathy, most executives feel toward strategic planning.

But companies can fix the process if they attack its root problems. A small number of forward-looking companies have thrown out their calendar-driven, business-unit-focused planning processes and replaced them with continuous, issues-focused decision making. By changing the timing and focus of strategic planning, they've also changed the nature of top management's discussions about strategy—from "review and approve" to "debate and decide," meaning that senior executives seriously think through every major decision and its implications for the company's performance and value. Indeed, these companies use the strategy development process to drive decision making. As a consequence, they make more than twice as many important strategic decisions each year as companies that follow the traditional planning model. (See the exhibit "Who Makes More Decisions?") These companies have stopped making plans and started making decisions.

Traditional strategic planning involves reviewing the situation, targeting goals and objectives, and mapping a path to achieve them. In what type of economic, sociocultural, and organizational environment would traditional strategic planning work best?

WHERE PLANNING GOES WRONG

In the fall of 2005, Marakon Associates, in collaboration with the Economist Intelligence Unit, surveyed senior executives from 156 large companies worldwide, all with sales of $1 billion or more (40% of them had revenues over $10 billion). We asked these executives how their companies developed long-range plans and how effectively they thought their planning processes drove strategic decisions.

The results of the survey confirmed what we have observed over many years of consulting: The timing and structure of strategic planning are obstacles to good decision making. Specifically, we found that companies with standard planning processes and practices make only 2.5 major strategic decisions each year, on average (by "major," we mean they have the potential to increase company profits by 10% or more over the long term). It's hard to imagine that with so few strategic decisions driving growth, these companies can keep moving forward and deliver the financial performance that investors expect.

Even worse, we suspect that the few decisions companies do reach are made in spite of the strategic planning process, not because of it. Indeed, the traditional planning model is so cumbersome and out of sync with the way executives want and need to make decisions that top managers all too often sidestep the process when making their biggest strategic choices.

With the big decisions being made outside the planning process, strategic planning becomes merely a codification of judgments top management has already made, rather than a vehicle for identifying and debating the critical decisions that the company needs to make to produce superior performance. Over time, managers begin to question the value of strategic planning, withdraw from it, and come to rely on other processes for setting company strategy.

The calendar effect • At 66% of the companies in our survey, planning is a periodic event, often conducted as a precursor to the yearly budgeting and capital-approval processes. In fact, linking strategic planning to these other management processes is often cited as a best practice. But forcing strategic planning into an annual cycle risks making it irrelevant to executives, who must make many important decisions throughout the year.

There are two major drawbacks to such a rigid schedule. The first might be called the *time* problem. A once-a-year planning schedule simply does not give executives sufficient time to address the issues that most affect performance. According to our survey, companies that follow an annual planning calendar devote less than nine weeks per year to strategy development. That's barely

Who Makes More Decisions?

Companies see a dramatic increase in the quality of their decision making once they abandon the traditional planning model, which is calendar driven and focused on the business units. In our survey, the companies that broke most completely with the past made more than twice as many strategic decisions each year as companies wedded to tradition. What's more, the new structure of the planning process ensures that the decisions are probably the best that could have been made, given the information available to managers at the time.

Here are the average numbers of major strategic decisions reached per year in companies that take the following approaches to strategic planning:

Annual review: focused on business units: **2.5** Decisions Per Year
Annual review: focused on issues: **3.5** Decisions Per Year
Continuous review: focused on business units: **4.1** Decisions Per Year
Continuous review: focused on issues: **6.1** Decisions Per Year

Source: Marakon Associates and the Economist Intelligence Unit

two months to collect relevant facts, set strategic priorities, weigh competing alternatives, and make important strategic choices. Many issues — particularly those spanning multiple businesses, crossing geographic boundaries, or involving entire value chains — cannot be resolved effectively in such a short time. It took Boeing, for example, almost two years to decide to outsource major activities such as wing manufacturing.

Constrained by the planning calendar, corporate executives face two choices: They can either not address these complex issues—in effect, throwing them in the "too-hard" bucket — or they can address them through some process other than strategic planning. In both cases, strategic planning is marginalized and separated from strategic decision making.

Then there's the *timing* problem. Even when executives allot sufficient time in strategy development to address tough issues, the timing of the process can create problems. At most companies, strategic planning is a batch process in which managers analyze market and competitor information, identify threats and opportunities, and then define a multiyear plan. But in the real world, managers make strategic decisions continuously, often motivated by an immediate need for action (or reaction). When a new competitor enters a market, for instance, or a rival introduces a new technology, executives must act quickly and decisively to safeguard the company's performance. But very few companies (less than 10%, according to our survey) have any sort of rigorous or disciplined process for responding to changes in the external environment. Instead, managers rely on ad hoc processes to correct course or make opportunistic moves. Once again, strategic planning is sidelined, and executives risk making poor decisions that have not been carefully thought through.

M&A decisions provide a particularly egregious example of the timing problem. Acquisition opportunities tend to emerge spontaneously, the result of changes in management at a target company, the actions of a competitor, or some other unpredictable event. Faced with a promising opportunity and limited time in which to act, executives can't wait until the opportunity is evaluated as part of the next annual planning cycle, so they assess the deal and make a quick decision. But because there's often no proper review process, the softer customer- and people-related issues so critical to effective integration of an acquired company can get shortchanged. It is no coincidence that failure to plan for integration is often cited as the primary cause of deal failure.

The business-unit effect • The organizational focus of the typical planning process compounds its calendar effects—or, perhaps more aptly, defects. Two-thirds of the executives we surveyed indicated that strategic planning at their companies is conducted business by business — that is, it is focused on units or groups of units. But 70% of the senior executives who responded to our survey stated they make decisions issue by issue. For example, should we enter China? Should we outsource manufacturing? Should we acquire our distributor? Given this mismatch between the way planning is organized and the way big decisions are made, it's hardly surprising that, once again, corporate leaders look elsewhere for guidance and inspiration. In fact, only 11% of the executives we surveyed believed strongly that planning was worth the effort.

The organizational focus of traditional strategic planning also creates distance, even antagonism, between corporate executives and business-unit managers. Consider, for example, the way most companies conduct strategy reviews — as formal meetings between senior managers and the heads of each business unit. While these reviews are intended to produce a fact-based dialogue, they often amount to little more than business tourism. The executive committee flies in for a day, sees the sights, meets the natives, and flies out. The business unit, for its part, puts in a lot of work preparing for this royal visit and is keen to make it smooth and trouble free. The unit hopes to escape with few unanswered questions and an approved plan. Accordingly, local managers control the flow of information upward, and senior managers are presented only with information that shows each unit in the best possible light. Opportunities are highlighted; threats are downplayed or omitted.

Even if there's no subterfuge, senior corporate managers still have trouble engaging in constructive dialogue and debate because of what might be called information asymmetry. They just don't have the information they need to be helpful in guiding business units. So when they're presented with a strategic plan that's too good to be believed, they have only two real options: either reject it—a move that's all but unheard-of at most large companies—or play along and impose stretch targets to secure at least the promise that the unit will improve performance. In both cases, the review does little to drive decisions on issues. It's hardly surprising that only 13% of the executives we surveyed felt that top managers were effectively engaged in all aspects of strategy development at their companies—from target setting to debating alternatives to approving strategies and allocating resources.

DECISION-FOCUSED STRATEGIC PLANNING

Strategic planning can't have impact if it doesn't drive decision making. And it can't drive decision making as long as it remains focused on individual business units and limited by the calendar. Over the past several years, we have observed that many of the best-performing companies have abandoned the traditional approach and are focusing explicitly on reaching decisions through the continuous identification and systematic resolution of strategic issues. (The sidebar "Continuous, Decision-Oriented Planning" presents a detailed example of the issues-oriented approach.) Although these companies have found different specific solutions, all have made essentially the same fundamental changes to their planning and strategy development processes in order to produce more, better, and faster decisions.

They separate—but integrate—decision making and plan making • First and most important, a company must take decisions out of the traditional planning process and create a different, parallel process for developing strategy that helps executives identify the decisions they *need to make* to create more shareholder value over time. The output of this new process isn't a plan at all—it's a set of concrete decisions that management can codify into future business plans through the existing planning process, which remains in place. Identifying and making decisions is distinct from creating, monitoring, and updating a strategic plan, and the two sets of tasks require very different, but integrated, processes.

Boeing Commercial Airplanes (BCA) is a case in point. This business unit, Boeing's largest, has had a long-range business plan (LRBP) process for many years. The protracted cycles of commercial aircraft production require the unit's CEO, Alan Mulally, and his leadership team to take a long-term view of the business. Accordingly, the unit's LRBP contains a ten-year financial forecast, including projected revenues, backlogs, operating margins, and capital investments. BCA's leadership team reviews the business plan weekly to track the division's performance relative to the plan and to keep the organization focused on execution.

The weekly reviews were invaluable as a performance-monitoring tool at BCA, but they were not particularly effective at bringing new issues to the surface or driving strategic decision making. So in 2001, the unit's leadership team introduced a Strategy Integration Process focused on uncovering and addressing the business's most important strategic issues (such as determining the best go-to-market strategy for the business, driving the evolution of BCA's product strategy, or fueling growth in services). The team assigned to this process holds strategy integration meetings every Monday to track BCA's progress

---

The Disconnect Between Planning and Decision Making

●

How Executives Plan
66% Periodically
Percentage of surveyed executives saying their companies conduct strategic planning only at prescribed times
67% Unit By Unit
Percentage saying planning is done unit by unit

How Executives Decide
100% Continuously
Percentage of executives saying strategic decisions are made without regard to the calendar
70% Issue By Issue
Percentage saying decisions are made issue by issue
No wonder only **11%** of executives are highly satisfied that strategic planning is worth the effort.

in resolving these long-term issues. Once a specific course of action is agreed upon and approved by BCA's leadership team, the long-range business plan is updated at the next weekly review to reflect the projected change in financial performance.

The time invested in the new decision-making process is more than compensated for by the time saved in the LRBP process, which is now solely focused on strategy execution. The company gets the best of both worlds—disciplined decision making and superior execution. BCA has maintained the value of the LRBP as an execution tool even as it has increased the quality and quantity of important decisions. Managers believe that the new process is at least partially responsible for the sharp turnaround in Boeing's performance since 2001.

They focus on a few key themes • High-performing companies typically focus their strategy discussions on a limited number of important issues or themes, many of which span multiple businesses. Moving away from a business-by-business planning model in this way has proved particularly helpful for large, complex organizations, where strategy discussions can quickly get bogged down as each division manager attempts to cover every aspect of the unit's strategy. Business-unit managers should remain involved in corporate-level strategy planning that affects their units. But a focus on issues rather than business units better aligns strategy development with decision making and investment.

Consider Microsoft. The world's leading software maker is a highly matrixed organization. No strategy can be effectively executed at the company without careful coordination across multiple functions and across two or more of Microsoft's seven business units, or, as executives refer to them, "P&Ls"—Client; Server and Tools; Information Worker; MSN; Microsoft Business Solutions; Mobile and Embedded Devices; and Home and Entertainment. In late 2004, faced with a perceived shortage of good investment ideas, CEO Steve Ballmer asked Robert Uhlaner, Microsoft's corporate vice president of strategy, planning, and analysis, to devise a new strategic planning process for the company. Uhlaner put in place a Growth and Performance Planning Process that starts with agreement by Ballmer's leadership team on a set of strategic themes—major issues like PC market growth, the entertainment market, and security—that cross business-unit boundaries. These themes not only frame the dialogue for Microsoft's annual strategy review, they also guide the units in fleshing out investment alternatives to fuel the company's growth. Dialogues between the P&L leaders and Ballmer's team focus on what the company can do to address each strategic theme, rather than on individual unit strategies. The early results of this new process are promising. "You have to be careful what you wish for," Uhlaner says. "Our new process has surfaced countless new opportunities for growth. We no longer worry about a dearth of investment ideas, but how best to fund them."

Like Microsoft, Diageo North America—a division of the international beer, wine, and spirits marketer—has recently changed the way it conducts strategic planning to allocate resources across its diverse portfolio. Diageo historically focused its planning efforts on individual brands. Brand managers were allowed to make the case for additional investment, no matter what the size of the brand or its strategic role in the portfolio. As a result, resource allocation was bedeviled by endless negotiations between the brands and corporate management. This political wrangling made it extremely difficult for Diageo's senior managers to establish a consistent approach to growth, because a lack of transparency prevented them from discerning, from the many requests for additional funding, which brands really deserved more resources and which did not.

Starting in 2001, Diageo overhauled its approach to strategy development. A crucial change was to focus planning on the factors that the company believed would most drive market growth — for example, an increase in the U.S. Hispanic population. By modeling the impact of these factors on the brand portfolio, Diageo has been better able to match its resources with the brands that have the most growth potential so that it can specify the strategies and investments each brand manager should develop, says Jim Moseley, senior vice president of consumer planning and research for Diageo North America. For example, the division now identifies certain brands for growth and earmarks specific resources for investment in these units. This focused approach has enabled the company to shorten the brand planning process and reduce the time spent on negotiations between the brands and division management. It has also given senior management greater confidence in each brand's ability to contribute to Diageo's growth.

They make strategy development continuous • Effective strategy planners spread strategy reviews throughout the year rather than squeeze them into a two- or three-month window. This allows senior executives to focus on one issue at a time until they reach a decision or set of decisions. Moreover, managers can add issues to the agenda as market and competitive conditions change, so there's no need for ad hoc processes. Senior executives can thus rely on a single strategic planning process—or, perhaps more aptly, a single strategic decision-making model—to drive decision making across the company.

Textron, a $10 billion multi-industry company, has implemented a new, continuous strategy-development process built around a prioritized "decision agenda" comprising the company's most important issues and opportunities. Until 2004, Textron had a fairly traditional strategic planning process. Each spring, the company's operating units—businesses as diverse as Bell Helicopter, E-Z-Go golf cars, and Jacobsen turf maintenance equipment—would develop a five-year strategic plan based on standard templates. Unit managers would then review their strategic plans with Textron's management committee (the company's top five executives) during daylong sessions at each unit. Once the strategy reviews were complete, the units incorporated the results, as best they could, into their annual operating plans and capital budgets.

In June 2004, dissatisfied with the quality and pace of the decision making that resulted from the company's strategy reviews, CEO Lewis Campbell asked

Traditional Planning

Companies that follow the traditional strategic planning model develop a strategy plan for each business unit at some point during the year. A cross-functional team dedicates less than nine weeks to developing the unit's plan. The executive committee reviews each plan—typically in daylong, on-site meetings—and rubber-stamps the results. The plans are consolidated to produce a company-wide strategic plan for review by the board of directors.

Once the strategic-planning cycle is complete, the units dedicate another eight to nine weeks to budgeting and capital planning (in most companies, these processes are not explicitly linked to strategic planning).

The executive committee then holds another round of meetings with each of the business units to negotiate performance targets, resource commitments, and (in many cases) compensation for managers.

The results: an approved but potentially unrealistic strategic plan for each business unit and a separate budget for each unit that is decoupled from the unit's strategic plan.

Stuart Grief, Textron's vice president for strategy and business development, to rethink the company's strategic planning process. After carefully reviewing the company's practices and gathering feedback from its 30 top executives, Grief and his team designed a new Textron Strategy Process.

There were two important changes. First, rather than concentrate all of the operating-unit strategy reviews in the second quarter of each year, the company now spreads strategy dialogues throughout the year—two to three units are reviewed per quarter. Second, rather than organize the management committee dialogues around business-unit plans, Textron now holds continuous reviews that are designed to address each strategic issue on the company's decision agenda. Both changes have enabled Textron's management committee to be much more effectively engaged in business-unit strategy development. The changes have also ensured that there's a forum in which cross-unit issues can be raised and addressed by top management, with input from relevant business-unit managers. The process has significantly increased the number of strategic decisions the company makes each year. As a result, Textron has gone from being an also-ran among its multi-industrial peers to a top-quartile performer over the past 18 months.

John Cullivan, the director of strategy at Cardinal Health, one of the world's leading health-care products and services companies, reports similar benefits from shifting to a continuous planning model. "Continuous decision

Continuous, Decision-Oriented Planning

Once the company as a whole has identified its most important strategic priorities (typically in an annual strategy update), executive committee dialogues, spread throughout the year, are set up to reach decisions on as many issues as possible. Since issues frequently span multiple business units, task forces are established to prepare the strategic and financial information that's needed to uncover and evaluate strategy alternatives for each issue. Preparation time may exceed nine weeks. The executive committee engages in two dialogues for each issue at three to four hours each.

The first dialogue focuses on reaching agreement on the facts surrounding the issue and on a set of viable alternatives. The second focuses on the evaluation of those alternatives and the selection of the best course of action. Once an issue is resolved, a new one is added to the agenda. Critical issues can be inserted into the planning process at any time as market and competitive conditions change.

Once a decision has been reached, the budgets and capital plans for the affected business units are updated to reflect the selected option. Consequently, the strategic-planning process and the capital and budgeting processes are integrated. This significantly reduces the need for lengthy negotiations between the executive committee and unit management over the budget and capital plan.

The results: a concrete plan for addressing each key issue; for each business unit, a continuously updated budget and capital plan that is linked directly to the resolution of critical strategic issues; and more, faster, better decisions per year.

making is tough to establish because it requires the reallocation of management time at the top levels of the company," he says. "But the process has enabled us to get sharper focus on the short-term performance of our vertical businesses and make faster progress on our longer-term priorities, some of which are horizontal opportunities that cut across businesses and thus are difficult to manage."

To facilitate continuous strategic decision making, Cardinal has made a series of important changes to its traditional planning process. At the corporate level, for example, the company has put in place a rolling six-month agenda for its executive committee dialogues, a practice that allows everyone inside Cardinal to know what issues management is working on and when decisions will be reached. Similar decision agendas are used at the business-unit and functional levels, ensuring that common standards are applied to all important decisions at the company. And to support continuous decision making at

Cardinal, the company has trained "black belts" in new analytical tools and processes and deployed them throughout the organization. This provides each of the company's businesses and functions with the resources needed to address strategic priorities that emerge over time.

They structure strategy reviews to produce real decisions • The most common obstacles to decision making at large companies are disagreements among executives over past decisions, current alternatives, and even the facts presented to support strategic plans. Leading companies structure their strategy review sessions to overcome these problems.

What are potential difficulties with continuous strategic decision making?

At Textron, for example, strategic-issue reviews are organized around "facts, alternatives, and choices." Each issue is addressed in two half-day sessions with the company's management committee, allowing for eight to ten issues to be resolved throughout the year. In the first session, the management committee debates and reaches agreement on the relevant facts—information on the profitability of key markets, the actions of competitors, the purchase behavior of customers, and so on—and a limited set of viable strategy alternatives. The purpose of this first meeting is not to reach agreement on a specific course of action; rather, the meeting ensures that the group has the best possible information and a robust set of alternatives to consider. The second session is focused on evaluating these alternatives from a strategic and financial perspective and selecting the best course of action. By separating the dialogue around facts and alternatives from the debate over choices, Textron's management committee avoids many of the bottlenecks that plague strategic decision making at most companies and reaches many more decisions than it otherwise would.

Like Textron, Cadbury Schweppes has changed the structure of its strategy dialogues to focus top managers more explicitly on decision making. In 2002, after acquiring and integrating gum-maker Adams—a move that significantly expanded Cadbury's product and geographic reach—the company realized it needed to rethink how it was conducting dialogues about strategy between the corporate center and the businesses. The company made two important changes. First, strategy dialogues were redesigned to incorporate a standard set of facts and metrics about consumers, customers, and competitors. This information helped get critical commercial choices in front of top managers, so that the choices were no longer buried in the business units. Second, senior executives' time was reallocated so they could pay more attention to markets that were crucial to realizing Cadbury's ten-year vision and to making important decisions.

Cadbury's top team now spends one full week per year in each of the countries that are most critical to driving the company's performance, so that important decisions can be informed by direct observation as well as through indirect analysis. Strategy dialogues are now based on a much deeper understanding of the markets. Cadbury's strategic reviews no longer merely consist of reviews of and approval of a strategic plan, and they produce many more important decisions.

Done right, strategic planning can have an enormous impact on a company's performance and long-term value. By creating a planning process that enables managers to discover great numbers of hidden strategic issues and make more decisions, companies will open the door to many more opportunities for long-term growth and profitability. By embracing decision-focused planning, companies will almost certainly find that the quantity and quality of their decisions will improve. And—no coincidence they will discover an improvement in the quality of the dialogue between senior corporate managers and unit managers. Corporate executives will gain a better understanding of the challenges their companies face, and unit managers will benefit fully from the experience and insights of the company's leaders. As Mark Reckitt, a director of group strategy at Cadbury Schweppes, puts it: "Continuous, decision-focused strategic planning has helped our top management team to streamline its agenda and work with business units and functional management to make far better business-strategy and commercial decisions."

ARTICLE 9.2

The Learning Organization and Strategic Change

Robert W. Rowden

INTRODUCTION

Imagine that you are taking a journey into the mountains. The nature of the experience will vary considerably from one mountain range to another. There are two kinds of mountain ranges. One type, like the North American Rockies, is dominated by prominent peaks, their majestic summits rising silently and austerely above the landscape. The foothills and smaller mountains, dwarfed in the foreground, dramatize the formidable scale of the highest peaks. On a trip, the summit dominates the horizon, an endpoint against which progress can be easily gauged.

But there is another type of mountain range, such as the Cascades in the Pacific Northwestern United States, composed of gradually rising peaks, the size of one peak not revealing itself until the last one has been conquered, the summit being but one final stage in the gradual ascent.

Aesthetically, each has an elegance and beauty—the first, awesome and inspiring, the second, mysterious and surprising.

Organizations also take journeys in their attempts to mount significant strategic change. Examples of these journeys include entering international markets, downsizing, forming strategic alliances, improving customer satisfaction, achieving quality improvements, pioneering new technical innovations, and introducing new products. Increasingly, a company's viability is being determined by its ability to make such systemic, organization-wide change happen, and happen fast.

Traditionally, firms have approached these journeys as if the business landscape resembled a mountain range like the Rockies. At the outset of the journey, the organization would scan the horizon and spot the summit. With the presumption of clear vision, it would set a goal and develop a precise roadmap to achieve its end target. Clouds of resistance, fog banks of shortsightedness, or storms of crisis might obscure the final destination now and then. However, the summit would still be reached if only the organization maintained momentum and stayed on course.

In the highly uncertain business conditions emerging in the early 21st century, the topography of the business environment might be more like the mysterious Cascades than the majestic Rockies. Clouds of swirling technological, competitive, marketplace, social, economic, and political changes obscure the final destinations. Until an organization takes some action and mounts the first hill, the size and scope of the next peak cannot be foreseen. Business environments are too chaotic and organizational change too complex to establish firm objectives, fixed plans, and concrete programs of change.

Amid sometimes unpredictable, always uncertain, and highly turbulent business conditions, an organization's capacity to learn as it goes may be the only true source of competitive advantage. No longer able to forecast the future, many leading organizations are constructing arks comprised of their inherent capacity to adapt to unforeseen situations, to learn from their own experiences, to shift their shared mindsets, and to change more quickly, broadly, and deeply than ever before. In other words, to become learning organizations. According to Kiechel, the notion of the learning organization is . . . a very big conceptual catchall to help us make sense of a set of values and ideas we've been wrestling with, everything from customer service to corporate responsiveness and speed (1990, p. 133).

The idea of the learning organization has been around quite some time. It derives from Argyris' work in organizational learning (Argyris & Schon, 1978) and is indebted to Revans' (1983) studies of action learning. It has roots in organization development (especially action research methodology) and organizational theory (most notably, Burns and Stalker's work on organic organizations). Its conceptual foundations are firmly based on systems theory (Senge, 1990a) and its practical application to managing a business has evolved out of strategic planning and strategic management (Fiol & Lyles, 1985; Hosley, Lau, Levy & Tan, 1994), which have recognized that organizational learning is the underlying source of strategic change (DeGeus, 1988; Jashapara, 1993). Much of the quality improvement movement of recent years, with its emphasis on continuous improvement, represented the first widespread, inchoate application of learning organization concepts (Senge, 1990b; Stata, 1989).

Learning organizations tend to have the following characteristics in common (Calvert, Mobley & Marshall, 1994; Watkins & Marsick, 1993):

- They provide continuous learning opportunities.
- They use learning to reach their goals.
- They link individual performance with organizational performance.
- They foster inquiry and dialog, making it safe for people to share openly and take risks.
- They embrace creative tension as a source of energy and renewal.
- They are continuously aware of and interact with their environment.

The label, "learning organization," is commonly used as if it represents a certain type of organization, implying that it is possible to designate certain firms as learning organizations and, at the same time, determine that others are not. In contrast, it seems more useful to think of the learning organization as a model of strategic change. In fact, the learning organization represents the fourth version in a series of strategic change models. The learning organization model is emerging to help firms plan and execute significant organizational change amid rapidly changing business conditions.

THE FIRST THREE VERSIONS

On an individual basis, each organization learns how to change by taking action, encountering obstacles, and discovering over time how to overcome them. Each version of this cycle (taking action, confronting problems, and adjusting course) is an opportunity for learning. In this process, organizations—at varying speeds and to differing degrees—become more sophisticated in their ability to introduce strategic change.

On a collective basis, organizations have also learned how to change over the past several decades. It is possible to identify three broad versions of this learning process, each of which is dominated by a generally prescribed model of strategic change. This model indicated the preferred methods of how companies can best go about introducing fundamental changes in their business.

THE FIRST VERSION—FORMAL PLANNING FOCUSED

If an organization uses a formal planning approach, what is the leader's role in ensuring it does not fail?

The first model focused almost solely on the planning of strategic change by senior management. Strategic planning, as traditionally practiced, reflected this first version approach to change, assuming that if executives came up with excellent plans, the plans would be easily executed, and successful strategic change would result (Gluck, 1986; Morrisey, 1996). This model emphasized the creation of formal, fixed planning documents through a staff-driven, once-a-year event restricted to the most senior executives. Underlying conventional strategic planning was a "predict and plan" premise, which presumed that incipient trends could be detected through the use of sophisticated environmental scanning methods. Based upon such advance warning signals, the organization could get a jump on the competition, formulating and implementing plans that would result in a competitive advantage when the predicted waves of change hit the shore.

This planning-dominated model of change has been seductive for several reasons. The approach is rational and unambiguous, rooted in the quantitative analytical tools of management science. Moreover, it is consistent with traditional command-and-control forms of management, reserving planning to an elite echelon of top management. Perhaps most important, it promises quick action and concrete results as specified by the planning document.

Over the years, even when companies used the most sophisticated scanning and profound planning methods, and even when the plans reflected brilliant and insightful approaches to future competitive positioning, they often failed. In reality, plans frequently stayed on the shelf. When it came down to the details of implementation, the desired changes were often much more complex than originally imagined, requiring more time and resources than previously thought. Speed was also an issue. Many business environments were themselves changing at rates exceeding the capacity or organizations to implement their plans (Henkoff, 1990). Finally, the actions of middle managers, rather than the words of top management, often determined how well plans are implemented. Because middle managers were not usually involved in the planning process, they were often not committed to the plans and, in fact, may not have fully understood them. Moreover, these same middle managers frequently had essential ideas and information that, when not taken into account, weakened the integrity of the plans.

THE SECOND VERSION— IMPLEMENTATION FOCUSED

A new model emerged in the late 1970s and early 1980s as an attempt to overcome the limitations of the planning-dominated approach. It recognized that coming up with great plans was often not sufficient. Detailed attention needed to be paid to how the plans were to be implemented (Fusch, 1997). For the first time in many companies, middle managers were included in the formulation of strategic plans, and in many cases, detailed execution schemes were developed. Often these implementation plans speculated about potential problems and made contingent plans to overcome them. Increased consideration was also given to the resources (financial, technical, human, and time) needed for plans to happen. A new emphasis was placed upon communicating strategic direction to all affected employees, including detailing any new responsibilities and tasks needed to be performed. Moreover, greater attention was paid to following up on plans, tracking progress, uncovering problems, and resolving impediments at the earliest possible point.

Nevertheless, companies still encountered many of the implementation problems identified earlier, such as unexpected delays, inadequate progress, and organizational resistance. Strategic change was clearly more complex than previously imagined. Broad systemic issues (culture, rewards, norms, policies, management styles, etc.) often affected implementation. Moreover, strategic change frequently called for skills and resources that could not be quickly developed in the narrow gap between planning and implementation. Senior executives often let short-term obstacles and internal considerations obscure their ability to provide strategic direction to the firm. Middle managers were occasionally resistant to the radical upheaval of past practices because they were often rewarded for short-term operational results, not long-term strategic successes. Front-line employees who execute the plans often did not understand the need to do things differently. They were ignorant of the competitive forces, technological changes, and marketplace demands that were combining to make their organization's environment so unpredictable and threatening. Nor were they aware of the strategic objectives the firm had established to deal with these uncertainties.

THE THIRD VERSION—READINESS FOCUSED

Second-version approaches often paid painstaking attention to the details of making strategic change happen. Still there were problems. Short-term considerations frequently diverted attention from long-term strategic goals. In many cases, broad-scale resistance to change persisted, prohibiting the initiatives from taking hold. Implementation often continued to take longer than planned, with new problems arising that no one could have anticipated, given what was known at the time.

Why? Why after involving middle managers in developing a plan for change? Why after fully communicating the new strategic direction to everyone involved? Why after creating detailed action plans for implementation that included contingency measures? Why after assigning sufficient financial, technical, and human resources? Why, after taking all of these steps did so many change efforts based upon the second iteration model still encounter major obstacles?

The reason was a fundamental lack of readiness for strategic change in the company. Rewards often reinforced the status quo. Management styles often clashed with the imperative to involve people in making change happen. People from throughout the company were often unaware of the need to change. And strong norms and culture prohibited change from taking form.

In response to these problems, a new model of strategic change developed. This third version placed as much emphasis upon the creation of readiness for change in the organization as it did upon planning and implementation. This new model of strategic change recognized the importance of three elements—readiness, planning, and implementation.

According to the third version, any successful strategic change was viewed as dependent on a certain degree of readiness for the change within the organization. As a result, it was proposed that any attempts to introduce significant organizational change should be prefaced by a series of steps to enhance readiness. These steps often included the following:

- Building awareness of the need for and communicating a vision of the desired change.
- Creating a climate that is supportive of the desired change by realigning organizational culture, rewards, policies, procedures, systems, and norms to support such change.
- Equipping people throughout the organization with the skills needed to participate meaningfully in planning and implementing strategic change (Barger & Kirby, 1995).

Planning tended to be seen as a more open process, with an emphasis on establishing general goals and direction and using pilot programs to build commitment within the organization. During implementation, there tended to be more concern for engaging frontline employees, as well as suppliers, customers, and other key stakeholders, in working out how plans should be executed.

Most quality improvement efforts of the late 1980s and early 1990s illustrate the third version. Quality improvement programs generally start with

Table 1   Versions of Strategic Planning

Version	Purpose	Emerged
First—Formal Planning Focused	Formal, Fixed Planning Documents by Senior Managers	1940s–'50s
Second—Implementation Focused	Complex Implementation of Strategic Change Plans	1970s–'80s
Third—Readiness Focused	Creation of Readiness For Change Along With Planning	late '80s–early '90s
Fourth—Integrated Organizational Learning Focused	Integrates Readiness, Continuous Planning, Improvised Implementation, and Action Learning	mid-1990s

ambitious preliminary preparations designed to create the readiness for change in the organization. A major focus is to build awareness of the critical importance of quality improvement and to convey top management's commitment to a radical new vision of the organization's future, a vision characterized by continuous improvement, employee involvement, and world-class leadership in quality. Another major target of readiness activities is to build a climate conductive to quality improvement by helping managers make a fundamental shift in their management practices, adopting more participative and facilitative styles that support employee involvement in the continuous improvement of quality. Still another target of preliminary readiness activities is the retooling of the workforce through intensive, up-front education and training in quality improvement philosophies and techniques.

TOWARD THE FOURTH VERSION

Each version of strategic change efforts emerges from the problems encountered in the previous version (see Table 1). So it is that, as a result of the limitations inherent in quality improvement programs and other third-version efforts, a new, fourth version of strategic change is taking shape: the learning organization.

Many quality improvement efforts have been highly successful. Numerous firms have achieved breakthroughs in product and service quality, significantly enhancing customer satisfaction and greatly strengthening their competitive positions (Watkins & Marsick, 1993). But there is also a dark side of quality. Several studies are showing that the quality improvement programs started over recent years, based upon the examples of Baldridge winners or the prescriptions of quality gurus, are experiencing a high mortality rate (Hosley, Lau, Levy & Tan, 1994; The Quality Imperative, 1991; Garvin, 1998). Even Florida Power & Light, the once-heralded example of world class quality improvement, hit the rocks. Its Deming Award-winning quality program was dismantled, and its president, the architect and champion of the effort, left the company under pressure (Main, 1991). In fact, studies indicate that change efforts, when treated as established programs and not unfolding processes, almost always fail (Beer, Eisenstat, & Spector, 1990; Fusch, 1997).

Over the years, even with full management support and substantial investments of time, people, and money, many third-version change programs are being designated failures, even by the people who initiated them (Barger & Kirby, 1995). This seems to be increasingly true for many total quality programs, for several reasons. First, the activities designed to create readiness also established unrealistic expectations that momentous change would happen, and happen fast. In addition, despite eloquent protestations to the contrary, many total quality initiatives were still introduced as fixed programs with short-term objectives. In many cases, organizations also failed to achieve a fully integrated, systemic approach to quality improvement, often neglecting the relationship of quality to business strategy, company structure, and information systems. Maybe most important, many quality programs have been primarily internally focused and past-driven—inducing incremental improvements in past procedures and products rather than the discontinuous disruptions needed to weather tempestuous and turbulent business environments.

Quality improvement efforts are teaching an important lesson. Change cannot be transplanted. It must follow its own natural cycle of planting, growth, and harvest in each organization. To do so, the ground needs to be prepared in advance; old soil must be churned and nourished. These seeds of change need to be sown on the organizational topsoil—the immediate issues facing the organization. These seeds then gradually sprout deep roots that wrap around the firm culture —its management practices, business strategies, structure, and information systems. As it grows, the final fruit takes shape over time. The emerging change is continuously pruned and shaped both by the natural forces of the environment and by the vigilant attention of the gardeners, who water and feed — not on a preplanned schedule, but through personal judgments formed from experience and experimentation. That is the fourth-version model of strategic change, and that is what is meant by the learning organization.

THE FOURTH MODEL—THE LEARNING ORGANIZATION

Today, a fourth model of strategic change has emerged to compensate for the limitations of the earlier versions — the learning organization. The learning organization can be defined as one in which everyone is engaged identifying and solving problems, enabling the organization to continuously experiment, change, and improve, thus increasing its capacity to grow, learn, and achieve its purpose (Daft & Marcic, 1998). Some authors agree that learning organizations start with the assumption that learning is valuable, continuous, and most effective when shared and that every experience is an opportunity to learn (Calvert, Mobley, & Marshall, 1994; Watkins & Marsick, 1993).

In one sense, becoming a learning organization increases the size of a company's brain. Employees participate in all thinking activities, including strategy, with few boundaries among employees in different departments or between the top and bottom. Everyone communicates and works together, creating enormous intelligence and flexibility to deal with rapidly changing environments.

There are four defining characteristics of the learning organization: constant readiness, continuous planning, improvised implementation, and action learning.

Constant readiness. Rather than building readiness for a predetermined change, the organization exists in a constant state of readiness, preparing itself not for any specific change, but for change in general, attuned to its environment and willing to question its fundamental ways of doing business.

Unlike the third version, readiness is no longer a one-time event designed to prepare the organization for a specific change. Instead, readiness consists of a perpetual state of preparedness for change since, amid highly turbulent conditions, the organization needs to be equipped to deal with anything and to reevaluate past assumptions and future directions.

Continuous planning. Rather than the creation of fixed plans by a few senior executives, the learning organization develops open, flexible plans that are fully shared and embraced by the entire organization. In learning organizations, the act of planning differs greatly from earlier versions, which often relied on formal, written, detailed programs and procedures. In learning organizations, "revision" may be more important than "vision," with rigid, fixed plans supplanted by flexible, open strategic directions. These plans are not merely top management visions and programs, but are fully embraced and shared by the people involved in making them happen.

Improvised implementation. Rather than executing plans by the numbers, the learning organization improvises change, encouraging experimentation, rewarding small wins, and institutionalizing success throughout the organization.

No longer does implementation consist of the note-by-note execution of a prescribed plan. Just as in jazz improvision, where every performer is a composer, in the learning organization, every member — whether on the front line or the executive suite — is a strategic partner. In the fourth version, individuals and teams act in creative and autonomous ways to interpret the strategic direction and make the plans happen. The actual nature of the change gradually reveals itself through the spontaneous and creative actions of people throughout the organization. They coordinate and collaborate with others in the organization who are also experimenting with change. Over time, successes and accomplishments are reinforced and institutionalized, modifying the formal structures, rewards, procedures, and systems of the organization.

Action learning. Rather than reevaluating change efforts only at once-a-year planning sessions, or waiting for the slow learning that derives from experience or the traumatic learning that occurs from crisis, the learning organization takes action, reflects, and adjusts course as it goes, seeking to enhance the speed and effectiveness by which it learns how to change.

In the fourth version, learning is not something that just happens. It is made to happen. Learning begins when those involved in an activity stop and examine how things are done. In learning organizations, attempts are made to provide frequent, ongoing opportunities for such action-based learning. Learning organizations do not wait for problems to emerge or for crises to arise to compel reevaluation. Reflection becomes part of "the way we do things around here" and is built into the implementation of strategic change. Through this process, they question the original assumptions and search for deep, system ("double-loop") solutions to the problems.

That organizations can learn to change is a captivating idea, with the potential to revolutionize our understandings of competitive positioning, strategic planning, and organizational change. There is a danger, however, that the learning organization will become the newest addition in a long succession of management fads, producing its own generation of quick-fix solutions in a box. That would be both sad and ironic, since what distinguishes this new model of change is the recognition that any fixed program or plan of change is doomed to failure. There is also the hazard that the learning organization will be prescribed as the ultimate cure for afflictions such as stagnancy and surprise. However, even the learning organization model, when perfectly implemented, will not be a panacea for all organizational ills. Companies will still experience problems in making change happen, and time will assuredly expose significant limitations of this fourth model of strategic change. Instead, the learning organization is best understood as part of a broad, fast-moving current of learning that is gaining speed as it heads downstream. The first version led to the second, the second to the third, and the third to the fourth. The fifth version is just around the next bend.

What are some of the unwritten implications of moving to the fourth model of decision making—the learning organization?

REFERENCES

Argyris, C., & Schon, D. (1978). *Organizational learning: A theory of action perspective.* Reading, MA: Addison-Wesley.

Barger, N., & Kirby, L. (1995). *The challenge of change in organizations.* Palo Alto, CA: Davies-Black.

Beer, M., Eisenstat, R. A., & Spector, B. (1990). *The critical oath to corporate renewal.* Cambridge, MA: Harvard Business School Press.

Calvert, G., Mobley, S., & Marshall, L. (1994). Grasping the learning organization. *Training*, 48(6), 38–43.

Daft, R., & Marcic, D. (1998). *Understanding management.* Ft. Worth, TX: The Dryden Press.

DeGeus, A. P. (1988). Planning as learning. *Harvard Business Review*, 66(2), 70–74.

Fiol, C. M., & Lyles, M. (1985). Organizational learning. *Academy of Management Review*, 10(4), 803–813.

Fusch, G. (1997). *Organizational change from scientific management to the learning organization: Implications for new work systems.* Washington, D.C.: National Institute of Education (ERIC Document Reproduction Service No. ED 417 329.

Garvin, D. (1998). Does the Baldridge really work? *Harvard Business Review*, 69(6), 80–93.

Gluck, W. F. (1986). Strategic management: An overview. In J. Gardner, R. Rachlin, & H. Sweeny (Eds.). *Handbook of Strategic Planning*, (pp. 1.1–1.36). New York: Wiley and Sons.

Henkoff, R. (1990). How to plan for 1995. *Fortune*, 122 (16), 70–79.

Hosley, S., Lau, A., Levy, F., & Tan, D. (1994). The quest for the competitive learning organization. *Management Decision*, 32(6), 5–15.

Jashapara, A. (1993). The competitive learning organization: A quest for the Holy Grail. *Management Decision*, 31(8), 52–62.

Kieschel, W. (1990, March). The organization that learns. *Fortune*, 122, 133–136.

Main, J. (1991, July). Is the Baldridge overblown? *Fortune*, 123, 62–65.

Morrisey, G. (1996). *Strategic thinking: Building your planning foundation.* San Francisco: Jossey-Bass.

Revans, R. W. (1983). Action learning: Kindling the touch paper. *Management Development*, 21(6), 3–10.

Senge, P. (1990a). *The fifth discipline: The art and practice of the learning organization.* New York: Doubleday/Currency.

Senge, P. (1990b, Fall). The leader's new work: Building learning organizations. *Sloan Management Review*, 7–23.

Stata, R. (1989, Spring). Organizational learning: The key to management innovation. *Sloan Management Review*, 63–74.

The quality imperative. (1991, October). Special issue *Business Week*.

Watkins, K., & Marsick, V. (1993). *Sculpting the learning organization: Lessons in the art and science of systemic change.* San Francisco: Jossey-Bass.

ARTICLE 9.3

The Genius Is in the Implementation

Mike Freedman

First you have to fomulate your strategy. Without it, it's like kicking a ball around with no goal and no goalkeeper in place. But this is not the end of the job, it's only the beginning. Each day you have to look at 'How can I achieve this strategy?' Implementing strategy becomes your work for the day. Strategy has to be translated into actions—a skill a lot of executives are lacking," says Alfred W.K. Chan, managing director of The Hong Kong and China Gas Company Ltd.

He's right. Best practice suggests that organizations must have a clear, robust, and motivating strategy, formulated using a proven process. Led by a CEO and his or her top team, it must be communicated effectively throughout the organization. Everyone must understand his or her role in ensuring flawless execution.

Unfortunately, implementation often gets short shrift. Setting strategy is glamorous. It truly is the preserve of CEOs. It reinforces their authority and their ego. However, the evidence shows that once strategy is set, interest among top team members falls rapidly away, implementation efforts pull up short, operational behaviors and short-term goals take over. The result is suboptimal performance; strategy becomes a byword for top management away days.

In fact, implementation pitfalls abound. Some of the deeper ones are:

- *Strategic inertia*—not getting started. Many executives resist change or fail to give it due priority.
- A lack of stakeholder commitment— not having everyone on board. This is particularly true of middle management who are frequently the block to progress.
- *Strategic drift*—not focusing on your destination. This can often start with a CEO if he or she ignores implementation. Without iron discipline throughout the organization, drift will occur.
- *Strategic "dilution"*—things are moving, but it's not clear who is driving. If ownership and commitment to the corporate strategy are not watertight in the top team, when team members return to their operations, divisional, functional, or geographic priorities are all too likely to take precedence. Confusing and contradictory direction results.
- *Strategic isolation*—things may be happening, but communication is ineffective. If every business unit of the organization, its performance system, key business processes, and role modeling by leadership is not

coherent, consistent, and in sync, there will be troublesome disconnects between the strategy and its implementation.

- *Failure to understand progress*—not knowing where you are on the journey. Without continuous measurement of a strategy's "vital signs," both quantitative and qualitative key indicators of strategic success (which are different metrics than traditional operational and financial ones), the destination proves illusive.
- *Initiative fatigue*—there's lots going on but nothing gets done. In overloaded organizations, the projects needed to implement strategy may be the straw that breaks the camel's back. Similarly, a cynical attitude of "this too will pass" will derail progress.
- *Impatience*—a demand that change take place now. Intellectually we know that strategy cannot be implemented overnight, but emotionally CEOs can be unreasonable.
- *Not celebrating success*—failing to recognize and reward progress can hold back the achievement of the ultimate goal.

World-class CEOs consciously avoid these traps. They recognize that true genius is required to implement strategy, and that the discipline and skill required for implementation is as rare as that needed to formulate strategy. They also know their involvement is essential.

This has never been truer than in today's dangerous world of uncertainty and adversity: Double-dip recession, asymmetric terror, war looming in the Middle East, questions about corporate governance, increased competition, skepticism about the merits of globalization. This background makes strategy implementation even harder. These are huge hurdles to overcome. Many CEOs face equally daunting internal critical issues, barriers to implementation. These include the need to reduce complexity, poor cultural and structural alignment, a lack of strategic thinking and implementation skills in middle management, and a performance system geared only to annual objectives and not to strategic ones.

So how, then, can a CEO ensure that no stone is left unturned in the quest to ensure flawless execution? To answer that question we must first examine the nature of the strategic task itself.

THE STRATEGY PROCESS

Our model indicates there are five phases to the strategy process, each of them iterative with the others. They are:

1. Strategic intelligence-gathering and analysis
2. Strategy formulation
3. Strategic master project planning
4. Strategy implementation
5. Monitoring, reviewing, and updating strategy

With phase 1 completed, there will be a firm foundation of assumptions upon which to base strategic decision making, together with an understanding of their implications for the organization. Phase 2 yields a clear strategic profile, which addresses these fundamental questions:

What is our strategic timeframe?

What basic beliefs and values underpin the organization?

What are the scope, emphasis, and financial mix of the products and services we will and will not offer?

What are the scope, emphasis, and mix of the markets (geographies, customers, and end users) we will and will not serve?

What key capabilities do we need to take our products to our chosen markets?

What are our priorities for growth and new business?

What is the basis of our competitive advantage?

What growth and return expectations do we have?

What critical issues—barriers to implementation—stand in the way of our success?

What vital few key indicators of strategic success should we track and measure?

Only when the leadership of an organization is convinced of the quality of its work in phases 1 and 2 of the process should implementation begin.

STRATEGIC MASTER PROJECT PLANNING

Even with these building blocks in place, there is a natural temptation to jump straight into implementation, especially when there is much to accomplish. But that would be a great mistake. Consider the experience of Lagoven, the State Oil Company of Venezuela, where there were more than 1,200 separate projects to plan and execute. To begin implementation without a master plan would have spelled chaos and disaster. And Lagoven's situation is the rule, not the exception. Emerging from every strategy formulation exercise, typically there will be hundreds of projects, sub-projects, and tasks. These will all compete for limited financial resources and top management's time and attention. Some will require major capital investment, others none, but nonetheless they may be more urgent.

Such projects can include:

- Launching new products/services
- Phasing down obsolete products
- Opening up new markets
- Acquiring companies
- Selling off unwanted plants, divisions, or subsidiaries
- Filling capability gaps
- Outsourcing nonessential competencies
- Creating alliance, partnership, or franchise networks

Figure 1   A Communications Matrix: "Who" and "What"

		Elements of the Strategic Profile and Implementation Plan							
Stakeholders		Strategy Process Adopted	Basic Beliefs	Vision Statement	Basis of Competitive Advantage	Product/ Market Matrix	Key Capability Requirements	Growth and Return Expectations	Strategic Master Project Plan
Internal	Board		✓	✓	✓	✓	✓	✓	✓
	Managers	✓	✓	✓	✓	✓	✓	✓	✓
	Employees	✓	✓	✓	✓	Sales force	✓	✓	✓
External	Trade Unions	✓	✓	✓	✓		✓	?	
	Key Investors	✓		✓	✓			✓	
	Analysts	✓		✓	✓			✓	
	Bankers	✓	✓	✓	✓			✓	
	Customers	✓	✓	✓	✓				
	Suppliers	✓	✓	✓	✓	?			
	Advertising, PR & Marketing Advisors	✓	✓	✓	✓	✓	✓	✓	?
	JV or Alliance Partners	✓	✓	✓	✓	✓	✓	✓	✓

✓ = Need to know; ? = May need to know, revisit criteria; Blank = Not applicable

Note: Clearly the content of each matrix will relate to the organization's stakeholders on the one hand and the subjects to be communicated on the other. Ticks indicate a definite need to know, question marks are for debate, and blank spaces represent no need to know.

- Developing new routes to market
- Repositioning the firm
- Innovation in product, design, marketing, and delivery
- Conducting market research
- Searching for new sources of supply
- Searching for acquisition candidates

When fully identified, each project needs to be defined, prioritized, resourced, sequenced, scheduled, executed, tracked and monitored, and closed out. Clearly, a process is required to coordinate and direct this effort.

We call this process the Strategic Master Project Plan (SMPP). This is usually developed by a strategy implementation team that reports progress to the CEO's top team. For the world-famous Savoy Hotel Group this meant first sorting projects into one of eight categories as follows:

What are characteristics of SMPP that ensure the plan will be implemented?

- Sales and marketing
- Customer care
- Business processes
- Information technology
- Human resources
- Finance and control systems
- The physical product, i.e., the hotels themselves
- General management

Within each category, managers defined sub-projects and set detailed and measurable objectives. They then deployed best-practice project management techniques in the remaining tasks of planning implementation. The Savoy's leaders took their tasks seriously and executed them in a world-class manner, achieving the chain's strategic goals more than a year ahead of schedule.

Particularly where resources are limited, a company may need to assemble an optimal project portfolio as a first step to ensure that the key projects that have the greatest influence on successful implementation are completed first. It would continually renew the portfolio as projects are completed and resources (time and money) are freed up.

The adoption of best practice project management processes creating a common language and methodology is a vital step in planning how to implement strategy most efficiently. Training all those who will be members of project teams in these processes is vital.

Once the top team has signed off on the SMPP, the organization can spring into action.

THE KEYS TO SUCCESSFUL IMPLEMENTATION

These keys lie not only in leadership's commitment and discipline. They also are found in the organization's ability to address the universal elements of implementation that our research and experience indicate are essential in every plan. Complete these activities, and a firm foundation for successful implementation will exist:

- Communicate the strategy
- Drive planning
- Align the organization
- Reduce complexity
- Install an issue resolution system

COMMUNICATING THE STRATEGY

World-class firms today ensure their internal and external stakeholders have a full understanding of their strategy, how it was arrived at, and what role each stakeholder must play in its implementation. Naturally, this is the first of all implementation projects to be completed.

Figure 1 illustrates a typical communications matrix. It shows what elements of the strategy should be communicated to whom. Each cell becomes a sub-project defining who would lead communication, when, what media to use, goals to be achieved, resources needed, and follow-up required.

One of the UK's leading banks, the Bristol & West, exemplified best practice when its leadership team embarked on a series of 47 presentations in the City of London to all major financial, institutional, and media stakeholders. This was complemented by an equally impressive exercise for their internal stakeholders. Key executives were trained to run two-day workshops for all employees who would have a role in implementation.

When the Bank of Ireland acquired the Bristol & West, one of the key reasons Bristol & West was so desirable was its total strategic coherence and the genuine commitment and ownership of every employee to their part in making the strategy happen.

DRIVING PLANNING

Strategy must drive planning. Unfortunately, in many organizations it doesn't. The planning community, often (and wrongly) part of the financial control function, will have ascendancy. As Figure 2 illustrates, strategy formulation and planning are very different. Strategy must be set first, and planning must be part of the strategy implementation process. In this context, combining the word "strategic" with the word "planning" creates a contradiction in terms.

Effective planning reflects the organization's strategy and becomes, like communicating the strategy, a key project in the SMPP. Experience suggests that in those organizations where strategy does drive planning, the end result is a more realistic and holistic long-range plan or budget, one that plays a key role in the transition from vision to action. Too often, without a strategic context providing direction and emphasis, planning is seen as an isolated,

Figure 2   Comparison of Strategy Formulation with Long-Range Planning and Budgeting

Strategy Formulation	Long-Range Planning and Budgeting
• Top-down	• Bottom-up
• Visionary	• Projective
• Driven by products and markets	• Financially driven
• Strategic time-frame dependent on industry and product cycles	• Tied to calendar time for accounting and reporting purposes
• Flexible and responsive	• Once completed, inflexible—change one number and they all change
• Led by the CEO	• Presented to the CEO by planners and financial controllers

unrealistic activity with unachievable goals and completed mainly for others in the organization.

Greeting card giant Hallmark International recognized these principles. After setting strategy, Hallmark's executive team designed a compatible planning process for both three-year and annual operating plans. Created from scratch, that planning process did not resemble at all the normal financially-driven process. More than 400 executives around the globe were trained in the skills necessary to use the process and in strategy implementation skills such as strategic decision making and situation appraisal.

ALIGNING THE ORGANIZATION

Amazingly, we are still approached by CEOs who have recently reorganized their company and who now want to set strategy. Our response is that of course we will help, but only if, when the strategy is complete, he or she will be prepared to reorganize once again to ensure alignment with strategic imperatives. Emotional and psychological resistance to this notion is frequently high, but in the end logic and rationality usually wins. Strategy must drive structure.

Structures should be designed against a set of clear criteria that will ensure strategic alignment. These include:

- Compatibility with the firm's competitive advantage
- Consistency with the two or three core processes that facilitate work flow and that support the strategy
- Support from central functions for the geographic nature of the business

- Alignment with the primary product and market segmentation variables
- Devolution of decision making authority to those positions that are closest to the ownership of the decision and thus the ability to implement it
- Compatibility with the organization's culture and leadership style

In the final analysis, however, a firm's structure, while it may be important to individuals and their need for status, is of relatively little importance in implementing strategy. Of vital importance, however, are best-in-class business processes that facilitate work getting done between the white spaces on the organization chart, a culture that supports superior performance, and a powerful issue-resolution system.

ISSUE RESOLUTION SYSTEMS

These are a set of rational processes that enhance flawless execution of the strategy. Installed organization-wide, they represent a compelling common language by which individuals are able to work effectively on their own or in teams to make their contribution in turning vision into action.

There are six of these. They are designed to facilitate:

- Making a choice between alternative courses of action—decision making
- Preventing things from going wrong—potential problem analysis
- Promoting further opportunities when things are going well—potential opportunity analysis
- Finding the true cause when things have gone wrong—problem analysis or troubleshooting
- Assessing complex situations, setting priorities, and planning action—situation appraisal
- Developing a plan to execute a key objective—project management

These processes are universal and are required in every function, business unit, and geography and at all but the most junior levels in organizations. Their effective deployment ensures a faster and a higher quality resolution of human, operational, and strategic issues. A significant investment and effort is needed to install them. Research shows, however, that the return on such investments can be significant. Those returns are measured in terms of the speed with which issues are resolved, the quality of the resolution, and its financial payback. With such processes and skills in place effective strategy implementation is considerably enhanced.

REDUCING COMPLEXITY

We have never seen an organization that cannot benefit from reducing its level of complexity. Complexity exists in a variety of strategic guises, including in the product base, the range and nature of customers served, and the number of suppliers used. Similarly, the number of business processes, the complexity of each, and the lack of a common language to resolve issues contribute to suboptimal strategy implementation.

Even after a clear and robust strategy has been set and which answers the questions around product and market scope posed earlier, companies often need to take a surgical look at where value is truly added. The "rule of 50/5" demonstrates that for many firms 50% of revenue comes from the top 5% of products, and that the bottom 50% of products represents only 5% of revenue. The same holds true for customers. When analyzed fully, this information often shows the status quo is costing money by hanging on to low-value, marginal products and customers rather than rationalizing the situation and improving profitability.

A European producer of domestic hardware had a product profile with the following characteristics:

There were 1,011 products in the product line
Total sales were $68 million
50% of all revenue came from 30 products, or 3.8% of the total
973 products, or 96.2%, accounted for the remaining 50% of sales
The lowest performing 50% of all products, 507 in total, accounted for less than 1% of all revenue

Despite the resistance of the marketing and sales teams, it was easy to show how absolute and relative profitability could be significantly enhanced by reducing the company's product range. Similar analyses applied to the customer base provided further guidance on how that could be profitably rationalized. Taking out activity clearly also leads to cost savings.

MONITORING, REVIEWING, AND UPDATING STRATEGY

Finally, a word about the fifth phase of the strategy process. In today's world of rapid, often unexpected change, increased uncertainty, the global nature of business, and rapid technological advances, this activity must be a constant, ongoing one for an organization's leadership. In particular, leaders must carefully track implementation progress. If it is insufficient then either the strategy itself may need updating or changing, or more effort, investment, skills, discipline, and resources may be required to ensure implementation is brought into line with the exigencies of the vision and its timeframe for completion.

The task of creating and implementing strategy is not for the faint hearted. It requires discipline, commitment, creativity, leadership, and superior thinking and execution skills. In other words, all it takes is genius!

Futuring: A Complex Adaptive Systems Approach to Strategic Planning

John Vogelsang

Strategic planning continues to be one of the most frequently requested nonprofit consulting services. Client's constructs of what strategic planning is, however, range from a one-day board and staff retreat to a six-month or longer process involving extensive research of trends, opportunities, and challenges. Most express the hope that the process will help them develop the "right" plan that will provide a map to the future or at least position their organization to survive for the next three to five years. Those who want to conduct extensive research often express the belief that if they can gather the right amount of quality information they can avoid predictable pitfalls and bring about desired outcomes.

To judge from the number of requests and the language people use to describe what they want, we are still in what Richard Pascale (1999) calls the "strategic era:"

> The decade following World War II gave birth to the "strategic era." While the tenets of military strategy had been evolving for centuries, the link to commercial enterprise was tenuous. Before the late 1940s, most companies adhered to the tenet "make a little, sell a little, make a little more." After the war, faculty at the Harvard Business School (soon joined by swelling ranks of consultants) began to take the discipline of strategy seriously. By the late 1970s, the array of strategic concepts (SWOT analysis, the five forces framework, experience curves, strategic portfolios, the concept of competitive advantage) had become standard ordnance in the management arsenal. (83)

However, as Pascale argues in his article about Complex Adaptive Systems, there are new approaches to planning. This article describes the current state of traditional approaches to strategic planning in nonprofits, some emerging approaches, and the potential for further rethinking offered by Complex Adaptive Systems Theory.

TRADITIONAL APPROACHES

Since its prominence in the 1970s and 1980s, strategic planning has become a method for examining the appropriateness of an organization's mission and for positioning an organization to deal with potential challenges in the future. If one were to include many of the refinements that have occurred over the past twenty some years, the method as they applied in nonprofit settings usually involves:

A set of underlying principles:

- There is a need for a clear, well-understood mission and vision
- The organizational culture must support trust, honesty, and accountability
- The participants need to have strategic/systems thinking and skills
- Well-informed cross-functional, cross group networks are important for gaining the best insights and sharing the process and decisions throughout the organization
- Good communication must be maintained at all times
- The coordinating team needs to define what they consider a successful planning process and articulate that definition clearly to those involved

The process usually includes:

- A Coordinating Committee and/or Planning Committee
- Task Forces to develop sections of the plan
- A planning retreat for internal stakeholders or their representatives and some external stakeholders
- A planning document developed by task forces and the planning committee with assistance from a consultant

The steps in the process, not necessarily in this order, can be:

- Review the organization's purpose, mission, vision and values
- Conduct an external environmental and internal organizational SWOT (What are our Strengths, Weaknesses, Opportunities, and Threats) scan
- Analyze the information from the scan
- Create a discussion document or a way to involve stakeholders in the information that was gathered during the environmental and organizational scan
- Revise the mission statement if necessary
- Revise or create organizational values (if not clarified)
- Create a vision of the future
- Develop strategies to implement the vision
- Identify specific long range goals/objectives
- Design a first year, detailed implementation plan
- Design an evaluation process for the plan

The strategic planning consultant and the coordinating/planning committee usually share responsibility for accomplishing each of those steps. In earlier approaches to strategic planning, the planning committee or an executive team usually developed the plan with some input from other staff and external stakeholders through surveys, interviews or focus groups. Currently, most agencies attempt to include as many internal and external stakeholders either through the information gathering and/or through a series of large/small group planning meetings to help formulate components of the plan.

EMERGING APPROACHES TO PLANNING

A number of approaches to planning have emerged over the past twenty years. They include: Whole-Scale (Dannemiller, 2000), Search/Future Search Conferences (Emery, 1996) (Weisbord and Janoff, 1992), the Conference Model (Axelrod, 2000), and FutureScape (Sanders, 1998). All of these approaches tend to use variations of the traditional process with the following differences:

- They emphasize large and small group ways to involve as many stakeholders in the system (both internal and external) in the planning process,
- They tend to do the environmental and organizational scan in "real time" at a large group meeting (with some scanning done before to shape the questions and process),
- They emphasize looking at the whole system and not parts; that is why they want to have as many representatives of the organization a part of the process,
- They favor visual and metaphoric approaches in addition to rational processes; and
- While developing the usual long-term goals, they tend also to look for short-term immediate changes that can help increase commitment to the overall plan.

Some use Appreciative Inquiry (Cooperrider, 1999) processes and emphasize how to nurture the effectiveness of those aspects of the organization that are valued by the internal stakeholders and produce value for the external stakeholders. Clarifying what the external stakeholders find valuable becomes the focus of the environmental scan. This scan can be done through interviews or focus groups (more traditional approach) or forums and large group meetings.

As practitioners incorporate the emerging approaches and attempt to connect them to clients' requests for more traditional strategic planning, they have developed some interesting hybrid variations. All of the following approaches assume the starting point is revisiting the organization's purpose and mission. In most cases there is a large group environmental scan, or a forum with external representatives, or the more traditional environmental scanning and report writing:

- Develop a three to five year Vision with long term strategies such as we will emphasize collaborative projects with other service providers, we will expand our capacity by emphasizing staff development. Specific goals and objectives are created on a yearly basis in an operational planning process.
- Develop a three to five year vision, affirm that the major strategy will be entrepreneurial development of opportunities, and identify criteria for how to decide among the many opportunities.

- Examine how people currently spend their time and energy and identify the emerging strategies and practices that are and could continue to move the organization forward. Choose how to support or further develop those strategies and design goals and objectives to accomplish that. The emerging strategies may lead to a re-examination of the mission.
- Instead of developing a plan, identify key strategic questions that become the topic of regular board and staff meetings. Such questions include: Who are our customers and how are they changing? How do we deal with an economic downturn? What are emerging service needs? As a product of the discussions the board and staff formulate long range strategies that inform operational decisions.

COMPLEX ADAPTIVE SYSTEMS THEORY'S INFLUENCE ON STRATEGIC PLANNING

Most of the practitioners of the new approaches to planning say they draw upon Theoretical Biology, Quantum Physics, and Chaos Theory, particularly theories of self-organization, nonequilibrium, complementarity, and the "butterfly effect"—minute fluctuations can produce large scale changes. Another influence on management theory and strategic planning is Complex Adaptive Systems Theory that attempts to understand how physical, biological and social systems operate. When people describe Complex Adaptive Systems they commonly include many of the following characteristics:

- **Agents with schemata.** The agents interact with each other constructing and reconstructing schemata (assumptions, expectations, values, habits) that organize their relations at the local level. They are continually coming together to understand the world and each other, form judgments, fashion the future, and to sustain their relations. Their act of responding to and interpret what they experience involves constructing, reconstructing, and modifying their schemata.
- **Global patterns of relationship emerge.** As the agents interact locally, adapt to each other, and generate variety and complexity in their schemata they construct coherent and global patterns of interacting: rituals, structured relationships, communication systems, commonly held criteria for making decisions (operating values), a shared purpose, and organizations. This emergence of self-organization comes from a range of valuable innovations to unfortunate accidents. Misunderstandings and miscues offer variable ways of interacting and opportunities to reshape the assumptions and expectations that have become global patterns. Each contributes to the continual change going on in the organization. Each time the members solve problems individually and together they self-organize and release variety into the system. The system will wind down unless replenished with energy generated by internal and external relations and the subsequent innovations and mistakes.

- **Coevolution at the edge of chaos.** Complex Adaptive Systems exist at the boundary regions near the edge of chaos where the frozen components of order begin to melt and the agents in the system coevolve in order to survive and optimize themselves in the changing environment. The agents often have conflicting goals that require them to adapt to each other's behavior. Complex Adaptive Systems are constantly creating variety and are at risk of death when they move toward equilibrium. One cannot predict which variation will have the greatest influence. Often, small variations can have huge effects and massive efforts may have little effect. Simple patterns can combine to generate great complexity and variety, and emerging complexity can create many possibilities and many possible futures. There are many small changes and infrequent, irregular massive changes.
- **System evolution based upon recombination.** In every interaction the agents enact historic patterns—the previously formed schemata—with slight or major variations. The agents are able to recognize the patterns, experience the difference, and choose to reconstruct them or construct new patterns. Thus there is consistency yet difference. The system generates novelty without abandoning the best elements of its past. The system is also resilient: flexible and open to learning in order to evolve while being durable and consistent with its schemata—purpose, values, rituals, and relations.
- **No one point of control.** For a Complex Adaptive System to survive it must cultivate variety, but it is an illusion to think that one can direct the variations. One can only disturb the system and be mindful of what is happening. At the same time one cannot be separate from the system—stand outside and influence its direction. One can only influence the rules, the relationships, the choices made as a participant in interactions while being influenced by others. (Anderson, 1999; Kauffman, 1995; Pascale, 1999; Rouse, 2000; Stacey, 2001)

Attempts to apply earlier versions of Complex Adaptive Systems theory to organizations often rejected or de-emphasized strategic planning in favor of organizational learning processes for challenging existing mental models of behavior in organizations in order to learn how to rapidly adapt to a changing environment (Phelan, 1995). If small variations can have huge effects and massive efforts may have little effect it is difficult to identify historic and emerging patterns that can be projected into the future in a planning process. Thereby, it is argued that the organization needs to develop learning processes that will enable it to adapt to the many unexpected changes. The emphasis on learning organizations has contributed to efforts to foster self-organization and coevolution in organizations through such techniques as learning circles, peer learning groups, communities of practice, and systems thinking. There may not be a predictable future but there is still a need to engage in futuring—continually constructing a future. We need ways to answer are we engaged in the most appropriate activities and relating in the most appropriate way to our stakeholders that contribute to our resilience and optimization in this particular patchwork of current and emerging relationships.

When we combine the emphasis on learning organizations and with the need to construct a future we have such planning concerns as:

- How can we be clear about our purpose and values and use them to structure modes of communication that support interconnectedness among the various stakeholders?
- How can we optimize and construct relationships in the organizations so to foster complexity, self-organization, and futuring?
- How can we encourage resiliency in the organization—the flexibility, durability, openness to learning, and decision making and problem solving skills to make complex, reliable decisions in the presence of massive and often conflicting input as we coevolve between order and chaos?
- How can we find the unique, alternative outcomes already contained in the current situation and its history, as different from creating an unknown future?
- How can we disturb/get the attention of the organizational system?

TECHNIQUES

If strategic planning is a way of asking are we engaged in the most appropriate activities and relating in the most appropriate way to our stakeholders that contributes to our fit and optimization in this particular patchwork of current and emerging relationships, there are some aspects of the traditional methods that are helpful and many that need to be modified. Instead of a rational, step by step planning process that produces the "right" goals that will allows us to exercise some control over the future, we need to develop mindfulness as we move between chaos and order. Some of the possible ways this can be done are:

Shaping the Context for Planning

As with traditional strategic planning the process can benefit from a well-informed, cross-functional, and representative coordinating group and an organizational system that supports trust, honesty, and accountability. The group needs to decide:

- How ready is the organization for developing a strategic plan? Are there far too many changes/crises happening or is the staff highly resistant to changing their patterns of work? If there are too many changes, the group may consider ways to foster relationships in the organization that encourage mutual learning and construction of adaptive techniques to the rapid changes (organizational learning approaches). Or they could use this time as an opportunity to revisit the mission and values and develop strategies that will help the immediate situation and provide some guidance for at least the next 2 years. If there is a high level of resistance, the group may want to look at ways to modify the relationships among the staff in order to develop possibilities that have been ignored. Are there some groups that could be cross-functional or work on joint projects?

- Is there sufficient trust and a sufficient functioning level in the relationships that would support honest feedback and discussion, and is there a willingness to learn and create together? If there is not, how can the process itself contribute to creating this atmosphere of trust and learning?
- Will the organization commit the needed time and money to the process?
- How can the coordinating group members be aware of the dynamics in their group in order to be more mindful of what is contributing to or hindering communication among the staff?
- What will be their criteria for deeming the planning process a success?
- Who will be involved and how?
- What will be the steps in the process?

Clarify, review, and affirm the core purpose, mission, values, desired outcomes, and criteria for making decisions that influence the stakeholders.

In Complex Adaptive Systems the agents are interconnected through commonly held criteria for making decisions (operating values) and a shared purpose that also informs the way they relate to each other and the stakeholders. As with the traditional and emerging processes described above, the coordinating group needs to involve the whole system in clarifying and reaffirming what difference (outcome) the agency is trying to achieve with its stakeholders, how they will know if they have achieved that difference, and what are the values/criteria that will influence what practices, methods, and resources they will use to achieve those outcomes.

Fostering Relationships and Systems and Modes of Communication

A Complex Adaptive System approach to Strategic planning is an opportunity to reconstruct relationships and construct possibilities through dialogue and networking among both internal and external groups. This means a shift in emphasis. As in traditional and emerging strategic planning approaches, meetings among stakeholders still have a role in generating information for decision-making, but they have a larger role in nurturing the relationships that contribute to constructing possibilities and encouraging self-organization. Instead of a traditional organizational and environmental SWOT analysis, the agency may use Appreciative Inquiry and other ways to look for the changes already happening or about to happen. There may be a series of large (whole system) and small group meetings of both internal staff and external stakeholders in order to create the opportunity for new relationships and better communication.

How does a Complex Adaptive System approach to planning differ from the learning organization approach as outlined by Rowden in reading 3?

The agency may try to understand the various relationships it has with its stakeholders and other community entities and how they and the stakeholders influence those relationships. The staff may want to explore their assumptions about the past, present and future and how those assumptions are affecting how the staff relates to each other and to the stakeholders. . . .

Choosing Strategies that Increase Resiliency and the Ability to Perform Complex and Reliable Decision Making

Beinhocker (1999) recommends that instead of choosing singularly focused strategies, organizations need to cultivate multiple strategies, many of which will operate in parallel in order to encourage co-evolution. The multiple strategies that can increase the resiliency of an organization are 1) those that deepen and extend current practices, 2) those that create new practices, and 3) those that plant the seeds for future developments. While emphasizing the first, organizations that continue to optimize in their particular fitness environment commit varying degrees of resources to the other two.

In forming strategies, the coordinating group (and the whole system through group meetings) can be mindful of the continual changes happening in the organization and decide how to foster those that fit the mission, values, and criteria. They can discuss what are the changes they want:

- To acknowledge—because they are already happening and they deepen and extend current practices
- To influence—because they need some support and direction to occur and they have the potential to further improve current practices and/or create new practices
- To make happen—because they are new possibilities: new practices or the seeds for future development

In order to contribute to continuing resiliency, planning strategies could include ways to foster the organizational learning processes mentioned earlier. These could include instituting and supporting opportunities for cross-functional and staff in the same program to come together for peer learning groups, case conferences, and mutual problem solving sessions.

A Complex Adaptive System approach to strategic planning builds upon organizational learning methods while it emphasizes mindfulness, mission and values based decisions, fosterng relationships and systems of communication, and continuing to construct possibilities that contribute to an organization's self-organizing and resiliency in its immediate and distant environment. A vision of a near or distant future and the strategic plan itself are not blueprints for a future state but ways to prepare an organization to be more mindful of the constant changes and possibilities happening in the present.

REFERENCES

Anderson, P. 1999. "Complexity Theory and Organization Science." *A Journal of the Institute of Management Sciences*, v. 10, 3, May/June.

Axelrod, R. 2000. *Terms of Engagement.* San Francisco: Berrett-Koehler Publishers, Inc.

Beinhocker, E. D. 1999. "Robust Adaptive Strategies." *Sloan Management Review*, Spring.

Cooperrider, D., P. F. Sorensen, and D. Whitney. 1999. *Appreciative Inquiry: Rethinking Human Organization Toward a Positive Theory of Change.* Champaign, IL: Stipes Publishing.

Dannemiller, K. and Associates. 2000. *Whole-Scale Change.* San Francisco: Berrett-Koehler Publishers, Inc.

Emery, M. 1996. *The Search Conference.* San Francisco: Jossey-Bass, Inc.

Kauffman, S. 1995. *At Home in the Universe.* New York: Oxford University Press.

Pascale, R. 1999. "Surfing the Edge of Chaos." *Sloan Management Review*, Spring, 83–94.

Phelan, S. 1995. "From Chaos to Complexity in Strategic Planning." Paper presented at the 55th Annual Meeting of the Academy of Management, Vancouver, BC.

Regine, B. and R. Lewin. 2000. "Leading at the Edge: How Leaders Influence Complex Systems." *Emergence*, v. 2, 2.

Rouse, B. 2000. "Managing Complexity: Disease Control as a Complex Adaptive System." *Information Knowledge Systems Management*, v. 2, 2.

Sanders, I. 1998. *Strategic Thinking and the New Science.* New York: The Free Press.

Stacey, R. 2001. *Complex Responsive Processes in Organizatons: Learning and Knowledge Creation.* New York: Routledge.

Weisbord, M. and S. Janoff, 1992. *Future Search.* San Francisco: Berrett-Koehler Publishers, Inc.

ISSUE SUMMARY

All organizations need to plan and look ahead. For decades, planning has been carried out in a formal manner, using analytical quantitative methods to predict actions that must be taken. The resulting plan was a carefully detailed document that may or may not have impacted daily organizational life.

Today, formal planning of the "review and act" type is being set aside for approaches that reflect new concepts and theories about organizations and the environment. These approaches can be clustered under the term "emergent." Many emergent approaches incorporate some aspects of traditional strategic planning: whole-scale, conference model, futuring, appreciative inquiry. Taken together, emergent strategies typically pay attention to the whole system and use images of change (visual or metaphoric) in addition to narrative and statistics.

Key to the success of emergent approaches is involvement of constituents at all levels of the organization. Planning becomes the work of everyone, not upper management or a select few. Kanter uses the metaphor of strategy as improvisational theater to describe the work of the organization: "It shifts attention from the dynamics among members of a project team to the way in which an organization as a whole can become an arena for staging experiments that can transform the overall strategy" (2002, p. 76).

For many organizational leaders, the process of looking ahead is more important than the resulting strategy plan document. By discussing the mission, creating action plans, and clarifying values, constituents think strategically about their organization. The document itself contains the plan, but the process of deliberation is what builds understanding and consensus about the future.

Deliberation and discernment are at the heart of a learning organization. An organization that has developed its own learning processes is better able to adapt and become resilient in ever-changing conditions. With an emphasis on learning and adapting rather than reviewing and perfecting, it is no wonder that strategic planning is evolving.

An additional approach to strategic planning that has much to recommend is appreciative inquiry. This model has three unique characteristics: assessment of current strengths and assets, involvement of all constituents, and extensive use of narrative and dialogue. As the term "appreciative inquiry" indicates, the process involves discovering what is going well and building on those strengths. More than asset mapping, this form of inquiry is strategic because it includes envisioning what the organization desires to be in the future.

ISSUE HIGHLIGHTS

- Calendar-driven, task-focused planning processes are becoming irrelevant for many organizations.
- Changing the timing and focus of planning also changes the nature of strategizing from "review and approve" to "discuss and decide."
- Planning that is continuous and decision-oriented leads to better long-term growth and profitability.
- Earlier versions of strategic planning have focused on detailed implementation schemes or on readiness for change.
- Quality and improvement initiatives often fail because they are not well integrated, are based on short-term expectations, and are limited to existing procedures.
- The strategic era is being replaced by the knowledge management era, which is leading to emergent strategic planning approaches.
- Organizations are realizing the need to continually construct a future and are using futuring strategies for their planning work.
- Complex adaptive system theory contributes a more holistic perspective to strategic planning, enabling an organization to do more "out of the box" thinking.

CRITICAL THINKING

In "Moving Beyond the Official Future," Doug Randall and Chris Ertel contend that new approaches to strategic planning involve a different kind of risk management. ". . . the definition of risk management for organizations has broadened, expanding beyond the tangible and quantifiable issues for which executives possess well-honed tools to the less tangible and more qualitative forms of risk that few have learned how to anticipate."

Physical, legal, and financial areas come to mind as types of risk that are tangible and quantifiable. Intangible risks are often ignored, simply because they cannot be placed on variable and actuary tables for analysis. Lack of knowledge, inefficient processes, or ineffective partnerships are all sources of great risk for organizations.

Many experts are advocating scenario thinking as an appropriate approach for managing these intangible risks. By creating scenarios—different versions of the future—constituents bring multiple perspectives to risk management. The result is a more comprehensive approach to risk management, one that can be integrated into strategic planning rather than remain separate.

ADDITIONAL READING RESOURCES

Syed H. Akhter, Strategic planning, hypercompetition, and knowledge management. *Business Horizons*, January/February 2003.

Eric D. Beinhocker & Sarah Kaplan, Tired of strategic planning? *McKinsey Quarterly*, Special Edition, 2002.

David J. Collis & Cynthia A. Montgomery, *Corporate Strategy*. McGraw-Hill/Irwin, 2005.

Rosabeth Moss Kanter, Strategy as improvisational theater. *MIT Sloan Management Review,* Winter 2002.

Carter McNamara, *Field Guide to Nonprofit Strategic Planning and Facilitation.* Authenticity Consulting, 2003.

Doug Randall & Chris Ertel, Moving beyond the official future. *Financial Times,* September 15, 2005.

Sherry Rockey & Laverne Webb, Organizational change inside and out: The impact of an appreciative inquiry. *Journal for Nonprofit Management,* 2005.

For more information check these sites:

http://appreciativeinquiry.case.edu/
www.strategyplus.org/
www.themanager.org/Knowledgebase/Strategy

How Will Organizations Function in the Future?

INTRODUCTION

The organization of the future has become a hot topic of speculation and debate. Will its fundamental shape change? Is collaboration the way of the future? Will size be a critical factor? Is process or outcome more important? How will communication change? Given the fluctuating nature of the global economy, leaders know that the transformation of organizations is occurring at a fast pace. What they do not know is the exact shape of the organization in the future.

No amount of assessment can give a sure answer to how organizations will be functioning and performing in days ahead. But there are plenty of indicators that make the shape fairly clear:

> The digital age organization is no longer a single corporate entity, but rather an extended network consisting of a streamlined global core, market-focused business units, and shared support services. This organizational model lends itself to the flexible teaming, select alliances, and increased outsourcing characteristic of competition in the electronic world. It is a networked, nonlinear, coherent organization that is neither centralized nor decentralized. Its dynamism, flexibility, and openness form the foundation of what some have dubbed the e.Org. (Malloch, 2001, p. 642)

There is no doubt that the Internet is transforming the organizational model and having a direct impact on work flow, service, and management. In a wired world, the Web becomes the business platform and capital becomes intellectual property. Doing e-business has implications for how organizations exchange information and stay connected. This is the focus of the first reading, "Fast Forward: Future Trends in Corporate Communication." Specialists in information flow paint a somewhat paradoxical picture of the trends. Some see a greater need for face-to-face communication while others see an increase in decentralized communication.

The second reading deals with the question: Why is it so hard for an organization to perform well and adapt at the same time? Evidently adaptation is written in some organization's DNA and is not in others. The author of "The Adaptable Corporation" contends that an organization learns one set of behaviors to deal with current demands but that set does not automatically transfer when conditions change. In other words, today's ways of conducting

315

business may become tomorrow's barriers to adaptation. Carrying out activities today may require tight control and close coordination but tomorrow's new activities may call for autonomy and openness. Very few organizations can be all of these things at once. The author proposes an organization can begin to overcome the barriers by addressing key aspects of its structure and culture.

One outcome of the globalizing economy is new opportunity for innovation. Connecting the two—globalization and innovation—is the focus of the third article, "Creation Nets: Getting the Most from Open Innovation." The authors, Brown and Hagel, believe the entire approach to business needs to change for organizations to function well in the world. The image of tight control over conventional pro forma tasks no longer fits with the kind of work and services needed for a global economy. We used to be able to predict what was needed, produce just enough so inventory didn't pile up, and tweak the process as the market shifted. Those days are gone, in part because the Internet makes us aware of market shifts second by second. Innovating, customizing, tailoring, remixing are at the heart of tomorrow's process networks. In essence, the authors' message is that organizational leaders need to play an orchestrator role in managing loosely coupled process networks.

The author of the final reading contends that the future of organizations is not in innovation or performance or product development but in relationships. Organizations that cultivate and retain clients/customers are poised for long-term profitability better than those that simply market products or services. The key for leaders is recognizing the subtle but real differences between relational exchange and transactional exchange. Once that difference is understood, the next hurdle is knowing how relational exchange differs across cultures: "Relationships are built on a cultural platform which means that the route to developing a good relationship can be very different in the Western and the Eastern cultures." For some leaders, gaining a competitive edge in the future will involve relationship-oriented strategies.

SOURCES

SCM Editorial Board, Fast forward: Future trends in corporate communication. *Strategic Communication Management*, December 2005/January 2006.

Eric D. Beinhocker, The adaptable corporation. *McKinsey Quarterly,* 2006.

John Seely Brown & John Hagel III, Creation nets: Getting the most from open innovation. *McKinsey Quarterly*, 2006.

Sabine Flambard-Ruaud, Relationship marketing in emerging economies: Some lessons for the future. *Vikalpa*, July–September 2005.

Fast Forward: Future Trends in Corporate Communication

SCM Editorial Board

This issue of Strategic Communication Management celebrates the journal's 10-year anniversary. To mark the occasion, we invited members of the SCM editorial board to comment on some of the major trends they believe will influence the profession over the next few years. If your communication strategy and personal development plans for next year don't incorporate these issues already, perhaps it's time to think about how they could.

Editor's Note

It's difficult to find the time to speculate on future trends when the phrase "doing more with less" is the business mantra of our times. Indeed, when members of the *SCM* Editorial Board were asked to share their thoughts on the challenges and developments they see ahead, one response reminded me that the ability to predict next week's events would be a blessing, never mind the next few years. Nonetheless, this group of industry experts has kindly indulged our request and the result is a valuable snapshot of the issues and priorities that should be on each practitioner's professional radar going into 2006.

—Roger D'Aprix
D'Aprix and Company, LLC
Author of *Communicating for Change*
USA

1. ENGAGING THROUGH MANAGEMENT

The major communication needs we must address as a profession are engagement and the communication role of line managers. Just recently, the new chairman of Delphi Corporation, Steve Miller, asserted that it would be necessary to reduce real union wages in his bankrupt company to $10 an hour if the company were to survive. In an interview with the *Wall Street Journal* he said that globalization means that labor-intensive products must be produced in low-wage countries and that "sophisticated" products will be made domestically by workers who have competitive, American industrial wages of

$20 an hour, including the cost of benefits. Bottom line that means $10 an hour before taxes!

Here's the point. Threatened workers—whether we are talking about hourly wage earners or salaried workers—are an uneasy audience. Human presence, human explanation by sympathetic bosses and effective face-to-face communication will be essential if we have any hope of engagement, increased productivity and the imagination to create real measures to improve competitiveness.

If Miller's dire views are correct and we find no other solutions but worker sacrifice, we face an unbelievable challenge in helping people to understand and cope with today's economic realities. If indeed the "receivers" in our audience become broken or tuned out, we have little hope of successful workplace communication. Engaging people who are constantly looking uneasily over their shoulders is our plight in the days ahead. It's a complex challenge that will stretch us all.

—John G. Clemons
Vice President, Communications
Raytheon Technical Services Co.
USA

2. PREPARING FOR CRISES

All indications are that the business, social, political, economic and human landscape will change dramatically in the next 10 years and, as a result, so will the way we communicate with fellow employees and one another in general.

The tragedy of September 11, 2001, and other terrorist attacks have had a profound, altering effect on the American psyche that has crossed the oceans and made us wary and on edge, wondering when and if there will be another major crisis. We are also experiencing natural disasters with greater frequency.

The impact on the communication profession over the next few years will mean a renewed focus on crisis management and the role communication plays to ensure companies, employees, clients and customers have the tools and mechanisms in place for business continuity, minimal confusion and chaos, and zero human casualties. Crisis communication planning and the ability to lead come hell or high water may become a required skill set for professional communicators. From executive kidnappings and tragic accidents to natural disasters and bioterrorism—will we be ready to step up?

It will be incumbent upon us to know how to:

- develop a crisis communications plan;
- form a crisis management team with functions and employees who need to be included; and
- prepare, rehearse and be ready to execute.

While we can never be fully prepared for the twists and turns of a crisis, communicators who have the skill to develop and implement a plan and stay cool under fire will be in demand.

—Stephen Windsor-Lewis
Employee Involvement & Communications Director
BAE Systems, UK

3. UNDERSTANDING EMPLOYEE DEMOGRAPHICS

It's often said that "we live in a changing world," and while this is certainly true, change can sometimes serve to emphasize those things that remain constant. One constant in the communications world is the influence of social demographics on an individual's predisposition towards information absorption.

Send a pension communication to a 25-year-old and watch their eyes glaze over as it goes straight in the bin. Send the same communication to a 60-year-old and watch their eyes light up as they read it and file it under "Important Documents."

As we progress through our working lives, so we also progress through our social lives. In generic terms, and without trying to paint stereotypes, an eager new employee in their twenties is looking for experience: they seek development, variety and challenge, but not at the expense of work-life balance. In their social lives, they are also looking for new experiences and are inclined to try new things.

By the time the average worker hits 30, they know what they want from their career. They're looking for promotion to middle management and are more inclined to work longer hours and take on more responsibility. In their social lives, they are more likely to live in an established social pattern, and often put their work first.

If we understand this progression, it provides clear guidance on what we should say, when and to whom if we want to improve information absorption and communication effectiveness.

The lesson for communicators is clear: know your audience and let that knowledge determine the method and manner of your communication.

—Fraser Likely
President and Managing Partner
Likely Communication Strategies Ltd.
Canada

How High-Tech Is Changing the Rules

Stuart Z. Goldstein
Managing Director
Corporate Communications
The Depository Trust and Clearing Corporation
USA

With the Internet leveling the playing field in communications, what are the unwritten implications for organizations in the future?

The internet has increased the quantity, quality and speed of information flow. As a result, transformational change in the world of media and in the practice of corporate communication is occurring at an accelerating rate of speed. The old rules no longer apply. For example:

• The press, which throughout history has been an arbiter of truth, is in decline. The standards of accuracy and rules of journalism are being eroded by the pressures to compete with internet blogs and web advocacy groups and the growing influence of the entertainment side of the media business. The media reporting of blog information increases their acceptance as legitimate news sources, adding fuel to this trend and undermining fact-checking as two sources becomes a basis for news reporting.

• Without a referee, companies face an enormous challenge in trying to communicate their messages clearly and effectively. The chatter and noise factor will grow. The internet has leveled the playing field and disgruntled stakeholders and advocacy groups will gain increasing influence.

• Communication strategists will increasingly look to adopt market research methods like focus groups and overnight polling to pre-assess and post-assess messaging strategies. Brand and messaging strategies will become more targeted and values-driven. And to compete, companies will create their own direct channels to reach stakeholders with internet broadcasting, e-mail and other direct marketing techniques. Companies will establish their own databases of shareholders and customers willing to defend the firm.

• Political campaigns have already become the laboratories for testing new communication theory and as a training ground for communication professionals who think strategically. In time, experience in politics will be as important as journalism as a criteria for corporate communicators.

• The art of writing will once again be the most valued skill a communicator can offer. In a crowded marketplace of ideas and opinions, the crafting of words that are impactful will be critical in distinguishing and differentiating your company—and your message.

4. APPLYING THEORY AND BEST PRACTICE

The opportunities for professional development in the public relations/communication (PR/C) field abound. The vast array of available resources provide practitioners with an all-you-can-eat intellectual feast. There is, though, a problem at this overloaded buffet table. Some dishes prepared for the feast are made from wholegrain wheat: some are made from the chaff. How is the typical practitioner to know what separates one from the other?

How do practitioners separate proven ideas from flavor-of-the-month—truly best practices from somewhat better practices? This need to have and to apply an approved standardized body of knowledge will be a major trend.

For example, standardization is lacking in such PR/C subject areas as media evaluation, return-on-investment (ROI) and engagement. In these areas, we do not have an accepted standard. We have a bunch of half-baked assumptions.

We will see the separation of wheat from chaff in the next few years. The resulting standardized body of accepted knowledge will become more useable. It will be in a form that practitioners can easily apply to their day-to-day work.

The first seeds of this separation and application process are being sown now. Soon, approved theorems and best practices will be built into issues management, communication planning and communication evaluation software. As practitioners create plans, they will be prompted to make decisions based on the highest level of accepted "truth."

Having experienced the power employed by this software, I believe it will change the PR/C field as we know it. It will change us from being practitioners to being applied theoreticians. It will do so by putting proven theories and best practices right into our planning and decisionmaking processes. What a change to the profession if every professional was working with the highest level of accepted knowledge available.

—Ayelet L. Baron
Senior Business Development Manager
Global Mobility
Cisco Systems
USA

5. ADAPTING TO NEW WAYS OF WORKING

The impact of new technological breakthroughs—and their unexpected consequences—continue to play a major role in shaping the way we work and manage our organizations. Employees will have to adapt to changing technologies and shifting product demand.

The workforce of the future will increasingly require seamless information flows as complexity and information overload increase. It will be important to leverage communication tools to create an organization where everyone has the information to do their jobs effectively. And also to ensure that relationships and trust continue to be a key component as organizations will become increasingly decentralized.

As teleworking and new employment contracts become more prevalent, managers will have to adjust to communicating to a more decentralized workforce and create new skills to manage virtual employees and teams.

As employees work more cross-functionally, what will be their challenges in the future?

We are continuing to move into a knowledge and values economy, where there will be a greater need to understand the values of employees and make sure highly knowledgeable people are motivated to contribute to the organization's success. Reality will also require people to work much more cross-functionally, and there will be a need to create a base of common understanding, shared beliefs and innovation. This will require a new capacity to learn and unlearn; challenge old models and create more productive ones that suit the time. We may find that we will have less managers and supervisors and more doers and thinkers.

Communicators will be challenged to help create new organizations with different demographics, different work arrangement and increased decentralization. Understanding organization design and how to create effective work teams will be critical to success.

When the notion of control decreases and belonging becomes more important in retaining and attracting employees, some new communication models will emerge.

—David Moorcroft
Senior Vice-President
Corporate Communications
RBC Financial Group
Canada

6. KNOWLEDGE, REPUTATION AND ENGAGEMENT

I see three areas of growing importance for communicators—business knowledge, corporate reputation and employee engagement.

As the world becomes more complex, transparent and competitive, organizations will increasingly look for communication professionals who understand business and can participate in strategic business discussions.

In light of the growing public distrust of big business, many organizations will also place greater emphasis on building and maintaining a good reputation. In fact, research shows that reputation is becoming a "tie-breaker" for consumers when they choose between firms with similar products and prices. So communicators who can identify and influence key drivers of reputation will become increasingly valuable.

And finally, organizations will continue to look for ways to enhance employee engagement in reaching their business objectives. In my view, there is a tremendous opportunity to unleash more discretionary effort from employees when they understand how their individual work contributes to an organization's overall strategy. Communicators who can help achieve this goal will be in growing demand.

—Bill Quirke
Managing Director
Synopsis Communication Consulting
UK

What Do Senior Leaders Expect?

Smooch Repovich Reynolds is CEO of The Repovich-Reynolds Group (TRRG), an international executive search firm headquartered in Pasadena, California. She has the following to say about attributes and criteria that she believes senior leaders will be looking for in future top-level communicators.

"My discussions with C-suite members include the structural considerations of the communication function. The trend emerging with the most momentum, and one that is gaining strength and credibility with senior management teams, is the notion of combining the Chief Marketing Officer role with the Chief Communications Officer role, in an effort to ensure a company's brand equity with a portfolio of constituencies that represent an international base.

"The resulting expectation of talent sets the bar at one of the highest levels ever in terms of the arsenal of experiences in which communication professionals must prepare themselves to prove credible. This incorporates knowledgeable leaders with exceptional business acumen (both traditional marketing as well as communications expertise); as savvy executives with financial analytical capabilities that enable the individual to assess complex global business challenges; and as professionals who leverage their intuition to glean the nuances of relationships that allow people to work effectively across the globe — a combination of both right and left brain abilities.

"Gone are the days when being an exceptional communication professional will suffice for senior communicators, or even in the one or two levels below the top communicator's position in a company. Senior leadership teams consider these expectations to be the basic price to entry and the basis for the future hiring of senior level communication executives."

7. HARMONIZING THE ORGANIZATION'S "VOICE"

Integrated communication will become a key issue, whether that's outside, within or across an organization. A blurring of organizational boundaries means "internal" communication is a distinction which will increasingly disappear. Outsourced partners, offshored call centers, joint ventures, supply chain partnerships will all fall into the remit of internal communication, in an attempt to harmonize the different voices customers hear from an organization.

Turf wars over where internal communication should sit will be replaced by cross-functional partnerships, as communica, for example, with HR on engagement, skills, appraisal and reward, and with employer branding, investor relations and finance on compliance and integrity.

The erosion of trust in management means internal communicators will have to become more challenging about the creation of messages and the credibility of leaders. This will mean coaching managers to crystallize what they mean, helping them to cut through the growing clutter.

Competition for people's time and attention will increase the need to manage the airspace, rein in would be communicators and reduce "vanity publishing." Internal communicators will be asked to act as gateways and will have to advise on not just reducing volume, but how to compete more effectively for shrinking employee brainspace.

Although importance will be placed on understanding the proliferation of channels driven by technology, the range of options available, and the strengths and weaknesses of each, a fascination with channels shouldn't distract communicators from addressing the bigger issue of having poor content to communicate in the first place.

The Adaptable Corporation

Eric D. Beinhocker

A ny business faces two basic demands: it must execute its current activities to survive today's challenges and adapt those activities to survive tomorrow's. Since both executing and adapting require resources, managers face an unending competition for money, people, and time to address the need to perform in the short run *and* the equally vital need to invest in the long run. This problem raises an important question—is it possible to do both well or is there an inevitable trade-off between executing and adapting?

EXECUTING VERSUS ADAPTING

Tom Peters and Bob Waterman were among the first popular writers to draw attention to the managerial implications of this challenge, in 1982's *In Search of Excellence,*[1] where they argued that organizations must simultaneously be "tight" in executing and "loose" in adapting. This dialectic has been a central theme in management literature ever since: James Collins and Jerry Porras, for example, note the importance of both control and creativity in *Built to Last,*[2] Richard Foster and Sarah Kaplan examine the need to balance operating versus innovating in *Creative Destruction,*[3] and Michael Tushman and Charles O'Reilly paint their vision of an "ambidextrous" organization that can operate as well as innovate in *Winning through Innovation.*[4] One of the best-known and most-cited academic papers on the topic, written in 1991 by Stanford's James March, used the memorable terms "exploration" versus "exploitation."[5]

Each writer's language and nuances may be different, but it is no coincidence that the yin-yang theme of opposing challenges keeps cropping up. The evidence suggests that most companies are far better at the executing half of the dialectic than at the adapting half. Very few do both well.

In two major studies, published in 2002 and 2005 respectively, Robert Wiggins, of the University of Memphis, and Tim Ruefli, of the University of Texas at Austin, show that while many companies can manage short-term bursts of high performance, only a few sustain it in the longer run. The authors stratified a sample of 6,772 companies over 23 years into superior, modal (middle), and inferior performers in their industries. Only 5 percent of these companies remained in the superior stratum for 10 years or more.[6]

Wiggins and Ruefli concluded that the short-term performers were successful executers that lost their way when the environment shifted. All sources of competitive advantage are temporary, and very few companies can create new sources of advantage after their historic sources decline.

Taking another angle on the problem, Foster and Kaplan point out (in *Creative Destruction*) that only a very small population of companies has endured for a very long time: for example, of the original Forbes 100 companies, in 1917, only 13 have survived independently to the present day. These companies must in some sense be highly adaptable, having endured the Depression, World War II, globalization, and enormous changes in markets and technologies. Yet as the authors observe, the long-term survivors, with the exception of GE, have been mediocre to poor performers relative to their industries and the overall market.

We thus have, on the one side, high-performing executers that can't sustain their performance and, on the other, long-term adapters that don't perform well. Companies that can both execute and adapt are very rare indeed. Wiggins and Ruefli found that fewer than 0.5 percent of the companies in their sample stayed in the top stratum for more than 20 years. Only three companies—American Home Products, Eli Lilly, and 3M, or 0.04 percent of the whole—made it to the 50-year mark. (This sample didn't include multibusiness companies, such as GE.)

Why is adapting *and* performing well so hard? The answer is that the demands of execution create deep barriers to adaptability, and these barriers afflict every organization. Overcoming them requires a fundamental rethinking of what GE's Jack Welch calls an organization's "social architecture"—the combination of individual behavior, structure, and culture—which shapes long-term performance.

BARRIERS TO ADAPTABILITY

Any organization faces many potential barriers to adaptability, some specific to itself. We will focus, however, on three that are deeply rooted in the nature of organizations and thus widely shared.

People: The Price of Experience

Much has been written about recent research in behavioral economics showing that managers and other decision makers are not as perfectly rational as traditional economic theory assumes.[7] This research tends to focus on common biases and errors, which affect the quality of decision making. Such biases can undermine adaptability; the well-studied bias of overoptimism, for example, can make organizational-change efforts seem less urgent.[8] What is less well known is that behavioral research also offers insights into why people become set in their ways and have difficulty adapting to change.

We've all had the experience of arguing with people and believing that the evidence for our position is crystal clear, though the other person "just doesn't get it." Why is it that people sometimes "just don't get it," even in the face of overwhelming evidence?

The answer may lie in the way we learn and categorize information in our mental models.[9] Many cognitive scientists believe that one important way people learn involves condition-action (or if-then) rules. A child might, for example, learn that, "If the stove is hot, then don't touch." Through experience, we accumulate a storehouse of such rules. Our environment gives us feedback about which do and don't work. Over time we tend to give more weight to those that have worked in the past. Mental models also organize rules into complex hierarchies and webs of relationships. A child, for example, might have a hierarchy of rules related to hot things, with a general rule—"don't touch"—as well as subcategories of specific forms of behavior for ovens, radiators, food, bathwater, and the like.

How can leaders keep their mental models flexible, open, and responsive to change?

This set-up of rules, weightings, and hierarchies has tremendous benefits. It enables us to learn from experience, to make decisions using ambiguous information, and to make inferences across experiences. (A child might, for example, categorize a radiator as *like* an oven; both are hot and not to be touched.) But the downside is that our mental models tend to become more rigid, more locked in, and more averse to novelty as we gain experience. . . .

The implications for organizational adaptability are critical. Companies tend to be organized as hierarchies, with the most experienced, successful people on top. This arrangement presents a trade-off: the mental models at the top are usually among the best for execution in a stable environment. These executives have extensive experience and a large storehouse of specific responses that are quite likely to be appropriate.

Yet when the environment changes significantly, such individuals may have difficulty recognizing the change and then, once they do, may draw too heavily on what has worked in the past. This kind of inertia helps to explain the *hero-rogue syndrome*: a CEO executes successfully in one environment, is lauded by the press and investors, and then falls off a cliff when the environment changes. It also helps to explain why many turnarounds involve wholesale changes in top management: it is often easier and faster to change which people occupy the executive suite than to change their mental models.

Structure: The Risk of Complexity Catastrophes

Organizations can be viewed as a form of network in which webs of people interact. A very general phenomenon in networks, called a *complexity catastrophe*, helps explain why large organizations often find it harder than small ones to adapt.[10]

The idea is simple. In any network with more than one connection per node, as the number of nodes grows, the number of connections or interdependencies grows even faster. (A three-node network where everything is connected to everything else has three connections, for instance, but a four-node network has six.) The more interdependences, the more potential for conflicts that constrain the range of solutions. Getting three friends to agree on where to meet for dinner might be easy, for example, but getting six friends to agree is much more difficult because one, say, likes meat, another is a vegetarian, yet another has to stay near home, and so on. Conflicting constraints make change difficult because a positive change in one part of the network can ripple through and have a negative impact somewhere else. Highly interdependent systems, such as large software programs, jet engine designs, and international trade agreements, can sometimes become so complex that they go into grid-lock and change becomes impossible. That is a complexity catastrophe. . . .

As an organization's size and complexity grow, its degrees of freedom drop. Yet size and complexity are just what execution demands. Scott Page, of the University of Michigan, has studied why some organizations are complex and hierarchical while others are simple and flat. He concludes that organizations evolve in response to the problems they have to solve. Complex problems that must be divided into lots of chunks and then carefully sequenced and coordinated require deep hierarchical organizations with many managers and traffic cops. Simpler tasks can be solved by simpler, flatter organizations.[11] The execution tasks of most large companies tend to be quite complicated, whether the challenge is getting oil from remote parts of the world into the cars of millions of consumers or coordinating risks in a global bank. This complexity of execution inevitably leads to interdependencies and organizational complexity, which in turn create the potential for gridlock: a complexity catastrophe.

Resources: The Path to Dependence

In 1959, long before the idea of a tension between exploration and exploitation became popular in management circles, Edith Penrose, an economist at the London School of Economics, published a slim but influential volume: *The Theory of the Growth of the Firm*.[12] Penrose viewed this growth as a process of search and exploration. Management teams seek out new opportunities in the environment and then use corporate resources to exploit them.

By resources, Penrose primarily meant physical assets and talent, but modern theorists have extended her definition to include less tangible but equally important resources, such as knowledge, brands, reputations, and relationships. In short, resources are whatever management uses to exploit opportunities.

This theory has two implications. First, the particular opportunities that management wants to exploit determine a company's resources. A team that sees opportunities in nanotechnology, for example, will find the relevant researchers and machines and then attempt to build a brand and a reputation for expertise in that field.

The flip side is that a company's resources define and limit its ability to explore. Say that a management team is running a fish-processing plant and the CEO wakes up one day enamored of nanotechnology. The opportunity may exist, but the company's resources (canning machines, its workers' skill at filleting fish, and a brand such as Taste o' the Sea) confine its real opportunities to fish processing.

According to Penrose, management's job is to search for profitable business plans. Naturally, the search is limited to plans the managers believe they can execute. The organization's resources determine what those plans will be. But in executing a plan, management changes a company's configuration of resources. As the company hires people, invests in assets, and so on to execute its current plan, those actions define its future opportunities. A coevolutionary loop thus links the resources a company employs to execute today with the business plans of tomorrow.

Another important barrier to innovation is the coevolution of plans and resources, which creates what researchers call "path dependence" in the structure of organizations. In other words, history matters because decisions that helped companies execute in the past constrain their ability to adapt in the future. A company therefore might be stuck with the wrong resources to go in a given direction because reconfiguring them would take too much time and money.

CREATING AN ADAPTIVE SOCIAL ARCHITECTURE

Thus three critical and widespread barriers to adaptability are a lack of flexibility in individual mental models, complexity catastrophes, and path dependence in resources. Overcoming these barriers isn't easy—if it were, far more than 0.5 percent of all companies would perform well over many decades. But by understanding the nature of the barriers, we can begin to address them.

Companies have two ways of overcoming these barriers. One is what Jack Welch called the "hardware" of an organization (its structure and processes), the other the "software" (norms and culture). The two sides must be consistent and mutually reinforcing to create a coherent social architecture.

Organizational Hardware

The hardware fixes for the adaptability problem, though challenging, are in many ways the easier ones. Companies can use three key approaches:

- Reduce hierarchy.
- Increase autonomy.
- Encourage diversity.

Reducing the level of hierarchy can help to prevent a small number of mental models from dominating the organization, while increasing the level of autonomy helps to reduce interdependences and to lower the risk of complexity catastrophes. Encouraging a diversity of mental models, resources, and business plans increases the odds that if the environment shifts, a company will have, somewhere inside it, the ability to respond.

Achieving this kind of shift requires changes not only in the organizational chart but also in important processes. Human resources (HR), for example, must support diverse mental models through hiring, training, and career paths. Likewise, strategic planning must support experimentation, and budgeting must promote appropriate trade-offs between efficiency and flexibility.[13]

In the 1990s, many organizations went down this path, chopping out layers of hierarchy and giving business units more autonomy. For some companies, these moves brought greater adaptability, but for many they created execution and control problems that forced the corporate center to reassert itself and often negated gains in adaptability. Why? Because hardware is only half of the story; an adaptable social architecture also requires critical changes to organizational software.

Organizational Software

Flatness, autonomy, and diversity are diametrically opposed to the control, coordination, and consistency that successful execution requires. But the software of norms and culture can help organizations have their adaptive cake and execute it too.

How can leaders instill norms that foster adaptation and innovation?

An organization's norms are "should" or "ought" statements about what it regards as the right, appropriate, or expected thing to do in a given situation. Taken together, norms create an organizational culture. Just as Tolstoy famously said, "All happy families resemble one another, but each unhappy family is unhappy in its own way," the norms of companies that are both high performing and adaptive have a family resemblance. These norms fall into three categories:

- *Cooperating norms.* One of the key roles of a hierarchy is to enforce cooperation among individuals — in particular, to ensure that people coordinate tasks and share information. Norms that encourage trust, reciprocity, and shared purpose can achieve the same effect, but in a more flexible way.
- *Performing norms.* One of the arguments against increased autonomy is the diminution of senior management's centralized control over performance. Companies can counter this problem by instilling norms that create strong expectations for individual performance, so that employees will go the extra mile, take the initiative, be honest and transparent, and believe that success will be rewarded.
- *Innovating norms.* Structures and processes that support experimentation and diversity must have norms to back them up. Vital innovating norms include the belief that facts matter more than hierarchy, that good ideas can come from anywhere, and (to borrow a phrase from Jim Collins and Jerry Porras) that "good enough never is.". . .

Executing and adapting appear to be irreconcilable opposites, and the empirical data suggest that most companies are destined to favor the former over the latter. But understanding the sources of this schism can help us to see the outlines of a potential solution. By creating a social architecture that marries a flexible structure to a cooperative, performance-driven, and innovative culture, companies can begin to overcome the problems that keep organizations from adapting to an ever-changing environment.

NOTES

1. Thomas J. Peters and Robert H. Waterman Jr., *In Search of Excellence: Lessons from America's Best Run Companies,* New York: HarperBusiness, 2004.

2. James C. Collins and Jerry I. Porras, *Built to Last: Successful Habits of Visionary Companies,* New York: HarperCollins, 1997.

3. Richard Foster and Sarah Kaplan, *Creative Destruction: Why Companies That Are Built to Last Underperform the Market—And How to Successfully Transform Them,* New York: Currency, 2001.

4. Michael L. Tushman and Charles A. O'Reilly III, *Winning through Innovation: A Practical Guide to Leading Organizational Change and Renewal,* revised edition, Boston: Harvard Business School Press, 2002.

5. James G. March, "Exploration and exploitation in organizational learning," *Organization Science,* 1991, Volume 2, Number 1, pp. 71–87.

6. Robert R. Wiggins and Timothy W. Ruefli, "Sustained competitive advantage: Temporal dynamics and the incidence and persistence of superior economic performance," *Organization Science,* 2002, Volume 13, Number 1, pp. 81–105; and Wiggins and Ruefli, "Schumpeter's ghost: Is hypercommunication making the best of times shorter?" *Strategic Management Journal,* 2005, Volume 26, Number 10, pp. 887–911.

7. Charles Roxburgh, "Hidden flaws in strategy," *The McKinsey Quarterly,* 2003, Number 2, pp. 26–39 (www.mckinseyquarterly.com//links/21100).

8. Dan Lovallo and Daniel Kahneman, "Delusions of success: How optimism undermines executives' decisions," *Harvard Business Review,* July 2003, Volume 81, Number 7, pp. 56–63 (www.hbr.com).

9. John H. Holland, Keith J. Holyoak, Richard E. Nisbett, and Paul R. Thagard, *Induction: Processes of Inference, Learning, and Discovery,* Cambridge, MA: MIT Press, 1986.

10. Stuart Kauffman, *At Home in the Universe: The Search for the Laws of Self-Organization and Complexity,* New York: Oxford University Press, 1995.

11. Scott E. Page, "Two measures of difficulty," *Economic Theory,* 1996, Volume 8, Issue 2, pp. 321–46.

12. Edith Penrose, *The Theory of the Growth of the Firm,* revised edition, Oxford: Oxford University Press, 1995.

13. Eric D. Beinhocker, "On the origin of strategies," *The McKinsey Quarterly,* 2000 strategy anthology: On strategy, pp. 167–76 (www.mckinseyquarterly.com/links/21101); and Eric D. Beinhocker and Sarah Kaplan, "Tired of strategic planning?" *The McKinsey Quarterly,* 2002 special edition: Risk and resilience, pp. 48–57 (www.mckinseyquarterly.com/links/21102).

ARTICLE 10.3

Creation Nets: Getting the Most from Open Innovation

John Seely Brown and John Hagel III

Thanks to the many books on open innovation[1] and to the prominence of open-source software projects such as Linux, most executives have at least a passing familiarity with the subject. Its central idea is that when companies look outside their own boundaries, they can gain better access to ideas, knowledge, and technology than they would have if they relied solely on their own resources.

Some executives may even be familiar with the many variants of open innovation, a number of which stray a considerable distance from traditional "closed" models of innovation management. Despite the familiarity of these ideas, persistent doubts and misunderstandings often make it hard to generate value from them. At one extreme, many people ask whether distributed models of innovation aren't notoriously hard to control, manage, and commercialize. At the other extreme, open innovation may seem to be mostly about narrowly defined joint ventures or transactions to acquire intellectual property created by others. If so, what's all the fuss about?

In truth, except for narrowly scoped forays (such as the licensing of technology) outside the confines of the enterprise, few top executives believe that they understand how best to create value with the open model of innovation. This uncertainty prevents many of them from taking advantage of the very real opportunities it presents.

The lack of confidence is understandable: although the roots of open innovation go back at least as far as the Italian Renaissance—when networks of apparel businesses in Piedmont and Tuscany were responsible for rapid innovation in techniques for producing silk and cotton fabric—today's variants on the model are anything but mainstream. That's why companies must visit the peripheries of today's commercial and scientific worlds to recognize the patterns that emerge across very diverse domains.

Such patterns reveal intriguingly promising "networks of creation" (or "creation nets"), where hundreds and even thousands of participants from diverse institutional settings collaborate to create new knowledge, to learn from one another, and to appropriate and build on one another's work—all under the guidance of a network organizer. These diverse participants often work in parallel and then fight and learn among themselves when the time comes to

332

integrate their individual efforts into a broader offering. The most widely publicized example may be the development of the Linux kernel by the open-source software movement. But creation nets are also visible in more unexpected fields and places, from the development of motorcycles in China and of consumer electronics products in Taiwan to the world's big-wave surfing beaches, where networks of sports enthusiasts push the technology and techniques required to ride 60-foot-plus waves, and the places around the globe where thousands of amateur astronomers operate telescopes tied together by the Internet to find and monitor celestial events.

These examples of open innovation are not undiscovered.[2] Yet few if any observers have pulled back from individual examples or stories to analyze the broader principles and mechanisms underlying the success of creation networks. Those principles and mechanisms, once understood, suggest specific moves that companies can make to profit from this ambitious form of open innovation and to create greater value than more conventional models of innovation can.

WHY CREATION NETS MATTER

The case for creation nets has its foundation in the speed of change in today's global economy.[3] In times of relative stability, a given stock of knowledge can create value indefinitely. If others acquire that stock, they can put it to work competing with its creators. During times of accelerating change, by contrast, the lifetime value of knowledge shrinks rapidly because it becomes obsolete more quickly. Now the game is using it to connect more rapidly and effectively with others in the creation of new knowledge. Rather than jealously protecting existing stocks of knowledge, institutions should offer them to others as a way of gaining access to broader knowledge flows.

Of course, knowledge doesn't really flow—it tends to be "sticky." Unlike information, which can be codified and disseminated more readily, knowledge tends to reside in individuals and is very context specific. You need close relationships with diverse sets of people and institutions when you want to create new knowledge jointly and deliver innovations to the market.

Narrower approaches to open innovation typically fail to create and encourage these rich, sustained interactions and collaborations. Joint ventures, for instance, typically involve a limited number of participants, but creation nets mobilize hundreds or thousands. The licensing of technology involves arm's-length transactions, but creation nets rely on long-term relationships. Some open-innovation initiatives focus on collaboration with lead customers; creation nets involve a broader range of participants, such as specialized technology providers, talented amateurs, suppliers, and customers.

The need for closer relationships with a broader set of participants brings with it a number of practical difficulties, however. Trust—in many ways the system's lubricant—can be hard to establish. What's more, large, distributed groups of people and institutions create their own difficulties.

As Mancur Olson points out in The Logic of Collective Action,[4] large groups of people don't work together easily toward a common goal. They may have different preferences and different tolerances for costs and effort. Some want a free ride. Others find it hard to determine who has made which valuable (or not so valuable) contribution.[5] These problems, which arise even in narrowly scoped corporate alliances, multiply as the number and type of participants increase. In fact, the more diverse the participants, the thornier the issues.

As we shall see, the institutional mechanisms of creation nets help overcome these very real difficulties and provide for the diverse kinds of collaboration needed to support sustained innovation in a world of far-flung knowledge and talent.

HOW CREATION NETS WORK

Although creation nets thrive in many different parts of today's global economy, they may not be fully visible to casual observers. Many Western executives, for example, go to original-design manufacturers (ODMs) such as Lite-On Technology and Compal Electronics, which are based in Taiwan but have expanding operations in mainland China, to source designs for a wide range of consumer electronics and high-tech products. From the perspective of these executives, they are dealing with a single outsourcing provider. Yet behind the scenes, the ODMs are mobilizing large creation nets to push the performance envelope of the products they design.

Executives stand in awe of Apple Computer's brilliant design for the iPod, for example, but overlook the important role that another company, Portal-Player, performed behind the scenes. Before being approached by Apple CEO Steve Jobs, PortalPlayer had already mobilized a broad network of specialized technology providers to solve the challenging problems of delivering high-quality audio in relatively inexpensive small devices.

Creation nets work by mobilizing hundreds or thousands of independent entities in the pursuit of distributed, collaborative, and cumulative innovation. The creation nets orchestrated by ODMs, for example, can bring together myriad highly specialized component and subsystem vendors from different business ecosystems, including disk drive manufacturers in Singapore, lens designers in Japan, semiconductor designers in Taiwan, and software engineers in Bangalore.

Mobilizing such a range of participants requires a precise set of institutional mechanisms to make clear who assembles the network, who can participate in it, how disputes will be resolved, and how performance will be measured. Creation nets thus begin with a network organizer, in the role of gatekeeper, which decides who participates in the network. ODMs, for instance, rigorously scrutinize not only the technological capabilities of prospective participants but also whether their corporate culture promotes collaboration and risk taking. The network organizer could be an individual, a small core team (as in the case of many open-source software initiatives), or a corporation or some other kind of large institution. Whatever it may be, it defines simple and informal participation protocols, such as how to resolve disputes and measure performance. An ODM, for example, will define clear performance milestones during the design process but allow participants to devise creative new ways of delivering the level of performance the client desires.

Creation nets typically organize their activities into modular processes, which make it easier to incorporate large numbers of participants and to give them the freedom to innovate within their own module of activity. Well-defined interfaces make it easier to coordinate activity across modules. The modularity of creation nets thus allows many participants to innovate in parallel and to pursue, simultaneously, a variety of ways of meeting a project's requirements.

While creation nets are loose in one dimension—the freedom to innovate—they are remarkably tight in another: defining clear "action points" when participants must come together and deliver outputs. Where inconsistencies or incompatibilities exist, participants must make clear choices to produce an integrated product or offer for use by others. If the design of the electronics in a digital still camera's sensor depends on the auto-focus functionality of the lens, for example, the two subsystem designers need to resolve any issues together.

Creation nets also rely on long-term incentives to motivate and align participants. To be sure, many creation nets are explicitly commercial, rewarding them with short-term cash or contracts for delivering successful innovations. But participants find that the real reward of even a commercial creation net comes in the longer term: by joining it, they can get better faster by working with others rather than alone.[6] For this reason, participants are motivated to do the right thing in the near term rather than pursue opportunistic short-term profits—a cooperative mind-set helping them to overcome many of the challenges to broad-based collaborative activity that Mancur Olson and others have described. Successful creation nets must therefore focus on building long-term relationships with participants and on creating opportunities for repeated interactions that demonstrate the value of cooperation.

What practical difficulties arise for individuals participating in creation nets?

BUILDING AND PARTICIPATING IN CREATION NETS

To harness the institutional mechanisms that give creation nets their power, executives will have to master new management approaches. Four are particularly relevant: choosing appropriate ways to coordinate the activities of the network, balancing local innovation with "global" integration, designing effective action points, and establishing useful performance feedback loops.

Choose the Right Approach to Coordination

Although creation nets share many characteristics, they differ in notable ways—for example, the degree of diversity among their participants.

Open-source software initiatives and extreme-sports networks, two of the best-known examples of creation nets, bring together participants who share relatively extensive sets of practices. Such groupings, which we call "practice networks," rely on looser forms of coordination.

Other types of creation nets—the design networks assembled by ODMs in Taiwan, for example, or the apparel production network created by Li & Fung in China—mobilize participants with very different practices and experiences. As a result, these networks, though still far too loose for the comfort of most executives of large enterprises, require more active forms of coordination. We categorize this subset as "process networks," a type of organization we have written about extensively to illustrate innovative ways of tapping into distributed expertise.[7]

Because of the diversity among the participants in process networks, their organizers play a more active role in mobilizing them—specifically, the part of orchestrator: recruiting participants into the network and then deciding which of them will be involved in each creation initiative, the specific role they will play, and the performance requirements they must satisfy.

In contrast, practice networks are coordinated much more loosely, both for recruiting participants and for managing specific creation initiatives. Network organizers tend to focus their coordination activity on the integration stage of the creation process, when the contributions of the participants are brought together and incorporated into a consistent or compatible release.

The general point is that executives must carefully consider how great a diversity of skills and experiences their creation networks require and then tailor their coordination approaches accordingly.

Balance Local Innovation with "Global" Integration

Some creation nets of all types involve looser forms of management. Others are managed more tightly. To strike the right balance, it is important to differentiate among three primary challenges in the creation process:

- accessing and developing highly distributed talent
- providing appropriate contexts for the participants to come together and engage in collaborative experimentation, tinkering, and innovation
- effectively integrating the creations of diverse participants into shared releases

Looking at the way creation nets address each of these challenges, you begin to discern interesting blends of emergent behavior (which occurs and evolves spontaneously, without an active, centralized manager) and managed behavior. Managed behavior is most pronounced at the integration stage, when the contributions of distributed participants must come together in a consistent or compatible release or offering. At this point, governance structures become critical to resolve differences that are often deeply held. Some of the greatest insights and innovations emerge as diverse parties clash and seek to address one another's concerns. In contrast, the aggregation and development of talent tend to be shaped more by emergent behavior, especially on the periphery of creation nets, which often rely on loosely organized environments (such as local business ecosystems and online forums) to attract, identify, and assemble talent.

Often, a creation net's collaborative experimentation, tinkering, and innovation activities are the least actively managed ones—perhaps the most challenging aspect for executives of traditional companies to embrace. After all, isn't the whole purpose of creation nets to drive innovation? If so, shouldn't the network organizers devote most of their time and attention to that? Surprisingly, the answer is no.

It is in this respect, perhaps, that creation nets represent the biggest break with more conventional approaches to open innovation. Executives are understandably tempted to develop detailed blueprints of what they require from their partners. For the sake of innovation, they must resist that temptation.

Design Effective Action Points

Organizers of a creation net play their most active role at the integration stage. In fact, the success of such nets hinges on the use of this stage as an action point to focus and align the efforts of diverse participants that must now come together and hand off their work to others, which either build on it or integrate it into a consistent or compatible release. By specifying when these activities must occur, the performance requirements that each participant must meet, and the protocols for escalating and resolving disputes, the network organizers create the institutional mechanisms necessary for productive friction.[8]

The essential point is that diverse participants must confront and resolve any significant differences in approach. Rather than determine outcomes by developing blueprints, the designers of effective action points specify high-level performance requirements and give the participants a substantial degree of freedom in meeting them. Greater freedom means a greater opportunity for divergence, especially in those parallel innovation initiatives, involving many participants, that modular approaches to management make possible.

When incompatibilities emerge across a product's modules or subsystems, the network organizer encourages the relevant participants to swarm the problem and resolve it on their own. Each participant understands that its designs will be included in the next release only if they work well with other parts of the product. Participants must therefore continually identify and make trade-offs between optimizing the performance of their own components and the broader performance requirements of an integrated product. On the margin, the ability to work effectively as part of a broader system determines which components are integrated into the final release.

Establish Performance Feedback Loops

Although creation nets may use much looser management techniques than more traditional approaches to open innovation do, they operate successfully in some of the most demanding global markets imaginable, from fashion apparel to enterprise software. Loose management doesn't mean sloppy performance; on the contrary, these creation nets perform at a very high level. More important, they continually improve their performance at a faster pace than conventional enterprises can match.

How? In part, the answer is the tight focus on relevant performance requirements. But something more is involved. Successful creation nets build explicit performance feedback loops to give participants a much better idea of how they are doing. Even in relatively loosely organized open-source software initiatives, the participants receive rapid feedback from others who have used their software. In these projects, the broad adoption of software modules ranks among the key drivers of status. Participants monitor this performance metric not only for their own software contributions but also for those of others, and they strive to learn from programmers whose modules gain the greatest acceptance.

To establish these performance loops, network organizers focus on three key design principles. First, they encourage rapid movement from concept to prototype. The faster participants can come up with prototypes, the easier it will be to test their performance, especially in concert with other components and subsystems. Second, the organizers define early and frequent rounds of performance tests so that participants gain early insights into performance issues and can make changes rapidly to solve any problems that arise. Finally, they establish broad-based communication mechanisms so that everyone in the creation net gains access to performance data quickly and easily.

GETTING THERE FROM HERE

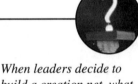

When leaders decide to build a creation net, what revisions in structure or practice will need to be considered?

The case for open innovation is clear: in today's rapidly moving world, companies can ill afford to retain outmoded closed models of innovation management. The case for creation nets as the best form of open innovation should also be clear: the institutional mechanisms embedded within them help to overcome its thorniest challenges. Furthermore, these networks focus solely on creation, so they promote innovation more than do stand-alone corporate enterprises, where executives must reconcile the competing demands of managing both innovation and routine operations.

Yet the case for creation nets does not extend to every corporate situation and endeavor. They work best in areas with three attributes: uncertain demand for goods and services, a need for the participation of many different specialists if creation and innovation are to occur, and rapidly changing performance requirements in the marketplace. In these areas, creation nets have their most distinctive value: the ability to mobilize dispersed and diverse talent for innovation in a flexible way, whatever the scale.

If these criteria do apply, executives must choose whether to participate in an existing network or to organize a new one. Too often, their instinct is to organize a new network. Those that try to do so late in the day may underestimate the network effects involved and wind up struggling to attract the attention and resources of relevant participants.

Once executives have decided to participate in or build a creation network, they will need to revise some corporate structures, aspects of corporate culture, and management and leadership practices, which often stand in the way of harnessing the network's full potential. Most institutions have been organized around push models of resource mobilization, but effective participation in a creation net requires a different skill set, focused on building, deploying, and managing pull models.[9]

At a more fundamental level, leadership teams will have to challenge conventional ways of thinking within their own groups and companies. One natural reaction to an accelerating pace of change is a desire to turn inward and tighten control in an attempt to protect what already has value—for instance, by strengthening a company's patent protection or limiting the number of business partners that have access to a company's intellectual property. Creation nets require a different way of thinking, built on the recognition that the key to success in a rapidly changing world is understanding how and why knowledge crosses institutional boundaries. This in turn requires an even more fundamental shift in mind-set: managers must move their focus beyond narrow efficiency gains and recognize that increased flexibility will help them embrace and explore the possibilities that uncertainty creates.

A creation net gives executives an opportunity to amplify open innovation's potential, but they can realize it only by challenging dominant ways of thinking. Those who do may, at long last, close the gap that has made open innovation a seductive mirage and an exercise in frustration for many of the companies that have tried to exploit its promise.

NOTES

1. See, for example, Henry William Chesbrough, *Open Innovation: The New Imperative for Creating and Profiting from Technology,* Boston: Harvard Business School Press, 2003; and Ron Goldman and Richard P. Gabriel, *Innovation Happens Elsewhere: Open Source As Business Strategy,* San Francisco: Morgan Kaufmann, 2005.
2. See, for example, John Hagel III and John Seely Brown, *The Only Sustainable Edge: Why Business Strategy Depends on Productive Friction and Dynamic Specialization,* Boston: Harvard Business School Press, 2005; Timothy Ferris, *Seeing in the Dark: How Amateur Astronomers Are Discovering the Wonders of the Universe,* New York: Simon & Schuster, 2002; Steven Weber, *The Success of Open Source,* Boston: Harvard University Press, 2004; and the wonderful documentary *Ruling Giants,* DVD, directed by Stacy Peralta (2004; Culver City, CA: Sony Pictures, 2005), describing the global innovations of big-wave surfers.

3. See, for instance, Martin Wolf, "The world must get to grips with seismic economic shifts," *Financial Express,* February 7, 2006.

4. Mancur Olson Jr., *The Logic of Collective Action: Public Goods and the Theory of Groups,* revised edition, Boston: Harvard University Press, 1971.

5. This part of the discussion draws on Steven Weber's first-rate examination of the open-source movement: *The Success of Open Source,* Boston: Harvard University Press, 2004.

6. This point is bolstered, by a 2002 Universum European MBA Survey, which found that European business school students are much less focused than past ones on job security. Instead, the top three priorities were constant opportunities for learning, variety in tasks and job rotations, and international career opportunities.

7. John Seely Brown, Scott Durchslag, and John Hagel III, "Loosening up: How process networks unlock the power of specialization," *The McKinsey Quarterly,* 2002 special edition: Risk and resilience, pp. 58–69.

8. For more on this topic, see John Seely Brown and John Hagel III, "Productive friction: How difficult business partnerships can accelerate innovation," *Harvard Business Review,* February 2005, Volume 83, Number 2, pp. 82–91.

9. For more about pull models, see John Seely Brown and John Hagel III, "From push to pull: The next frontier of innovation," *The McKinsey Quarterly,* 2005, Number 3, pp. 81–91.

Relationship Marketing in Emerging Economies: Some Lessons for the Future

Sabine Flambard-Ruaud

The past two decades have brought dramatic changes in the marketing environment leading to a rethinking of the marketing discipline. As markets mature and customers become scarce resources, the concept of relationship marketing has emerged as a big new idea and has become increasingly important for many Western companies. Today, relational, as opposed to transactional exchange, is the norm in the more affluent industrialized economies.

At the centre of this contemporary philosophy is the notion that making the most out of existing clients is essential for long-term profitability. Retaining clients by developing relationships with them is crucial to establishing and maintaining a competitive advantage in the market. Numerous companies use structures (for instance, key account management) and instruments (databases, direct marketing, efficient consumer response, and customer relationship management) developed by relationship marketing. Certain companies implement individual or dyadic relationship marketing based on the personalization of the offer and interpersonal interaction while certain other companies prefer a community or associative relationship marketing where emphasis is on the collective behaviour of clients (feeling of belonging, level of participation, etc.). But, perceptions on what exactly constitutes relationship marketing may differ in various cultural settings. As a result, an exchange method which has worked well at home may fail in a culture with different values. Failure to adapt methods of exchange may bring about a marketing failure. This leads us to question whether the concept of relationship marketing can be transferred, especially to new markets such as emerging markets, which offer amazing opportunities to the firms. . . .

BUSINESS AND CULTURAL VALUES

From the Westerner's point of view, a market is a market. But, the formulations of relationship marketing based on contemporary Western norms of behaviour may not function well when transplanted into emerging countries where the economic, social, and cultural environments differ significantly from the country for which a relationship marketing policy was originally formulated.

Using an inter-cultural approach to explain marketing and general business practice has been supported by academics such as Hofstede (1991) who emphasized that cultural differences have a vital impact on the results of all aspects in business such as marketing management, leadership, decision-making, etc. As a result, it was felt that, in order to understand the contextual background of generating relationships with customers, cultural factors should be included (Gilbert and Tsao, 2000).

Though there are various definitions of culture, a more agreed upon definition seems to be that of Hofstede (1980): "culture is the collective programming of the mind." In other words, culture can be defined as the deep-seated, unwritten system of shared values and norms within an organization (Peck *et al.*, 1999). People from different cultures behave and interact differently because their minds are programmed differently.

Thus, when relationships cross national borders, any cultural differences that exist will impact the nature of relationships, what flows through them, and how successful they are (Ambler and Styles, 2000). Consequently, there are subtle differences between the Western and the Eastern ways of doing things (Buttery and Wong, 1999).

In Western societies, the analysis of relationships has come from transaction cost theory, social exchange theory, and interaction theory. *Transaction cost theory* takes the view that transaction costs are associated with exchange such as research, information, and the cost of monitoring contractual performance. Such costs are generated by the exchange process and are in addition to the market price of goods and services. Transaction cost analysis has been applied to explain the behaviour of a wide range of organizational activities including bureaucracy (Williamson, 1979), vertical integration of production (Williamson, 1971; Klein, Crawford and Alchian, 1978), clan-like relations among firms (Ouchi, 1980), and organizational culture. *Social exchange theory* is a framework for analysing different social interactions which are defined as a process in which two parties are engaged in activities directed towards one another with the expectation of the exchange of valuable resources (Dwyer, Schurr and Oh, 1987). The social exchange theory (Blau, 1964, Emmerson, 1962, and Schurr and Ozanne, 1985) explains, for example, the importance of inter-firm adaptation and trust. The limitations of both the approaches—economic and social theories—lie in their static nature when, in fact, relationship building is dynamic, and in the assumption of rational behaviour by those involved in the process of negotiation and this too does not always apply. *Interaction theory* has brought in a dynamic element into the analysis such as the mutual influence of, and communication in, the transactions process (Kutschler, 1985). Similarly, Häkansson (1982) and Cunningham (1980) have captured the factors leading to close relationships and exchange episodes over time in a framework in which actors adapt to one another. This approach has also been the focus of the work of the European IMP Group (as previously mentioned). Also, such writers as Grönroos (1994) and Gummesson (1994) consider the study of relationships so important that they have called for a new theory of marketing based on relationships rather than exchange.

In contrast, the relationship dimension of business has always been integrated in the Asian and the African cultures. In these societies, it is often the success of established relationships that condition successful business transactions. The relationship is built before transactions take place and is closer to a client-seeking strategy. For example, the Chinese prefer to deal with people they know and trust. On the surface, this does not seem to be much different from doing business in the Western world. But, in reality, the heavy reliance on relationship means that Western companies would have to make themselves known to the Chinese before any business can take place. Furthermore, this relationship is not simply between companies but also between individuals at a personal level. The relationship is not just before the sales start taking place but is an ongoing process. The company has to maintain the relationship if it wants to do more business with the Chinese. In other words, in the strongly capitalist economies (Western society, for example), transaction creates and develops the relationship (transaction is the centre of the exchange) whereas in the less capitalist economies (Asia, Africa, Middle-East), relationship creates and develops the transaction (Figure 1).

Based on the work of Tsapi (1999), the comparison of the terms *individualism* and *community* enables us to better understand this difference. In the community philosophy, the most important attributes revolve around self-awareness as a member of a community (family, working group, nation). The objectives of the group take priority over personal objectives. The norms and values of the group are more important than the personal attitudes such as behavioural determiners and the pre-eminence of the needs of group members on which an individual determines social behaviour. Durkheim (1973), the French sociologist, qualifies this form of social link as *mechanical solidarity* dominated by the primacy of the collective conscience, i.e., "all beliefs and feelings common to members of a same society."

How does the Western world's preference for individualism impact business and innovation elsewhere in the world?

Figure 1   Two Universes, Two Visions of Business

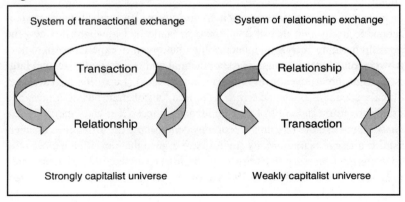

In slightly capitalist societies (i.e., traditional and less individualistic), the individuals prefer to work in teams and interdependence is a basic fact. The collective conscience is, thus, maximized and the individual conscience practically does not exist. The success of the group is more important than that of the individual and, as a result, the individual gives great importance to how his/her actions will affect the other members of the group. Conversely, the 'individualists' define themselves as being autonomous compared to a group, give priority to personal objectives, behave mainly according to their attitudes, and pay attention in priority to their own needs. For Durkheim (1973), these societies are characterized by a form of *organic solidarity* which essentially is based on the division of labour which makes persons economically dependent on one another.

In strongly capitalist societies (modern and, therefore, highly individualistic), recognition and self-fulfilment give great satisfaction and there is competition between individuals to achieve these goals. Social functions are totally distinct and inequalities appear more difficult than in traditional societies. In these rather competitive societies, the psychological structures and the politico-economic systems reward individual contributions and encourage competition between individuals. This distinction is relevant because it is linked to the distinction made today in marketing, i.e., between '*relational*' which is close to the community (traditional) society and to '*transactional*' which is close to an individualistic (modern) society. In this logic, a system with low individualism requires greater connections in the process of exchange and the members involved respond favourably according to the degree of interpersonal dynamism.

THE CONCEPT OF *GUANXI*

While marketing theory has advised Western firms to choose rationally between a relationship marketing approach for key customers and a transactional approach for the majority of less important customers, Eastern firms tend to prefer long-term personalized relationships and mutual cooperation as the basis for most of their business dealings (Hamzah-Sendut, Madsen and Thong, 1990).

As emerging economies are not homogenous or clearly identifiable and recognizable groups, we look at Asia, more particularly, China which is now the biggest emerging economy. Indeed, China has recently experienced a rapidly growing economy with huge market potential and is already the second largest foreign direct investment recipient in the world (Luo, 1997b). However, China's economy is characterized by a lack of coherent business laws and strong governmental control over limited resources (Xin and Pearce, 1996). These characteristics of China's economy demonstrate the difficulties of entering this massive market. Many studies have argued that developing close relationships is a necessary step to succeed in China (Ambler, 1994; Hall and Hall, 1987; Johansson, 1995; Luo, 1997b). By developing personal relationships, firms can enhance their marketing effectiveness and efficiency (Sheth and Parvatiyar, 1995).

In fact, Chinese business persons prefer to work with others with whom they have empathy, trust, and share a process that produces mutual benefits (Chen, 1996; Luo, 1997a). This special kind of relationship is called *guanxi* (it can be translated as 'relationship' or 'connections' or 'networking' or even 'entering through the back door') and it has been identified as a key feature of doing business in China (Abramson and Ai, 1994; Chen, 1995; Davies, 1995; Buttery and Wong, 1999).

However, only limited research is available on this complex notion of *guanxi*. Misunderstandings and misconceptions concerning this significant topic persist. We make an attempt here to explore the concept of *guanxi*, discuss its origin and ethics, and analyse its major benefits, risks, and implications for management.

In the Chinese culture, much emphasis has been placed on the teaching of Confucius and the impact it has had on the Chinese population in the past and in current times. According to this philosophy, all relationships are dictated by five major *wu-lun* or relationships: emperor-subject, father-son, husband-wife, elder-younger brothers, and friend-friend (Ordonez de Pablos, 2002). To ensure social harmony, order, and stability, appropriate behaviours are needed. In business practice, the word used to refer to the latter is *guanxi*.

However, because *guanxi* refers to a cultural phenomenon, it is not a precise term of art and, as such, it carries several different connotations. In the most general sense, *guanxi* simply means relationship. The second usage refers to a sub-set of relationships that work according to norms of reciprocity. A third usage exhibits a negative connotation related to bribery and corruption: the usage of someone's authority to obtain political or economic benefits by unethical person(s); *guanxi* or *guanxixue* represents a way to bypass regulations, laws or norms through personal connections with people who control limited resources.

In this paper, we focus on the first and the second usage of the term *guanxi* which essentially refers to emotional bonds, trust, and friendship that originated from previous satisfactory experiences of dealing with each other and frequent contacts.

The foundation of the process of *guanxi* is conceptualized as having four dimensions (Abramson and Ai, 1997). Trust was viewed as the basis for shared goals which were the basis of cooperation driven by self-interest. Under conditions of trust, one would expect disagreements to be handled using collaboration or compromise-based methods. *Guanxi* also seems to require extensive networking efforts. The four dimensions were combined into a single *guanxi* construct in an attempt to test an authentic construct. This was done despite Thompson's (1996) concerns related to the use of multi-causal variables.

Because *guanxi* and relationship exchange in the West have several similarities—exchange partners have long-term perspectives; they focus on the relationship itself rather than on a single transaction, make efforts to preserve the relationship, try to resolve conflicts in harmonious ways, and engage in multi-dimensional roles rather than simple buying and selling (Alston, 1989; Xin and Pearce, 1996; Gomez Arias, 1998)—some authors (Bjorkman and Kock, 1995; Wong and Chan, 1999, imply this in the title, if not the discussion) have identified *guanxi* with a traditional form of relationship marketing.

However, *guanxi* has its own unique characteristics distinguishable from relational exchange in the West (Lee, Pae and Wong, 2001). For instance, although often criticized as favouritism in Western society (Anderson, 1995), the reciprocal exchange of due favours is widely accepted and used in Chinese business (Luo, 1997b; Xin and Pearce, 1996). Exchange partners in *guanxi* have affective and personal involvement in the relationship resulting in affective commitment (Geyskens *et al.*, 1996). In contrast, relational exchange partners in the West tend to have economic and impersonal involvement which leads to calculative commitment (e.g., commitment based on cost and benefits). Besides, partners in *guanxi* tend to have implicit role expectations which often go beyond the existing role expectations. That is, expectations in a *guanxi* relationship often go beyond the existing roles to include reciprocal exchange of personal favours, mutual protection, and enhancement of social status. The guiding principles of relational behaviours in *guanxi* are morality and social norms (Gomez Arias, 1998) and the underlying motive for reciprocal behaviours is face-saving. In other words, *guanxi* is an informal relationship based on personal affiliations (Alston, 1989; Hwang, 1987). Exchange partners in a Western-style close relationship will have more explicit role expectations. The guiding principles of a relational exchange in the West are legality and rules. One of the main motives for reciprocal behaviours is mutuality in the relationship.

Several empirical researchers have examined the outcomes of *guanxi*. Most studies focus only on the positive outcomes of developing *guanxi*. For example, the empirical study conducted by Davies (1995) suggests three major benefits that arise from the establishment of *guanxi*: key sources of information, sources of resources, and other areas (smoothing transport arrangements, smoothing collection of payments, and building up the firm's reputation and image).

However, in a recent survey of Chinese managers (Guthrie, 1998, mentioned in Dunfee and Warren, 2001), we noticed that some perceptions about the practice of *guanxi* are increasing in importance while others believe that it is of less or even no importance in the emerging Chinese legal framework. Guthrie summarized the views by stating that *guanxi*, while still an important institutional system, is diminishing in importance due to both increasing competition and legalism. Managerial perceptions of *guanxi*'s importance varied according to the firm's *position in the industrial hierarchy of the former command economy*. Specifically, Guthrie found that managers in the higher institutions of the Chinese industrial hierarchy perceive *guanxi* as less important than managers in institutions that hold lower positions in the industrial hierarchy. He interprets the difference as a reflection of the manager's ability to access high-level officials. Those managers in higher institutions already have access to the bureaucrats who facilitate business transactions and, therefore, do not need to rely on *guanxi* as much as those managers in lower institutions.

In short, China is enjoying rapidly increasing foreign investment while, at the same time, it must cope with local changes influenced by Western forms and concepts. This evolution of the Chinese market is bringing about the need for a relationship marketing approach to serve more sophisticated consumers who demand better products and services. Understanding the role *guanxi* plays in the Chinese society and business is part of the process of learning about the Chinese market that Western companies need to be aware of and provides one of the most dramatic examples of an entrenched cultural norm under pressure from international business trends.

Besides, the practice of *guanxi* is not unique to China; it occurs in many societies (Li and Wright, 1999 in Wright, Szeto and Cheng, 2002). It also pervades other business cultures such as Japan (called *Kankei* or *Toyama* or *Kusuri*), Korea (known as *Kwankye*), India, Russia (called *Svyazi*), and other managed economies where intimacy with those in authority, be they political, military or bureaucratic, is important (Lehtinen, 1996; Robins, 1996).

COMPARISON OF ASIAN VS WESTERN MANAGEMENT

An in-depth examination of Asian culture reveals the advantages of certain practices. One of the most striking characteristics of Asian societies is the remarkable stability of their civilizations. More precisely, Cova and Pras (1995) have identified four major permanent features to differentiate Asian management from Western management:

- the family rather than the firm as basic economic actor
- a long-term horizon rather than a short-term horizon
- a consensus approach to decision-making rather than a conflictual approach
- a risk reduction approach rather than a risk-creation approach.

Two hypotheses can be put forward to explain the existence of these permanent features:

Hypothesis 1: The traditionalist hypothesis which insists on the duration of traditional customs and habits in Asia contrary to modern (or post-modern) Western societies which continually try to rid themselves of the matrix of traditional bonds and archaic beliefs.

Hypothesis 2: The cultural hypothesis which evokes the existence of the same basic culture made up of contextual specificities (values, nature of social relations, . . .) as opposed to the Western society which is fragmented and pluralist.

However, even if one succeeds in identifying common Asian features and finding an ethical grounding, following the image of management in Western countries, it is still possible to highlight numerous features specific to a local managerial approach (Dubinsky *et al.*, 1991) such as:

- the rhythm and process of economic development of each country
- the role played by the state in each country
- the political orientations of each country
- the structural differences of a socio-economic issue
- the strategic choices of companies
- the societal context in which the economic activity is embedded (language, writing system, social system, etc.).

An analysis of the environmental and cultural constraints of Western countries combined with the previous reflection on the local Asia specificities enables us to draw the following conclusions:

Western societies are more differentiated and pluralist than Asian societies. A majority of the Western societies have developed other centres of authority and power than that of the family and the state. In the same way, CEOs are generally less dependent on political power than in Asia, relationships between business leaders and politicians being closer in the West. Relationships with authority are not influenced by the omnipresence of the state but by the development of legal and institutional systems which have given a legal base common or close to most Western societies.

The greater importance of the individual and the legislature in the West has led to more formalized procedures centred on individual performances within the structure and to a high level of confidence for formal contracts. The development of law in the West has reduced the authority of the business leader of the firm compared to that of Asian leaders. In the same way, the importance of the contract has reduced flexibility, given less weight to confidence in one's partners' word, and made easier the development of imposing hierarchical structures and impersonal networks.

CONCLUSIONS

Theory transgresses economies whether they are emerging or not. Marketing has always studied relationships between institutions (B2B) and relationships between institutions and customers. The basic rules of marketing, therefore, remain the same whatever the economy. What changes is the context.

In Western economies, fundamental changes in the market environment have forced marketers to reconsider marketing strategies. A transaction-oriented marketing strategy encounters more and more difficulties in finding an appropriate answer to challenges such as increasing numbers of product varieties, shortening of product life cycles, and higher customer expectations. These developments require firms to become more customer-oriented. As technological developments in data collection and data processing as well as in communicating and interacting with customers provide opportunities to meet these requirements, companies are increasingly shifting their focus from transaction-oriented to relationship-oriented strategy so as to build a competitive edge.

The recognition of the importance of establishing and maintaining long-term relationships has led both marketing theorists and practitioners to focus on an emerging framework termed relationship marketing.

However, relationship marketing cannot be a universal paradigm capable of having uniform global application. The environment is and remains multi-cultural. In that sense, the dangers of ethnocentrism must be avoided and, on the contrary, the phenomena of acculturation and local appropriation need to be taken into consideration.

What issues should leaders consider in helping an organization adopt relationship marketing in another culture?

As seen previously, in the Chinese society, *guanxi,* which is based upon social activities and business activities, is significant as a basis of conducting business. As such, it is not a simple matter to transpose relationship marketing, which is based upon a different set of cultural values, into a Chinese-dominated culture.

Relationships are built on a cultural platform which means that the route to developing a good relationship can be very different in the Western and the Eastern cultures. Not only are the methods for building relationship different, but also the relative importance of the attributes which make up the relationship are valued differently in different parts of the world. In other words, cultural factors play an important role in the development of relationship marketing. It is, therefore, suggested that more cultural studies need to be carried out in order to understand what kind of cultural elements can have a positive or magnified impact on relationship marketing applications in a business context.

In essence, this exploratory study has taken a step forward towards a better understanding of the ways in which relationship marketing has emerged in the Western economy and suggests a few rules which need to be observed in order to apply it efficiently in emerging countries. It also shows how the management of *guanxi* can help in enhancement of sustained competitive advantage taking into consideration the idiosyncrasies of the Eastern and the Western national and organizational cultures.

REFERENCES

Abramson, NR and Ai, X (1994). "Taking the Slow Boat to China," *Business Quarterly*, Winter, 27–36.

Abramson, NR and Ai, X (1997). "Using Guanxi-Style Buyer-Seller Relationships in China: Reducing Uncertainty and Improving Performance Outcomes," *The International Executive*, 39(6), November—December, 765–804.

Alston, JP (1989). "Wa, Guanxi, and Inwha: Managerial Principles in Japan, China, and Korea," *Business Horizons*, 32(2), March–April, 26–31.

Ambler, T (1994). "Marketing's Third Paradigm: Guanxi," *Business Strategy Review*, 5(4), 69–80.

Ambler, T and Styles, C (2000). "The Future of Relational Research in International Marketing: Constructs and Conduits," *International Marketing Review*, 17(6), 492–509.

Anderson, E (1995). "Relationships in Business Markets: Exchange Episode, Value Creation, and their Empirical Assessment," *Journal of the Academy of Marketing Science*, 29(2), 18–34.

Bjorkman, I and Kock, S (1995). "Social Relationships and Business Networks: The Case of Western Companies in China," *International Business Review*, 4(4), 519–535.

Blau, PM (1964). *Exchange and Power in Social Life*, New York: John Wiley.

Buttery, E A and Wong, Y H (1999). "The Development of a Guanxi Framework," *Marketing Intelligence & Planning*, 17(3), 147.

Chen, GB (1995). *Asian Management Systems*, Boston, MA: International Thomson Business Press.

Chen, GB (1996). *Negotiating with the Chinese*, London: Dartmouth Publishing.

Cova, B and Pras, B (1995). "Que Peut-on Apprendre du Management Asiatique?" *Revue Francaise de Gestion*, 103, March–April–May, 20–32.

Cunningham, MT (1980). "International Marketing and Purchasing of Industrial Goods: Features of a European Research Project," *European Journal of Marketing*, 14(5), 322–338.

Davies, H (1995). "Interpreting Guanxi: The Role of Personal Connections in a High Context Transitional Economy," in Davies, Howard (ed.), *China Business: Context and Issues*, Hong Kong: Longman.

Dubinsky, AJ; Jolson, MA; Kotabe, M and Lim, CU (1991). "A Cross-National Investigation of Industrial Salespeople's Ethical Perceptions," *Journal of International Business Studies*, 22(4), Fourth Quarter, 651–670.

Dunfee, TW and Warren, DE (2001). "Is Guanxi Ethical? A Normative Analysis of Doing Business in China," *Journal of Business Ethics*, 32(3), 191–204.

Durkheim, E (1973). *De La Division Du Travail Social*, Paris: PUF.

Dwyer, FR; Schurr, PH and Oh, S (1987). "Developing Buyer-Seller Relationships," *Journal of Marketing*, 51(2), April, 11–27.

Emmerson, RM (1962). "Power-dependence Relations," *American Review*, 27, 31–34.

Geyskens, I; Steemkamp, JEM; Scheer, LK and Kumar, N (1996). "The Effect of Trust and Interdependence on Relationship Commitment: A Trans-Atlantic Study," *International Journal of Research in Marketing*, 13(4), 303–317.

Gilbert, D and Tsao, J (2000). "Exploring Chinese Cultural Influences and Hospitality Marketing Relationships," *International Journal of Contemporary Hospitality Management*, 12(1), 45–53.

Gomez Arias, J T (1998). "A Relationship Marketing Approach to Guanxi," *European Journal of Marketing*, 32 (1/2), 145–156.

Grönroos, C (1994). "From Marketing Mix to Relationship Marketing: Towards a Paradigm Shift in Marketing," *Management Decision*, 32(2), 4–20.

Gummesson, E (1994). "Broadening and Specifying Relationship Marketing," *Australia Marketing Journal*, 2(1), August, 31–44.

Häkansson, HG (1982). *International Marketing and Purchasing of Industrial Goods: An Interaction Approach*, New York: John Wiley.

Häkansson, HG and Snehota, I (1995). *Developing Relationships in Business Marketing*, London: Routledge.

Hall, ET and Hall, MR (1987). *Hidden Differences: Doing Business with the Japanese*, New York: Anchor Books.

Hamzah-Sendut, TSD; Madsen, J and Thong, TS (1990). *Managing in a Plural Society*, Singapore: Longman.

Hofstede, G (1980). *Culture's Consequences: International Differences in Work-related Values*, Beverly Hills, CA: Sage.

Hofstede, G (1991). *Cultures and Organisations: Software of the Mind*, London: McGraw Hill.

Hwang, K (1987). "Face and Favour: The Chinese Power Game," *American Journal of Sociology*, 92(4), 944–974.

Johansson, J (1995). "International Alliances: Why Now?" *Journal of the Academy of Marketing Science*, 23(4), 301–304.

Klein, B; Crawford, RG and Alchian, AA (1978). "Vertical Integration, Appropriable Rents and the Competition Contracting Process," *Journal of Law and Economics*, 21(2), 291–326.

Kutschler, M (1985). "The Multi-organisational Interaction Approach to Industrial Marketing," *Journal of Business Research*, 13, 383–403.

Lee, DJ; Pae, JH and Wong, YH (2001). "A Model of Close Business Relationships in China (Guanxi)," *European Journal of Marketing*, 35(1/2), 51–70.

Lehtinen, U (1996). "Relationship Marketing Approaches in Changing Russian Markets," *Journal of East-West Business*, 1(4), 35–49.

Luo, Y (1997a). "Guanxi: Principles, Philosophies and Implications," *Human Systems Management*, 16(1), 43–52.

Luo, Y (1997b). "Guanxi and Performance of Foreign-Invested Enterprise in China: An Empirical Study," *Management International Review*, 37(1), 51–70.

Ordonez de Pablos, P (2002). "Guanxi and Relational Capital: Eastern and Western Approaches to Manage Strategic Intangible Resources," http://www.iacmr.org/03-065.pdf.

Ouchi, W (1980). "Markets, Bureaucracies, and Clans," *Administrative Science Quarterly*, 25(1), 129–162.

Peck, H; Payne, A; Christopher, M and Clark, M (1999). *Relationship Marketing Strategy and Implementation*, Oxford: Butterworth Heinemann.

Robins, F (1996). "Marketing in a 'Managed' Economy," *Marketing Intelligence & Planning,* 14(3), 45–56.

Schurr, P H and Ozanne, JL (1985). "Influences on Exchange Process: Buyer's Preconceptions of a Seller's Trustworthiness and Bargaining Toughness," *Journal of American Research,* 11, March, 939–953.

Sheth, JN and Parvatiyar, A (1995). "Relationship Marketing in Consumer Markets: Antecedents and Consequences," *Journal of the Academy of Marketing Science,* 23(4), Fall, 255–271.

Tsapi, V (1999). "Marketing Relationnel: De Quoi Parlet-on ?" *La Revue des Sciences de Gestion,* 177, 13–26.

Thompson, AG (1996). "Compliance with Agreements in Cross-Cultural Transactions: Some Analytical Issues," *Journal of International Business Studies,* 27(2), 375–390.

Williamson, OE (1971). "The Vertical Integration of Production: Market Failure Considerations," *Journal of Law and Economics,* 22, October, 3–6.

Williamson, OE (1979). "Transaction-Cost Economies: The Governance of Contractual Relations," *Journal of Law and Economics,* 22(2), October, 233–261.

Wong, YH and Chan, RYK (1999). "Relationship Marketing in China: Guanxi, Favouritism and Adaptation," *Journal of Business Ethics,* 22(2), 107–118.

Wright, P; Szeto, WF and Cheng, LTW (2002). "Guanxi and Professional Conduct in China: A Management Development Perspective," *Journal of Human Resource Management,* 13(1), 156–182.

Xin, KR and Pearce, JL (1996). "Guanxi: Connections as Substitutes for Formal Institutional Support," *Academy of Management Journal,* 39(6), 1641–1658.

ISSUE SUMMARY

Several themes emerge in the readings selected for this issue of forecasting an organization's future: adaptation, networked, global core, partnering. But there are many more themes that could have been chosen for this section. The choice was subjective and merely points to the fact that we are in an age of hyperchange and the organization of the future is likely to be reshaped frequently and rapidly.

Gone are the days when an organization could count on being able to offer a broad range of products or services to a steady stream of loyal clients/customers. Gone too are the days when communication was top-down, in the form of memos, delivered to personnel at their in-office mail boxes. And long gone is the notion that "made in America" really meant something was made in America. At the broadest level, what is gone is the security of a stable organization that knows where it is headed because it has a sensible long-range plan.

The reality of the organization in constant flux has direct implication for organizational leaders. What leaders knew in the past does not necessarily shape what will happen in the future. Instead the dazzling pace and shape of change brings with it unimagined opportunities. The wise leader will "stop marveling about the coming age of information and knowledge and get serious about coping with it and capitalizing on it" (Albrecht, 2006, p. 29). This means taking a positive attitude about the future, anticipating opportunities, and maintaining a holistic perspective. No doubt leaders will need to think clearly and more quickly:

> Executives will have to stand back and let individual employees identify and mobilize resources and collaborators at the right time. In many cases, it will be necessary to transform not-invented-here cultures that prevent organizations from effectively leveraging third-party resources. Instead of wondering what companies can get from their business partners, executives will have to ask what they and their business partners can learn from one another.
>
> —(Brown & Hagel, 2005, p. 90)

What does this bode for the future of organizational leadership? In many ways, leadership will continue to be about culture, strategy, process, and ideas. Clear thinking, seeing the patterns, discerning good-better-best, and making wise decisions will continue to be the building blocks of good leadership. What is most likely to change for organizations and their leaders is that knowing won't be as important as learning.

ISSUE HIGHLIGHTS

- Calendar-driven, task-focused planning processes are becoming irrelevant for many organizations.
- The role of communication will be heightened to ensure business continuity and crisis management.
- The workforce of tomorrow will require seamless flows of information.
- Three barriers to adaptation shared among organizations are: (1) people are set in their ways and have difficulty changing, (2) highly interdependent systems are resistant to change, and (3) an organization's resources define and limit its ability to innovate and change.
- For organizations to be adaptable, structures and processes need to be consistent with norms and culture.
- Innovating, customizing, and remixing are organizational means of survival in the future.
- Companies are increasingly shifting from transaction-based marketing to relationship-based strategies.
- Relationship marketing does not have global application; it has different implications that are dependent on the culture.

CRITICAL THINKING

Some experts believe that organizations of the future will be defined by generative capabilities that are more comprehensive than simply the power to innovate and invent. Generative refers to capabilities that are foundational drivers of the organization. Scholars are naming a number of such capabilities that vary somewhat, depending on the nature of the organization. A cluster of generative capabilities that is consistent across organizations is learning, collaborating, and strategy making. These three principles are named by Saint-Onge and Armstrong in their work, *The Conductive Organization: Building Beyond Sustainability.*

The idea behind generative capabilities is the presence of these foundational principles set in motion a range of other organizing behaviors and capabilities that enable an organization to move into the future. Compare the ideas presented in the readings for the issue of how organizations will function in the future with this list of emerging principles of the conductive organization:

- New technologies impacting on human communication drive new organizing principles and structures.
- Technology is short-circuiting all the linear ways in which we've structured our organizations.
- A highly conductive organization has formulated a new way of looking at the world through the eyes of the customer.

- A new order of risk is associated with increased reliance on intangible assets—it's more complex, difficult to detect, and lethal if ignored.
- High-quality relationships support core values.
- The brand is a qualitative reflection of the organization's character as expressed by its core values.
- Performance gives freedom to be who we want to be, to express our collective greatness as individuals, to actualize our full potential, and to realize our destiny.
- Strategy making is an action verb as opposed to a noun or an object. It's an embedded process as opposed to a finite set of activities in a defined time cycle. It's a key capability geared to ensure constant renewal-creating relevance in the marketplace (adapted from www.conductiveorg.com).

ADDITIONAL READING RESOURCES

Karl Albrecht, Eight supertrends shaping the future of business. *The Futurist*, September/October 2006.

John Seely Brown & John Hagel III, The next frontier of innovation. *McKinsey Quarterly*, 2005.

Theodore Roosevelt Malloch, Corporations in the world economy: Dynamic innovation. *The Global Century: Globalization and National Security,* National Defense University, 2001.

Hubert Saint-Onge and Charles Armstrong, *The Conductive Organization: Building Beyond Sustainability.* Elsevier, 2004.

Edie Weiner & Arnold Brown, *FutureThink.* Pearson Education/Prentice Hall, 2005.

For more information check these sites:

www.conductiveorg.com
www.conference-board.org
www.futurist.com
http://hbswk.hbs.edu/archive/4020.html
www.innosight.com

CONTRIBUTORS TO THIS VOLUME

EDITOR

JOYCE HUTH MUNRO, Ph.D., has worked with nonprofit organizations and professional associations and is currently the dean of the school of graduate studies at Chestnut Hill College. She has experience conducting program assessments and reviews, research projects, and strategic planning processes. Dr. Munro has published articles on professional development and leadership issues. Her current interest is helping professionals in nonprofit organizations and educational institutions become systems thinkers. Dr. Munro holds graduate degrees from the University of South Carolina and Vanderbilt University.

STAFF

Larry Loeppke   *Managing Editor*
Susan Brusch   *Senior Developmental Editor*
Jill Peter   *Senior Developmental Editor*
Beth Kundert   *Senior Production Manager*
Jane Mohr   *Project Manager*
Lenny J. Behnke   *Permissions Coordinator Lead*
Maggie Lytle   *Cover*
Tara McDermott   *Design Specialist*
Nancy Meissner   *Editorial Assistant*
Julie Keck   *Senior Marketing Manager*
Mary Klein   *Marketing Communications Specialist*
Alice Link   *Marketing Coordinator*

AUTHORS

RUSSELL ACKOFF is author of books on management and systems thinking. He is Anheuser-Busch professor emeritus of management science at The Wharton School and a former president of both the Operations Research Society of America and the Society for General Systems Research.

ROB ANDERSON is executive vice president of change, a branch of Golin-Harris that offers services in strategic philanthropy and corporate social responsibility to corporations, nonprofits, and government agencies.

LYNN BARENDSEN is project manager of Project Zero, an educational research group at the graduate school of education of Harvard University.

ERIC D. BEINHOCKER is a senior fellow at the McKinsey Global Institute, where he conducts research on economic, management, and public policy issues. He has held research appointments at the Harvard Business School, the MIT Sloan School, and has been a visiting scholar at the Santa Fe Institute.

T. E. BOSTOCK is a special counsel to the Melbourne (Australia) office of Gadens Lawyers, after completing 34 years as a partner of Mallesons Stephen Jaques.

DEAN L. BOTTORFF is principal of Ethics Quality, Inc., which specializes in business ethics training, governance, and culture management aspects of process and organizational improvement. He also has more than 25 years of business development and marketing experience in the engineering and construction industry and is a fellow of the American Society for Quality

JOHN SEELY BROWN is the former chief scientist at Xerox Corp. and is currently a visiting scholar at the University of Southern California. He is coauthor with John Hagel of *The Only Sustainable Edge: Why Business Strategy Depends on Productive Friction and Dynamic Specialization.*

NELDA CAMBRON-MCCABE is a professor of educational leadership at Miami University in Miami, Ohio. She is coauthor, along with Luvern Cunningham, James Harvey, and Robert Koff of *The Superintendent's Fieldbook: A Guide for Leaders of Learning.*

SANDRA EUNYOUNG CHA is a doctoral candidate in organizational behavior at the Harvard Business School.

JENNIFER A. CHATMAN is the Paul J. Cortese Distinguished Professor of Management at the Haas School of Business, University of California. Her area of research explores the psychology of leadership and culture within organizations and how organizations can design and manage teams to maximize both productivity and individual experience.

JOSEPH F. COATES is the coauthor of *Future Work, What Futurists Believe,* and *Issues Management: How You Can Plan, Organize, and Manage for the*

Future. As president emeritus of Joseph F. Coates Consulting Futurist, Inc., he is a writer and speaker on emerging technologies and future trends.

KAREN CRENNA is a Milan-based senior executive in the Accenture Growth & Strategy group. She oversees the development of Accenture's business strategy and is responsible for its implementation companywide. Crennan also leads Accenture's research and competitor intelligence organizations.

LUVERN L. CUNNINGHAM is an emeritus professor and former dean of the College of Education at Ohio State University. She is coauthor, along with Nelda Cambron-McCabe, James Harvey, and Robert Koff of *The Superintendent's Fieldbook: A Guide for Leaders of Learning*.

ANNE D'INNOCENZIO is an Associated Press business news editor, assigned to the AP New York office.

SUSAN DAVIDSON is founder and president of Beyond Borders Inc., an intercultural training and coaching consultancy. She has worked with U.S. and multinational corporations for more than 20 years to improve business performance.

DEBORAH DOANE is chair of CORE, a coalition of NGOs, organizations, and individuals campaigning for stronger regulation of business vis-à-vis their social and environmental responsibilities. Doane is also an associate at the New Economics Foundation, a not-for-profit think tank.

WILFRED H. DRATH is a senior fellow and director of the New Lenses Initiative at the Center for Creative Leadership in Greensboro, North Carolina.

SUSAN P. EISNER is a professor of management at Ramapo College, New Jersey, and consultant with senior practitioner experience in national ventures of major organizations including a leading television station, a prominent health care foundation, a presidential campaign, a public interest group, and a national political party.

TIM FIELD is the vice president of organizational consulting for the Southern California Region of Right Management Consultants, a global consultancy that specializes in helping organizations execute their business strategies. His doctorate in psychology is from the University of Southern California.

SABINE FLAMBARD-RUAUD teaches marketing at Edhec Business School in Lille, France. Her research interest is customer relationship management. She is the author of *Le Marketing Relationnel: Nouvelle Donne du Marketing E-theque*, which was awarded the Prize of Excellence for 2002–03.

MIKE FREEDMAN is former president of worldwide strategy practice at Kepner-Tregoe, an international consulting firm. Freedman, who lives in the United Kingdom, has extensive experience facilitating strategy formulation and implementation with business, government, and nonprofit organizations.

HOWARD GARDNER teaches cognitive psychology at the Harvard Graduate School of Education. Among his recent books are *Good Work: When Excellence and Ethics Meet* and *Changing Minds: The Art and Science of Changing Our Own and Other People's Minds.*

DAVID GEBLER is president of Working Values, Ltd., a business ethics training and consulting firm specializing in developing behavior-based change to support compliance objectives.

HOWARD M. GUTTMAN is the principal of Guttman Development Strategies, Inc., a management consulting firm specializing in executive development, management development, and organization development. His corporate experience includes Johnson & Johnson and Automatic Data Processing.

JOHN HAGEL III is an independent management consultant who spent 16 years with McKinsey & Co. and continues to serve as a senior advisor to the firm. He is coauthor with John Seely Brown of *The Only Sustainable Edge: Why Business Strategy Depends on Productive Friction and Dynamic Specialization.*

MARCIA A. HALFIN is a senior manager in the Accenture Growth & Strategy group. Her work includes helping financial services and consumer products clients on a number of strategy issues. Ms. Halfin's articles have appeared in the financial trade press, including the *Journal of Private Equity.* She is based in New York.

DAVID HENDERSON is former chief economist at the Organisation for Economic Co-operation and Development in Paris and has held senior positions at the World Bank and in the British government. Among Henderson's publications are *The Role of Business in the Modern World, Misguided Virtue,* and *The Changing Fortunes of Economic Liberalism.*

RALPH JACOBSON is a principal of The Leader's Toolbox, author of *Leading for a Change: How to Master the Five Challenges Faced by Every Leader,* and faculty member at the Physician's Leadership College, University of St. Thomas.

RICHARD LEPSINGER is president of OnPoint Consulting and has over 20 years experience as a human resource consultant and executive. He is coauthor (with Gary Yukl) of several books as well as author of articles on leadership.

NANCY R. LOCKWOOD is human resource content expert for the Society for Human Resource Management. She is certified as a senior professional in human resource management and as a global professional in human resources by the Human Resource Certification Institute.

ANDREW LONGMAN is a partner and vice president of marketing at Kepner-Tregoe. He is responsible for the worldwide promotion of the company's brand and consultants. Longman is coauthor of *The Rational Project Manager: A Thinking Team's Guide to Getting Work Done.*

MICHAEL C. MANKINS is a managing partner of Marakon Associates, a strategy and management consulting firm. Based in San Francisco, he advises business leaders on strategic and organizational initiatives to drive performance and long-term value growth. Mankins holds an MBA from The Wharton School of the University of Pennsylvania.

DICK MARTIN is former EVP of public relations, employee communications and brand management with AT&T. He is the author of *Tough Calls: AT&T and the Hard Lessons Learned from the Telecom Wars.*

JENA McGREGOR is management editor at *BusinessWeek.*

GARY L. NEILSON is a senior vice president based in Booz Allen Hamilton's Chicago office. He is a member of Booz Allen's board of directors and operating council and holds an MBA in finance from Columbia University.

PAUL F. NUNES is an executive research fellow at the Accenture Institute for High Performance Business in Wellesley, Massachusetts, where he directs studies of business and marketing strategy. His work has appeared regularly in *Harvard Business Review* and other publications. His most recent book is *Mass Affluence: Seven New Rules of Marketing to Today's Consumers.*

BRUCE A. PASTERNACK is president and chief executive officer of Special Olympics, Inc., and a former senior vice president at Booz Allen Hamilton. He has coauthored two business books, *The Centerless Corporation* and *Results.* Pasternack has also authored articles in *Harvard Business Review* and *Strategy+Business.*

GEORGE E. REED is the director of command and leadership studies at the United States Army War College in Carlisle, Pennsylvania. He has 25 years of experience as a military police officer. Reed holds a doctorate in public policy analysis and administration.

ROBERT W. ROWDEN is associate professor of management in the Stetson School of Business and Economics at Mercer University in Georgia. His research is in workplace learning and human resources.

RICHARD SELINE is the founder and principal of New Economy Strategies, a consulting firm in Washington, DC.

RICHARD STEELE heads the Global Diversity Initiative of Marakon Associates. He has been published in *Harvard Business Review, Harvard Management Update, MIT Sloan Management Review,* and *The Financial Times.*

AMEY STONE is an associate editor at BusinessWeek Online, where she cowrites the daily "Street Wise" column and writes many of the lead stories on business trends, technology, and the economy.

KAREN E. VAN NUYS is a principal with Booz Allen Hamilton, a consulting firm that provides services in strategy, operations, organization and change, and information technology for government and commercial clients.

CURTIS C. VERSCHOOR is the Ledger & Quill research professor, school of accountancy and MIS, DePaul University in Chicago and research scholar in the Center for Business Ethics at Bentley College, Waltham, Massachusetts.

JOHN VOGELSANG is associate director of the Support Center for Non-profit Management in New York. He has published articles and monographs on organization development and leadership issues. He also serves on the editorial board of the *OD Practitioner.*

GARY YUKL is a professor of management in the school of business at the University at Albany, State University of New York, and the author of books on organizational leadership. His areas of research are leadership, power and influence, and managerial skills.

CREDITS

1.1 From *Leadership in Action*, September/October 2005, pp. 20–21. Copyright © 2005 by John Wiley & Sons. Reprinted by permission.

1.2 From *Leadership in Action*, March/April 2003, pp. 3–7. Copyright © 2003 by John Wiley & Sons. Reprinted by permission.

1.3 From *Leader to Leader*, Fall 2004, pp. 43–50. Copyright © 2004 by John Wiley & Sons. Reprinted by permission.

1.4 From *Media and Entertainment Insights*—The Lastest New in Media, Entertainment & Technology Law & Business, October 2003. Copyright © 2003 by PriceWaterhouseCoopers. Reprinted by permission.

2.1 From *The State of Corporate Citizenship 2005*, pp. 1–4. Copyright © 2005 by GolinHarris. Reprinted by permission.

2.2 From *Journal of Financial Planning*, August 2005, pp. 10–14. Copyright © 2005 by Financial Planning Association. Reprinted by permission.

2.3 From *Stanford Social Innovation Review*, Fall 2005, pp. 23–29. Copyright © 2005 by Stanford Social Innovation Review. Reprinted by permission of the publisher and author.

2.4 From *National Observer*, Spring 2005, pp. 49–53. Copyright © 2005 by National Observer. Reprinted by permission.

3.1 From *Strategic Finance*, December 2005, pp. 19–20. Copyright © 2005 by Institute of Management Accountants (IMA). Reprinted by permission via Copyright Clearance Center.

3.2 Reprinted by special permission from *Business Week*, February 19, 2004. Copyright © 2004 by The McGraw-Hill Companies, Inc.

3.3 From *Quality Progress*, April 2006, pp. 25–33. Copyright © 2006 by American Society for Quality. Reprinted by permission.

3.4 From *Strategic Finance*, May 2006, pp. 29–34. Copyright © 2006 by Institute of Management Accountants (IMA). Reprinted by permission via Copyright Clearance Center.

4.1 Copyright © 2006 by Associated Press. All rights reserved. Distributed by Reprint Management Services.

4.2 From *Executive Action*, May 2006, pp. 1–5. Copyright © 2006 by Conference Board, Inc. Reprinted by permission.

9.2   From *SAM Advanced Management Journal*, Summer 2001, pp. 11–16, 24. Copyright © 2001 Society for Advancement of Management. Reprinted with permission.

9.3   From *Journal of Business Strategy*, March/April 2003, pp. 26-31. Copyright © 2003 by Emerald Group Publishing Ltd. Reprinted by permission.

9.4   From *Support Center for Nonprofit Management*, March/April 2003, pp. 1–11. Copyright © 2003 by John Vogelsang. Reprinted by permission of the author.

10.1 From *Strategic Communication Management*, December 2005/January 2006. Copyright © 2006 by Melcrum Publishing Ltd. Reprinted by permission.

10.2 From *McKinsey Quarterly*, 2006, pp. 77-87. Copyright © 2006 by McKinsey & Co.. Reprinted by permission.

10.3 From *McKinsey Quarterly*, 2006, Number 2. Copyright © 2006 by McKinsey & Co.. Reprinted by permission.

10.4 Reproduced with permission from the July–September 2005 issue of *Vikalpa: The Journal of Decision Makers* published by Indian Institute of Management, Ahmedabad, India.

Opener photo Part 1: Keith Brofsky/Getty Images

Opener photo Part 2: PhotoLink/Getty Images

INDEX

Abasta-Vilaplana, Naomi, 55

abuse of power, 79

academic links, innovation and, 194

Accenture, 198

accountability: as corporate value, 92; diffused, 11–12; growing public demand for, 204–5; for workplace diversity, 137–38, 140–41

Ackoff, Russell L.: on learning systems, 214–30; on machine metaphor, 232–33

ACL Services, 71

acquisitions, 204, 216, 275

action learning, 291–92

action points in creation nets, 337

adaptable corporations, 325–31

adaptation: execution versus, 325–26; improvement through leadership, 6; learning and, 222–24, 327

adaptive challenges to leadership, 10

Addams, Jane, 16

Adisseo, 104

advertorials, 156

agents with schemata, 306

aggressive behavior, 26

agility, 26–27

agreement over culture, 111

alignment of values, 92–93

Altier, William J., 216–17

Amazon.com, 197

American corporate cultures, 103–8. See also organizational cultures

American dream, 181

analytics, 197, 202–3

Anderson, Rob, on corporate citizenship, 34–42

anonymous authority, 75

anti-Americanism, 174–76, 182, 184

Anti-Slavery Society, 16

appeals to force, 75

Apple Computer, 203, 334

appliances, energy-efficient, 53

Arthur Andersen, 71

Ashoka, 17

assessment (performance). See performance assessment

assessment for workplace diversity, 144

assimilation approach to diversity, 135

assumptions, complex challenges to, 10

Audi, 177

authority, unclear, 119–20, 124

awareness, situational, 7

awareness training, 140

Baby Boomers: attributes of, 157, 158, 165–66; management strategies for, 162

Ballmer, Steve, 278

bandwagon effect, 75

Bank Austria, 204

Barabba, Vincent P., 219–20

Barendsen, Lynn, on social entrepreneurs, 16–23

Baron, Ayelet L., 321

barriers to adaptability, 326–29

barriers to innovation, 189–90, 193–94

begging the question, 75

Beinhocker, Eric D., on adaptable corporation, 325–31

beliefs of social entrepreneurs, 19–20

benefits, 51, 102, 200–201

biases, 326

Big Dig, 252

bioeconomy, 205

blogs, 320

boards of directors, 57, 138

Boeing Commercial Airplanes, 277–78

BOGSAT, 231

bonuses, 128. See also rewards

bosses, American deference toward, 105–6. See also management

Bossidy, Larry, 24

Bostock, T. E., on corporate social responsibility, 57–61

Boston Globe, 156

bottom-line mentality, 79

Bottorff, Dean L., on ethics management, 73–85

BOVESPA, 205

BP, 50
brain chemistry, 176–77
brainstorming sessions, 113
Brambles, 105
brands: localization of, 178–79, 199–200; perceived corporate citizenship of, 39, 40, 41–42, 179–80; power of, 176–77; success factors for, 180–82
Bristol & West, 299
British American Tobacco, 52
Browne, John, 50
Brown, John Seely, on creation nets, 332–39
BT Retail, 201
burden of proof fallacy, 76
Bush, George W., 177
business processes, corporate values for, 92
business strategies. *See* strategies
business units, strategic planning by, 275–76
busyness, 233–34
Cadbury Schweppes, 282
Cairns, Tom, 24
Cambron-McCabe, Nelda, on systems thinking, 237–42
Campbell, Lewis, 279–80
capability sourcing, 199
capitalism. *See* globalization; market forces
Cardinal Health, 280–82
career paths for minority workers, 151–52
cash bonuses, 128. *See also* rewards
catalytic converters, 54
categorical imperative, 77
categorizing diversity, 149
cause branding, 41
challenges: complex, 9–15; reframing, 22; social entrepreneurs' views of, 20–21, 22
Chanel, 177
Change (GolinHarris program), 41–42
Change Corporate Citizenship Index (CCI), 37–39
changes: agility in addressing, 26–27; needed by passive-aggressive firms, 125–29; program versus process approach, 290; promoting, 310; reactions against, 238, 326–27; required by complex challenges, 10–11; social entrepreneurs' views of, 20; unexpected effects, 7. *See also* innovation

changing subject, 76
chaos, 307
character attacks, 75
Chatman, Jennifer A., on organizational cultures, 109–16
Chemtura, 250
chief executive officers (CEOs), 109, 126
China: as emerging economy, 198; innovation in, 186; Proctor & Gamble entry, 178; relationship marketing, 344–47; working conditions in, 55
Cisco Systems, 50, 114
CitiGroup, 138
Clark Consulting, 70
Clean Air Act (U.S.), 54
Clemons, John G., 318
Coates, Joseph, on workplace diversity, 148–56
Coca-Cola Company, 176–77
codes of ethics, 70–72. *See also* ethics
coevolution, 307
coffee house communities, 181
collective leadership, 9–15
commission, errors of, 223
commitment: building, 8; cultures based on, 112; lack of, 294
common-good values, 92–93
communications: about corporate citizenship, 36, 37, 40–41; about strategies, 299; basic corporate values for, 91–92; future trends, 317–24
community, individualism versus, 343
compensation for diverse employees, 152–53
competencies, 259, 261–63, 264. *See also* performance assessment
competitive advantage: innovation and, 185, 190–92; in pricing, 197; in response to emerging economies, 198; top contributors to, 185, 191; from workplace diversity, 134–45
complete learning systems, 223
Complex Adaptive Systems, 306–8, 309–10
complex challenges, 9–15, 237–42
complexity catastrophes, 327–28
complexity, reducing, 301–2
compliance programs for corporate ethics, 78, 80
CompUSA, 115
computerized diagnostics, 218

concealing ethics breaches, 80
condensing information, 225
conflict avoidance, 105
conflict on teams, 255
congestion pricing, 201
Conklin, Renee, 260
connected leadership, 13–14
consensus on ethics, 82
constant readiness, 291
consumer behavior, corporate citizenship influence
    on, 36
continuous assessment of systems, 235–36
continuous planning, 279–82, 291
contradiction, 75
control, unclear, 119–20
control subsystems, 229
cooperating norms, 330
coordination of creation nets, 335–36
core ideologies, 8. *See also* values
core organizational competencies, 264–65
corporate citizenship, 34–42. *See also* corporate
    social responsibility
corporate communications trends, 317–24
corporate cultures. *See* organizational cultures
Corporate Responsibility Coalition, 54
corporate social responsibility: criticisms of, 43–47;
    current opinions about, 34–42, 174, 179–80; as
    dimension of corporate value systems, 93; left-
    wing politics of, 57–61; myths about, 48–56
corporate structures, changing, 53–56
Corporation 20/20, 54, 55–56
corrective actions in learning support systems,
    227–28
Costco, 51
costs, optimizing, 199
Coughlin, Tom, 102
creation nets, 332–39
creativity, innovation versus, 112
Creditanstalt, 204
Crennan, Karen, on top business trends, 196–206
crisis communications, 318–19
critical competencies, 262, 265
cross-cultural competence, 140
Cullivan, John, 280–81

cultural values, 341–49
Culture Risk Assessment model, 90–93
cultures (corporate). *See* organizational cultures
Cunningham, Luvern L., on systems thinking,
    237–42
D'Innocenzio, Anne, on Wal-Mart culture, 101–2
DaimlerChrysler, 252
Danforth Superintendents' Forum, 238, 239
data, 215, 225
Davidson, Susan, on U.S. corporate culture, 103–8
decentralized workforces, 322
decision making: in passive-aggressive organiza-
    tions, 120, 123, 124, 127; shrinking time frames,
    202–3; strategic planning versus, 272–83;
    support systems for, 225–28
decision records, 226–27
decision rights, unclear, 124, 127
decision support systems, 219, 225–28
defense transportation systems, 233
definitional distortion, 76
Deloitte & Touche, 71
Delphi Corporation, 317
demographic trends for diversity, 136
Department of Defense, 232, 233
deutero-learning, 214, 223
developing nations, corporate social responsibility
    in, 55
development: growth versus, 216, 221; of passive-
    aggressive firms, 121; sustainable, 44, 55,
    58–59, 93
deviations in learning support systems, 227
Diageo North America, 278–79
diagnosis and prescription function, 227–28
differentiation approach to diversity, 135
diffused accountability problem, 11–12
dilution, strategic, 294
direct feedback assessment methods, 263–64
directors, 57, 138
disabled workers, 139–40, 149
diversionary tactics, 76
diversity. *See* workplace diversity
Doane, Deborah, on corporate social responsibility,
    48–56
Doing Well by Doing Good 2005, 34–42

double-loop thinking, 239, 240

Dow Jones Sustainability Indexes, 49

Drath, Wilfred H., on leadership challenges, 9–15

Drayton, William, 17

Dresdner Kleinwort Wasserstein, 197–98

drift, strategic, 294

Drucker, Peter, 179

dual-income households, 150–51

DuPont, 137

duty-based ethical principles, 77

education, training versus, 217

effectiveness, 221, 222, 262

efficiency: effectiveness versus, 221, 222; improvement through leadership, 6; measuring, 215

Eisner, Susan P., on Generation Y, 157–67

e-mail wars, 105

emerging economies, 198, 341–49. *See also* globalization

emotional intelligence, 24–27

emotional power of brands, 176–77

employee benefits, 51, 102, 200–201

employee councils, 139

employee demographics, 136, 319

employees: as barriers to adaptability, 326–27; corporate citizenship influence on, 36, 40; leading through culture, 110–15; misconduct observed by, 67–68, 69; as most important assets, 189–90; trends concerning, 200–201; values for communicating with, 91–92. *See also* workplace diversity

Employment Equality Directive 2000/78/EC, 143

energy-efficient appliances, 53

Enron scandal, 71, 87

enterprise performance management, 202–3

entertainment industry, 26, 27

entrepreneurs, social, 16–23

environmental issues, 51

errors of comission, 223

errors of omission, 216, 223

ethics: consumer views of, 51; enforcing codes, 70–72; managing implementation of, 73–85; myths about, 52; in organizational cultures, 67–69, 87–94; of social entrepreneurs, 21–22; wisdom and, 229–30

ethics committees, 85

Ethics Quality (EQ), 73–74

Ethics Resource Center, 67–68

Eubanks, Gordon, 126

Eunyoung Cha, Sandra, on organizational cultures, 109–16

European Union, 46, 143–45

evidence for efforts, 123

example setting, 8, 79

execution, 109–10, 325–26. *See also* implementation

executive management. *See* management; senior management

experience as barrier to adaptability, 326–27

expert systems, 217

ExxonMobil, 182

failure mode and effects analysis, 82

fallacies (ethical), 75–76, 81, 83–84

false analogy, 75

false authority, 76

false benefit mentality, 79

false dilemmas, 75

false pretexts, 79

false win-win, 79

farm agents, 180

fast-food industry, 151

FBI (Federal Bureau of Investigation), 252

feedback loops, 234, 235, 337–38

fidelity principle, 77

fiduciary duties of directors, 57

Field, Tim, on emotional intelligence, 24–27

filtering information, 225

financial stability, 91

Flambard-Ruaud, Sabine, on relationship marketing, 341–49

flexible benefits, 200–201

flexible leadership, 6–8, 26–27

flexible work arrangements, 150–51, 154

Florida Power & Light, 289–90

Forbes, Steve, 43

forced ranking systems, 249–51

foreign employees, 103–8, 150

fragility of business environments, 201–2

Freedman, Mike, on plan implementation, 294–302

free markets. *See* globalization; market forces
frontline managers, support for workplace diversity, 155
Gahn, David, 260
Gardner, Howard, on social entrepreneurs, 16–23
Garrison, William Lloyd, 16
Gebler, David, on creating ethical cultures, 87–94
gender diversity, 142–43. *See also* workplace diversity
General Electric: anticipated overseas growth, 176; brand strength, 177; longevity of, 326; performance assessment system, 249–50; recruiting values, 113
Generation X: attributes of, 157, 158–59, 165–66; management strategies for, 163
Generation Y: attributes of, 157, 159–62, 165–66; fit with current workplace trends, 164–67; management strategies for, 162–64
Georgia Institute of Technology survey, 193
Gleevec, 205
Global Compact, 48–49
globalization: branding and, 174–84; hostility toward, 45; impact on wages, 317–18; innovation and, 185–94; myths about, 52–53; top business trends, 196–206
global patterns of interacting, 306
global salvationism, 46–47
goal displacement, 231–32
goals of project teams, 253, 255
Golden Rule, 77
Goldstein, Stuart Z., 320
GolinHarris, 41
Governance Metrix, 71
gray zone ethical issues, 78–81
Grief, Stuart, 280
growth, 121, 216, 221
guanxi, 344–47
guilt by association, 75
Guttman, Howard M., on project team evaluation, 252–58
Hagel, John III, on creation nets, 332–39
Haier Group, 198
Hakim, Catherine, 152
Halfin, Marcia A., on top business trends, 196–206

Hallmark International, 300
Halpin, James, 115
Hamburger University, 179
Harari, Guy, 104
hardware of organizations, 329–30
Harrah's Entertainment, 197
hasty generalization, 75
Hatch, Mary Jo, 232
Hawthorne studies, 110
Hayes, Randall, 180
health sciences economy, 205
Heifetz, Ronald A., 10, 237–38
helping principles, 77
Henderson, David, on corporate social responsibility, 43–47
Herceptin, 205
hero-rogue syndrome, 327
hierarchies: adaptability and, 327; in American corporate culture, 105–6; in passive-aggressive organizations, 125; problem-solving within, 328; reducing, 329
hiring for culture fit, 113–14. *See also* recruiting
Holcim, 107
honesty stereotype, 103–4
hostile humor, 75
Hudson Highland Group, 69
Hull House, 16
human resources departments, support for diversity, 154
human resources leadership, 6
Hurricane Katrina, 252
Hyperion Solutions, 71
IBM, 177
IDEO, 113
ideologies, 8. *See also* values
implementation, 291, 294–302. *See also* execution
implementation-focused planning, 287
improvised implementation, 291
inactive memory storage, 226–27
incentives: of creation nets, 335; Generation Y preferences, 161–62; in passive-aggressive organizations, 122–24, 128; for project teams, 254; for workplace diversity, 137–38, 152–53
inclusion approach to diversity, 136

inclusive leadership, 9–15

inclusiveness principle, 77

individualism, 344

individual leadership, challenges to, 9–15

inertia, strategic, 294

information, 215, 225

information sharing: advantages of workplace diversity, 155; by NGOs, 180; in passive-aggressive organizations, 125, 127–28. *See also* communications

information sources, 36, 37, 180

information technology: impact on communications trends, 320; security of, 202; telemedicine, 205; top global trends, 196–98

initiative fatigue, 295

innovating norms, 330

innovation: cultures promoting, 112–13; growing importance, 203; national survey findings, 185–94; open approaches, 332–39. *See also* changes

insect infestations, 234–35

inspection, ethics compliance as, 78

instructions, defined, 225

integrated communications, 324

integration and learning approach to diversity, 135–36

Integrity Interactive, 71

Intel, 177

intelligence (defined), 217

intelligence (emotional), 24–27

intensity of culture, 111

intentions, 218

interaction theory, 342–43

internal barriers to innovation, 193–94

International Organization for Standardization, 46

interpersonal dynamics on teams, 255–56, 257–58

investments, 49, 189–90

iPod, 203

isolation, 19, 294–95

issue resolution systems, 301

Jacobson, Ralph, on assessment alternatives, 259–65

job satisfaction for Generation Y, 161–62. *See also* incentives

job security, 107, 161, 164

journalists, 21

judgment, 222

justice principles, 77

Kaiser Permanente, 203

knowledge, 215–17, 219. *See also* learning

knowledge management, 155, 219, 220

Kraft Foods, 139

labeling mentality, 79

Lagoven, 296

lawsuits, fear of, 107

leader development, leadership development versus, 12

leaders' competencies, 262

leadership: American deference toward, 105–6; complex challenges to, 9–15; development, 12, 260–61; emotional intelligence for, 24–27; flexible approaches, 6–8; of organizational cultures, 109–16; of project teams, 256, 257; of social entrepreneurs, 16–23; systems thinking and, 231–36; for workplace diversity, 137–38

leadership tasks, 12–13

learning: adaptation and, 222–24, 327; in community approach to school reform, 240; content variations, 214–15; of data and information, 215; design of systems for, 222, 223, 224–28; implementing systems for, 228–30; obtaining knowledge, 215–17; obtaining understanding, 217–18; obtaining wisdom, 218–22

learning organizations, 284–92, 307–8

learning support systems, 222, 224–28

left-wing politics, 57–61

Lepsinger, Richard, on flexible leadership, 6–8

Levi's, 181

Levitt, Ted, 178

life sciences economy, 205

lifestyle centers, 201

Likely, Fraser, 319

limited companies, 57–58

line extensions, 192

line managers' support for workplace diversity, 155

Linux, 333

localization of brands, 178–79, 199–200

Lockwood, Nancy R., on workplace diversity, 134–45

logical errors, 80

Longman, Andrew, on project team evaluation, 252–58

long-range planning. *See* strategic planning

Lucas, Tim, 238, 239

machine metaphors, 232–33

management: American deference toward, 105–6; Asian versus Western styles, 347–48; support for project teams, 254; support for workplace diversity, 137–38, 144, 145, 153–55

management learning and adaptation systems, 224–28

management programs, 6–8

Mankins, Michael C., on planning versus decision making, 272–83

market forces: CSR advocates' view of, 43, 46; myths about, 50–53; support for, 174; workplace forces versus, 107–8. *See also* globalization

Marshall, George C., 234

Martin, Dick, on globalization, 174–84

master project planning, 296–98

McDonald's: apple sales, 53; brand localization, 178–79, 199; brand power, 176; as globalization scapegoat, 175

McGregor, Jena, on performance assessment, 249–51

mechanical solidarity, 343

mental models, 327, 329–30

Mercedes, 177

mergers, 204, 216, 275

messaging strategies, 320

Microsoft, 177, 278

Miller, Steve, 317–18

minimum wages, 54

minorities. *See* workplace diversity

mirror sites, 202

mission, 8, 140

mistakes, learning from, 223

Montreal Protocol, 54

Moorcroft, David, 322

moral issues, 74–76. *See also* ethics

motivational messages, 225–26

motivators: Generation Y preferences, 161–62; in passive-aggressive organizations, 122–24, 128; for workplace diversity, 137–38

MTV, 178

multinational enterprises as special interest targets, 60

Myers, David, 87

myths: about brands, 181–82; about market forces, 50–53

name calling, 75

National Business Ethics Survey, 67–68, 88–89

national innovation, 185–94

Negroni, Peter, 237, 238, 240

Neilson, Gary L., on passive-aggressive organizations, 119–29

Networking Academies (Cisco), 50

New Coke, 176

Nike, 47, 49

nongovernmental organizations: as corporate partners, 180, 182–83; promotion of corporate social responsibility, 46, 48

nonprofit organizations, strategic planning by, 303–10

Nordstrom, 111

norms, 110–11, 330

Nunes, Paul F., on top business trends, 196–206

objectivity, 222

obligations of social entrepreneurs, 23

observations, 215

older workers, 138–39

omission, errors of, 223

Omotani, Les, 238–39, 240

open innovation, 332–33

open-source software initiatives, 333, 336, 338

opportunities, identifying, 228

optimizing costs, 199

organic solidarity, 344

organizational charts, 125. *See also* hierarchies

organizational cultures: adaptive, 330; American, 103–8; incorporating ethics in, 67–69, 87–94; as leadership tools, 109–16; major ethical factors in, 81, 82–84; passive-aggressive, 119–29; Wal-Mart changes, 101–2

organizational hardware and software, 329–31

organizational structures, 300–301. *See also* hierarchies

organization man, 120

organization-wide competencies, 261, 264–65

original-design manufacturers (ODMs), 334–35

outcome-based ethical principles, 77

outsiders, 19, 126

outsourcing, 199

overdelegation, 80

oversimplification fallacy, 75

part-to-whole fallacy, 75

passive-aggressive organizations, 119–29

Pasternack, Bruce A., on passive-aggressive organizations, 119–29

path dependence, 329

pattern recognition, 235

peak consumer experiences, 111

Penrose, Edith, 328

people skills, 24–25

performance: difficulty of maintaining, 325–26; improving through flexible leadership, 6–8; management processes, 202–3; of project teams, 252–58; top global trends, 196–206; workplace diversity and, 141–43. *See also* productivity; profitability

performance anatomy, 200

performance assessment: acknowledging diversity in, 137; alternatives, 259–65; continuous, 235–36; forced ranking systems, 249–51; for project teams, 252–58

performance feedback loops, 337–38

performance workspaces, 201

performing norms, 330

personalities of social entrepreneurs, 18–19

persuasion mentality, 79

Peterson, Terry, 260–61

pharmacogenomics, 205

planning. *See* strategic planning

poisoning the well, 76

policies, unethical, 79

political campaigns, 320

politics of corporate social responsibility movement, 57–61

PortalPlayer, 334

positive reinforcement, 104–5

predictive analytics, 197

prejudicial language, 76

pressures, unethical, 79

pricing, 197, 201

processes, basic corporate values for, 92

Proctor & Gamble, 178, 199–200

product design, 149

productivity: growing need to increase, 200; innovation and, 190; technology's impact on, 197–98; workplace diversity and, 142. *See also* performance; profitability

profitability: as corporate responsibility, 53–54, 58, 174; importance of emotional intelligence for, 25; of innovation, 192; organizational health and, 128, 129; shrinking windows of, 203; workplace diversity and, 137, 141–43

profits: CSR advocates' view of, 45; ethical view of, 85; from innovation, 192

progress, inability to recognize, 295

project teams, 252–58

promotion paths for minority workers, 151–52

proportionality principle, 77

public relations/communications, 321

public relations mentality, 79

puffing mentality, 79

purposeful entities, 218

puzzles, 219

Quaker Oats, 137–38

quality: approach to ethics as, 73–85; improvement programs, 288–90; of leadership, 6; of life, 221

Quirke, Bill, 323

Racial Equality Directive 2000/43/EC, 143

readiness, constant, 291

readiness-focused planning, 288–89

readiness reporting, 233

reasoning, ethical, 74–77

recognition, 104–5

record of comparisons, 227

recruiting: for culture fit, 113–14; for Generation Y workers, 164; for workplace diversity, 138–39

red herrings, 76

reducing complexity, 301–2

Reed, George E., on leadership and systems thinking, 231–36

reframing challenges, 22

regression fallacy, 75

regulations, 53, 54

relationship marketing, 341–49

religion, social entrepreneurs' views of, 20

renorming, 77

Repovich Reynolds, Smooch, 323

reputation, 322

research and development, 186, 194

resilience, 119, 122

resources, as barriers to adaptability, 328–29

resource shortages for teams, 253–54, 257

rewards: of creation nets, 335; Generation Y preferences, 161–62; organizational culture and, 115; in passive-aggressive organizations, 122–24, 128; for project teams, 254; ranking systems, 251; for workplace diversity, 137–38, 152–53, 154

Richard Barrett & Associates, 90

risk taking, 112–13

role expectations, 346

Rowden, Robert W., on learning organizations, 284–92

rule of 50/5, 302

SAP ethics code, 70

Savoy Hotel Group, 298

scheduled planning, 274–75

schemata, 306, 307

schools, systems thinking in, 237–42

scientists, 21

scorecards for workplace diversity, 141

Sears Roebuck, 179–80

Securities & Exchange Commission, 89

security, growing need for, 202

selective truthfulness, 79

self-awareness, 25

self-regulation, 25–26

Seline, Richard, on national innovation, 185–94

Senge, Peter, 234

senior management: American deference toward, 105–6; for communications, 323; support for project teams, 254; support for workplace diversity, 137–38, 144, 145, 153–54

sense-making, shared, 13–14

7-Eleven, 127–28

shared leadership, 9–15

shared sense-making, 13–14

shared values, 92–93

shareholders, duties to, 57–58, 59

short-term mentality, 79

similarity-attraction effect, 114

Simon, Bill, 24

simplicity, 234

single-loop thinking, 239, 240

situational awareness, 7

Six Sigma, 78

skill-based diversity training, 140

Smart car, 252

Smith, Rosa, 238, 241

social controls, 110–11

social entrepreneurs, 16–23

social exchange theory, 342

socialization to organizational culture, 114–15

social labeling, 53

socially responsible investment, 49

social skill, 26

Society for Human Resource Management, 156

SoftBrands, 260–61

software of organizations, 330

Southwest Airlines, 109–10

special interest groups, 60

spirituality of social entrepreneurs, 20

sport-utility vehicles, 51

stakeholders, 59

standard of living, 221

Starbucks, 181

Steele, Richard, on planning versus decision making, 272–83

stock options, 128

Stone, Amey, on ethics codes, 70–72

stories, of brands, 180–82

Storti, Craig, 103, 104

straight talk stereotype, 103–4

strategic drift, 294

Strategic Master Project Plans, 298

strategic planning: approaches used by nonprofits, 303–10; decision making versus, 272–83; importance of implementation, 294–302; in learning organizations, 284–92

strategies: aligning diversity goals with, 140–41; building commitment to, 8; communicating, 299; importance of execution, 109–10; for outsourcing, 199; relation to wages paid, 193

straw man tactic, 76

strength of organizational culture, 111–12

structures, aligning with strategies, 300–301

success measures, 23, 89–90

Sullivan, Scott, 87, 88

supply chain analytics, 197

sustainable development: as corporate goal, 44, 55, 58–59; as dimension of corporate value systems, 93

Symantec, 126–27, 128

symptoms of threats and opportunities, 228

systems: basic corporate values for, 92; to facilitate learning, 214–30; machine metaphor, 232–33

systems thinking: approach to knowledge, 219; leadership and, 7, 231–36; in schools, 237–42

talent organizations, 200

teams, evaluating, 252–58

technical problems, 10, 239–40

telecommuting, 150–51

Telefónica, 204

telemedicine, 205

Textron, 279–80, 282

Thompson, John, 126–27, 128

threats, 228

three C's of culture, 115–16

360-degree assessment, 259, 262, 263

tikkun olam, 20

timing problems with strategic planning, 274–75

Tofteland, Randy, 260

toolbox training, 260–61, 264

too-many-chefs problem, 11–12

top management. See senior management

Toshiba Corporation, 199

total quality programs, 290

Toyota Motor Corporation, 197

Traditionalists: attributes of, 157, 158, 165–66; management strategies for, 162

traditional planning model, 272–76, 280, 286–87, 303–4

training: for career advancement, 151; education versus, 217; ethics, 67, 71, 85; for Generation Y workers, 163; for project teams, 254; to promote workplace diversity, 140

transaction cost theory, 342

transaction-oriented strategies, 348–49

transformative experiences, 18

transforming thinking, 75–76

traumatic events, 17–18

trucking industry, 153

trust, in relationship marketing, 345

Tulgan, Bruce, 164–67

UFI Filters USA, 107

Uhlaner, Robert, 278

understanding, elements of, 217–18

unemployment, fear of, 107

United Nations, 48–49

universal ethical principles, 77

university links, impact on innovation, 194

unlearning, 223, 229

UPS, 199

upward mobility for minority workers, 151–52

urban congestion, 201

vacuous cultures, 111

validating ethical decisions, 77

validity of performance assessments, 259

values: building commitment to, 8; distinctly American, 181; diversity of, 9; generational, 165; levels of, 90–93; in organizational cultures, 110, 111–12; relationship marketing and, 341–49; of social entrepreneurs, 19–20; wisdom and, 221–22. *See also* ethics

Van Nuys, Karen E., on passive-aggressive organizations, 119–29

Verizon Communications, 138

Verschoor, Curtis C., on ethical cultures, 67–69

Vinson, Betty, 87–88

violence, 17–18

virtue, 77

vision, 305

vision statements, 140

Vogelsang, John, on strategic planning by nonprofits, 303–10

WakeUpWalMart.com, 101

Wal-Mart: consumer views of, 50–51; organizational culture, 101–2; questionable labor practices, 151

Walt Disney Company, 113

Walton, Sam, 101

Wamberg, Tom, 70

weak analogy, 75

weapons systems, 252

websites, recruiting via, 114

Welch, Jack, 249

Whirlpool Corporation, 199

2008 10/19

376 Index

whistle blowers, 79
whole-to-part fallacy, 75
"Why CEOs Fail," 109
wiki software, 198
Windsor-Lewis, Stephen, 319
wisdom: acquiring, 229–30; decisions lacking, 216–17; elements of, 218–22
wishful thinking, 75
women, career orientations among, 152
worker treatment, 36
working at home, 150–51

workplace diversity: company-wide implementation, 148–56; competitive advantage based on, 134–45; Generation Y, 157–67. *See also* employees
World Bank, 182
WorldCom scandal, 87–88, 94
World Council for Sustainable Development, 58–59
wrong thinking (ethical), 75–76, 81, 83–84
Yahoo!, 200, 250–51
Yates, Buford, 87
Yukl, Gary, on flexible leadership, 6–8